Bahamas' oldest and most extensive Real Estate service

Since 1922

Prime Real Estate in:
OUT ISLANDS
NEW PROVIDENCE
FREEPORT

*Management *Rentals
*Developments
*Condominiums

h.g. Christie
REAL ESTATE LTD.

"Cascadilla"
Millars Court
P.O. Box N-8164
Nassau, Bahamas

Tel: (809) 322-1041
Cable: CHRISTLAND

Vacation & Business

It's not surprising that after nearly a century and a quarter's experience in the business we've become pretty knowledgeable about what ingredients blend best into the ideal vacation.

Of course, we started out with the matchless natural advantages of superb beaches and translucent waters which vary in colour from palest green to darkest blue, and a landscape which is enlivened year-round by the flamboyant blooms of tropical trees and shrubs against a lush background of gently sloping green hills.

To all of that, over the years we've added luxury hotels, sparkling night clubs where entertainment runs the gamut from Las Vegas-type cabaret to exciting native shows, casino gambling, shopping for merchandise from around the world and often at bargain prices, and gourmet restaurants — but try our Bahamian delicacies of conch, crawfish, grouper and guava duff as well. Take a sightseeing tour of Nassau and the countryside to learn something of our colourful history and environment.

One aspect of the city you're certain to notice is the extraordinary number of banks and other financial institutions which are established here. This international financial community exists primarily because of the absence of taxation, stringent bank secrecy laws, political stability and the attractive atmosphere in which to do business.

Sound investment opportunities abound here, and you could well find it worthwhile on your vacation to consult any one of the professional experts here about your own future financial planning.

Nassau & Paradise Island

Nassau and Paradise Island are joined by a graceful bridge which spans the busy, picturesque harbour, but they remain distinctly separate in atmosphere. Both share the natural attractions of sun, sea and sand, but Nassau retains much of the charm which evolved through its long colonial history, while Paradise Island has emerged as a vibrant and luxurious resort during the past two decades.

We fly at 540 smiles an hour.

Bahamasair flies direct to the United States from Nassau and Freeport, Bahamas. Think about it. All that time you used to spend changing planes can now be spent changing into your bathing suit. So come fly with us to Nassau, Freeport and all twenty of our fabulous Family Islands. We're only a smile away!

For reservations, call Continental U.S.A. 800-327-8080; Florida (excluding Miami) 800-432-1375; Miami 442-8585; Nassau 5-1487/8 or 7-8451/7-8511; Freeport 352-8341/6.

Bahamasair
The National Airline of the Bahamas

Freeport/Lucaya

Started just 28 years ago as an international free trade port, Freeport has mushroomed into a bustling residential, industrial and business complex. Adjoining it, Lucaya is a modern resort of luxury hotels, de luxe casinos, fine restaurants and an exciting International Bazaar. There are excellent facilities for all types of seasports, golf, tennis and squash, and scuba diving.

Family Islands

More and more visitors are discovering the Family Islands experience of quaint villages and towns, friendly people, lovely secluded beaches and an atmosphere of timeless tranquility. Vacation amenities vary from large modern hotels to smaller inns and clubs and modest guesthouses. All of the islands share a matchless natural beauty, and some cater for special interest groups, such as divers.

Island Days

The problem is not what to do, but rather how many of the attractions Nassau offers you can fit into your vacation days. Spend a day sightseeing ...test your skill on our challenging golf courses...try tennis or squash... soak up our sunshine on a gleaming white beach, and snorkel around nearby reefs in crystal-clear warm seas.

Island Nights

Warm, scented tropical nights provide an exquisite backdrop for whatever entertainment excitement appeals to you. Savor the international and Bahamian cuisine of our gourmet restaurants, then take in a sophisticated cabaret or a joyous native floor show; bring Lady Luck with you to our two casinos, dance the night away to hip-twitching goombay rhythms, or disco into the dawn.

Greenfire®
Emeralds Ltd.
A history of Quality

Finest Emeralds and Jewelry
From Colombia.

Bahamianisms

Basically we speak English in the Bahamas, but we've also developed variations in our vocabulary that would raise the Queen's eyebrows (and Elizabeth II is Queen of the Bahamas, too).

The first colonists came, via Bermuda, in the 1640s from the cities and shires of England, then in the 1780s Loyalists, who were also transplanted Englishmen, arrived from the rebellious American colonies. The speech idioms they brought with them have survived in many of the islands they settled and the people who live there still omit the "h" in certain words where it normally belongs, and add it before a vowel where you don't expect it to be. We change our Vs and Ws around, too: you don't become vexed, you "get wex", for example.

We sometimes become so excited by joy or anger that run-of-the-mill Queen's English is totally inadequate to express our emotions — "confusion", for instance, can be much too tame a word in certain situations, so we use the stronger sounding "exfusion". Similarly, "excitement" can be much too ordinary, so we change it to "combruction" or "concitement".

We can sometimes be a bit vague about distance directions, so if you're in the islands and you ask how far away another location is, you'll likely be told that it's "just round the p'int".

But we're a friendly people, so if you become "exfused" by our chatter, just "axe" us what we're talking about!

Shaving Brush of the Bombax family is one of the exotic flowering trees that bloom in the Bahamas in May and June.

Sailing the Bahamas

The Bahamas is a yachtsman's paradise, with miles of brilliant sea which surrounds an incredibly lovely necklace of islands and cays. With Nassau as a base, you can explore the delightful cruising areas of the Exuma Cays in the south, Abaco and its cays in the north, Eleuthera to the east and the Berry Islands to the west. Each area offers a unique and unforgettable sailing vacation.

BIMINI BIG GAME FISHING CLUB

Bimini Big Game Fishing Club, a place of unspoiled charm and simple pleasures. . .
We can offer you spacious double guest rooms, luxurious penthouse apartments or delightful cottages with kitchen facilities - the choice is yours.
Enjoy our fresh-water swimming pool; tennis court; liquor store; dining room and of course our lounge for sipping your favourite island drink.
Each of our sixty boat slips has power (115 - 240 volts), and fresh water hook-ups. And the visiting yachtsman's building offers showers and facilities.
At this tropical Bahamian retreat you can relax. . .
really relax.

P.O. Box 699
Bimini, Bahamas
Tel. (809) 347-2391

Fishing the Bahamas

Whether you're an expert with rod and reel or an amateur angler who prefers a handline, the Bahamas offers the world's most exciting deep-sea and shallow water fishing. We've racked up 29 world record catches covering 12 species of game fish to prove it, no less than 16 of which were boated off Bimini. If you're looking for marlin or giant tuna or the fast, elusive bonefish, we've got them — and every fighting salt-water fish in between.

NASSAU, BAHAMAS

For the businessman on a working vacation, The Pilot House offers the relaxing solution.

Minutes away from downtown business houses. Yet world's away from the rush.

Because a hard day's work deserves a room with a balcony view. Then a poolside lunch at the **Three Ladies** or **Under the Dilly Tree**, dinner in the **Regatta Room** and cocktails and dancing in the **Captain's Lounge**. The **Windward Mark** is another attractive new cocktail lounge.

Golf, tennis, fishing and diving are easily arranged. Unlimited free local phone calls with touch-tone direct dialling.

And we're just across the bridge from the world-famous Paradise Island Casino.

Corporate rates available. For reservations call:
(outside Florida)
800-327-0787
(in Florida)
800-432-5549
(in Hialeah)
305-446-8466

P.O. Box N-4941, Nassau, Bahamas.
Tel: 2-8431

Bahamas Ministry of Tourism Offices Abroad

CANADA:
MONTREAL
1255 Phillips Square
Suite 1105
Montreal, Quebec H3B 3G1
(514) 861-6797
TORONTO
85 Richmond Street West
Toronto, Ontario M5H 2C9
(416) 363-4441
VANCOUVER
470 Granville Street #129
Vancouver, British Columbia
V6C 1V5
(604) 688-8334

ENGLAND:
LONDON
23 Old Bond Street
London W1X4PQ
01-629-5238

FRANCE:
PARIS
9, Boulevard de la Madeleine
75001 Paris
261-61 30, 261-60 20

WEST GERMANY:
FRANKFURT AM MAIN
6000 Frankfurt am Main
Zimmerweg 10
Second Floor
0611/25 2029

UNITED STATES:
ATLANTA
1950 Century Blvd., N.E.,
Suite 26
Atlanta, Georgia 30345
(404) 633-1793

BOSTON
1027 Statler Office Building
Boston, Mass. 02116
(617) 426-3144
CHICAGO
875 North Michigan Avenue
Suite 1816
Chicago, Illinois 60611
(312) 787-8203
DALLAS
2825 Southland Center
Dallas, Texas 75201
(214) 742-1886
LOS ANGELES
3450 Wilshire Boulevard #208
Los Angeles, Calif. 90010
(213) 385-0033
MIAMI
255 Alhambra Circle
Coral Gables, Fla. 33134
(305) 442-4860
NEW YORK
30 Rockefeller Plaza
Room 52
New York, N.Y. 10020
(212) 757-1611
PHILADELPHIA
42 South 15th Street
Philadelphia, Pa. 19102
(215) 564-1704
SAN FRANCISCO
44 Montgomery Street
San Francisco, California 94104
(415) 398-5502
WASHINGTON, D.C.
1730 Rhode Island Ave., N.W.
Washington, D.C. 20036
(202) 659-9135

Cat Cay, Bahamas

Bahamas
Handbook
and Businessman's Annual

1984

EDITORIAL DIRECTOR/*S.P. Dupuch*
MANAGING EDITOR/*Benson McDermott*

PUBLISHER/*Etienne Dupuch, Jr.*

ETIENNE DUPUCH, JR. PUBLICATIONS
P.O. BOX N7513   NASSAU, BAHAMAS

Contents

Features

Leisure & Vacation

The Family Islands

Business & Finance

Bahamas Information

Freeport/Lucaya

Freeport Information

Government

Foreword

by the
Governor General
Sir Gerald Cash,
G.C.M.G., K.C.V.O., O.B.E.

I am delighted to write the Foreword for this edition of The Bahamas Handbook and Businessman's Annual.

As the pages of the Handbook are unfurled, one becomes more knowledgeable about Bahamians and others, past and present, who have made, and who continue to make, contributions to the Commonwealth of the Bahamas. In addition, it gives valuable data about the historical, agricultural, economical and social situations of this archipelago nation. The Handbook can be useful to Bahamians and foreigners alike, for its contents can be appreciated by and beneficial to persons from all walks of life, especially students and business and professional persons.

Much research and hard work must go into the preparation of each edition. I wish to pay high tribute to the publishers for their untiring efforts in publishing this worthwhile source of information, which is an asset not only to the community, but also to tourists and future investors in our country.

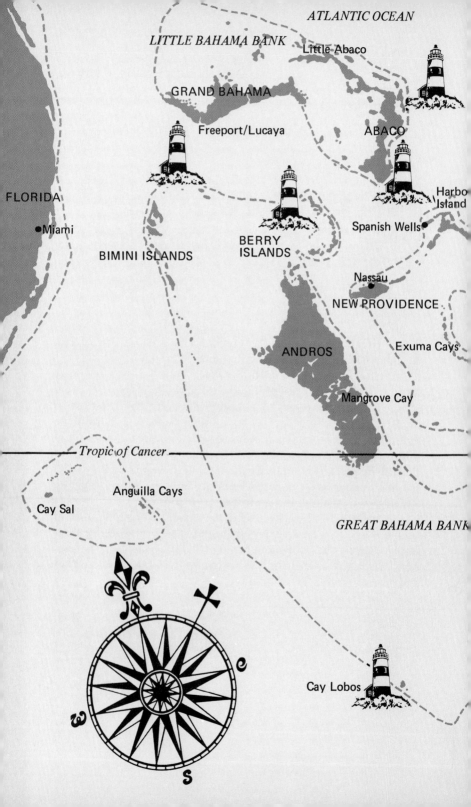

Introduction

Each year, for over two decades, **Bahamas Handbook** has fashioned a literary rainbow of our country's colourful history combined with current developments in a broad spectrum of subjects.

The response of our readers suggests that it is a satisfying formula, and certainly those concerned in its annual preparation have invariably found it a fascinating and professionally rewarding assignment.

So, in this new edition, we've again brought together a versatile and varied cast of those who *were*, in another era, and who *are* today actors in the often fast-paced

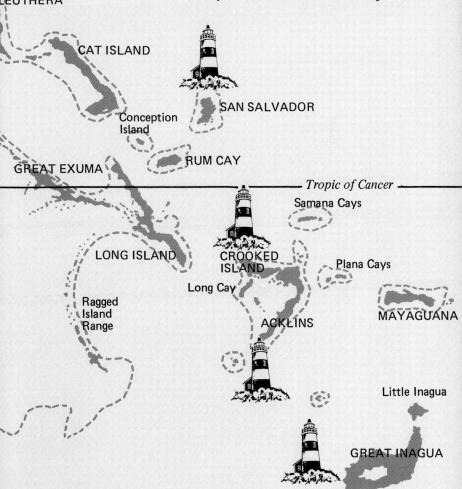

LEUTHERA

CAT ISLAND

Conception Island

SAN SALVADOR

GREAT EXUMA

RUM CAY

Tropic of Cancer

Samana Cays

LONG ISLAND

CROOKED ISLAND

Plana Cays

Long Cay

Ragged Island Range

ACKLINS

MAYAGUANA

Little Inagua

GREAT INAGUA

Bahamian drama.

There's Walton Young, the poor boy from the native New Providence village of Fox Hill who became one of the most powerful and controversial politicians of his day; and investment genius John Templeton, founder of the prestigious and rich annual award for Progress in Religion, who tells about his life in Nassau, and how he developed his deep involvement in the Christian and other religious philosophies.

For those who come to cruise our matchless seas, five veteran Bahamian yachtsmen talk about the areas they most enjoy visiting, and offer advice for first-time boaters here. For landlubber vacationers, we've compiled a six-day holiday itinerary which is designed to keep you pleasantly busy.

Six of the country's leading architects describe their favourite homes, and explain why they especially enjoyed designing them; and we've talked with several old-time former politicians to report on some of the election shenanigans candidates indulged in before the secret ballot.

The Bahamas National Trust is energetically concerned with the preservation of our wildlife, historical associations and the vast natural beauty of the islands. In separate features we record the Trust's work in Inagua, where once-threatened flamingos now thrive in an environment of mystical appeal, and in the Exuma Cays where a Land and Sea Park is maintained for the enjoyment of those who visit this uniquely lovely part of our Commonwealth.

In the sphere of business and finance, experts relate why the Bahamas has become an important offshore centre, and how investors can utilize the tax-free advantages it offers. New legislation to attract more captive insurance and reinsurance business is examined in depth, and there's a detailed report on activities in the real property market.

The Freeport/Lucaya section features a lively description of the world's longest underwater cavern and the marine and historical treasures it has revealed. There are updates on new developments in tourism, industry and agriculture, and an exploration of the attractive investment opportunities available in our second city.

For those who rely on **Bahamas Handbook** primarily as an accurate reference book, our Blue Pages information sections again provide concise and comprehensive answers to questions about living, vacationing and doing business here.

Features

L.W. Young:

Formidable Force from Fox Hill

— BY BENSON MCDERMOTT

L eon Walton Young served in the House of Assembly for over 30 years as one of the two members for the Eastern District. A singularly clever politician and volatile debater, he was feared by some of his House colleagues, admired by others and disliked by yet others.

Young also became a prominent builder and land developer in his constituency, and enjoyed a considerable degree of prosperity.

What made his career both remarkable and controversial was that Young, of Yoruba descent, achieved his powerful position in parliament and success in his business at a time when politics and the economy of the Bahamas were generally dominated by a relatively small clique of white men.

Young's style was not to try to buck the establishment, but rather to become integrated with it as a political equal. His natural shrewdness persuaded him that that was the practical means of serving his own people and the then-colony generally, and for him it proved to be a successful formula.

Young's mother, Caroline Pratt, was a full-blooded Yoruba. Her mother had been among the first generation of children born

15

in Fox Hill after a settlement of freed slaves was established there following emancipation in 1834. Nothing much can be discovered today about Walton Young's father, Roger. The Rev. Leopold Cox, 83, whose father, Jeremiah, was the son of Caroline Pratt's sister, remembers that the senior Young was "always dressed up in a suit and tie", but he cannot recall what his occupation was or when he died. In the register of births, he is identified as a labourer. Walton Young was born out of wedlock on May 11, 1876, in Congo Town in the western section of Fox Hill. He had no brothers or sisters.

Living in the pleasant settlement, as the Rev. Cox remembers it in the early years of this century, was close to idyllic. "Life was like I think it should be," he says. "Everybody knew everybody and treated each other like brothers and sisters. We never had locks on our doors—just a bent nail to keep the breeze from blowing the door open when you went out. The whole area was like a huge garden, with fruit trees of all kinds everywhere." He still lives in Fox Hill, where he has been the pastor of Mount Carey Union Baptist Church since 1958.

Young learned the trade of a ship's and house carpenter, and Cox remembers that he often made trips to Andros to build the sturdy dinghies for which the island was well known. Later, he would become a successful building contractor, and from the knowledge he acquired of reading plans he became adept at drawing his own. But even for a skilled young artisan, it was difficult to make an acceptable living in New Providence at the turn of the century, and while he was in his 20s Young emigrated to Key West, Florida, where the opportunities seemed wider. But unlike many others who left it, Young soon felt the pull of his island-home, and he returned to it after a few years, wiser in the ways of the world and more experienced at his craft.

For many years before Prohibition in the United States brought bootleg prosperity to the Bahamas, skilled construction workers were paid four shillings a day (then the equivalent of $1). Young's reputation as a reliable, intelligent and productive worker attracted the attention of Charles E. Bethell, a prosperous liquor merchant and property developer. It became the talk of the community when it was learned that Bethell had hired Young as his building superintendent at the astonishing pay rate of one pound ($5) per day.

Sir Etienne Dupuch, 84, editor/publisher of *The Tribune* in Nassau from 1919 to 1972 and now its contributing editor, recalls that when the New Colonial Hotel (now the Sheraton-British

Rev. Leopold Cox remembers Young "like a father".

Sir Etienne Dupuch admired Young in later years.

Colonial) was being built in 1922, American artisans were brought in to speed up the work at rates which were considerably higher than the one pound a day which had by then become the scale for local workers. Soon there was pressure on the contractor by the Bahamians on the project for equal pay, so one day the foreman placed the ring-leader of the disgruntled Bahamian painters on a scaffold beside an American, facing a plastered wall of the hotel. At the end of the day the American worker could be seen to have painted a considerably larger area than had his Bahamian counterpart, so the foreman called the latter in and asked him to explain what had happened. Shaking his head sorrowfully, the Bahamian confessed: "Boss, I guess I'se just a pound-a-day man!"

So well known and successful a builder had Young become by 1926 that when construction of the Fort Montagu Hotel was begun that year he was awarded lucrative sub-contracts. The Rev. Cox had emigrated to the U.S. in 1917, but he kept in touch with Young, who had trained him as a carpenter, and at Young's invitation he returned to Nassau to help with the hotel project. "He was always like a father to me," he says. Although he had been lured abroad because he "wanted to see the bright lights, and lots of my friends were in the States", he was happy to return home for "it was rough on coloured people in the South in those days".

Dr. Cleveland W. Eneas, Sr., 68, a Bahamian dentist who obtained his degree from Meharry Medical College in 1941,

17

records that when he was a boy he knew of Young as "a figure to be held in awe and looked up to and respected as a 'big man'. In a way, I was close to him because he was a friend of my father and was kin to my step-grandmother whom he visited often."

In appearance Young was formidable, and he was well known for the quickness and violence of his temper. "He would flare up suddenly," the Rev. Cox relates, "but he came down just as quickly."

Dr. Eneas gives this description of him: "He was of medium height, but broad of shoulder. He had a broad face, a very strong mouth, and eyes that were like gimlets which seemed to bore right through you, especially when he was angry."

In their years together in the House of Assembly, Sir Etienne and Young were always antagonistic, although they became friends during Young's last years.

"We always fought," Sir Etienne comments, "because we were different people with different values, but he was a very colourful character and a most interesting person. He was not prepossessing, but he generally dressed well. He was stocky, and very powerfully built."

Sir Alvin Braynen, 79, who also served in the House with Young for many years, and who was Speaker from 1967 to 1972,

Dr. Cleveland Eneas knew Young as an awesome figure.

Sir Alvin Braynen recalls Young as intimidating.

18

*This photo from his passport
shows Young when he was
66 years old.*

recounts that members were always careful not to cross Young in debates because "he could be acrimonious—he would say anything he wanted, and how he liked. He looked ferocious with his heavy eyebrows knitted, and he often intimidated younger members. He was physically powerful, and could lick his weight in wildcats".

T. A. Toote, a lawyer and politician who fought bitterly with him during their parliamentary careers, was a diminuative man who was physically in awe of Young. He once had to write a letter to him, on behalf of a client, threatening to take civil action against Young through the courts. Young responded promptly: "Dear Mr. Toote, I have your letter before me. Soon it will be behind me."

Because there was not enough continuing activity in the building trade to keep him fully occupied, Young turned to shopkeeping among his other activities. He operated an "odds and ends" store and real estate office on the north side of Bay Street opposite Dunmore Lane. It became a meeting place for his friends, young and old, who gathered there daily to discuss the political events of the day.

Young possessed unlimited energy and a restless mind which was always busy with new projects. It is a trait of Yorubas to enjoy acquiring land, and Young became a successful property developer for many years. Among his purchases was extensive acreage in Fox Hill, mainly in the Congo Town area. Dr. Eneas, himself a descendant of Yorubas, is quick to point out that Young "was no

19

Congo, however. He was a N'Oonga of the best Yoruba stock, but, nevertheless, he owned most of Congo Town".

Young owned two contiguous estates, one on the south side of Bernard Road, which was known as Windsor Estates, and the other on the east side of Soldier Road, which he named Village Estates.

Windsor Estates was only partly developed by him by the sale of a few building lots. A large part of the tract was acquired and developed in the 1950s by Dr. R. M. de Gregory as an attractive residential area, retaining the name Windsor Estates Subdivision. The site of the present L. W. Young Junior High School, on another part of the tract which Young once owned, is where he started but did not complete, the building of what Dr. Eneas describes as "a castle". It is believed that all of the Windsor Estates tract was disposed of by Young before he died.

Village Estates was his major development. Its southern boundary extended to the roadway, north of and parallel to Prince Charles Drive, and ran east from Soldier Road to the Telecommunications Transmitter Station. It was in that area that he constructed his final home, which he built himself, and in which he lived during the last years of his life. The house sits on approximately four acres of land. On the same parcel he also built a small nightclub and hotel which he named the Walleyou Hotel, from the first letters of his full name, transposing the "Walton" and the "Leon".

"The hotel was never a success," comments Mrs. Eva McPherson Williams, whose father, S. C. McPherson, represented the Southern District in the House for many years and was a close friend of Young. "He made some money from his bar operation," Mrs. Williams adds, "but the location was really too remote then."

When he had nearly finished building the hotel, Young phoned Sir Etienne one day to ask him to send a photographer to take a picture of it for *The Tribune*. "He must have been over 80," Sir Etienne remembers, "and when my photographer got to the Walleyou he was astonished to find Young up on the roof nailing down some final shingles."

The Walleyou Hotel was demolished about 15 years ago. Immediately to the north of this area is a 10-acre parcel of the Village Estates tract which Young never developed. He sold it shortly before his death to a company of which Orville A. Turnquest, M.P., a prominent barrister, and Ervin Knowles, M.P., a builder and land developer, are the principal shareholders.

Government junior high school in Bernard Road honours the memory of Leon Walton Young.

The property was developed as a commercial garden cemetery, known as Woodlawn Gardens, which is today well established. The northern part of Village Estates was developed by Young in the late 1950s as a residential subdivision extending north into the Danottage Estates.

At the time of Young's death there was a small portion of the undeveloped remainder of Village Estates, comprising between 10 and 20 acres. His Will provided that his executors should give a parcel of five acres to his son, David Young, who was one of two "natural" sons reputedly born to him out of wedlock. It is believed that there were also a few individual lots remaining unsold in Village Estates when he died.

Perhaps the most elaborate structure Young ever designed and built was a home for himself and his second wife in the 1920s on a property at the northwest corner of Shirley and Armstrong streets. He called it "Windsor" and it was a large wooden structure, by far the most imposing residence in the vicinity.

"It was a house filled with gaiety," Dr. Eneas remarks, "and when I was a young man we used to enjoy going to parties there. He had fine furnishings in that house, and it was a joy to all of us."

Young later transformed the home into "The Windsor Club",

21

and finally sold the property, which now stands vacant.

According to Bert A. Cambridge, 82, who was elected to the House in 1942 and served as a member for the Southern District until 1957, Young "always had an eye for the girls". Rev. Cox concurs: "Yes, you'd have to say that he was a ladies' man."

Young married three times. By his first wife, Rhoda Dickson, of Grant's Town, he had three children—Henney, Maria and Daisy. The latter, who was born on August 28, 1913, is the sole survivor. She was married in November 1949 to David Moore, a New York realtor, and they live in Hollis, N.Y.

Young's marriage was a stormy one, and Rhoda left with the two older children when they were very young for New York. Daisy remained with her father until she was 15, then joined her mother and brother and sister.

She remembers that when she was a young girl the people she knew in Nassau had "deep self-respect, and they respected others, too".

According to Mrs. Moore, Young provided for his children's education and living expenses. She maintained a very good relationship with him. "He spent as much time as possible with me," she reminisces, "and always kept in touch by letter. He was a loving and concerned father, and made sure that I had a good education. I remember him as a very dignified gentleman, who loved to help people who wanted to better themselves."

Mrs. Moore became an interior decorator in New York. She visits Nassau frequently, and still owns property, which she inherited from Young, in the eastern section of New Providence. She was one of the two executors of his estate, and his principal beneficiary.

His second wife, Gladys, was born on Acklins Island but had been taken as a child to Florida where her father, S. A. Sampson, became a well-known Baptist minister. According to Sir Etienne and Cambridge, she was a pretty, light-skinned girl and considerably younger than Young. Mrs. Moore recalls that her stepmother was "a very lovely and educated lady". Gladys was already married, but the appearance of Young's wealth and position in the community evidently appealed to her and she got a divorce in order to marry him.

Young could not have been an easy man to live with, and Cambridge reports that Gladys, who was very friendly with both him and his wife, often came to spend the night at their home after a disagreement with her husband. They had a daughter, Marjorie, who was taken to Miami when her mother decided that her

Young's daughter, Mrs. Daisy Moore, left, with lifelong friend Mrs. Eva McPherson Williams during a 1983 Nassau visit.

freedom was more valuable than any benefits she might ultimately receive as Young's widow. In any event, she predeceased her former husband, and it is not known whether Marjorie is alive today.

Katie Basden, a young Turks Island girl, became Young's third wife, but that marriage did not last long either. They had no children, and Katie returned to Turks Island, and evidently did not retain contact with any of her Nassau friends, so what happened to her afterwards is also unknown.

Politics was the very core of Young's life, and it was in that area that he often became a controversial figure. He was first elected as a member for the Eastern District of New Providence on January 6, 1912, and he represented the same constituency until May 21, 1942.

Dr. Eneas points out that in those days the Eastern District included what is now the constituencies of Montagu, Shirlea, Fox Hill and Yamacraw. He explains how Young was able to win and hold his House seat for over 30 years thus: "The majority of the population was made up of Fox Hill people, who owned most of the land and were of Yoruba stock. With them were some old settlers of mixed (tribal) blood and a few whites who were mostly fishermen

23

and tomato growers. None of these groups wasted any love on the power structure and the merchant class who lived west of the Eastern Parade. The East was too far in the bush, the roads were too bad and transportation too poor for 'The Bay Street Boys' to get to the voters to influence them, and, anyway, their livelihood didn't depend on Bay Street so they were free to vote for whom they pleased—so they voted for Walton Young."

Bert Cambridge remembers that as a young man he often joined others who met regularly at Young's Bay Street shop. "We talked politics all day," he says, "but in those days there was never any consideration of race."

Young was entirely self-educated. "Every penny he could spare he used to buy books," Sir Etienne recalls. Sir Asa Pritchard, 92, who was first elected to the House in 1925 for the Eleuthera constituency and served as Speaker from 1946 to 1962, remembers that Young "always read a lot and kept abreast of world events".

What also impressed Sir Asa about him was his deep knowledge of and respect for the rules of the House of Assembly. "He was always very outspoken, but he handled the English language extremely well, indeed. He could be aggressive in the House, but he was always courteous and adhered strictly to proper procedure. He might attack another member's views vehemently, but when they left the House he'd put his arm around the shoulder of that member and joke with him. In those days there was no thought of race at all—there were no prejudices."

Sir Alvin was not one of Young's admirers, although he concedes that he was "well read, expressed himself well and had some ability". He remembers that during a debate he once told the Speaker that Young caused him to doubt the veracity of the scriptures which recorded that God decreed that "the serpent should forever walk on his belly—but (pointing to Young) that man stands up!"

Sir Etienne comments that "in Young's day, for a black man to do anything for his country he had to work through the white bosses". Sir Alvin confirms that: "Young was in with the white boys, and he stuck with them. They could always call on him for help, and they used him extensively in campaign meetings. He was a fluent speaker, and when he had to 'talk black' he could do it. Young was a man who would do anything for money."

Young became extremely close to two powerful political figures of the day. William Christopher Barnett Johnson, O.B.E., a successful businessman, was Deputy Speaker of the House and

24

Hon. and Mrs. R.W. Sawyer celebrate their 1952 golden wedding anniversary. Sawyer and Young worked closely in parliament.

would succeed Harcourt Malcolm, C.B.E., Q.C., as Speaker on December 29, 1936 (see **Bahamas Handbook, 1975**). Johnson operated a large tomato and pineapple canning plant on Bay Street where No. 1 Dock is now located, and he also owned extensive sisal plantations at Cable Beach, Prospect and The Caves. He was, therefore, the principal employer of labour in New Providence.

Richard William Sawyer served in the House for some 45 years between 1903 and 1948 and became a member of the Legislative Council (now The Senate) in the latter year. As a member of Executive Council from 1943 to 1948 he acted as Leader for the Government in the House on occasions when Sir Kenneth Solomon (see **Bahamas Handbook 1982-83**) was absent. Sawyer became wealthy through his grocery and shipping interests.

Young spent much of his time with Johnson and Sawyer, and gained their trust. It was an arrangement of mutual usefulness.

Says Sir Alvin: "Harcourt Malcolm used W.C.B. Johnson to do his dirty work, and Johnson used Young to do his."

"Young was Sawyer's mouthpiece in the House," Cambridge comments. "He would often introduce measures which had been agreed on outside the House between him, Johnson and Sawyer, although I remember one occasion when Young became furious with Sawyer because he'd moved for the appointment of a committee at Sawyer's wish, then when the motion was put Sawyer had a change of mind and voted against it!"

Sir Alvin once remarked in the House that he thought "the member for the East (Young) must be a carbon copy of the member for Eleuthera (Sawyer) because every time the latter speaks, the former leaps to his feet to support him".

Sir Alvin claims that on one occasion Young, at Sawyer's instigation, moved for a committee to consider an inter-island mailboat contract, it being understood that the committee's report would recommend awarding the government-subsidized contract to an agreed-upon ship-owner. "I'm sure Young was rewarded for getting that committee," says Sir Alvin. "He always supported the white element, and they paid for it."

He remembers a meeting of the House Finance Committee, of which he was then chairman, when Young couldn't get the support of other members for a vote of funds. "Young became very angry," Sir Alvin recalls, "and stormed outside the door of the committee room, pausing to shout at me: 'Now get on with your meeting!' But we couldn't because he'd deprived us of a quorum."

Sir Etienne tells of another committee meeting which was held in the chamber of the House. Members who had not been appointed to a committee nevertheless had the right to listen in on any deliberations as long as they did not participate in them. Young, having taken a seat outside the Bar on this occasion, continuously heckled members and Sir Etienne finally became so exasperated with him that he appealed to the chairman, Sir Kenneth Solomon, to demand that Young either be silent or remove himself. Young overheard this and retorted: "You want me out, you put me out."

Sir Etienne says he was so incensed that he left his seat, strode up to Young and struck him with his fist. Young got up from where he had fallen from the unexpected blow, and departed without another word.

One of the strong bonds between Young and Sawyer was the fact that the latter was for many years chairman of the Board of Education, and that was a subject which interested Young deeply.

"He always spoke eloquently, forcefully and honestly on questions of education," Sir Asa remembers. "He was a good representative," adds Cambridge, "as well as being one of the most outstanding politicians of his day. He never missed an opportunity to plead for better educational facilities for the masses."

Sir Etienne reports that at one period Young, Herbert J. "Gully" Russell (Young's one-time colleague for the East) and Lorenzo G. Brice (a member for Long Island) "were the dominant influence in the House – they all spoke on every issue that was

26

Bert Cambridge remembers Young's efforts for better education for the masses.

brought up, and Young, particularly, was an effective voice in debates.

"During the bootleg prosperity," he adds, "Young, Brice and 'Gully' were forceful proponents of a policy of spreading the revenue around on public works as fast as it came in, and they prevailed. The result was that when Prohibition ended, the Treasury was as empty as it had been in 1919."

In the 10 years prior to Prohibition, revenue often dropped below £100,000 annually. By 1922-23 it had climbed to £850,000, and from 1926 to 1930 it was over £1 million each year, but a year after the repeal of the Volstead Act receipts slumped to £270,000.

Interestingly, Young, Russell and Brice were able to win support for their short-sighted policy over the protests of one of the "Bay Street" establishment. James Ronald Clerihew Young, a representative for Abaco, was the son of Sir James Young, a former president of the Legislative Council. J.R.C. Young was firmly opposed to the spending spree advocated by Walton Young, "Gully" and Brice, and instead urged the House to invest its new wealth through the Crown Agents in London, and limit public works expenditures to the income from that source.

"J.R.C. Young," Sir Etienne comments, "was a very sound, conservative individual, but members of the House preferred to go along with Walton Young's crowd. Time showed that J.R.C. Young was right, and they were wrong."

Although Young could work successfully and effectively with the majority of leaders, Sir Etienne relates how on one occasion, at least, he picked the wrong man to approach for a political favour. Sir

27

George (Harry) Gamblin was Leader for the Government at the time (he was later president of the Legislative Council), and he once told Sir Etienne with shocked disapproval that Young was the only member of the House who had "ever dared" suggest a course of action to him regarding a matter that was before the House. "I always admired Gamblin greatly," Sir Etienne says, "and there could never be any involvement in political manoeuvering for him."

Young was never specifically concerned with the cause of black people because, as has been noted, racial divisions were not a burning issue at the time.

"To say that he was a fighter for the black cause could be disputed," Dr. Eneas concedes. "It might be more correct to say that he was a champion of the underdog, and especially of his Fox Hill people. I have heard him criticized as being clannish – that is, that he looked out for his own."

"Young didn't really accomplish anything specifically for black people," Sir Etienne feels.

There is no doubt that Young used his influence energetically on behalf of his Eastern District constituents, but it is impossible at this distance in time to point to any specific accomplishments of his to improve conditions in what was then a very poor parliamentary constituency.

"I can't recall that he actually did very much for Fox Hill," Sir Asa muses, "but then in those days none of us could do a lot because we didn't have any money in the Treasury – but everyone seemed happy with what they had."

For a number of years Young's House colleague for the East had been Wilfred Gladstone Cash, father of the present Governor General of the Bahamas, Sir Gerald Cash, G.C.M.G., K.C.V.O., O.B.E. But in the 1935 general election, the powerful R.T. Symonette (later Sir Roland and the country's first Premier) switched from his Harbour Island constituency to the East, defeating Cash. Then in the general election of 1942, after he had represented them for over 30 years, the voters rejected Young and elected Symonette and Cash.

Young never tried to regain his seat. Cambridge says that he was satisfied that he had always served to the best of his ability, and he accepted the collective voice of the electorate without rancour or bitterness. Mrs. Moore confirms that: "His attitude was that everything had an end, and that the old should make way for the young with new ideas."

28

In 1960, when he was 84, Young suffered a severe stroke and was bedridden for a while. "But he had tremendous willpower and determination," Sir Etienne says. "He had a rail made out of pipes built at his hotel, and he forced himself to walk by holding on to it. He told me he was too young to die!"

With their political differences long behind them, Sir Etienne and Young developed a close relationship. "He telephoned me one day to come and visit him, and so I went," Sir Etienne remembers, "and later my wife and I often went to see him on Sundays, and we always enjoyed those occasions."

It was during this period that Young made a singularly generous gesture to a young black family in distress. According to Sir Etienne, sometime during 1961 a policeman was fatally stabbed by a burglar while he was on patrol in a new suburban shopping area. He left a young widow and children of whom he had been the sole support. Sir Etienne appealed through his *Tribune* for aid from the public to build them a home, and the response was heartening. Additionally, Sir George Roberts offered construction materials at cost through his City Lumber Yard, several artisans promised their services free, Sir Etienne's half-brother, the late Hon. Eugene Dupuch, C.B.E., Q.C., agreed to do the conveyancing without a fee, and the late J.S. Johnson offered free insurance for the projected house.

All that was needed was a plot of land on which to build, and one day Sir Etienne received a message that Young was in the *Tribune's* parking area and wanted to see him. He had had himself lifted into his car and driven to the newspaper's offices to tell Sir Etienne that he was prepared to give a piece of land provided the latter would agree to act as trustee of the property until the eldest of the murdered policeman's children reached the age of 21. Young wanted to protect the children against their mother deciding to sell the home, or marrying someone who might try to take the house from her or put her children out of it. Sir Etienne promptly agreed, and construction went ahead.

There is no evidence that religion was a particularly strong influence in Young's earlier life, but after his first stroke he became a convert to Roman Catholicism. He suffered a second, fatal stroke on July 30, 1962, and his funeral service at St. Francis Xavier's Cathedral was attended by a large and representative crowd. He had lived 86 eventful years, during which, in the words of Dr. Eneas, "he became a sort of local hero, and to the Yorubas of Bain Town and Fox Hill he *was* a hero".

In this fish-eye view of Parliament Square from the Senate balcony, the building at left is the most important house in the Bahamas — it's the home of our 254-year-old House of Assembly. Architectural styles and tastes change, but after 171 years the buildings which form this square retain an imposing dignity. While the architect in this instance is unknown, in the following pages we present the designs of six contemporary architects whose work has also enlivened and enhanced our island environment.

Six Architects Describe their
Favourite Bahamian Homes

Houses have a great fascination for most people. Visitors, of course, tend to be exposed only to those aspects of Bahamian life they encounter while enjoying our holiday attractions, so to provide a more in-depth look into the way we live, **Bahamas Handbook** has invited six prominent architects to tell about the favourite home they have designed in the Bahamas, and the reasons why they like it.

Three of the architects are Bahamian-born; one was born in Sarajevo (when it was under Austrian rule); another is a former Londoner long resident in Nassau; and the sixth was born in Sri Lanka when it was still Ceylon.

The homes they have chosen to describe are located at Lyford Cay, at the western end of New Providence and about 15 miles from Nassau; at Love Beach, a few miles east of Lyford Cay; at Long Island (see map, page 119); and at Danottage Estates in New Providence's Eastern District.

Their work is presented in the following pages in the alphabetical order of the architects' names.

The Chambers House
at Long Island

DONALD CARTWRIGHT,
A.A. Dipl., A.R.I.B.A. *was
born in Nassau and has been in
practice here since 1965. Before
opening his own office he was on
the staff of the Ministry of Works
in Nassau.*

"No one house I have designed can be an exclusive favourite, for each one which is commissioned by a client is highly individual and suited to the needs of that person's way of life. It is also designed to respond to the particular locality of the site, so all these variables add up to a building which is special to its situation, and the architect attempts to make every house a 'favourite'.

"In choosing a favourite house, then, the criterion must be that the client likes living in it. Such is the case with 'The Chambers House' at Cape Santa Maria, Long Island. From the earliest sketches for the design to their occupancy of the house, I felt the clients' complete identification with the design.

"It is located on an isolated, flat, rocky site which looks across a small shelling beach to the ocean on one side, and, from the first floor, to a calm bay on the other side. A most idyllic setting.

"It was designed to be built in two stages. Stage one consists of a single living/sleeping room in one 'pod', and a garage/storeroom in another 'pod'. Eventually a separate master bedroom suite will be built in a third 'pod'. The main 'pod' is designed as a single, high space with a mezzanine sleeping area. The living room, with a temporary guest sleeping space, and kitchen are on the ground floor. Large sliding windows and doors at both levels provide access to open porches and views of the sea and across the bay.

"Although fully air-conditioned, the house is designed to be entirely cross-ventilated, thus allowing cooling by natural means when the mosquitos are not rampant. Water is supplied from a large rainwater tank under the house, and electricity is supplied by a diesel generator.

"The style of the building attempts to evoke a feeling of white sails when viewed from a distance across the water, and that feeling will be even more pronounced when the third 'pod' has been constructed.

"Mr. and Mrs. Chambers are themselves interior designers (they own House and Garden at Lyford Cay), so the house has been furnished and appointed in a style which is sympathetic with the architecture. They have occupied the house as often as their busy schedule allows, and it is the obvious pleasure they have in using and maintaining it that makes it a home for them and one of my favourite houses."

The Nesbeth House
at Love Beach

JOHN DARVILLE, Dipl. Arch. (Hons.), R.I.B.A., *was born on the Bahamian island of Eleuthera, and has practised in the Bahamas since 1973.*

"This house was designed in 1980 for Mr. and Mrs. Lloyd Nesbeth and their family. The site is located on a hill overlooking Love Beach to the north, and the view to the south overlooks the island. It is accessible directly off West Bay Street.

"Due to the nature of the site, the house was designed on three levels. It is entered through a lower courtyard, at which level the garage and utility room are also located, and there is an internal staircase leading up to the kitchen from this level. External steps lead up from the courtyard to the main entrance of the house on the ground floor level.

"All living accommodation is located at this level, and consists of living room, dining room, kitchen, family room and music room. The living room opens to the north and south views, and to the swimming pool terrace. All other rooms on this level open principally to the ocean view to the north.

"All bedrooms are located on the first floor level, and all open to north and south views. The master bedroom, with its private balconies, is separated from the other bedrooms, affording complete privacy. The overall general arrangement of the planning, in fact, provides for privacy of the individual, and takes full advantage both of the views from this superb site and of the prevailing breezes.

"The architecture respects the climatic conditions with large roof overhands and covered patios. All of these elements have been assembled into a building which, I believe, is not only successful as a dwelling but succeeds also as a piece of architecture."

Serendip Cove
at Lyford Cay

MLADEN M. JOJKITCH, Dip. Arch. (Technische Hochschule, Dresden), *was born in Sarajevo and practised in Yugoslavia and in London, England, before coming to Nassau in January 1953.*

"I was very lucky that my clients gave me a free hand to design a home which, I believe, has all the features best suited to the climate of the Bahamas.

"'Serendip Cove' is at Lyford Cay and faces Clifton Bay. The basic layout is an 'H-shaped' plan enclosing an atrium, and is similar to houses found in ancient Greece and Rome, which has been my favourite design since my schooldays. I, therefore, welcomed the opportunity to design and build this kind of home in the Bahamian environment, for there is hardly any other design with similar features more suitable, if properly conceived and properly located, to allow prevailing breezes to flow through the living area, introducing clean, unpolluted air without depending on air-conditioners, which really only circulate stale air.

"The house has an area under the main floor high enough to walk through, and all water pipes and electrical conduits are placed under the floor so that they can easily be inspected and maintained. No tide-rise less than eight feet above highwater mark will affect the main floor, which was proven by 'Hurricane Betsy' when all houses in the Clifton Bay area were flooded except 'Serendip Cove'.

"Why I like this house from the artistic point of view is the fact that all proportions of rooms and other areas are 'mathematical' (classical proportions), which give an overall pleasing and beautiful effect. The ancient Greeks used the same formula to create their most memorable buildings.

"In the 30 years I have lived in the Bahamas the climate may have changed slightly, but it will always be warm and sometimes humid, and if we want an attractive, comfortable, practical and energy-saving house, I believe the best design is, in principle, a modern adaptation of classical architecture."

The Cox House
in Danottage Estates

RAY J.H. NATHANIELS,
Dipl. Arch. F.R.I.B.A., *was
born in Sri Lanka, and practised
in England, Libya, the Middle
East and India before coming to
Nassau in 1957.*

"A home should relate in a loving way to its environment. I see it then evolving as a natural variation on the regular and irregular themes which nature provides on its doorstep, packed with hidden interest and drama. No rules of 'style' are necessary; its vocabulary is that of imagination.

"A creative architect is unhappy when he has to produce a design for expediency, or to meet the unreasonable needs of demanding clients. But I felt great pleasure in designing this home for Mr. and Mrs. George Cox because of their understanding and co-operation. They were receptive to all ideas, and this freed me from preconceptions. As a result this hillside setting freely offered solutions in much profusion, ready to be expressed in three dimensions.

"Although I used conventional shapes, they were never allowed to remain static, and the tyranny of the 'right angle' was constantly broken up visually to dissolve into the overall concept, with patios and balconies inviting the garden and distant horizon to participate in the scheme of things. However contrasting each element happened to be, I endeavoured to make it relate to its neighbour, so that when a door suddenly disappeared into a wall creating an abrupt end to their conversation, a new dimension with a new voice appeared. This always satisfied me, for it suggested that the building was coming to life.

"I tried to relate all diverse elements actively or passively with a message of unity, and this was difficult. I felt that the elements of the fireplace, essentially for burning logs, could express themselves in other ways also. So, the flat surfaces of the chimney were broken up with illuminated niches for objects of special interest, and reached up to the cathedral ceiling to articulate the rigid lines of the timbers by the irregular fashion in which it related to the adjoining walls. The form of the brick hearth invited the pot of flowers, and creeps along the wall to offer seating.

"The swimming pool, at the lowest level, displays its shapes to the two decks which lead out of the house at different levels above it. It snuggles in its own domain and becomes part of the exposed natural rock on which the house rests. Such are the things that satisfy in this home, and I would like to think that the owners are enriched by them in the course of their household activities."

Whitecaps
at Love Beach

PATRICK RAHMING, B.Arch.
(McGill University), R.I.B.A.,
*was born in Nassau and has
practised here since 1970.*

"The building sits dramatically on a hill, an angular, carved, white block with a flat top, turned carefully to receive the prevailing winds, and to appreciate the magnificent views both to the north and to the south.

"'Whitecaps', overlooking fabulous Love Beach, is the home of Dr. and Mrs. Anthony Davis. They are young, avant-garde Bahamians with a zest for life, and their house was designed to reflect their personal tastes.

"In spatial organization as well as detailing, the building is reminiscent of traditional Bahamian houses – the covered porch is, in fact, a transposed verandah; the home is cooled by a system of cross-ventilation; rainwater is collected and stored, then heated by solar collector panels; a well supplies much of the other water needed to service the building; and the vertical louvres are translations of a traditional balustrade detail.

"Yet the image is fresh and contemporary, with clean white walls, clear, natural wood partitions and ceilings, and earth-toned ceramic tiled floors creating a natural texture which helps the spaces flow easily from inside to outside – from the complete protection of the family room, through the outdoor room of the family porch to the sun-drenched pool deck. The good ventilation and lighting throughout the building help the exterior planting to move easily inside, there to compliment the simple, elegant furniture.

"The plan is simply zoned on both floors. On the ground floor, the foyer distributes traffic left to the two-levelled living and dining area (guest area) or right to the kitchen and family room (family area). At the top of the simple spiral stair, the master suite is left, and the children's bedrooms are right. And, as noted, every occupied space in the building has access to either a balcony or to the porch.

"'Whitecaps' is a part of an effort to integrate the principles of traditional Bahamian houses with the innovative lifestyles of young Bahamians who are increasingly more concerned that their personal environment reflects their personal direction. In a world of package deals and mail-order houses, I am proud to share this celebration of the purpose-made home."

Weatherside
at Lyford Cay

ARNOLD F. ROBJOHNS,
R.I.B.A., *was born in London,
England, and opened his practice
in Nassau in 1948.*

"It's awkward for a practising architect to name his favourite house because it involves that necessary evil, his client. A client thinks that his particular house must be his architect's favourite if only because of the valuable input he himself provided, and he could be offended should the architect choose another's house.

"A way out of this dilemma is to write about a house for a client who has passed away. So I am writing about 'Weatherside', at Lyford Cay, which I designed for the late Mrs. Connie Mellon Burrell. The house is a favourite of mine because the design process ran along the lines of my particular philosophy of house designing.

"The organization of succession and sizes of rooms to suit the client's life-style and then drawing the plans is not enough. The architect should perceive, or guess at, those pleasurable subliminal elements peculiar to the client, and include in the design spaces or forms evocative of them.

"Mrs. Burrell had spent her childhood holidays in Nassau at Clerihew House (now a parking lot next to John Bull in central Bay Street), and she obviously fondly remembered the casual beach days of shelling and the style of the Porcupine Club at Hog Island (now Paradise Island). She also had a bad hip, liked to pad around barefoot and didn't fancy slippery floors. She had an Irish house in Ireland, a New England house at Woods Hole, and she wanted a Bahamian house here, which made sense.

"The Bahamian character was achieved with large porches, minimal roof eaves overhangs, chamfered wooden columns, and chimney details as in the old 'slave' kitchens. The entrance facade is a free interpretation of that delightful porch treatment of the Adderley Building, which used to stand on Bay Street about 100 yards from her childhood house.

"The style, for want of a better word, was obtained by height. The house stands on a ridge to begin with, then the house itself is raised again with wide, simple steps, then the porches are tall, as is the living room, which is proportioned on the 'golden cut' ratio, much better than the 'double cube'.

"All very evocative of her happy environment long ago, but what really polished it off was the paving stone which my gardener and I developed from coral pieces from dredged waste dumps and conchshells from the harbour dumps. So, she had a non-skid flooring and steps which needed only an occasional treatment with bleach to maintain, and which must have sent pleasant sensations to her subconscious. I know that she enjoyed it all."

Like "the Red Glow
of a Blazing Prairie Fire"

Flamingos Flourish at our Farthest Island

To some, nature might appear to have forgotten Inagua, the Bahamas' southernmost island, when she distributed her lavish gifts of flamboyant flowering shrubs and trees, pine forests and gently sloping green hills among the rest of the archipelago.

But, despite the bleakness of its landscape, Inagua possesses a unique charm which casts a spell of wonder and awe upon those who venture into its interior. Barren it may be, but it manages nevertheless to create an atmosphere of peacefulness, serenity and a strange sort of wild beauty.

That is not altogether contradictory, for more than half of this third largest of our island-group has been transformed over the past more than three decades into a wildlife sanctuary. It is there that the last remaining large flock of flamingos (*Phoenicopterus ruber*) in the Bahamas lives and breeds in the protected environment of the Inagua National Park, and under the vigilant eyes of Bahamas National Trust wardens.

To the north of the flamingo retreat lies Union Creek, also within the Park boundaries, where protected green turtles are raised and studied – much of the world's knowledge of this fascinating marine reptile has been acquired through the continuing research at Inagua.

Writing about Union Creek for the 1981 edition of **Bahamas Handbook,** former Trust president Michael E. Lightbourn commented: "It has no spectacular scenery, and on a still summer night there are hordes of blood-thirsty sandflies and mosquitos. Yet to the relatively few persons who have known the Creek it seems to hold a strange and lingering fascination."

Alexander (Sandy) Sprunt IV, who has known the flamingo sanctuary intimately for over 20 years, has written that all who have visited there "have found a beautiful place in the midst of a forbidding landscape".

It was just over 30 years ago that the first concerted move was launched in Nassau to protect the Bahamas' flock of West Indian flamingos, whose numbers had then become alarmingly depleted.

Ornithologists believe that at one time there were about 100,000 of these birds in nesting colonies scattered through the Bahamas, the West Indies and the Caribbean. By the beginning of the 1950s, however, it was estimated that, in common with the trend elsewhere, the Bahamas' flock had dwindled to about 2,500 birds or less. Today, there are approximately 40,000 flamingos, now the National Bird of the Bahamas, thriving in the sanctuary on Inagua.

Although energetic and spirited in the wild, and extremely strong fliers, flamingos are shy and live by preference in isolated places too remote to be frequented by humans. Throughout history the birds have been hunted for their brilliant feathers and for food, but in recent times the main reason for the depletion in flamingo flocks has been the ever-expanding human population, which has overflowed into areas which once provided safe breeding grounds.

A practical reason why flamingos choose to live in uninhabited places is that they build their mud nests on the ground, and both eggs and chicks are vulnerable to predators against which the birds have no defences.

Before World War II there was a fairly large flock on the west side of Andros, which provided an ideal environment for them. But when Nassau became a Royal Air Force training base in the early 1940s, the flamingos were exposed to the disturbance of low-flying aircraft, and they left their Andros sanctuary for the salt swamps and uninhabited wilderness of north-central Inagua.

Concern about the dwindling flamingo population in this part of the world had been formally recorded some 78 years ago. At their first meeting, directors of the National Audubon Society of the United States, which was incorporated on January 30,

1905, resolved to appeal to "the Governor and Assembly of the Bahamas to give the birds of those islands such legal protection as will ensure their preservation..." The Society's solicitude applied to Bahamian birdlife generally, and to the West Indian flamingo in particular.

Robert Porter Allen   *Arthur S. Vernay*

The Bahamas Government, then administered by Sir William Grey-Wilson, acted expeditiously in response to the Society's request, and, as it turned out, incidentally created a historic precedent. Passage through parliament in 1905 of The Wild Birds Protection Act was, the Audubon Society's records noted, "the first occasion in the history of mankind that special protection for the flamingo had been proposed and then established by law". By an Order-in-Council in 1920 further protection was extended to the flamingo, and in 1952 an amendment to the Act established protected reserves and a fine and/or imprisonment on conviction of killing the birds.

Undeterred by two world wars and the depression years between them, the Audubon Society's interest in the Bahamas continued, and in March 1951 their Research Director, the late Robert Porter Allen, was requested to devote his time over the ensuing three years to a field study and analysis of the causes of the decline of flamingos.

A few months later, Allen met in Nassau with the late Arthur S. Vernay, a distinguished explorer and conservationist who had a home here, and with L. E. W. Forsyth, an authority on Bahamian wildlife and many other local subjects. When Bob Allen published his research report, *The Flamingos: Their Life History and*

47

Trust president Basil T. Kelly with Velma Knowles, secretary (centre), and education officer Susan Holowesko.

Survival, Vernay, in his preface to the work, recalled that at his 1951 meeting with Allen "I realized ... that the Bahamas constituted the largest remaining stronghold (of the flamingo) .... and the best chance for their survival ... is here".

That year Vernay spearheaded the formation of The Society for the Protection of the Flamingo in the Bahamas, and Forsyth became its first president. The following year Vernay was elected president and he served for a number of years.

During his early years at Inagua, Allen hired Sam and James Nixon as wardens to ensure the flamingos' protection, and they continue to serve in that capacity today. Plans were later made for the construction of a camp on Long Cay, and when it was completed in April 1962, the Flamingo Protection Society honoured their long-serving president, who had died on October 25, 1961, by naming it Camp Vernay.

On July 13, 1959 The Bahamas National Trust was established by act of parliament, and on May 1, 1963 it officially took over the work of the Society, forming its own Flamingo Protection Division. Two years later, on April 28, 1965, the Trust was granted a 99-year lease by the Government of 287 square miles on Inagua for a nominal sum, and the Inagua Park, comprising approximately half of the island's land area, was created.

Mrs. William (Lynn) Holowesko, president of the Trust from 1976 to 1982, notes that Bob Allen "who spent so much time, energy and love on our flamingos — who camped in the open with the Nixon brothers on Jackass Cay in sight of the camp — never saw Camp Vernay. His health failed him early in life, and to the opening of the camp he sent his young associate, Alexander Sprunt IV. Bob Allen died a short time later".

For Sandy Sprunt that occasion marked the commencement of an association with Camp Vernay which still continues. In March 1982 he made his 25th visit to Inagua, and observed that three generations of Sprunts have stayed at the camp "and all have gone away refreshed and wanting to come again".

In the more than 20 years since Camp Vernay was opened, nearly 1,000 visitors have gone there to enjoy the beauty of the birds and peacefulness of the surroundings in which they thrive.

The Park has also become an important breeding area for other bird species as well. Spoonbills, Olivaceous Cormorants, Brown Pelicans, Black-necked Stilts and other waders gather there, as do Reddish Egrets, Louisiana Herons, the Common Egret and Bahamas Parrots.

One of Camp Vernay's most spectacular sights occurs during the spring when the flamingos assemble for their annual pairing-off ritual. Bob Allen has left us this description: "When it is time to build their nests and lay their eggs, wild flamingos will start proceedings by gathering in a huge flock and going through elaborate and very noisy ceremonies. It is almost like a very large

The spectacular pairing dance of the flamingos occurs in the spring.

49

dance, the massed birds prancing around shoulder to shoulder, long necks waving and twisting this way and that, and a thousand voices setting up a fearful hue and cry. But it is an impressive sight, and a picture of great beauty, the red glow of so many flamingos seen from a distance looking like a blazing prairie fire. And when it is over, the pairs are formed and the building of the nest mounds begins."

The eggs hatch in about a month, and the male and female flamingos take turns in feeding the chicks. Young flamingos can fly by the time they are some 75 days old, and during the ensuing year they venture off to nearby islets. Eventually, their brown, white and pink feathers turn to scarlet, and the young birds join the adults in the spring ceremonies which precede nest-building and the raising of a new generation of flamingos.

Those who cannot take the time to fly to Inagua can still discover the beauty of our National Bird by visiting The Ardastra Gardens in Nassau. There are some 50 flamingos, all of them born at Inagua (and a goose who thinks she's a flamingo!), who perform twice daily for fascinated visitors, going through a marching drill and then mingling shyly with spectators for photographs to be taken.

The Gardens were opened by Hedley Edwards in 1937, and it was he who first trained a small flock of flamingos to march in response to vocal and visual directions. Following his death in 1979, however, the Gardens were abandoned until in 1982 they were acquired by Norman S. Solomon, owner of Mademoiselle fashion shops, and Jeanne I. Thompson, an attorney-at-law. Hap-

Sam, left, and James Nixon have served as wardens since the early 1950s.

50

Flamingos surround Alexander Sprunt IV at Nassau's Ardastra Gardens.

pily, the Ardastra's five acres of tropical gardens and birdlife again offer a sanctuary of peacefulness, entertainment and education within a mile or so of downtown Nassau.

"We take pleasure," says Solomon, "in the fact that substantial portions of the gardens are once again almost in perfect condition. I say 'almost' because Mother Nature will not be hurried, and plant growth is a measured and gentle thing."

Of the nearly 1,000 visitors to Camp Vernay to date, Sandy Sprunt writes: "Some have come doubtfully, not knowing what to expect; others have come expectantly, looking for adventure. All have found a beautiful place in the midst of a forbidding landscape. Its beauty is quiet and many times subtle. Only those who have spent days and nights there, through the blinding light and heat of noon and the cool darkness of night, can appreciate it fully. It changes constantly – but is never dull. Perhaps its best times are early morning and late evening – long sun rays, still water and the incredible flamingos flying low in lines with their reflections looking back at them. To know that it is there – a place that changes and yet does not change – is an anchor in a world of restlessness."

John Marks Templeton speaks with gentle authority.

52

In the Gracious Templeton Home

Riches and Religion Blend Compatibly

To some 240 people, John Marks Templeton is deeply respected as the financial wizard who manages their $2 billion worth of mutual assets with spectacular success through his Templeton Growth Fund. Anyone who had the foresight – and the wherewithal – to put $50,000 in the Fund when he started it in 1954 would now have $1,850,000, for each dollar invested then is now worth $37.

But to hundreds of thousands of others, John Templeton's fame is based on his Templeton Prize for Progress in Religion, the largest cash prize awarded annually since 1972.

And that is precisely the way Templeton wants it, for when the award of the prize calls global attention to new spiritual research and development, that is far more exciting to him than progress in any other sphere of human endeavour.

"The message I want the Templeton Prize to convey," he says, "is that to us progress in religion is more important than progress in anything else, and one way to do that is by making the prize the largest in the world."

When he is not travelling on either his Fund's or his Foundation's business (and that takes about half of the year), Templeton lives with his second wife, Irene, in an elegant, plantation-style home at Lyford Cay, an exclusive resort about 15 miles west of Nassau. The house, surrounded by fluted pillars, sits on a hilltop overlooking a golf course and the Atlantic.

The Templetons moved to the Bahamas 20 years ago and bought an apartment at Cable Beach in which they lived while the Lyford Cay residence, "White Pillars", was being built.

"We searched all over the world for the most pleasant place in which to live," he states, "and while other places had obvious advantages, the Bahamas seemed to us to have more advantages than any other. We wanted to live where Jesus lives, and the Bahamian people live their religion. They open their hearts to God, and we decided we wanted to live in the minds and hearts of the people we found here."

Templeton's day starts early, at around 6:30 a.m. He has an office above the Lyford Cay Shopping Centre where he deals with the management of his five mutual funds. He employs a staff of 140 in offices located in Toronto (The Templeton Growth Fund is incorporated in Canada), Fort Lauderdale and St. Petersburg.

For exercise and recreation he swims daily. A trim and healthy 70, he reluctantly gave up golf a few years ago because he found that the three hours it required to play 18 holes was more than he could afford out of his daily religious and financial work schedule.

Templeton speaks with a gentle authority, and his style is naturally low-key. Every statement he makes is first carefully considered, and his time is deliberately planned. "I have found," he says, "that I can leave my office, have a swim and return to my desk in exactly an hour."

Because of the continuing pressures of his deeply felt responsibilities to his shareholders and the demands on his time exerted by his Foundation, Templeton has to limit his reading to religion (of any denomination) and financial reports and journals.

Since he and his wife spend half of the year travelling, they never plan a vacation. "But on our travels," he adds, "we often do things just for fun – like shopping for antiques." He says he is mildly interested in the theatre, but hasn't had time over the past five years or so to see a play.

He rates Toronto high among the list of cities he visits regularly, and he always enjoys his time in London. Oxford, where he studied economics as a Rhodes Scholar after graduating from Yale, is another of his favourite cities, and in 1983 he attended the first organized reunion of Rhodes Scholars ever held there.

A year after returning from Oxford to New York, Templeton married his first wife, Judith, who died in Bermuda in 1951 after

Mr. and Mrs. Templeton on the verandah of their Lyford Cay home.

a traffic accident. They had three children, two of whom, John, Jr., and Anne are surgeons, while the youngest, Christopher, is the leader of a charismatic religious community in North Dakota.

"About 10 years ago," Templeton explains, "Christopher found an old house near Jamestown and he established a community there. They find young people with problems and take them in and help them to straighten out."

Templeton married his present wife, the petite and attractive former Irene Reynolds Butler in 1958. She has a son and a daughter, and he refers to all of their offspring collectively as "our five".

The Templetons are obviously devoted to one another. When

55

she demurred that she was not dressed well enough to have her photograph taken with him during an interview, he prompted her affectionately to "go change, then". And when she returned, he was quick to respond with an admiring: "Well, that looks charming!"

After his freshman year at Yale in 1931, his father had to tell him that he could no longer pay college fees as the depression had wiped him out. Templeton, typically, looks upon that as "my luckiest break because it taught me very quickly to rely on myself". He won scholarships and worked his way through Yale, graduating Phi Beta Kappa at the top of his class.

Templeton first tested his investment theories in 1939 with a borrowed $10,000 fund. "It was," he reports, "the first and last time I borrowed any money." He bought $100 worth of any stocks on the American and New York exchanges selling for less than a dollar and held them until his original stake had grown to $40,000. He started his own investment fund in 1941.

Although he is a lifelong Presbyterian and an elder in the United Presbyterian Church, Templeton's devoutness and dedication have led him to develop a consuming interest in all faiths and in all religions.

"My whole heart is in the Christian gospel," he says sincerely, "and I think it is my duty to help send missionaries to people who haven't heard the gospel message. But, by the same token, I don't see why I shouldn't welcome a missionary from the Buddhist faith whose heart is in his scriptures, and who wants to explain it to me. I think it is only open-mindedness to listen carefully to that Buddhist missionary. We rejoice in diversity. We think that no one has the whole truth, and that we can learn more about God and grow spiritually if we listen to what all the different people are saying."

In a brochure he has written to explain his Prize, he notes: "This is not a prize for religion. It is not a prize for saintliness, nor mere good works, nor social justice, nor racial justice, nor peace. It is a prize for progress...It is imperative that progress in religion be accelerated as progress in science and other disciplines takes place."

The 1982 winner of the Templeton Prize was Dr. Billy Graham, who held a one-night crusade in Nassau in December of that year. The 10 winners of the prize to that time have included a Hindu scholar, a professor of theology and the founder of a Buddhist lay organization.

In 1983, the award was presented to Aleksandr Solzhenitsyn as "a pioneer in the renaissance of religion in atheist countries".

Winners are selected by a rotating eight-member panel of judges from around the world who are advised by a 60-member international panel of religious leaders. One of the current judges is the Rt. Hon. Sir Lynden Pindling, Prime Minister of the Bahamas. Templeton plays no part in choosing each year's winner. Prizes are presented at the Guildhall, London, by H.R.H. The Prince Philip.

Dr. Graham is the first evangelist to win the prize, and Templeton believes that his visit to Nassau had "an absolutely marvellous and lasting effect on Christian Bahamians". It is his hope to establish the Bahamas as a centre for religion, and to help build that reputation the Templeton Foundation plans to bring prizewinners to Nassau for three days each year so that, through the international media, attention will be focussed on the Bahamas as the place from which the Templeton Prize emanates.

Each year the Foundation offers prizes to high school students here for the best essay on "The Greatest National Treasure in the Bahamas", which, in Templeton's view, is "the religious spirit in the hearts of the Bahamian people". Also, 15 partial bursaries to Princeton Theological Seminary are provided annually to enable ministers in the Bahamas to become better educated for the Christian ministry. Free investment counsel is given by the Foundation to any denomination in the Bahamas requesting it to improve its financial resources.

Templeton believes that the whole world, including the Bahamas, faces "a marvellous future. More books are being written than ever before, more goods are being produced than in any earlier era, and scientific knowledge is doubling every 20 years".

In Lyford Cay's rarefied atmosphere of wealth and high society, God and millions seem utterly compatible in the gracious Templeton household. He plans to retire from all business activities in 10 years to devote himself fully to his religious studies. "I do not think," he smiles, "that I should remain on as chief executive beyond my eightieth birthday."

Gazing out of a tall northern window of his living room, across the bright green of fairways to the sun-dappled ocean, Templeton remarks: "Learning the total joy of religion is a slow growing process, and I still regard myself as a student. God is a million times greater than human beings, so I can only hope to learn a small part of Him."

Agent flees irate voters demanding anticipated payment.

Election Shenanigans

They added Zest to
Political Campaigns

A s recently as 35 years ago the Bahamas lagged behind the rest of
the civilized world in the way political campaigns were conducted. Some candidates seeking election to the House of Assembly
openly flaunted the law which prohibited vote-buying, and while
the practice did not have official sanction, no serious efforts had
been made then to eliminate it.

A retired senior parliamentarian, in fact, recalls that an
English Commissioner of Police once admitted he knew perfectly
well what went on in elections here, but he had come to regard paying for votes as "a Bahamian tradition".

In many of the undeveloped out islands, a general election was
about the only "cash crop" the residents harvested. Subsistence
farming might provide a primitive standard of living, but the money
which was passed out by a candidate's agent to get them to the polls
brought to many settlements the kind of cash flow they only experienced at election time.

And it could be a long wait between elections, although most
"representors" became resigned to having to dig in their pockets
again whenever one of their constituents managed to come to Nassau. Prior to 1962 the life of a House, unless dissolved sooner, was
seven years, a term which had been stipulated in the Septennial Act
of 1795. Since the former date general elections are held every five
years.

The secret ballot was not introduced in New Providence constituencies until 1939, and it was another 10 years before it was extended to the out islands. "Open voting", as can be imagined, invited bribery, for each elector was obliged to declare verbally to the returning officer how he wanted his vote recorded. In most cases, that was likely to be in favour of the candidate who had promised the highest reward for his ballot. With a check list of the register of voters in front of him, a candidate's agent in the polling station would know precisely who had earned a monetary reward. With the establishment of the secret ballot, candidates who paid out on speculation before the balloting took place exposed themselves to a very uncertain gamble.

There can be no question, of course, that it was lawbreaking in an outrageously blatant form, but in point of fact the practice was not as thoroughly corrupt as it must appear from this distance in time and outside the contemporary Bahamian context.

Most of the Bahamas was relatively poor country then, and voters with very little education did not understand the concept that the vote they had been given was a right they should not abuse. From the voter's point of view, if he went to the trouble to cast his ballot he felt that the person for whom he voted was under an obligation to reward his effort. Candidates, on the other hand, who were offering to serve the country in the House without a parliamentary salary, faced the practical fact that the only way they could secure election was by promising money for each vote in their favour.

In most cases, then, victory went to the candidate with the most money to spend. There were no political parties at the time, but the establishment leaders, known as the "Bay Street Boys", invariably assembled a singularly potent and efficient election machine. Planes and boats were chartered, far enough in advance to deprive the opposition of vital transportation, and "generals" from Nassau were distributed among the islands to liaise with local "generals". Shipments of food, liquor and, of course, money were quickly organized when needed in the constituencies.

These "blitzkrieg" tactics were especially effective in the days when the dates of out island elections were staggered, and groups of powerful political leaders and their Nassau supporters moved from one constituency to another, ahead of the polling, for last-minute public meetings in a show of strength on behalf of the establishment candidate.

The 1949 general elections witnessed the end of wholesale open bidding for votes in exchange for money. In the Acklins and Crooked Island constituency the voting was extremely close, but in favour of the

Secret ballot cleaned up elections but never dampened enthusiasm. Eleuthera winning candidates in the 1960s were brothers George and Useph Baker (standing, second and third from left), shown with barrister E.A.P. Dupuch (fourth from left).

machine's candidate. The loser, a brilliant young lawyer, was in the constituency the day after the polls were held, collecting affidavits from his supporters swearing that they had been given money to vote for his opponent. He turned the affidavits over to the English Attorney General and to the Elections Committee of the House, and as a result a number of prominent politicians and well-known citizens received summonses. The winning candidate resigned, and the young lawyer won the by-election unopposed.

The Attorney General was known to be anxious to prosecute, but by the time those who had been summonsed appeared before the English magistrate for a preliminary hearing of the charges, the government had been advised by the Colonial Office not to proceed. With great reluctance, *nolle prosequis* were entered by the Crown.

One of those charged, who was a social friend of the magistrate, recalls that after his appearance in court they met at a nearby pub. As he was toasting his deliverance from the possibility of a prison term, the magistrate looked him in the eye and said: "You have no idea how much I was looking forward to sending the lot of you up for trial!" The two then proceeded to have a few more drinks, the one celebrating his good fortune, while the other calmed his disgust at the withdrawal of documented bribery charges in the middle of the 20th century. Only those who were in the top echelon of the power group knew what transpired behind closed doors before that decision was reached.

Many candidates arranged to give their local "generals" an agreed sum after the election results were announced for distribution among their supporters. At an election in Grand Bahama many years ago, the Bay Street candidate agreed to pay his "general" at Eight Mile Rock £500 (then about $2,000) if he delivered that polling division. He did so, overwhelmingly, so he later approached the winner and said: "Mr. K., you know dat's wort' more 'an £500 — mus' be more like £2,000."

Without a word, the candidate took out his cheque book and wrote a cheque for £2,000 payable to his "general". It was not until the latter presented it for payment at The Royal Bank of Canada in Nassau that he discovered the cheque had been signed "Pine Tree". The disconsolate man looked at the teller who had returned the cheque to him and complained: "Oh my Gawd, Mr. K. done put one over on muh!" Later he met with Mr. K. and happily accepted £500 in cash.

Back in the 1940s, an out island election campaign could cost a candidate anywhere from £3,000 to £5,000 and then for the next seven years he could count on having to pay out £2,000 or more annually to look after supporters who came to him for financial assistance in a variety of forms. A retired House member recalls that in those days his income was around £4,000 a year, "and half of it would go to looking after my supporters in the islands".

Plural voting used to be common. At one time a director of a limited liability company was entitled to vote on behalf of the company, and a man owning or renting properties in a number of constituencies could vote in all of them, in addition to the one in which he voted on a residence qualification. It was not unusual for a candidate in the islands to buy a plot of land in the constituency in which he was offering, then subdivide it and have small parcels conveyed to supporters he would bring in from Nassau so they would be qualified to vote for him. After the election they would sell their parcels back to him at the price for which they had "bought" them.

Although members of the power bloc were usually business or professional men who lived in Nassau, occasionally it happened that in a few of the more sophisticated islands ambitious local leaders were able to exercise control over the electorate. Before World War I, the Harbour Island District, a three-member constituency which included a part of North Eleuthera, was in the pockets of two brothers named Johnson, and whoever they decided to put on the ticket with them was certain of being elected.

At the time, senior English civil servants — Colonial Secretary, Receiver General and Treasurer and Attorney General — were allowed to run for House seats as candidates, and in a Harbour Island election the Receiver General decided to challenge the Johnson ticket. He was a popular figure in the colony and believed that he had strong independent support in the constituency.

But he reckoned without the wily Johnsons. As soon as his nomination papers were in they spread the rumour that, because he was Receiver General, as soon as he was elected he intended to introduce new taxes. They hired a man to walk around settlements in North Eleuthera, where the Receiver General might have been a threat to them, with a book and pencil in his hand, and as he stopped in front of each house he could be seen making notes in his book. When curious residents asked him what he was doing, he told them that the Receiver General planned to tax each house by the number of window sashes it had, "but," he would add, "don't tell anyone".

When on election day the Receiver General arrived at each polling station, he was greeted by groups of men who told him "don't put your foot ashore, or we'll throw you overboard". He later left the colony, never knowing why the Harbour Island voters had turned against him en masse.

Savannah Sound at one time was known as "the Athens of Eleuthera" because the people there were all well-educated and the men were first-rate public speakers. John Solomon Gibson, decades ago, was the settlement's undisputed leader. The late Gilbert Albury was the resident justice there and Gibson was his best friend. In the 1925 general election Gibson was caught red-handed buying votes, and charges were laid. He tried desperately to see Albury, who refused to meet with him. Later, Albury admitted: "I sweated John Solomon", but when he appeared before the resident justice the latter dismissed the case because Gibson was basically a fine man and a strong community leader.

Once when a Bay Street merchant offered in an out island constituency, he was visited in his clothes shop by one of the voters who said he couldn't possibly go to the poll as badly dressed as he was. So the merchant outfitted him completely since he was an influential person in one of the settlements. But when the man came into the station to declare his vote, he looked the merchant in the eye and boldly called out the name of his opponent.

Around the same time, a man named Gussie, the catechist in an out island village, accepted money for his vote from the two opposing candidates. However, when he went to the poll he was horrified to find that both candidates were present at the station. Asked what he did then, he replied: "Man, I put muh shoulder-basket on, and I gone into der field — what else I cudda do?"

An old-time former House member says, "I never paid a penny for a vote for the same reason I've never taken a drink of liquor — I'm afraid of it." But he remembers an election in the Eastern District of New Providence when he acted as agent for one of the candidates. He was also asked to take on the task of paying off the voters as well, but he refused, he says.

However, "out of hellery", as he puts it, he carried around a bag containing about £20 so that the voters would think he would be paying them off. It became known that the price agreed by the candidate was £2 for each vote in his favour, but one of the voters kept following the agent around and asking for £3. When the voter went into the polling station, the agent accompanied him, but before declaring his vote he looked at the agent and wheedled: "Come on, gimme three!" The agent glanced around nervously and found himself staring at the Commissioner of Police. Collecting himself, he grabbed the voter's arm and called loudly: "Three what?" and he hustled him from the poll.

During another election in the East, another agent led the voters to believe that if his candidate won they would be paid off, but in the confusion following the counting of ballots he was unable to make contact with the person who actually had the money. In one division the voters cornered him in a school room, and pressed him to pay them. Fortunately for the agent, a prize-giving had been held recently in the school yard, and bleachers had been left there. "The voters were getting rambunctious," he relates, "and I was getting scared, so I jumped up on the platform and told them I would have to go for the money. But they rushed the platform, so I leaped out of the window onto the bleachers and kept running for my life!"

Throughout the 1950s a great deal of pressure was exerted to secure votes for women. The ladies who spearheaded the movement were strongly backed by opponents of the Bay Street Boys in the belief that the majority of women would vote to oust the power group, who resisted their appeals for the same reason. Finally, in 1960 women were enfranchised, but in the general election held two years later the Bay Street Boys were returned with an even larger majority than they had held previously.

Electioneering in the old days was a colourful and often amusing exercise, and despite the fact that the electorate was exploited there were times when voters, who were more sophisticated, perhaps, than

64

they appeared to be, managed to turn the tables on candidates who incurred their displeasure.

Candidates, too, sometimes succeeded in confounding their opponents with a surprise tactic. In his book, *A Salute to Friend and Foe*, Sir Etienne Dupuch recounts how he was once able to disconcert the supporters of the man running against him in an election in the Inagua and Mayaguana constituency, where he was the incumbent.

The power bloc, which then wanted Sir Etienne out of the House, had nominated Charlie Sargent, who was well-liked and respected in Inagua, and Sir Etienne felt sure that he himself would be defeated, although he still retained some support in the island. He was, though, extremely popular in Mayaguana, but because the two islands are separated by over 100 miles of ocean, transportation problems had always prevented the voters of Mayaguana from getting to the single polling station at Mathew Town, Inagua.

On this occasion, however, Sir Etienne had been loaned a motor vessel, the *Marmaduke*, for his campaign, and aboard it he travelled to Mayaguana. There he picked up all of the excited and delighted registered voters for the voyage across the Caicos Passage.

"We arrived at Inagua the next day," he writes, "accomplishing a complete surprise. We steamed past Mathew Town singing songs of victory. All the men crowded on the side of the boat facing the town. I even had men hanging from the riggings..."

The Inagua leaders attempted to board the *Marmaduke*, but they were repulsed.

"The opposition wanted to reach my Mayaguanans, of course, to corrupt them," Sir Etienne recounts. "After all, these people were poor ... And so a little bribery might go a long way."

What the opposition also wanted to find out, naturally, was exactly how many men were aboard the *Marmaduke*.

On election day, Sargent's Inagua supporters gave him an early comfortable lead, so Sir Etienne sent a boat load of Mayaguanans ashore and he moved ahead, which encouraged his supporters on the island.

"Every time Sargent took the lead I sent a boat load ashore and took it from him," Sir Etienne records triumphantly. "No one had any idea how many voters I had on my boat. They must have seemed inexhaustible to the people in Mathew Town. By 11 o'clock the Sargent camp was demoralized and I won the election."

As one experienced campaigner notes: "Even more so than today, in years past you always had to be at least one jump ahead of your opponent if you had any hope of winning, especially in the out islands."

The New Charmant Coordinates Luxury with Economy.

Small-car economy and
big-car luxury in the same vehicle? Yes!
Daihatsu's new Charmant proves
that an efficient compact can be big enough for comfort.
The new Charmant is bigger than current models (LGX and LE models
are 90mm longer and LGX, LE and LC models are 95mm wider).
That means wider seats, and enough space for deluxe interior features.
But the quality and comfort of a high-class saloon is
actually contained in an economy-class compact.
The new Charmant gives big performance with small fuel consumption,
especially if you choose the economical 1,290cc engine.
For bigger power, select the 1,588cc version.
Mileage. Power. Space. Luxury. And gorgeous new styling.
Daihatsu's new Charmant has the big things you want,
and the small things you need.

DAIHATSU CHARMANT

Model LE

Model LE (Moquette full fabric seats with split rear seatbacks: option)

Model LE

KC NEW CAR SALES LTD.

Victoria Avenue and Dowdeswell Street, P.O. Box N-273,
Nassau, Bahamas. Tel: 5-4825/6, 5-2500.

Leisure
and Vacation

The Sunley Building marks the western end of Rawson Square, which is on the harbour in the centre of Nassau.

Your Special Vacation Guide to

Six Days of Fun in the Sun

After weeks of planning and anticipation, you've finally arrived at New Providence Island, on which Nassau is located, and ahead lie six glorious days of vacationing in the sun. Left far behind are the pressures of business and the sometimes monotonous routine of everyday living—for the next six days you're going to enjoy a relaxing, carefree and entertaining holiday in one of the world's most beautiful resorts.

If you arrive by plane, you will land at Nassau's International Airport, which is about 12 miles west of the capital city. You'll pass through an immigration check (for details of documents required, see **Immigration** on page 296), and into the customs area where you'll collect your luggage for examination.

Here a word of caution – do not attempt to bring with you any type of dangerous drugs, even in very small quantities for your own use. If you're caught (and chances are you will be) you'll be arrested and, on conviction, given a heavy fine and, possibly, imprisonment.

Unless you are already familiar with New Providence you'll want to take a taxi to your hotel. If you do decide to rent a car from one of the international agencies at the airport, remember that in the Bahamas we drive on the left, and because of the relative narrowness of most roads our speed limits are deliberately low.

If you've booked into one of the Cable Beach hotels, taxi fare for two should come to around $11; should your hotel be in or near the city, the fare will be about $14. Taxi rates to hotels on Paradise Island average $16. All taxis are required by law to be equipped with meters in good working condition. If you've booked your holiday through a tour company, a representative of the firm will meet you outside the Customs room and transport you to your hotel.

So, having settled comfortably into your room, let's take a day-by-day look at some of the things you can enjoy during your stay in what Christopher Columbus described 491 years ago as these "isles of Perpetual June".

DAY ONE – If you're staying at a beach hotel, one look out of the window on arising will convince you that the irresistible way to start the day is with a swim in our astonishingly clear and beautiful sea. The early mornings and late afternoons, incidentally, are the safest times to start acquiring that golden tan you'll want to show off back home.

After breakfast, a good suggestion is that you spend an hour or two on the beach and in the sea to get rid of the tensions of travelling and any left-over strain from the work-week that's now behind you. It's a relaxing way, too, to meet other vacationers with whom you may later want to share some of your holiday activities.

It's only about a 10- or 12-minute drive by taxi from Cable Beach into Nassau, or you may want to take one of the small "jitney" buses. Their western schedules are fairly reliable, and they make convenient stops in the area of the oceanfront hotels. Guests of the smaller hotels near the city can enjoy a stroll along the harbourfront, past the Sheraton-British Colonial Hotel, through Navy Lion Road and Woodes Rogers Walk into Rawson Square in the centre of Nassau.

There are several small restaurants where local business and professional people meet for lunch (always a good guide to quality of food and service), with menus offering Bahamian specialties, European and American dishes and English "pub" fare. Try one of our exotic tropical drinks with a leisurely lunch – rum, of course, is the "wine of the country" and the Bacardi Rum company has a large distillery in New Providence – then take a sightseeing stroll around Bay Street, which is the main thoroughfare, and the interesting side-streets.

Visit the native straw markets to buy a colourful straw hat and other souvenirs; do some window-shopping, too, but save the

A horse-drawn surrey wheels down Bay Street at a leisurely pace.
Parallel to the harbour, Bay Street is Nassau's "downtown".

more important aspects of bargain-hunting for personal purchases and gifts until you can make that a special project another
day. Stop in at one of the tour agencies, or engage a taxi for a
morning of island-sightseeing the next day.

You can board a "jitney" or Paradise Island bus to take you
back to your hotel for another swim before cocktails and dinner.
Chances are that you'll want to spend the first night at the hotel
where you're staying, and it can be as quiet or exhilarating an evening as you feel like making it. All of the major hotels offer a variety of restaurants and late-night entertainment.

DAY TWO — one advantage of a relaxed first night is that
you can make an early start on your sightseeing — and don't forget to take your camera along, too.

Until you've become more familiar with the island's roads
and our driving customs, it's best to visit the sights by taxi or tour
car and learn about the points of interest from their drivers.
Later, you can rent a car, scooter or bicycle and with a Trailblazer

Map (free at your hotel) to guide you, you'll be able to move about the city and suburbs in your own time. (See **Transportation** on page 348 for rental rates.)

Your guided tour will include visits to one or more of the 18th century forts on New Providence. Fort Charlotte, the largest of the three, was completed in 1789, and is built on a ridge which commands a view of the harbour entrance west of the city.

The hill continues south of Nassau to Fort Fincastle (built in 1793) and the Water Tower which stands at the top of the Queen's Staircase, all of which points will be included in your tour. Named for Queen Victoria, whose statue presides over Parliament Square in the centre of Nassau, the treads and risers of the "staircase" were cut by slaves into the solid hillside and bricked. Take the elevator to the top of the Water Tower for a spectacular panoramic view of the city and the surrounding countryside and suburbs.

The drive along East Bay Street takes you past three marinas and the Nassau Yacht Club, Fort Montagu (erected in 1741), lovely Montagu Bay where local and international regattas are sailed, the Royal Nassau Sailing Club and onto the Eastern Road.

The eastern section of New Providence is where many prosperous Bahamians live, and in that area you will see some of our most splendid homes and attractively landscaped gardens, alive with the brilliant colours of the blooms and foliage of tropical trees, plants and shrubs.

Your tour may include a visit to Blackbeard's Tower, which the infamous pirate is reputed to have built so that he could post a lookout there while he roistered in Nassau. The return trip will take you to Fox Hill, a picturesque native village which was originally settled by freed slaves, then you drive past St. Augustine's College and Monastery where the Benedictine monks in the Bahamas live.

Back in Nassau, and after a relaxing lunch, complete your day's sightseeing on foot with visits to the Public Library (built in the 18th century as a gaol, but used as a library and museum since 1879). Walk along Shirley Street west to Frederick Street where the Central Bank of the Bahamas stands, and stroll south on Frederick to Princes' Street and Government House. There's a statue there of Columbus, who discovered the gateway to the West when he made his first landfall in the New World at the Bahamian island of Guanahani (he re-named it San Salvador) in 1492. From Government House, walk back to the city down tree-lined George Street, stopping en route for a look inside Christ

Church Cathedral, which was built in 1840.

Get back to your hotel in time for a refreshing swim and, perhaps, a rest so that you can enjoy an evening sampling some of the island's exciting nightlife. A few of Nassau's gourmet restaurants have gained international reputations, and all of them offer excellent cuisine, imaginative wine lists and attractive settings. Your best bet is to study a free copy of What-To-Do Magazine, and select a restaurant which offers the type of food you enjoy, or whose menu tempts you with a new dining experience.

The choice of entertainment around New Providence and Paradise Island is excitingly varied. There's everything available from a spectacular Vegas-type cabaret to native shows featuring fire and limbo dancers, expert congo drummers and artists on the steel drums, and goombay rhythms. Again, check your What-To-Do to find out what's playing and where.

Casino gambling is available at the Ambassador Beach Hotel and at Paradise Island. Both casinos are owned by the Government's Hotel Corporation. (See **Gambling**, page 289.)

DAY THREE — If you ended your night on the town with some cool disco dancing into the early morning, you'll want to sleep in late and then enjoy a reviving swim and lie in the sun before lunch.

As a fascinating change of pace, try a nature tour for some educational entertainment. Start with the early afternoon show at the Seafloor Aquarium where you can view some of our colourful reef fish, turtles, sharks, sea lions and dolphins.

In the same area as the aquarium is the Botanic Garden where, for a peaceful interlude, you can stroll around 16 acres of beautiful and fascinating tropical flora. Then it's a short walk to the Ardastra Gardens to enjoy the afternoon performance by 50 marching flamingos, and wander through the garden's aviary and miniature zoo (see page 50).

To complete a relaxing day, take a dinner cruise through the harbour — check with your hotel's social hostess to arrange bookings.

DAY FOUR — Having got a glimpse at the aquarium of some of the marvels of the Bahamas' underwater wonderland, you'll want to see more of it. Several companies offer diving tours to nearby shallow reefs, generally around Rose Island, and a few hours spent exploring spectacular coral formations and the beautifully coloured fish which live in and around them will form one of the most memorable experiences of your vacation.

73

If you really get bitten by the diving bug (and many thousands of visitors have), you can enroll for a short course of instruction in scuba-diving and widen the scope of your underwater explorations. Perhaps next year you'll want to book one of the exciting dive holidays that are available on several of the outer islands.

After lunch, to make this a day under and on the sea, arrange to rent a sail- or powerboat through your hotel and get away to one of the nearby small cays where you can have a secluded beach all to yourselves. The protected waters off Cable Beach and Paradise Island are ideal for water-skiing and windsurfing, and for a different view of the island try a parasail ride.

DAY FIVE — Since this will be your last evening in Nassau or on Paradise Island, have a chat after breakfast with the social hostess to discover what's happening on the local scene that might offer a new and different experience. For instance, there might be a play, a musical or ballet being staged at the Dundas Centre for the Performing Arts, and often soloists and musicians of international repute fill engagements at one of the major hotels. Performances usually end at around 11 p.m., so there would still be lots of time left for night clubbing, dancing or another visit to one of the casinos.

On your earlier visits to the city you will have browsed around many of Nassau's attractive shops where luxury goods from around the world are displayed — and many of them at bargain prices. No doubt you will have made mental notes, and done some cost comparisons, of the items which appeal to you as gifts for friends and relatives and for personal use or adornment, and now you can devote the whole morning to shopping.

The attitude of Bahamian sales personnel is generally helpful, but low-key — nobody is going to try to pressure you into buying — so shopping here becomes another relaxing and pleasant experience.

After all of the gourmet dining and wining you've indulged yourself with and the occasional late night of island entertainment, you'll probably feel the need for some healthy exercise.

If you're staying at one of the large resorts, you'll be able to rent a tennis court there, and hire racquets if you haven't brought your own. There'll also be a qualified pro for coaching, and he or she can probably arrange a doubles game with other guests who play to your standard.

If you're a squash enthusiast, there are two clubs on New

United Shipping Company (Nassau) Ltd.

**SHIPPING AGENTS
PASSENGER SERVICES
AND STEVEDORES**

REPRESENTING: *Norwegian Caribbean Lines *Royal Caribbean Cruise Line *Carnival Cruise Lines *Yugoslav Line *Sun Line *Hellenic Mediterranean Line *American Atlantic Lines, *Mitsui O.S.K. Line *United States Line (Freight) *Marine Agents & Brokers Ltd. *D.S.R. Line *Independent Gulf Line.

Nassau * Bahamas - P.O. Box N-4005. Tel: 2-1340/3. Telex: 20 160
Freeport * Bahamas - P.O. Box F-2552. Tel: 352-9315. Telex: 30 048
Cables: "UNITEDSHIP"

Providence where visitors can book a court, but as this has become a very popular sport here it would be best to make your arrangements well in advance.

Both New Providence and Paradise Island have some great 18-hole golf courses, and all major hotels are located near one of them. Perhaps the most testing layout is at South Ocean Beach Hotel, and scenically it is one of the most attractive.

After your game, the sea will beckon, and perhaps there'll be time for a snorkelling trip to a shallow inshore reef before preparing for whatever evening entertainment you've planned.

DAY SIX— What you do on the last day of your vacation depends, of course, on your flight time. If your departure is scheduled for early afternoon, you'll probably only have time before packing for a final swim and a session in the sun to perfect the bronze tan you will have acquired.

An evening flight gives the opportunity for another visit to Nassau for last-minute shopping and some more leisurely sightseeing. Try a surrey ride for a restful tour of the city, and enjoy the informative, and often amusing, patter of the driver-guide.

If you can arrange to prolong your stay for a few days, plan to visit one of the beautiful out islands. We call them the Family Islands, and many of them offer an atmosphere of tranquillity and charm that has remained virtually unchanged by the passage of time. There are quaint villages to explore and incomparably lovely beaches to enjoy.

Accommodations in the islands vary from the luxurious to the unsophisticated comfort of small clubs, inns and guest houses. Bahamasair, the national carrier, operates scheduled flights to all of the principal islands — there are several charter services, too — and any local travel agent will help you select the resort which provides the amenities that suit your taste in out island-living.

Inevitably, though, the time comes when you have to leave, but your departure will be cheered by the happy memories you'll have of your Bahamas' vacation — and, of course, the islands will still be here on your return.

Native crafts like straw-work
(above) and woodcarving appeal
to Bahamas vacationers.

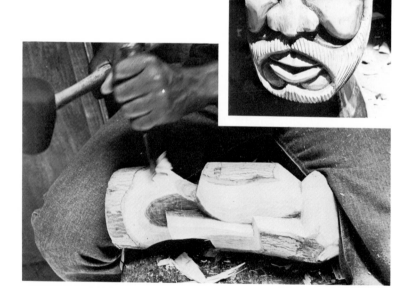

Tourism Update

Hitting the Magic Two Million Mark

Tourism is the national business of the Bahamas. Two out of every three Bahamians who hold jobs owe their employment, directly or indirectly, to the industry, which also produces about 60 per cent of the country's foreign currency earnings, and more than half of the government's annual revenue. Visitor spending in 1982 was estimated at $695 million, with a projected increase of over 10 per cent during 1983 from more than two million tourists.

The pattern of tourism has gone through many changes since the doors of Nassau's first major hotel, The Royal Victoria, were opened to visitors 122 years ago. It was the hope of its forward-looking promoters that The Royal Vic would attract at least 500 visitors annually, an estimate that proved to be under-stated initially because of the outbreak of the American Civil War.

Nassau then became prosperous overnight as a trading station for the sale of European-made armaments to the Southern States, and for the trans-shipment of cotton from the South to the mills of Lancashire. The Royal Victoria's accommodations were often taxed to capacity by the presence of Confederate Army officers, daring blockade-runners, agents of Southern cotton planters and representatives of English mills.

But tourism was to experience many transmutations before the 1861 anticipated yearly total of 500 visitors would grow to the two million, plus, tourists who come to the Bahamas today.

At the conclusion of the war in America, the briefly buoyant economy here sank swiftly, bringing a recession that was to last, in varying degrees, through World War I until the illusionary experiment of national prohibition was begun in 1920 in the United States.

It was during the 1920s, also, that the speculative land boom in Florida spread to Nassau, and the newly acquired wealth of both Americans and Bahamians was reflected in the construction of large new homes along Cable Beach, Prospect Ridge, The Grove and the Eastern Road. By the 1930s, Nassau, like Palm Beach, had established a reputation as an exclusive winter resort for those rich enough to be able to afford a holiday home in the sun from around mid-November to Washington's Birthday on February 22.

By 1937 the visitor count had soared to 34,000, and because of World War II that total would not be exceeded until 1951. The year previous to that the late Sir Stafford Sands had been appointed Chairman of the Development Board (precursor of the Ministry of Tourism), and under his dynamic leadership highly successful programmes were implemented to promote tourism as a year-round industry, as opposed to the previous three- or four-month winter season activity. By the time Sir Stafford resigned as Minister for Tourism in 1967, the total visitor-arrivals figure was over 800,000, and continued to climb through the decade of the 1970s.

The Bahamas came close in 1980 to the magical figure of two million tourists, with a total of 1.90 million, but due to the recession in the U.S., 1981 witnessed a drop back to 1.7 million. However, despite continuing worldwide economic problems during 1982, visitor-arrivals again climbed, to 1.94 million, and early in 1983 the Ministry predicted an increase of between 10 and 12 per cent to surpass the previously elusive two million mark.

The country is fortunate in having an energetic and imaginative Director-General of Tourism in the person of Baltron Bethel. A former civil servant, Bethel has an extensive background in administration, and since being appointed Deputy Director-General in May 1978 and *de facto* Director-General from January 1979 he has revealed a flair for promotional planning, and developed an understanding of and expertise in all areas of the tourist market.

It is from the U.S. that the Bahamas draws the greatest percentage of its visitors, and during 1981 Americans were hard hit by high interest rates, rampant inflation, reduced consumer spending, an erratic stock market and a sharp reduction in air transportation due to the air controllers' strike in mid-year.

Bethel explains how he and his senior colleagues in the Ministry were able to effect such an impressive turn-around during

Minister of Tourism, Perry G. Christie, left, discusses a promotional brochure with the Ministry's Director-General, Baltron Bethel.

1982 thus: "Three years ago it was evident to us that a recession in the U.S. was approaching, and that it would last longer than was then predicted. Also, we recognized that the recession in Europe would be deeper and even longer lasting.

"We, therefore, began, in addition to our normal marketing plans, to concentrate on co-operative marketing with airlines and cruise lines, major wholesalers and travel agents. We were able to increase our profile in the travel trade press, and through travel writers and with agents. Thus, despite escalating transportation costs, we were able to maximize the use of joint funds and resources on co-operative space buying, and we made sure that way that sales personnel pushed the Bahamas."

The Ministry also maintained a close dialogue with hoteliers who agreed to offer a wider range of room prices at the lower end of their rates, while leaving luxury accommodation costs at regular levels. Attractive packages were offered, based on economy air fares during low-traffic days (Tuesdays, Wednesdays and Thurs-

81

days), and better group fares were negotiated with some airlines.

"We also kept up a constant dialogue with the airlines," Bethel adds, "to obtain more services from existing, and new, gateways at competitive prices allied to the cost of flying to south Florida. We concentrated most of our efforts in the traditional markets in the U.S., Canada and Europe, but while we were able to increase travel from America we lost out in Europe because of the loss in value of European trading currencies in relation to the dollar."

Up to three years ago the Bahamas attracted a substantial number of European visitors, especially from Germany. They tended to take longer holidays here than the average North American tourist, and were generally pretty free-spenders. But the gradual strengthening of the U.S. dollar (with which the Bahamian dollar is at par) against European currencies, particularly the Deutschmark, persuaded many former and prospective visitors from Europe to look to other resort areas where they felt they got better value for their money.

The sharp reduction in demand for passenger-seats from Germany to Nassau led Lufthansa to cancel its Frankfurt-Nassau-Mexico City flights in April 1981, and about the same time International Air Bahama, which for years had been an important carrier out of Luxembourg, went out of business.

Since then visitors from England and Europe have, in the majority, arrived via the U.S. because the density of traffic allows airlines to charge lower fares than is the case on direct U.K.-Nassau flights.

"Our strategy over the last three years," Bethel explains, "has been to maintain a presence in Europe, and that has paid off in the U.K. British Airways has instituted promotional fares to the Bahamas, via Miami, on the theme 'You Can Afford the Bahamas'. Fortunately for us, too, while hoteliers here were able to hold the line, prices in the traditional English resort markets of Spain and the Mediterranean shot up. In Europe we're re-directing our efforts towards encouraging large industries and businesses there to offer holidays in the Bahamas as employee incentives for sales production."

In early March 1983 British Airways announced that during the coming summer months it would be reducing its previous tri-weekly direct service from London to Nassau to twice-weekly. However, its Tristar aircraft would be replaced by more fuel-efficient and larger Boeing 747s, thus actually offering more seats weekly to Nassau than previously.

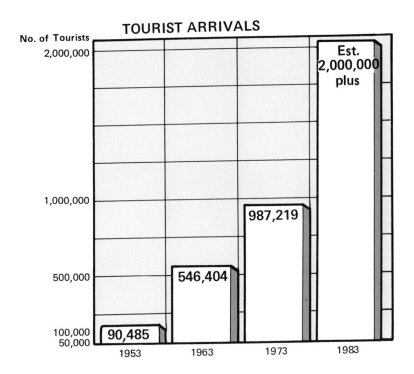

TOURIST ARRIVALS

No. of Tourists

2,000,000 — Est. 2,000,000 plus

1,000,000 — 987,219

500,000 — 546,404

100,000 / 50,000 — 90,485

1953   1963   1973   1983

The Ministry's projected increase of between 10 and 12 per cent in visitor arrivals during 1983 is a conservative estimate, Bethel feels. The budget for 1982 was $21.1 million, which, it was thought, did not really keep pace with inflated media and promotional costs. For 1983, estimated expenditure was set at $29.3 million, a significant increase which Bethel regards as the government's recognition that expansion of the country's overall economy depends directly on an increase in tourism. The 1983 vote of funds to the Ministry made it the fourth largest expenditure item in the budget, below public debt financing, education and health.

The Ministry's strategy to ensure continued growth in 1983 involved, according to Bethel, "more emphasis on quality of product in terms of what we have on shore. We want to add to our attractions and emphasize delivery of product".

Following the June 10, 1982 general election, the Prime Minister, Sir Lynden Pindling, K.C.M.G., P.C., M.P., announced a major Cabinet change by making 40-year-old Perry Christie the new Minister of Tourism. A barrister by profession, Christie, who was previously Minister of Health, has brought a refreshing enthusiasm and elan to his new responsibilities. He has developed a definite and pleasing aptitude for promotion, is an impressive public speaker and a dedicated ambassador from the Bahamas to the travel industry.

His aim is to involve all Bahamians in as many aspects of tourism as possible, and to expose visitors to every facet of the Bahamas, particularly its culture and its history, through special promotions. "I want to mobilize all agencies related to tourism to integrate with the Ministry in promoting the Bahamas," he says. "I have a total commitment to selling the Bahamian product and to enhancing it wherever possible."

To fill the gap in the tourist ranks left by the loss of volume European business, the Ministry has also been concentrating on developing potential markets in South America, from where there is already a constant stream of visitors to Miami. Working with the airlines, the Ministry is evolving travel/vacation packages which are competitive with what Miami offers, and intensive marketing is being done in Colombia, Venezuela, Ecuador, Chile and Brazil.

The Ministry has also been able to increase by some 40 per cent the number of air-seats available to the Bahamas from traditional U.S. markets in the southwest and northeast. In late February 1983 Bethel was able to report: "As the result of a great deal of research – in-house and outside – in close collaboration with marketing experts, carriers and the hotel industry, we are very much on course for 1983. We have been able to move quickly – but only after indepth research."

The Ministry's efforts are primarily directed towards attracting visitors with incomes in the middle and upper-middle levels, and to catering for special interest groups, such as scuba-divers, private aircraft owners, yachtsmen, anglers, honeymooners and others.

"If we're going to increase our revenue," Bethel explains, "we've got to be competitive with those people who have money to spend, otherwise our efforts are going to be counter-productive."

Marketing today is directed at people with an average annual household income of $30,000, plus.

The Bahamas has already become the number one destination for scuba-divers, and the Ministry plans to further upgrade its promotion and publicity in that area. There are now 17 facilities throughout the islands – more than any other part of the world.

The Bahamas National Trust and the Dive Resort Association planned during 1983 to approach the Ministry of Agriculture and

Outstanding

From its multimillion-dollar marina, with all yacht and fuel services, to its beautiful sandy beaches with crystal-clear waters, Cape Eleuthera Resort has it all.

Bruce Devlin-designed golf course, six tennis courts, fantastic scuba diving and snorkeling, dock-side immigration and customs, laundromat, showers, marina and tackle shop, and villas, if you want to come ashore. Make your next cruise to Cape Eleuthera Resort.

For reservations call 800-327-5753.

Fla. 800-432-6577. Reservations worldwide by Utell International and British Caledonian.

Fisheries to set aside specific areas as fishing reserves. "We not only have a great variety of dives here—shallow diving, wall diving and drops – but we also have a fascinating variety of marine life," Bethel points out, "and today most serious divers are not interested in spearing fish, but rather in looking at them and photographing them."

According to the Ministry's research, the general appeal of the Bahamas to tourists is still very much environmental – sun, sand and sea. But the average visitor today, Bethel points out, is looking for action as well as relaxation. He wants to be able to enjoy water-sports—boating, sailing, diving and fishing—and land sports such as golf, tennis and squash.

In the area of entertainment, visitors tend to look for something more than traditional night club acts; they're interested more in cultural experiences, whether imported or indigenous, but with a preference for the latter. Surveys have shown that although 12 per cent of our visitors come here specifically to gamble, 50 per cent visit one of our casinos during their holiday, although the Ministry, Bethel says, does not promote gambling in isolation from other activities.

The need to fill the several hundred additional guest rooms which became available during 1982 provides a very real incentive to Bethel, and the industry generally, to succeed in promoting increased tourism. New hotels have been built and others enlarged in Nassau and Paradise Island, with the largest of them – the government's 730-room Cable Beach Hotel—due to open at the end of 1983. In March, construction was two weeks ahead of schedule, and already the government's Hotel Corporation was seeing the results of its advance promotion of room sales. "I'm told they've got bookings three or four years down the road," Bethel reports.

"The competition," he adds, "is bound to make pricing more realistic and aimed at a reasonable margin of profit, and it will induce hotel operators to display increased initiative in their own marketing programmes."

Some eight years ago the Ministry adopted "It's Better in the Bahamas" as the signature to all of its advertising. That has become the best known slogan for any resort destination, and Bethel and his associates are absolutely convinced that they have the finest product in the area to sell. They are very much aware, too, that the future economic growth of the country depends on the results of their efforts to persuade increasing numbers of vacationers that it is, indeed, "Better in the Bahamas".

The Family Islands

Friendly grouper welcomes a Reef visitor.

Exploring Exuma's Land and Sea Park

S un, sand and sea! The essence of the Bahamas, and few places can rival the magnificent combination of these elements found in the Exumas.

This chain of cays in the centre of the Bahamas' archipelago has long been regarded as one of the world's best areas for cruising in a small boat. There are hundreds of islands (locals claim there are 365 — one for each day of the year), miles of beaches and reefs, and, of course, dozens of secure anchorages. Situated near the middle of this chain is the Exuma Cays Land and Sea Park.

The Park grew out of the concern for conservation which was shared by a group of farsighted individuals in the mid-1950s. In 1956 the government tentatively set aside an area 22 miles long in which no land sales would be permitted pending a survey and study of the area to ascertain the feasibility of a park reservation.

The survey team, which included the late Colonel Ilia Tolstoy, a leading proponent of the Park scheme, and Oris S. Russell, C.M.G., O.B.E., then Director of Agriculture and Fisheries, compiled a 40-page report on the types of vegetation and animals found on the cays, and the fish and corals discovered while diving.

They saw as the main thrust of their report "recommendations that will ensure the perpetuity of the things that people come to see in the Bahamas, as well as to assure a lasting supply of those natural resources that are so necessary for the livelihood of Bahamians themselves".

A serious problem appeared to be, in the words of team-member the late Hon. Herbert McKinney, to make "people aware of the pressing need for conservation. The attitude of the people seems to be that the good Lord will always send more". Unfortunately, that attitude is still apparent on the part of some persons, but hopefully they are fewer in number now than 25 years ago.

Following the survey report, the Bahamas National Trust Act of 1959 established the Trust as a non-profit organization to promote conservation and preservation of Bahamian animal and marine life, and submarine areas of natural beauty, as well as places of historical interest. The government then leased to the Trust an area eight miles wide by 22 miles long, now known as the Exuma Cays Land and Sea Park.

The Park's 176 square miles is only about five per cent land area (8.75 square miles), consisting of nine large cays, 50 smaller cays and innumerable rocks, lying between Wax Cay Cut in the north to Conch Cut in the south. Three of the four largest cays — Shroud, Hawksbill and Warderick Wells — are leased by the Trust, while Cistern Cay, Hall's Pond, Soldier Cay, O'Brien's Cay, Bell Island and Little Bell Island are privately owned.

During the 1960s and 1970s when the Park was visited by thousands of people, the enforcement of Park Regulations depended on voluntary compliance. Volunteer wardens, who were members of the Trust, travelled through the Park occasionally and warned violators of the rules of the possible consequences of their actions. The Park bye-laws, drawn up by the Trust, have the power of Bahamian law, and offenders are liable to a fine and seizure of any vessel or equipment used while violating the law.

In 1973 an expedition brought to the Park some rare endangered hutias, the only endemic Bahamian mammal. Hutias are closely related to the porcupine, and are brown and furry. Nocturnal creatures, they previously existed only on East Plana Cay, a small island between Crooked Island and Mayaguana, until they were introduced onto Little Wax Cay at the Park's north end.

Hutias possess at least two characteristics which scientists consider worthy of more study. One is their non-aggressive social behaviour in crowded conditions, and the other is their ability to survive in an arid environment—they exist during dry periods on the moisture in the plants they eat.

Iguanas are a protected species in the Park.

During the 1973 expedition, also, several Acklins Rock Iguanas (another endangered species) were released on Bush Hill Cay, just north of Little Wax Cay. Again, it was felt that diversifying the location of iguanas would lessen the threat of extinction. Populations of the various species of iguanas throughout the Bahamas have been severely reduced by their most dangerous enemy – the man who eats them. They have no other significant enemies.

During the late 1970s and into the 1980s, the Park has come under increasing pressure from commercial fishermen as fish, conch and crawfish become more difficult to obtain in other areas. Also, more people have been visiting the Park in their own or charter boats.

In early 1981 a Trust planning committee declared that "the greatest priority of the Trust's human and financial resources should go toward the creation and implementation of a sound management programme (in the Park) and to its development as a recreational centre". As part of that programme, a special committee was appointed to formulate policy and oversee the Park.

The aim in managing the Park is environmental control, recognizing that land and sea areas are inter-dependent and man is an integral part of the natural system. Man should be able to reap harvests and enjoy the beauty of nature, but never endanger resources beyond their ability to replenish themselves.

Signs and information boxes were placed throughout the Park in the Fall of 1981, and stocked with copies of new information brochures about the Park. In January 1982 the author was engaged as the first fulltime Warden.

The goals of my appointment were announced at a press conference that month, during which Mrs. Lynn Holowesko (then president of the B.N.T.) and Basil Kelly (current president), Egbert Wallace and Colin Higgs (both of the Ministry of Agriculture and Fisheries) and I explained our future plans. The Ministry of Agriculture and Fisheries assists and supports the Trust in our efforts to conserve the marine resources of the Bahamas. Mr. Wallace joins me from time to time on my patrols in the Park to see at first hand what is involved.

I live onboard my 40-foot houseboat in the Park, moving from anchorage to anchorage. I also patrol the entire area, as weather permits, in a 14-foot boat clearly marked Park Warden. I monitor radio traffic between boats in the area and assist those on board when necessary. I am in daily radio communication with Bahamas Air Sea Rescue in Nassau, and just having me within VHF radio range is often reassuring to persons cruising the Exumas.

It has been necessary for me to caution a number of people who were fishing illegally in the Park. The limits allowed are: 12 conchs per boat per day; one each of grouper, rock fish, mutton fish and hog fish per boat per day; and during the open season from August 1 to March 30, six crawfish per boat per day. At present when I approach a violator I just warn him of the consequences, and photograph his vessel for identification. This information is forwarded monthly to the Trust and to the Ministry of Agriculture and Fisheries. Hopefully, the warning process will prove sufficient for most first offenders, and legal action will not be necessary in most cases.

In addition to conservation enforcement, I have completed a more detailed chart of the Park, showing more anchorages, diving sites and other points of interest. Persons visiting the area are quick to purchase the various field guide booklets produced by the Trust which identify plants and animals found in the area.

Until you have an opportunity to visit the Park, let me describe some of the pleasures which await you. Arriving at the north end of the Park, only about 40 miles southeast of Nassau, good anchorages can be found near Shroud Cay, which is really

Park visitor enjoys a stop at Camp Driftwood.

an archipelago of small islands divided by swamps and creeks. In
years past these cays had separate names, such as Hungry Hill,
Pigeon Cay, etc., but now the whole group is collectively known
as Shroud Cay.

The creeks, as one would expect, are tidal, and the "swamps"
are actually tidal marl flats, or swashes, which lie bare at low
water and awash at high tide. Perhaps it is the creeks which lend
Shroud its greatest charm. Hours may be spent exploring their
winding courses in a small boat, and there are several deep areas
where colourful tropical fish can be observed in a very protected
environment.

You might even see one of the small loggerhead turtles we
have released around Shroud. They were donated to the Trust by
Nassau's Seafloor Aquarium, where they were born, and released
with the help of the Research Vessel *Coral Reef*, which is owned
by the Shedd Aquarium in Chicago. Crew members assisted us in
weighing, measuring and tagging the turtles prior to their release
on the beach near the northern creek exit to Exuma Sound. We
hope the turtles will survive and breed in the area.

A spot not to be missed at Shroud is Camp Driftwood — an
inspiring result of one man's stay in the Park. Ernest Scholtes
spent many months in the creek at Shroud aboard his sailboat,
and constructed the camp on a hill overlooking the entire area.
He built steps up the 50-foot hill, carried sand by the sailbag full
up the hill and constructed such a pleasant grouping of driftwood
furniture that visitors feel they have come upon Robinson Cru-
soe's island. Truly, a unique spot from which to watch the rare
and beautiful Tropic Birds wheel and dive over the azure waters

94

of Exuma Sound. The beauty of these graceful birds, with their 12 to 14 inch long tail feathers, must be seen to be believed.

The natural well near the west side of Shroud Cay is one of the best in the Bahamas, and has provided good fresh water to visitors for more than a century. The well was a popular stop for sponging boats which worked in Exuma during the early part of this century. In 1927 the government improved the well with a cement curb around it, and I have cut steps into the stone path which leads towards the well from the south. The handrail for these steps is a 35-foot spar from a Haitian vessel which was wrecked off Wax Cay in 1980.

A visit to Bush Hill Cay, north of Shroud, will enable you to see the iguanas, or "baby dinosaurs", as some visitors call them. We discourage people from feeding them so that their behaviour will remain natural. The iguanas on Allen's Cay, five miles north of the Park, are fed so often that they tend to rush toward anyone coming ashore.

A night-time visit to Little Wax Cay is a treat when you realize how rare are the hutias thriving there. When going through the bush they waddle like porcupines, but on the open beach they hop like rabbits. I've measured their hops in excess of two feet. Hutias are interesting creatures to observe on the beach in quiet moonlight.

At Hawksbill Cay you can explore the most extensive ruins in the Park. Squatters lived at Hawksbill in the 19th century, raising sisal and other crops there and on many of the surrounding cays. We have cut some trails around the ruins. There is a good well near the Park sign on the beach towards the south end of Hawksbill, and from there it's only a short dinghy ride to observe one of the osprey nests in the Park. These ospreys, or fishhawks as they are called locally, build large nests on top of a promontory, such as the one at the west end of Little Hawksbill. They return year after year, and their nests of sticks become architectural marvels. They catch fish with their talons, not with their beaks as do most sea birds, and their attack-dive is something awe-inspiring.

A drift-dive in the cut off Cistern Cay takes you across some of the most beautiful corals in this area. If you are a trained cave diver, you'll want to investigate the Blue Hole near a small cay in Wide Opening. I call it the Sea Dragon Hole, not because of any dragons I've seen in it, but because divers from the Research Vessel *Sea Dragon* discovered it. Wide Opening has long been

Visitors to Warderick Wells leave mementos of their stay there.

known as an excellent fishing area, and, hopefully, the offspring of fish protected there will enrich other areas of the Bahamas.

Near Long Cay, in Wide Opening, are some blow holes which spew impressive geysers of water, given the right amount of tide and surge. From there you can go into the northern anchorage at Warderick Wells, avoiding the wreck of a sailing vessel which burned and sank there about five years ago. It makes an interesting snorkel dive at slack tide. You are welcome to tie to the mooring buoy which I maintain just off the Park sign there. Be sure to go ashore and leave a note in the book in the mailbox there, and wherever else you stop, and check to see if any of your friends have been in the Park recently.

If you go into the southern anchorage at Warderick Wells, try snorkelling through the tunnel which passes clear through Hog Cay near the north beach inside the anchorage. But watch out for sea urchins!

Going south from Warderick Wells you may choose to stop and admire the natural bridge on White Bay Cay, dive on the beautiful coral heads southwest of the old Hall's Pond Club, or visit another osprey nest on Sandy Cay.

Don't miss the anchorage between Bell and Little Bell islands. You could spend weeks in this idyllic, storm-proof harbour and find new delights every day. Coming in from Exuma Sound,

ELEGANT BLACK
CORAL JEWELLERY

All
Jewellery
and
Sculpture
made in
the Bahamas

Located at the
Sheraton British Colonial Hotel
P.O. Box SS-6187, Nassau, Bahamas
Tel: (809) 32-53364

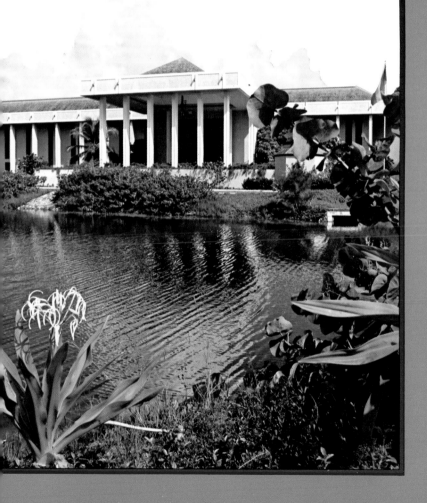

CONTROLLING SHAREHOLDERS

The **Ro**yal Bank of Canada Group and
National **W**ᴇꜱᴛminster Bank PLC

Well-protected anchorages can be found throughout the Park.

use the range markers I have set up to keep you in a channel at least 10 feet deep clear into the anchorage. Or, if you come in from the south, look for the stone beacon on Kiss Cay, so called because you have to come almost close enough to kiss it in order to stay in the deep channel. While there be sure to climb Bell Rock, a 50-foot bell-shaped rock on the shore of Exuma Sound — and take your camera with you, for the view is spectacular.

In a 1928 survey of Bell Island, a Mr. Aranha tells of two female residents he found there. They were, he wrote, "diminutive but independent octogenarians, who took up their abode in 1862. They rely on a dog and a gun stock for protection, and make their living by farming, fishing and by diving turtles. They allow only a favoured few to land, and will assail any trespasser who dares to land without permission. They claim ownership of the surrounding sea and all that is in it to a distance only limited by their eyesight, and demand, and even attempt to exact a toll of fish or conchs from any boat that stops to fish nearby. On account of their age and stature, it is humoured — though it is said that a sailor once threw one of them overboard while she was exacting her tax.

"During the storm of 1926, their house was destroyed, and they live in an improvised shack, but have refused all offers of

assistance in building another shack". The photograph of their shack which accompanied Mr. Aranha's report certainly leaves no doubt as to their hardiness and independence.

The stories you still hear about the 1926 hurricane are fearful, and locals will point to the four-foot high wall of empty, unbroken conch shells piled on Rocky Dundas and explain that they were washed there to rot by that storm.

Many unforgettable diving trips can be made around the Bell Island anchorage. You can dive near the southeast point of Little Bell and see spectacular staghorn corals, or explore a veritable forest of coral near the brown bar north of the northern Rocky Dundas.

Don't miss the caves in the south Rocky Dundas, with their beautiful stalactites and stalagmites, and pick up some of the conchs which gave Conch Cut its name. Also, you should visit the first two "natural seaquariums" we have set aside near Pasture Cay. These reefs are protected from all fishing in an attempt to establish areas where the fish are not afraid of divers. I feed fish here whenever possible.

I have tried to give you an idea of the beauty of the area, but words can only do so much. Come to the Park and give me a call on the radio — I'd enjoy sharing with you the continuing surprises and discoveries the Park offers.

Call the Bahamas National Trust in Nassau for more information about conserving our Bahamian heritage. John O'Reilly of *Sports Illustrated*, who was a member of the 1958 Park survey team, made this comment at the time: "Everyone goes to a place for something, and when it disappears they go somewhere else." That's worth remembering, so help us to protect the beauty we have in the Bahamas.

The author of this article about the Exuma Cays Land and Sea Park, Warden Beryl Nelson, first came to the Bahamas in 1969. He has a background of commercial fishing, and is experienced in yacht maintenance and operation. He holds a United States Coast Guard Captain's Licence (100 tons), and the 95-foot schooner 'America' is among the charter yachts he has captained. For a period he was employed by Bahamas Underwater Research Foundation at Lee Stocking Island, Exuma, as a diver/laboratory technician in a spiny lobster mariculture research project. Raised a Quaker, he was educated at Earlham College, Richmond, Indiana, where he studied marine biology.

Geoffrey Johnstone describes a cruise through the Exuma Cays.

Our Veteran Yachtsmen
Advise About
Safe Cruising Through the Islands

From Walker's Cay in the north to George Town, Exuma, and even further south, increasing numbers of yachtsmen are again enjoying exploring the island's beautiful cays, islands and beaches in the secure and peaceful atmosphere which in the past attracted them to the Bahamas.

If you're an old-hand at cruising through the islands, you'll know what to look for and what areas you've found offer the most rewarding experiences. But for those who plan to set out on their first venture into Bahamian seas, we've asked five veteran local yachtsmen to give their advice and guidance regarding safety precautions to be taken, and to tell all about their own favourite cruising and fishing grounds.

The most popular cruising areas have always been the Abaco and Exuma cays, and the argument will probably never be settled among experienced yachtsmen as to which has the greater attractions. Both contain sheltered passages and modern facilities for refuelling, as well as other vacation facilities and amenities.

Actually, our Bahamian boaters are unanimous in recommending a cruise through the Exuma Cays (see map, page 116). Captain Geoffrey G. Brown, who has 38 years of experience in these waters, prefers the Pipe Creek area of Exuma. "The cays are only 28 miles southeast of Nassau," he says, "with a maximum depth of five fathoms during the crossing, and after reaching Ship Channel Cay in the north you can enjoy 70 to 80 miles of continuous islands and cays."

Brown, a realtor and former harbour pilot with wide experience in many types of boats, uses a 30-foot twin-225 h.p. outboard Scarab for whatever casual cruising he can fit into his business schedule today.

Geoffrey A. D. Johnstone, a barrister, started cruising in 1948 and now owns a 46-foot Bertram Sports Fisherman. He concurs with Brown's view of the Exumas: "They are truly the gems of the Bahamas, and they provide numerous safe anchorages and an atmosphere of appealing tranquillity."

He suggests this cruising itinerary: "Make a landfall at Allan's Cay or Highborne Cay, which are within a few hundred yards of each other. The former is totally uninhabited, while the latter has marina facilities and a commissary. The journey across the Yellow Banks to Allan's or Highborne cays is straightforward. The visitor is now positioned to explore the Exuma Cays.

"Depending on the draft of the yacht and weather conditions, the voyage can be made either by the ocean route, on the southeastern side of the cays, or the Banks route on the northwestern side, or a combination of both. Proceeding southeastwardly, I recommend the following route: Allan's Cay/Highborne Cay to Shroud Cay, bypassing Norman's Cay. The Exuma Cays Land and Sea Park, protected by the Bahamas National Trust (see page 89), stretches from Wax Cay Cut at the northwestern end of Shroud Cay to Conch Cut at the southeastern end of Little Bell Island, and the visitor will pass through the Park on this suggested route.

"There is a good anchorage at Shroud where a day or two of exploration will prove interesting. From Shroud proceed to Hawksbill Cay—two anchorages on the western coast—and thence to Warderick Wells, where there are two good harbours. The next leg of the journey—Warderick Wells to Staniel Cay—is perhaps the loveliest in the Bahamas, and is best enjoyed in a yacht with a draft not exceeding 4'6", which will permit a passage along the eastern side of the cays. As an alternative, the ocean route can be followed.

"The journey is from Warderick Wells's southern harbour, past Hall's Pond Cay, Soldier Cay and O'Brien's Cay to the appealing and comfortable anchorage of Little Bell Island where two or three days should be spent. Little Bell permits easy access to the beautiful Pipe Creek, a miniature archipelago providing totally safe anchorages in the loveliest surroundings, ending at Staniel Cay at its southeastern extremity. The cay has a small settlement on it and two marinas, which both sell fuel and food. The yachtsman may then continue to George Town at the southeastern portion of the Exuma Cays, or retrace his steps to New Providence."

Ben Astarita, left, founded BASRA in 1963, while Nicholas Wardle established SEARCH five years ago.

Another Exuma booster is David M. Lightbourn, a merchant, who cruises in a 38-foot diesel Bertram. "For family cruising," he comments, "the Exumas are the jewels of the Bahamas." He adds that he also enjoys the Berry Islands "for a trip 'with the boys' because the fishing is outstanding." He has known the islands and seas of the Bahamas for some 50 years.

Noel S. Roberts, another barrister, agrees that the Berry Islands offer superb fishing, but for cruising he, too, prefers the Exumas "because of the tranquillity of the cays and the great beauty of the surroundings". He began exploring these waters some 20 years ago, and now owns a 40-foot Pacemaker.

Well-known photographer Stanley Toogood became a boating enthusiast as soon as he arrived in Nassau from England in 1934. Now a Bahamian citizen, he lives aboard his cruising houseboat, and includes the Exuma Cays among his favourite areas. He has an extensive knowledge of the islands, and also enjoys short cruises to Spanish Wells (see map, page 115), to Bimini and the Berry Islands (see map, page 112- 113), and to San Salvador (see map, page 121).

"All of these islands," he observes, "are within a short sea-distance of each other, and they can easily be reached by simple piloting." He adds: "From Nassau to the Abacos (see map, page 109) is very pleasant, too, with calls at Marsh Harbour, Hope Town and Green Turtle Cay."

Now that you have some educated suggestions about where to go, here are some tips on how to get to your Nassau cruising base, and a few words of caution.

Brown, Lightbourn and Roberts all advise anyone piloting in

103

these waters to obtain a current copy of the *Yachtsman's Guide to the Bahamas.*

"Read it before leaving the United States," Brown suggests, "especially all about the area you intend to cruise."

"A non-Bahamian," Lightbourn warns, "must first learn that in coastal waters and around shaols we navigate by eye in determining depth of water. The *Guide* spells this out quite clearly, and it should be read and read again. A depth-finder is of little use when it often happens that your bow can be on a shoal and your stern in 20 feet of water. Beginners would do well to avoid dark and shoaly waters, and stick to the sandy bottom areas. It should be remembered, too, that our tide rise and fall is only three feet."

"You should have a *Yachtsman's Guide* with you at all times," Roberts advises. "It gives full details of all yachting areas and safe anchorages, as well as how to approach them. It also includes tide tables, which can be extremely useful."

Brown suggests that visiting yachtsmen make sure before starting out that their boats' radio and other equipment are all in perfect condition. "Take along as many spare parts as possible, as sometimes they can be hard to find in the islands. Also, have your compass swung before leaving Florida—it only costs about $70 and is good insurance."

Brown and Roberts both caution that all cruising should be done in daylight, and Roberts and Toogood suggest also that it might be advisable to travel in the company of another boat.

Lightbourn adds that although the danger of being boarded by narcotics smugglers has greatly diminished today, "speaking for myself, I would still avoid North Andros".

Johnstone recommends entering the Bahamas (see Ports of Entry, page 314) from Florida "via Gun Cay to Northwest Channel Light, stopping at Chub Cay. This will permit an inspection of the southern Berry Islands for a day or two—Whale Cay, Bond's Cay and Frozen Cay/Alder Cay. I would suggest one night at that location, and the visitor should then proceed to New Providence Island, spending a few days in the capital of Nassau".

Toogood advises a stop at Bimini or Cat Cay en route from Florida. "Then across the Banks to the Berry Islands," he adds, "and on to Nassau and beyond—Spanish Wells, Eleuthera, the Exumas and as far as San Salvador."

American yachtsmen are accustomed to relying on their numerous Coast Guard establishments should they experience difficulty while cruising their home waters, but once they venture into

Bahamian and Caribbean waters, the Coast Guard cannot help them unless a direct request is received from the government concerned.

Fortunately, that is not a deterrent to them to cruise through the 100,000 square miles of the Bahamas because of the presence here of a highly efficient volunteer organization called the Bahamas Air Sea Rescue Association, or BASRA for short. Founded in 1963 by Ben Astarita, a former New York advertising executive and now a Bahamian citizen, the search and rescue unit is recognized today as the most active and best organized operation of its kind in this part of the world.

BASRA enjoys a close working and communications relationship with the U.S.C.G., and in appropriate situations is able to call on it for swift co-operation in rescue missions. Because it is a purely volunteer group, BASRA relies entirely on donations from the public, membership dues and its own fund-raising efforts in order to continue and expand its facilities.

It receives and responds to over 1,000 calls each year from boats and aircraft (about half of them owned by Americans), and often its volunteers risk their own lives, boats and aircraft to search in bad weather for distressed craft. BASRA owns a 31-foot Bertram, but no aircraft, and must frequently call on members to loan their own planes and boats for rescue work.

With BASRA as a model, other similar volunteer organizations have been established in the Netherlands Antilles, Turks and Caicos Islands, the Cayman Islands and the British Virgin Islands.

In order to complement the fund-raising initiatives of these associations, five years ago Nicholas Wardle, an English chartered accountant and 19-year resident of the Bahamas, established the Search and Rescue Charitable Foundation (SEARCH).

Headquartered in Fort Lauderdale, Florida, it is incorporated as a qualified charitable corporation. All of SEARCH's net income is used to support search and rescue activities in the islands, after paying for information publications as well as basic administrative costs.

Wardle is a former vice-commodore and director of BASRA, which he joined in the early 1970s, but when he founded SEARCH he resigned all posts in the group, except that of senior control officer, so as to avoid any appearance of conflict of interest between his BASRA and SEARCH activities.

Because of his years of experience in the Bahamas, Wardle was aware that the principal need was the establishment of an effective communications system throughout the archipelago. He is, there-

fore, concentrating SEARCH's efforts for the Bahamas on the creation of VHF radio marine shore station facilities in co-operation with the Bahamas Marine Council, which is formed of individuals and organizations sharing the common interest of promoting safe boating in the Bahamas.

At the present time, Wardle explains, if you get into trouble on the sea or in the air in the Bahamas and use VHF equipment, your voice is likely to be one crying in the wilderness, unless you happen to be within reach of, say, the Abaco Cays, where a lot of people own VHF sets.

In 1982 SEARCH donated $5,000 to BASRA for the purchase of a special direction-finding VHF receiver for its Bertam, and a compact single-sideband radio for the association's Nassau headquarters.

Wardle, who is SEARCH's president and treasurer, reckons that what is required for effective VHF-FM communications here is at least 30 remote relay stations, and it is towards that end that SEARCH, BASRA and the B.M.C. are working. Phase 1 of the plan would provide for the establishment of five local stations, and the B.M.C. has arranged for the necessary equipment to be donated through SEARCH.

Phase II is SEARCH's automatic system for bringing emergency radio traffic into Nassau from as far away as Walker's Cay and Long Island, or further, on a 24-hour per day listening watch facility.

Recent years witnessed a fall-off in the numbers of those who came to cruise the incomparable waters of this picturesque archipelago, or go after the big ones with rod and reel, because of several tragic incidents which resulted from the occasional presence of people who were engaged in smuggling drugs from the south into the United States.

By and large, those involved in this illicit traffic were not Bahamians, but the word spread that travel through these islands could occasionally be unsafe, and, in fact, after reviewing the existing circumstances the Ministry of Tourism made the deliberate decision to cut-back temporarily on promoting and publicizing the attractions of cruising the islands.

The concerted efforts of the Royal Bahamas Defence Force, and the Royal Bahamas Police Force, in close collaboration with the U.S. Coast Guard and Drug Enforcement Agency, have now virtually eliminated the presence of drug "pirates" in Bahamian waters, and the Ministry is again actively recreating the image of the Bahamas as one of the world's loveliest and most fascinating cruising and fishing areas.

"The Bahamas," says David Lightbourn, "offers a wealth of pleasure to yachtsmen. If you are a loner who craves your own safe, private anchorage, we have them by the hundreds. But if you are the type who prefers modern dockage with good accommodations and fine food, there are dozens of such marinas ready to cater to your every need."

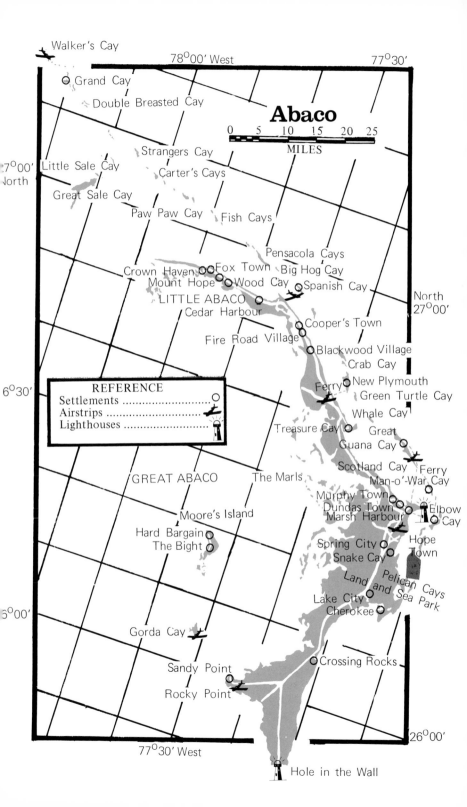

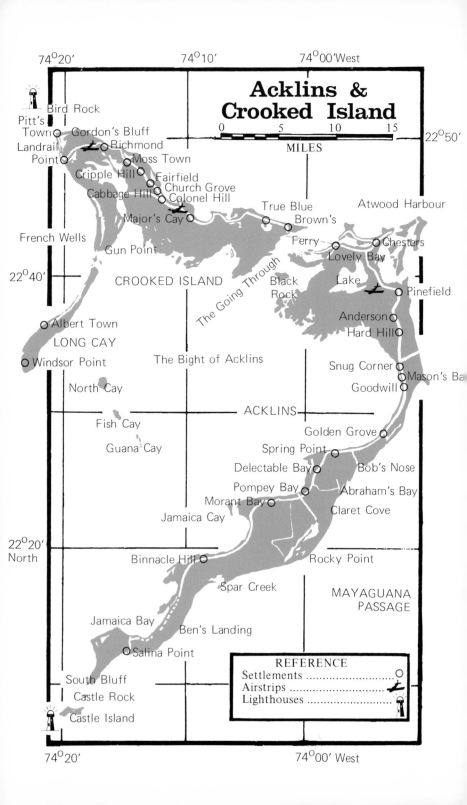

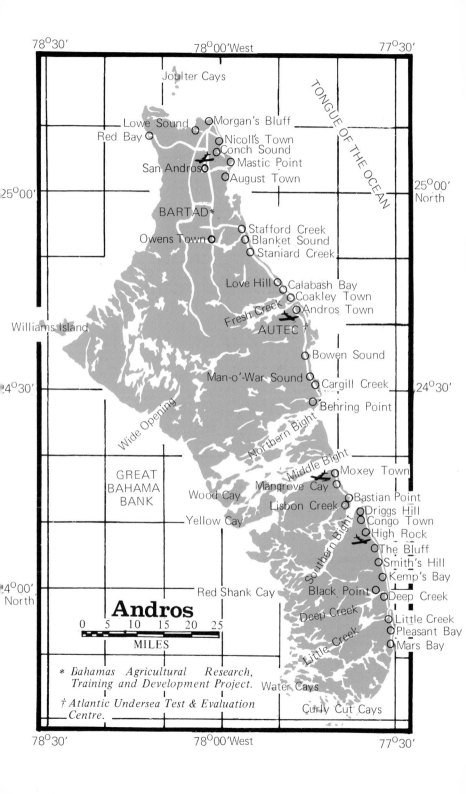

78°30' 78°00'West 77°30'

Joulter Cays

TONGUE OF THE OCEAN

Lowe Sound   Morgan's Bluff
Red Bay
Nicoll's Town
Conch Sound
Mastic Point
San Andros
August Town

25°00'   25°00'
                                          North

BARTAD *

Stafford Creek
Owens Town   Blanket Sound
Staniard Creek

Love Hill   Calabash Bay
            Coakley Town
Fresh Creek   Andros Town
AUTEC †

Bowen Sound

Williams Island

24°30'   Man-o'-War Sound   Cargill Creek   24°30'

Behring Point

Wide Opening

Northern Bight

Middle Bight   Moxey Town
GREAT   Mangrove Cay   Bastian Point
BAHAMA   Lisbon Creek   Driggs Hill
BANK   Wood Cay   Congo Town
             Yellow Cay   High Rock
                                     The Bluff
                                     Smith's Hill
                                     Kemp's Bay
24°00'   Red Shank Cay   Black Point   Deep Creek
North   Deep Creek
                                       Little Creek
Andros   Pleasant Bay
0   5   10 15 20 25   Mars Bay
MILES

Southern Bight

Little Creek

* *Bahamas Agricultural Research,*
  Training and Development Project.
  Water Cays
† *Atlantic Undersea Test & Evaluation*
  Centre.   Curly Cut Cays

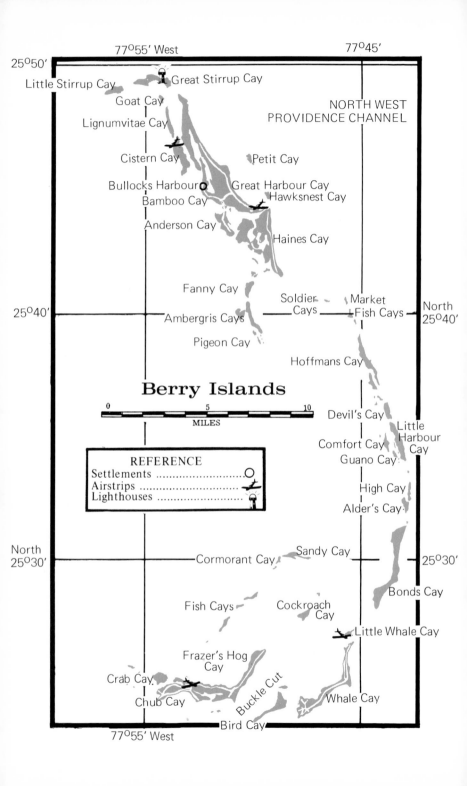

Berry Islands

REFERENCE

Settlements	○
Airstrips	✈
Lighthouses	🗼

0   5   10
MILES

77°55′ West   77°45′

25°50′

Little Stirrup Cay   Great Stirrup Cay

Goat Cay

Lignumvitae Cay   NORTH WEST
PROVIDENCE CHANNEL

Cistern Cay   Petit Cay

Bullocks Harbour   Great Harbour Cay
Bamboo Cay   Hawksnest Cay

Anderson Cay

Haines Cay

Fanny Cay

Soldier   Market
Cays   Fish Cays   North
25°40′   25°40′

Ambergris Cays

Pigeon Cay

Hoffmans Cay

Devil's Cay   Little
Harbour
Cay

Comfort Cay
Guano Cay

High Cay

Alder's Cay

North
25°30′   Cormorant Cay   Sandy Cay   25°30′

Bonds Cay

Fish Cays   Cockroach
Cay

Little Whale Cay

Frazer's Hog
Cay

Crab Cay

Chub Cay   Buckle Cut   Whale Cay

Bird Cay

77°55′ West

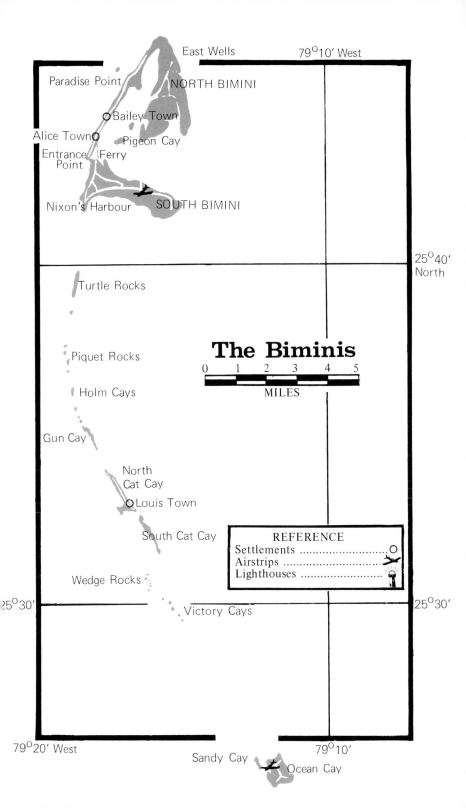

East Wells

79°10′ West

Paradise Point

NORTH BIMINI

○ Bailey Town

Alice Town ○

Pigeon Cay

Entrance ｜Ferry
Point

Nixon's Harbour

SOUTH BIMINI

25°40′
North

Turtle Rocks

The Biminis

Piquet Rocks

| 0 | 1 | 2 | 3 | 4 | 5 |

MILES

Holm Cays

Gun Cay

North
Cat Cay

○ Louis Town

South Cat Cay

REFERENCE
Settlements .... ○
Airstrips .... ✈
Lighthouses ....

Wedge Rocks

25°30′

Victory Cays

25°30′

79°20′ West

79°10′

Sandy Cay

Ocean Cay

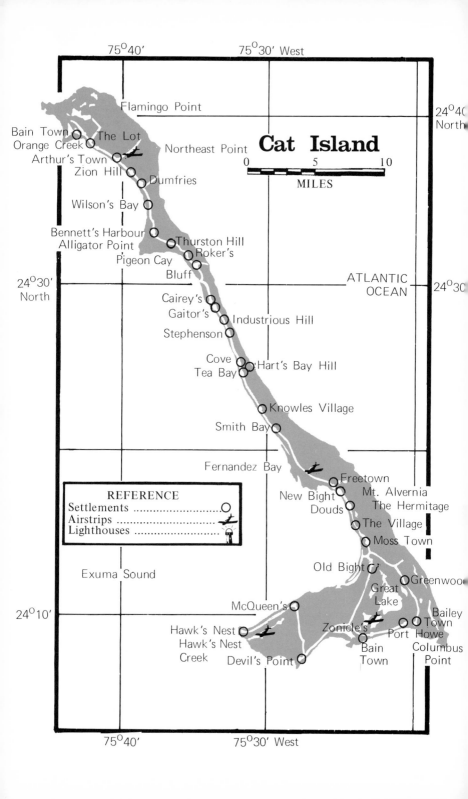

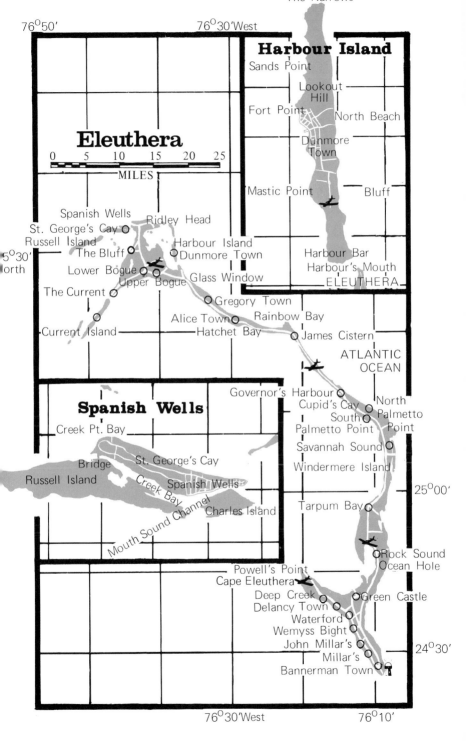

The Narrows

Harbour Island

Sands Point

Lookout Hill

Fort Point

North Beach

Dunmore Town

Mastic Point

Bluff

76°50'   76°30'West

Eleuthera

0   5   10   15   20   25
MILES

Spanish Wells   Ridley Head
St. George's Cay
Russell Island
The Bluff
Harbour Island
Dunmore Town
Lower Bogue
Upper Bogue   Glass Window
The Current
Current Island   Gregory Town
Alice Town   Rainbow Bay
Hatchet Bay
James Cistern

Harbour Bar
Harbour's Mouth
ELEUTHERA

5°30'
North

ATLANTIC OCEAN

Governor's Harbour   North Palmetto Point
Cupid's Cay
South Palmetto Point
Palmetto Point
Savannah Sound

Spanish Wells

Creek Pt. Bay

Bridge   St. George's Cay
Russell Island   Creek Bay
Spanish Wells
Charles Island
Mouth Sound Channel

Windermere Island

25°00'

Tarpum Bay

Rock Sound
Ocean Hole

Powell's Point
Cape Eleuthera
Deep Creek   Green Castle
Delancy Town
Waterford
Wemyss Bight
John Millar's
Millar's
Bannerman Town

24°30'

76°30'West   76°10'

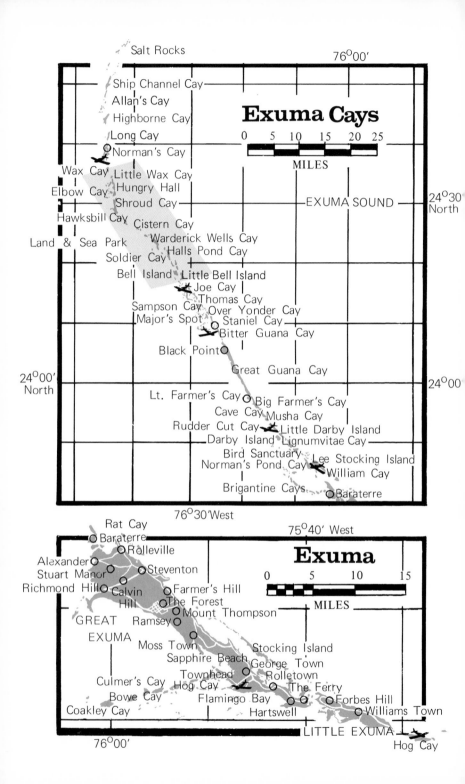

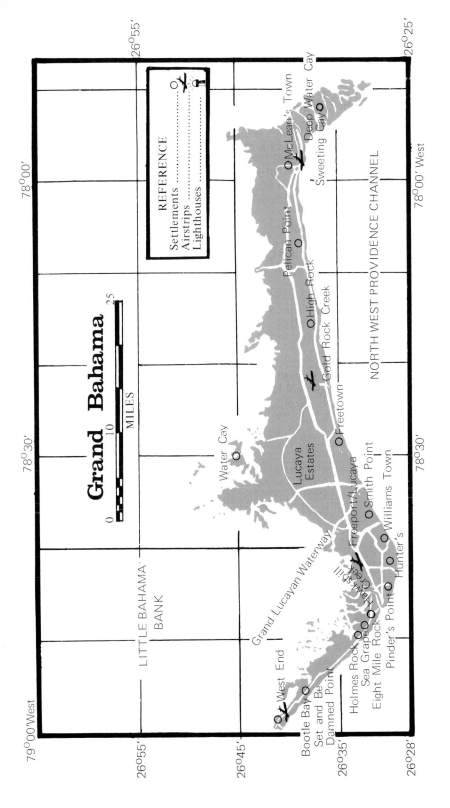

Grand Bahama

REFERENCE
Settlements .... O
Airstrips .... ✈
Lighthouses .... ⌁

MILES
0   10   25

79°00'West   78°30'   78°00'   78°55'

LITTLE BAHAMA BANK

Grand Lucayan Waterway

West End
Bootle Bay
Set and Be Damned Point
Holmes Rock
Sea Grape
Eight Mile Rock
Pinder's Point
Hawksbill Creek
Hunter's
Williams Town
Smith Point
Freeport/Lucaya
Lucaya Estates

Water Cay

Freetown

Gold Rock Creek

High Rock

Pelican Point

McLean's Town
Deep Water Cay
Sweeting Cay

NORTH WEST PROVIDENCE CHANNEL

78°30'   78°00' West

26°55'   26°45'   26°35'   26°28'

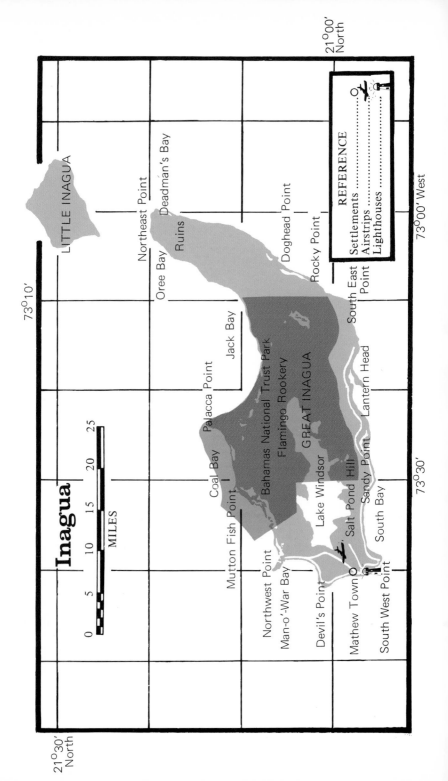

Inagua

MILES

0   5   10   15   20   25

21°30' North

73°10'

73°00' West

73°30'

21°00' North

LITTLE INAGUA

Northeast Point

Oree Bay

Deadman's Bay

Ruins

Doghead Point

Rocky Point

Jack Bay

Palacca Point

GREAT INAGUA

Bahamas National Trust Park

Flamingo Rookery

Coal Bay

Mutton Fish Point

South East Point

Lantern Head

Sandy Point

Lake Windsor

Salt Pond Hill

South Bay

Northwest Point

Man-o-'War Bay

Devil's Point

Mathew Town

South West Point

REFERENCE

Settlements .... O

Airstrips ....

Lighthouses ....

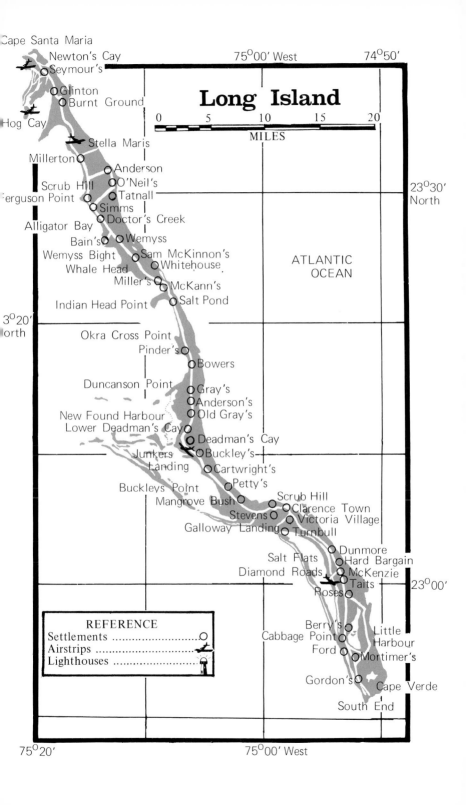

Cape Santa Maria
Newton's Cay
Seymour's
75°00' West   74°50'
Glinton
Burnt Ground
Hog Cay

Long Island

0   5   10   15   20
MILES

Stella Maris
Millerton
Anderson
Scrub Hill   O'Neil's   23°30'
Ferguson Point   Tatnall   North
Simms
Doctor's Creek
Alligator Bay
Bain's   Wemyss
Wemyss Bight   Sam McKinnon's
Whale Head   Whitehouse
Miller's   McKann's
Indian Head Point   Salt Pond

ATLANTIC
OCEAN

3°20'
North

Okra Cross Point
Pinder's
Bowers
Duncanson Point
Gray's
Anderson's
New Found Harbour   Old Gray's
Lower Deadman's Cay
Deadman's Cay
Junkers   Buckley's
Landing
Cartwright's
Buckleys Point   Petty's
Mangrove Bush   Scrub Hill
Clarence Town
Stevens   Victoria Village
Galloway Landing   Turnbull

Dunmore
Salt Flats   Hard Bargain
Diamond Roads   McKenzie
Taits   23°00'
Roses

REFERENCE
Settlements .... O
Airstrips ....
Lighthouses ....

Berry's   Little
Cabbage Point   Harbour
Ford   Mortimer's

Gordon's   Cape Verde
South End

75°20'   75°00' West

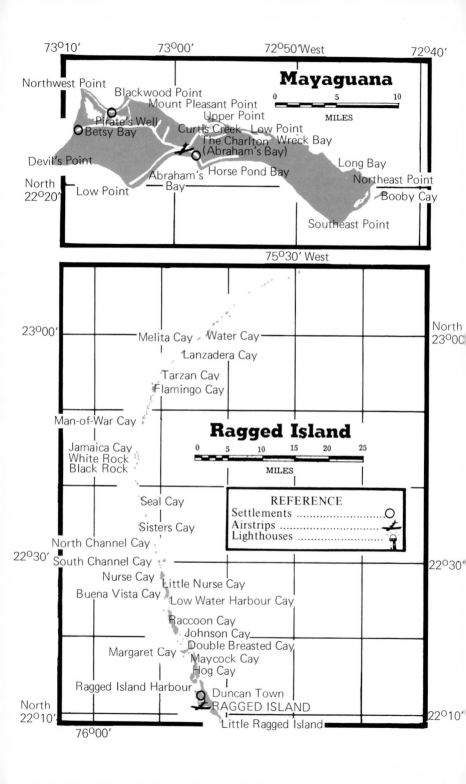

Mayaguana

73°10' 73°00' 72°50'West 72°40'

Northwest Point
Blackwood Point
Mount Pleasant Point
Upper Point
Pirate's Well
Betsy Bay
Curtis Creek Low Point
The Charlton Wreck Bay
(Abraham's Bay)
Devil's Point
Abraham's Horse Pond Bay
North Bay
22°20' Low Point
Long Bay
Northeast Point
Booby Cay
Southeast Point

0   5   10
MILES

Ragged Island

75°30' West

23°00' Melita Cay Water Cay North
23°00'
Lanzadera Cay
Tarzan Cay
Flamingo Cay
Man-of-War Cay
Jamaica Cay
White Rock
Black Rock
Seal Cay
Sisters Cay
North Channel Cay
22°30' South Channel Cay 22°30'
Nurse Cay Little Nurse Cay
Buena Vista Cay Low Water Harbour Cay
Raccoon Cay
Johnson Cay
Margaret Cay Double Breasted Cay
Maycock Cay
Hog Cay
Ragged Island Harbour
North Duncan Town
22°10' RAGGED ISLAND 22°10'
Little Ragged Island

76°00'

0   5   10   15   20   25
MILES

REFERENCE
Settlements .... ○
Airstrips .... ✈
Lighthouses .... 🗼

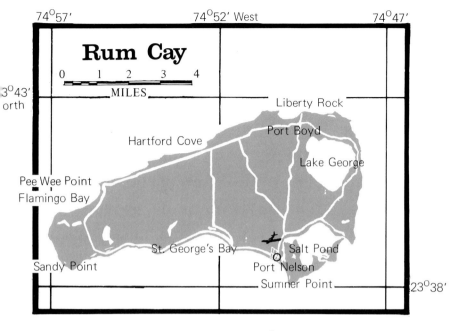

Rum Cay

0 1 2 3 4
MILES

74°57'   74°52' West   74°47'

23°43' North

Liberty Rock

Port Boyd

Hartford Cove

Lake George

Pee Wee Point
Flamingo Bay

St. George's Bay

Salt Pond

Sandy Point

Port Nelson

Sumner Point

23°38'

San Salvador

0 1 2 3 4 5
MILES

74°34'   74°30' West   74°26'

Graham's
Harbour

Northeast Point

Reckley Hill
United Estates

Quarters

Harbour Estate

North
Victoria Hill

Dixon's

Brandy Hill
Polly Hill

24°05' North

24°05'
North

Riding Rock
Point

Hard Bargain

Cockburn Town

Storr's Lake

Granny Lake

Fernandez Bay

Great Lake

Fortune Hill

Holiday Track

Long Bay

Farquharson

South Victoria Hill

Columbus Monument

Olympic
Flame
Monument

Sugar Loaf

Pigeon Creek

Old Place

Trial Farm

Allen

Montreal

Watling's Castle
Ruins

French Bay

High Cay
Middle Cay
Low Cay

Sandy Point

24°00'
North

The Lanier
No Problem® Typewriter.
It does more than just type.

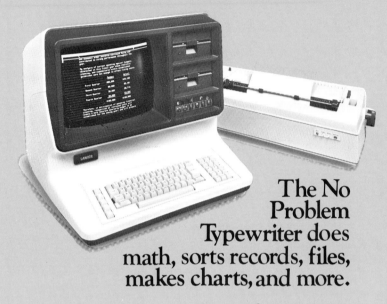

The No Problem Typewriter does math, sorts records, files, makes charts, and more.

LANIER BUSINESS PRODUCTS, INC.

The Lanier **No Problem** electronic typewriter is multi-use with extraordinary powers.

The **No Problem** typewriter is many typewriters in one. It speeds up everyday typing and can perform additional tasks by simply inserting different **No Problem Smart Discs.**[TM]

Why not see Lanier **No Problem** typing in action.

Distributed in the Bahamas by

Bay Street, P.O. Box N-3737, Nassau, Bahamas. Tel: 2-4252/3

Business
and Finance

Nassau Keeps Growing as a

Leading Offshore Financial Centre

At the opening of the 253rd year of our parliament in 1982, the government reaffirmed its intention "to further strengthen the position of the Bahamas as a leading financial centre, and to aggressively promote overseas our superiority as a site for banking, trust operations, insurance and ship registration".

How important, then, *is* its financial sector to the Bahamas? How did these pleasant, sunny, carefree islands come to develop such a sector at all, and what are the prospects for the future?

Banks and trust companies alone provide over $100 million a year in direct contributions to the Bahamian economy, of which over $50 million is by way of salaries to employees. Some 3,500 people are employed in the banking, trust and insurance businesses in Nassau, only 1,000 less than the total of around 4,500 persons employed in the major hotels on New Providence and Paradise Island.

Parliament Square, the heart of Nassau and New Providence, surrounds the seated statue of Queen Victoria. The white-columned building is where the Senate meets.

Licence fees paid direct to the government total $4.5 million, and the remaining approximately $45 million represents general administrative expenses, ranging from the construction of new buildings, fees to local lawyers and accountants, the provision of training for Bahamians (locally and in foreign countries), bankers' lunches and entertainment in local hotels and restaurants, and substantial donations to a wide range of local charities and to the arts.

The present $100 million direct contribution to the Bahamian economy has increased by some 300 per cent over the past 10 years (in 1973 it was $36.3 million), but, of course, the direct contribution is only part of the story.

Economists at The Central Bank of the Bahamas calculate that every job created in the financial sector has a multiplier effect of four or five other jobs in the rest of the economy. These jobs include not only lawyers and accountants, employees of the Central Bank, of the Ministry of Finance, of the Immigration Department, of the Bahamas Telecommunications Corporation, and educators at the College of the Bahamas, especially in its banking faculty, but go right the way through to maids and gardeners of more senior bank personnel.

There are now some 340 banks and trust companies registered in the Bahamas, of which about 80 have a physical presence, and more are coming in every month. These banks and trust companies include branches and subsidiaries of many of the largest banks in the world, and staffs vary in size from a handful up to about 250 people. In addition to this, over 25,000 companies are administered from the Bahamas.

The eurodollar assets administered by the banks in Nassau amount up to $150 *billion*, or approximately one-tenth of the worldwide eurodollar market. By that criterion, Nassau is the world's second largest eurodollar centre after London.

This much quoted and apparently very impressive statistic is, however, not of great significance to the wellbeing of these islands for, from the local point of view, the question is not how big the banks' balance sheets are (that is simply a paper number), or how much profit they make (the government does not tax profits or income), but how many people are employed, and how much money is injected into the local economy.

A BOOST TO TOURISM INCOME STATISTICS

The banking and financial community also provides other benefits which are less statistically quantifiable. International financial institutions, as a matter of course, provide good training and development in office skills and disciplines, and, for the more promising local employees, provide courses, scholarships and educational programmes in North America and Europe. Their modern air-conditioned offices are naturally considered a desirable place to work, and salaries in the financial sector are among the best in Nassau.

A high proportion of the elegant and very well-dressed Bahamians who grace Bay Street, Nassau's shopping centre, at lunch time, and add to its charm and attractiveness for tourists, spend their working day behind desks or next to computers in the City's banks and trust companies.

Many hotel rooms and restaurant tables are occupied by people who come to Nassau not only for a holiday, but also to see their offshore banker. Indeed, the constant comings and goings of international bankers, inspectors, auditors, trust specialists, taxation, insurance and shipping executives and their clients probably contribute a more useful addition to the income statistics of the Ministry of Tourism than is generally recognized. And these visitors, when they get an opportunity to relax and go shopping, usually buy more than just a straw hat. Moreover, they are good "up-market" advertising for the Bahamas when they return to their home countries.

There are several other advantages to encouraging the continuing development here of an international financial centre. For example, because the financial sector cannot operate without a well-functioning overseas telecommunications system, the Bahamas has had to develop such a system, and there are plans for further major developments in the coming years, including satellite communications.

The revenues which the Telecommunications Corporation derives from international telephone and telex traffic, particularly from the international banks, is sufficient to enable all local telephone calls on the island to be made free of charge, except for a fairly nominal monthly rent.

It is, therefore, not surprising that the government recognizes the significant role which the international financial community plays, and intends to aggressively promote further development.

TEN REASONS WHY THE BAHAMAS

But why have international banks and financial institutions of so many countries decided to come here in the first place, and why are more still coming in every month?

Ten principal reasons can be given for this development:

1. The absence of income taxes, withholding taxes, corporation taxes, capital gains taxes, death taxes and gift taxes;

2. The fact that there is now a large, well-established community of international banks;

3. The existence of bank secrecy laws comparable with those of Switzerland;

4. The flexibility to operate in a relatively unregulated environment, coupled with the benefit of a strong and efficient Central Bank, which has the responsibility of keeping out undesirables;

5. A long, uninterrupted record of political stability;

6. The opportunity to enjoy a beautiful climate and pleasant environment while doing business here;

7. Relative proximity to and direct air links with the principal North American business centres, and with London, and being in the same time zone as New York and Miami.

8. Excellent overseas telephone and telex services, including direct long distance dialling all over North America, and banks can also arrange direct lines to Europe, via New York;

9. Maturity gained through long years of experience as an offshore centre; and

10. A highly qualified financial community, and the availability of a satisfactory supply of administrative and clerical personnel. On the professional side, it is worth noting that all but one of the world's "Big Nine" accounting firms have offices in Nassau, and there are 10 firms of attorneys having six or more partners.

While these are the main attractions *to* the Bahamas for banking and financial services, let's also take a look at the circumstances throughout the world which tend to push business *from* onshore centres to seek an offshore haven, and which are cur-

YOUR SWISS BANKING PARTNER IN NASSAU

Banca della Svizzera Italiana
Nassau Branch

Norfolk House, Frederick Street
P.O. Box N-7541

Telephone: 322 13 32
Telex: 20 312
Cable Address: BSI Nassau

Head Office: Lugano, Switzerland

YOUR PARTNER
FOR INTERNATIONAL
BANKING SERVICES

Banca della Svizzera Italiana (Overseas) Ltd.

Norfolk House, Frederick Street
P.O. Box N-7130

Telephone: 322 13 31
Telex: 20197
Cable Address: BSI Overseas

Banking and Trust Services

Current and deposit accounts in all major currencies

Trading and custodianship of securities and precious metals

Portfolio management

Trust company functions, including trusteeships, executor duties and acting as escrow agent

Swiss Bank Corporation (Overseas) Limited
Nassau, Bahamas

a wholly-owned subsidiary of

Swiss Bank Corporation
Basle, Switzerland

Nassau (Bahamas)
P.O. Box N-77 57
Claughton House
Corner Shirley and
Charlotte Streets
Phone: 2-7570/3
Telex: 20 181/20 348
Cables: Swisbank

rently multiplying rapidly. One clear indication of this is the number of Swiss banks which have recently set up operations here – there are now over 20 of them.

These circumstances include: high and increasing taxation; over-regulation; lack of secrecy; cut-throat competition; left-wing socialism; right-wing extremism; and political uncertainty. All are factors which encourage the development of business in the Bahamas.

Among the more recent world problems, which make the quiet, stable and industrious banking community here seem more attractive than ever, both to banks and to their customers, have been turmoil in Iran and the blocking of Iranian assets in the United States; war in Lebanon; financial and political strains in Poland and other Comecon countries; the Falkland Islands episode; the disastrous state of the Argentinian economy and the blocking of assets in the United Kingdom; guerrilla wars in Central America; and political and economic problems in Mexico.

But, of course, it is simplistic to suppose that financial institutions in the Bahamas and their clients have somehow avoided *all* the problems of the outside world by conveniently setting up operations in the pleasant environment of Nassau. Indeed, if that were the case, the rush to these small islands would rapidly convert them from a tourist and financial paradise into being thoroughly unpleasant and over-crowded, and the fiscal and regulatory authorities of major countries all over the world would be exercising the strongest pressure to bring down this sector of the offshore banking system.

An occasional journalistically promoted image of the Bahamas which demands correction is that the lack of taxation here, coupled with strong secrecy laws, provides an ideal haven where all sorts of people can hide their possibly questionable financial resources from the sharp eyes of the tax collector in the U.S. and more distant lands. The concept that you can engage in a kind of updated Bahamian buccaneering where doubloons (denominated now in dollars) are buried in bank vaults instead of sandy coves may be appealing to some imaginations, but the reality is far less romantic and vastly more complex.

First of all, a large proportion of banks registered here represent subsidiaries of U.S. banks — there are, in fact, some 89 of these. Because they are branch operations of U.S. domiciled banks, their books and records are physically maintained in duplicate within the U.S., where they are available for inspection by

the authorities. Moreover, the profits of such branches are consolidated with those of the U.S. parent organization's, and tax is paid in the U.S. in a normal way.

You may ask, since there is nothing very secret or sensational in that, why bother to have a branch here at all?

The answer to that question is connected very little either with tax avoidance or with secrecy, but rather with the avoidance of complex domestic regulations in the U.S. and other countries relating to such things as liquidity requirements, gearing ratios and minimum deposits. Banks which set up branches in the Bahamas, and thus avoid these regulations, do so with the agreement, specific or implied, of the authorities in their home countries.

The home authorities will often agree to the setting up of a Bahamas branch for perfectly sound domestic reasons. For example, in the case of the U.S., the domestic authorities recognized in the late 1960s that their domestic regulations were making it impossible for U.S. banks to compete in the international markets, except by establishing new operations in less restricted banking centres offshore, such as London. Larger U.S. banks could usually justify the expense of doing this, while smaller banks frequently could not. A solution to the problem was thus found through the Bahamas, with U.S. authorities agreeing that only a smallscale presence was needed here for U.S. tax purposes, while much of the real work would still be carried on in the U.S. itself.

BUSINESS IS BETWEEN BANKS FOR MUTUAL BENEFIT

This somewhat artificial arrangement was largely corrected at the end of 1981 when U.S. authorities introduced new regulations permitting banks to do business territorially *in* the U.S. under very much the same conditions which previously applied only in offshore centres such as the Bahamas. These are known as the International Banking Facility (IBF) regulations, and as a result of their introduction nearly 200 banks have set up IBFs in New York, and are beginning to move some of their assets back from offshore centres. This has led to the quip that the newest offshore island financial centre is Manhattan!

There has, however, been no significant reduction in real banking activities in the Bahamas or other offshore centres, since once banks have been established in a centre, they have a tendency to remain – especially when their presence provides a form of

131

ALL THE WORLD'S OUR STAGE

Barclays Bank International is on stage throughout the commercial world. Anything to do with money, ask us first. We can help you with a personal chequing account. Or a savings account. Or a business account — large or small. Through our associated company **Barfincor,** we can even help you buy your own home!

We can help you overseas too. **Barclays Visa Travellers Cheques** are known and accepted throughout the world. And when you buy them there's no commission to pay.

Come on in — we'll be glad to see you.

Branches on
New Providence, Eleuthera,
Grand Bahama and Great Abaco Islands.

insurance against U.S. regulations being tightened up again.

There is currently some $80 billion of loans on the books of U.S. branch and subsidiary banks in the Bahamas, and much of it is likely to stay here. It should, however, be stressed that the money to fund this massive amount of loans comes principally through parent bank offices in New York, and through the international inter-bank market.

In other words, the vast majority of the billion dollar business in the Bahamas is a business conducted openly between banks, and for the benefit of banks, in arranging their international structures around the world.

On a much smaller scale, so far as amounts of money are concerned, there are also financial institutions in the Bahamas, such as the subsidiaries of Swiss banks and some locally registered trust companies, whose business is related to personal banking, rather than to the inter-bank market. This sector has grown in recent years, not least because of the desire of wealthy individuals to transfer some of their wealth from Europe and elsewhere to what is perceived as the more hospitable climate of North America, and at the same time, so far as the law permits, to avoid be-

134

coming unnecessarily involved in the complexities of U.S. regulations.

The local trust companies and related banks provide a wide range of specialized services which, in an article of this length, one can do little more than list. They include deposit, savings and current accounts in all major currencies, formation and management of companies and trusts, investment management and advice, tax and estate planning, management of offshore mutual funds, re-invoicing services, employee benefit programmes and offshore pension plans.

LONGTERM INTERESTS PREDOMINATE

Unfortunately, and perhaps inevitably, in a very small number of cases the hospitable financial climate of the Bahamas *may* be abused. But, it should be noted, this is the same kind of problem that is encountered in other countries, and not least in nearby Miami, which is developing very rapidly as a banking centre, and benefitting from the large flow of funds stemming from South America.

However, most of the banks with branch operations here are part of large international networks. Although the favourable tax

135

environment and secrecy laws can be, and are, used to find flexible solutions to complicated international, fiscal and regulatory problems for individuals, for companies and for banks themselves, the banks here and their head offices abroad are fully aware that it is not in their own longterm interests to encourage the development of business which, while entirely within the letter of Bahamian law, is known to offend the laws and regulations of other countries in which business is done.

Quite apart from any moral considerations, it is simply not a good longterm business proposition for a bank to risk creating problems for its often substantial organization in other countries for the sake of the relatively insignificant benefits which could be obtained by the small local entity if it were to ignore such foreign laws and regulations.

Moreover, the very rare incidents where the benefits offered by the Bahamas have been abused are much regretted by the local financial community, which is fully aware that such incidents detract from the reputation this country is building up as a financial centre.

Bankers here are glad that there is a strong and mature Cen-

OUR OFFICE HAS ALL THE RESOURCES OF A BANK MANY TIMES ITS SIZE.

As a branch and a subsidiary, our banking office and trust company have access to all the capabilities of the 17th largest bank in America.

The First National Bank of Boston.

Backed by over $18 billion in assets and the expertise of 12,700 people, worldwide, we can help you with all your financial needs. Eurodollar deposits and loans. Letters of credit. Trust and investment management services.

But because we're local, we can also provide you with personal and confidential service.

For more information, write: Russell F. Ploss or J. Richard Evans, P.O. Box N-4294, Nassau, Bahamas. Or call: (809) 322-8531.

And get all the resources of a bank many times our size, without going to a bank that big.

BANK OF BOSTON
(NASSAU BRANCH)

BANK OF BOSTON TRUST COMPANY LTD.
(BAHAMAS)

tral Bank which, while allowing individual banks to operate with the minimum of supervision and regulation, nevertheless carefully controls all potential newcomers to ensure that undesirables are kept out. This policy has helped Nassau to develop as the largest and most successful offshore financial centre in this part of the world, and will continue to ensure that it remains such in the future.

The author of this article, Ian M. G. Ross, was chairman of the Association of International Banks and Trust Companies in the Bahamas, and managing director of S.F.E. Banking Corporation Limited in Nassau before his return to his bank's head office in Paris at the end of 1982. He was educated at Charterhouse School in England, and at the universities of London, Munich and Madrid. He started his business career as a solicitor with  *the City of London firm of Slaughter & May, and also worked previously for seven years in Paris and three in Geneva. He has an M.B.A. from the European Institute of Business Administration in Fontainebleau, and an LL.B. from London University.*

Churchill Building, overlooking Rawson Square in the centre of Nassau, is where the Cabinet meets. The government is keen to establish the Bahamas as an important situs for captive insurance companies.

New Insurance Legislation is Aimed at

Going After the "Captives"

Well established in the western hemisphere as the premier off-shore banking centre and a playground for North and South American and European tourists, the Bahamas is now embarking upon a new frontier: establishing itself as an important situs for captive insurance companies and as a flag-of-convenience for foreign ship registrations.

To give fruition to this objective the government and the private sector are collaborating in both fiscal and promotional initiatives which have already produced positive results, and show exciting future potential. The subject of this article is restricted to the captive insurance developments and initiatives, which are the focus of both domestic and international attention.

One of the most substantive moves which is demonstrative of the co-operative mood which exists between the government and the private sector is the creation of the Bahamas Association of International Insurance whose founding members and officers comprise representatives of relevant government departments and executives from the insurance industry itself. According to a serving officer of this organization, the main purpose of the institution is "to encour-

age and direct co-operative efforts between the government and the private sector to produce an international insurance sector in the Bahamas which will be equal in size to the prestigious and significant banking community already operating efficiently and safely in the country". There are now 42 captive insurance companies registered in the Bahamas, more than 50 per cent of which have been established since 1979 when the preoccupation with attracting captives began in earnest.

In 1979 the Non-Resident Insurer (Exemption) Act 1978 impacted on the industry. This Act essentially offered more fiscal incentives than were available under the Insurance Act of 1969, which controlled the industry at the time. The three main exemptions which were focused on by the Act were:

1) Non-Resident Insurers (defined as registered insurers who issue policies covering underlying or primary risks on property, lives or any other risks located outside of the Bahamas) were exempted from publication of their accounts. It was still required, however, that they submit annual accounts to the Registrar of Insurance Companies (the Registrar being subject to non-disclosure rules, of course);

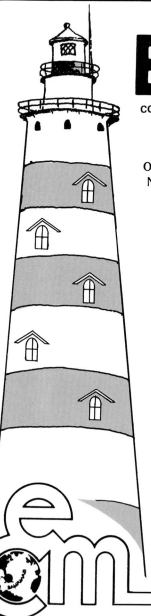
144

2) Exemption from the one per cent premium tax assessed against companies insuring risks within the Bahamas; and

3) The new "non-residency" classification implied the absence of restrictions on the investment of premium income and reserves which relate to the insurance of risks outside of the Bahamas.

Although these were very positive and noteworthy concessions, which made the Bahamas more competitive with other captive insurance centres, comparison with insurance laws in these centres still left something to be desired. This gave rise to rather intense lobbying by the local insurance industry for the introduction of comparable captive-oriented laws, resulting in the passage of a distinct and separate "External Insurance Act" (the short title of the Act) dealing with the international insurance issue in a most favourable manner. Before discussing the contents of this Act and its implications, perhaps an overview of the captive insurance phenomenon and its *raison d'être* would be appropriate.

The basic attractiveness of a captive insurance operation is that it is essentially "self-insurance", which carries very intrinsic economic benefits and inherent risks, both economic and fiscal, of course. The popular concensus is that the captive insurance concept

REPUBLIC NATIONAL BANK
OF NEW YORK
(International) LIMITED

A wholly-owned subsidiary of:

REPUBLIC NATIONAL BANK OF NEW YORK
452 FIFTH AVENUE, NEW YORK CITY, N.Y., U.S.A.

Address: P.O. Box N-3001
                                  Beaumont House,
                                  Nassau, N.P.,
                                  Bahamas.
Telephone: (32) 2-7568/(32) 2-7569/
                                  (32) 2-2263
Telex: 20 154 & 20 157
Cable Address: BLICBANK

TRADE DEVELOPMENT BANK
NASSAU BRANCH

Head Office

TRADE DEVELOPMENT BANK,

2, PL. DU LAC, GENEVA, SWITZERLAND

Address: P.O. Box N-3001
                                  Beaumont House,
                                  Nassau, N.P.,
                                  Bahamas.
Telephone: (32) 2-7568/(32) 2-7569/
                                  (32) 2-2263
Telex: 20 154 & 20 157
Cable Address: SUDAFIN

emerged out of shipping and petroleum industries which saw it, in the early 1900s, as a vehicle for tapping the international reinsurance market which offered comprehensive risk coverage at supposedly cheaper premium rates: the captive would carry little liability, transferring most of the risk to the reinsurance market.

From this crude form, incidental and contrived benefits evolved from the captive concepts: large institutions saw the opportunity to control and re-invest the vast insurance premium payments; smaller institutions appreciated it as a medium for reduced insurance costs and thus, more rapid growth. The most popular reasons for the formation and use of captive insurance companies are:

1) **Insurance Cost Savings** — premiums can be greatly reduced by using captives in a cost-effective manner;

2) **Risk Coverage** — some risk coverage is not available from conventional insurance companies, but captives can provide such cover;

3) **Regulatory Circumvention** — some insurers find it difficult to operate in some jurisdictions where there is "offensive" regulation and "excessive" reserve requirements. They find refuge by establishing captives in places where such requirements are more favourable;

147

PICTET BANK & TRUST LTD.

Affilated to:
Pictet & Cie, Geneva (Switzerland)
Private Bankers since 1805

*Investment
Management Services*

Tel: (809) 32-23938/9,
24703, 24895
Telex: 20 308

P.O. Box N-4837
Charlotte House
Nassau, Bahamas

4) **Tax Avoidance** — it is possible (with proper planning and under the appropriate circumstances) to form a captive in a tax haven to accumulate tax-free premium income, and at the same time obtain tax deductions at home for premiums paid;

5) **Premium Investment Yield** — some large companies with huge insurance bills find it feasible to establish captives just to retain the yield on investment of the ordinary premiums they pay;

6) **Window to the Reinsurance Market** — some institutions see captives as a window to the vast international reinsurance market, where profits can be high, and capital can be more easily moved across frontiers than in conventional insurance;

7) **Overall Profitability** — conventional insurance companies have overhead costs which can approach the 50 per cent to 60 per cent mark of premium income. Commissions and promotional expenses can further erode premium income and threaten to deplete funds which should be set aside for paying claims. Captives have, or can have, the advantage of large premium income from fewer policies with a minimal need for administrative work outside of the required risk management.

Most captives have been created by very large organizations

Let's talk about the Bahamas.

We're a Bahamian bank helping Bahamians achieve financial independence. Some of the ways we're helping are by providing a full range of personal and corporate banking services.

* **Chequing Accounts**
* **Savings Accounts**
* **Term Deposits**
* **Business Loans**
* **Safety Deposit Boxes**
* **Travellers Cheques**
* **Foreign Exchange**

So let's talk.
You can stop in and see us
at any of the addresses
listed below.

Bank of Montreal
(Bahamas & Caribbean) Limited

Head Office: Harrison Building, P.O. Box N-7118
            Nassau. Telephone (809) 322-1690
Main Nassau Office: P.O. Box N-3922, Nassau
Bay and East Streets Office: P.O. Box N-3922, Nassau
Freeport Office: P.O. Box F-2608, Freeport

whose operations are extensive enough to accommodate their own risk-spreading pool, but smaller companies are now getting into the act in greater numbers. The "lead" company pays premiums to its captive as it would under normal circumstances, but premium payments are usually smaller because costs are lower and brokerage commissions are avoided. Also profits which accrue from investment of reserves go back to the "lead" company at some point.

A few years back Fuqua Industries Inc. (FII) formed a captive subsidiary, Fuqua Insurance Co. (FIC). FII self-insured its workmen's compensation programme in 1971 and estimated that it saved $2 million in premiums by so doing. FII, which is a diversified manufacturing and services company, wanted to expand on such a saving. When its regular insurer raised its annual premium for liability and auto coverage from $1 million to $1.7 million in 1975, FII insured such risk with FIC.

In the two years that followed FII paid its captive (FIC) premiums totalling $2.3 million which it asserted was $2.2 million less than it would have paid to a regular insurer. Claims totalling $1.2 million were paid out—some $200,000 less than in the previous two years.

Despite these impressive economic results, however, FII was to derive a supplemental benefit, that of "flexibility". Subsequent to the formation of its captive company, FII acquired National Industries, Inc. According to FII, to accommodate this acquisition they were able to put together an insurance programme, under the aegis of its captive, in just 60 days — a feat which takes six to nine months working with an outside insurance company.

Between 1973 and 1978 Risk Planning Group estimated that there were some 350 captives formed. The number of captives in existence in 1980 was placed at slightly over 700, reflecting a two-year increase of 100 per cent. Most experts believe that new captives are now coming on stream at the rate of approximately 200 per annum. There is now a wide disparity in the size of captives, ranging from over $500 million to $250,000 in assets. The majority of these are denominated in dollars (which gives rise to a very interesting opportunity for the Bahamas).

The captive insurance industry does not lack credibility as it is patronized by blue chip companies and promoted within borders of some countries from which a large volume of this business originates

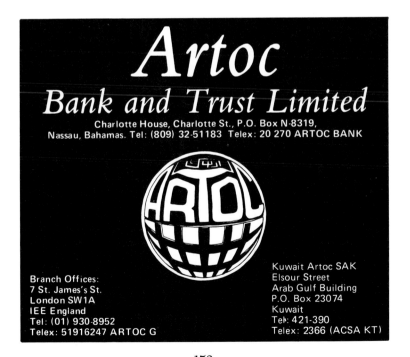

S.F.E.
Banking Corporation Limited

& ITS WHOLLY-OWNED SUBSIDIARY

S.F.E. Bank & Trust (Bahamas) Limited

Post Office Box N-100, Nassau, Bahamas
Telex: 20 103, Cable: SOFINEUR, Telephone: 2-7480

BANKING	**FOREIGN EXCHANGE &**	**TRUST**
Mr. A. O. Scarrow	**TREASURY**	Mr. B. Lynch
Managing Director	Mr. H. Webb	Vice President
Mr. Evan R. Cox	Telephone: 2-7480	Trust Company
Vice President		Telephone: 5-2811
Telephone: 2-7480		

EQUAL SHAREHOLDER BÁNKS

Algemene Bank Nederland N.V.	Holland
Banca Nazionale del Lavoro	Italy
Bank of America NT & SA	U.S.A.
Banque Bruxelles Lambert S.A.	Belgium
Banque Nationale de Paris	France
Barclays Bank International Limited	Great Britain
Dresdner Bank A.G.	Fed. Rep. of Germany
The Sumitomo Bank Limited	Japan
Union Bank of Switzerland	Switzerland

—namely, the United States. Patrons include such names as Exxon, Mobil Oil, Ford Motor, Gulf Oil, Phillips Petroleum, Murphy Oil, B. F. Goodrich, Sperry Rand, Weyerhaeuser, International Flavors & Fragrances, the University of Pittsburgh, the University of Minnesota, and so on.

The fact that the captive insurance industry is inherently compatible with the Eurodollar market should be underscored when considering the Bahamas as a captive base. Most of the captives are denominated in dollars by their parents and this gives them little option but to invest the lion's share of their funds in Eurodollar Bonds. As a matter of fact, should the captive industry flourish in the Bahamas, an ancillary industry of investment management can viably emerge.

A good example of this is Oil Insurance, Ltd. (OIL), a group of captives controlled by several oil companies. OIL controls vast funds which are invested (mostly in Eurodollar Bonds) by London investment managers. As the Bahamas is the leading offshore centre for Eurodollars, getting captive funds close to the marketplace is, indeed, a compelling reason to locate captives here.

Before moving on to discuss the incentives the Bahamas offers

Corramar Bank & Trust Limited

affiliated with

Hentsch & Cie, Geneva

Private bankers in Switzerland since 1796

Management and advisory services for International Investments of individuals and institutions.

Norfolk House
Frederick Street
P.O. Box N-4232
Nassau, Bahamas

Tel: (809) 325-4485/
3-8034/3-8169
Telex: 20 128

as a captive situs *vis-a-vis* the External Insurance Act, it should be noted, that most advisors in the captive insurance industry hold that unless you have a minimum of $500,000 in annual premiums, formation and operation of a captive would not be economically feasible.

Once the proper funding (annualized premium) is ascertained, coupled with preliminary risk management work, the flexibility would exist to effect the kind of strategy most advantageous under the circumstances. For example, should the premium payments be tax-deductible, the parent may opt to pay high premium rates to the captives. Conversely, however, if the payments are not deductible, low rates may be desirable. The matter of rates may be governed by inter-company pricing rules or "arms-length" provisions. However, in the U.S. the Internal Revenue Service has challenged the practice of treating a company's premium payments to its captive as a tax-deductible business expense. The celebrated Carnation Co. case highlighted this IRS objection. The case is being appealed, but this area of contention continues to be a point of nebulosity in the tax code.

When luring foreign investors to the Bahamas the most prominently mentioned attractions are: tax-free status; political stability;

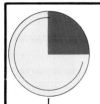

158

bank secrecy; absence of bi-lateral disclosure treaties; and excellent infrastructure (communications, banking, a substantial corps of professionals, etc.)

More specifically, however, for captive insurance company operators the potential attractions to be explored are embodied in a group of rules and regulations known as the External Insurance Act (EIA). For the most part, this Act replaces the Insurance Act 1969 for external insurers, but in some places the EIA is *pari passu* with the 1969 Act.

The first purpose of the EIA is to control the conduct of business by external insurers, and underwriting managers of external insurers. An external insurer is described by the Act as "a body corporate incorporated in the Bahamas, or registered in the Bahamas under the Foreign Companies Act, and which carries on only external insurance business". An "underwriting manager" is defined as a company incorporated in the Bahamas which, operating from or within the Bahamas as manager or consultant (but not as a *bona fide* employee) provides underwriting and insurance expertise for one or more external insurers.

A summary of the more important requirements and benefits

of the Act are as follows:

1.) The paid-up capital requirement is $200,000 (**Part II, Sec. 8**);

2.) The external insurers must have their accounts audited annually by an independent auditor (**Part II, Sec. 11**);

3). a) Application for a licence as either an external insurer or an underwriting manager is to be made out on the same basis as that suscribed in the Insurance Act, 1969 (**Part IV, Sec. 20**);

b) Non-resident designation from the Central Bank of the Bahamas has to be submitted with the application before any registration can take place (**Part IV, Sec. 28**).

Two most important clauses are at the heart of this piece of legislation, and they are so compellingly significant that they are quoted here verbatim:

Sec. 21(1) Except for the purposes of the carrying out of his functions under this Act or when lawfully required to do so by any Court of competent jurisdiction within the Bahamas, neither the Registrar nor any person acting under his authority shall disclose any information relating to any application by any

International financial planners for people who value their privacy.

Independent Bank
and Trust Company,
Limited

E.D. Sassoon Building
Shirley & Parliament Streets
P.O. Box N-3908
Nassau, Bahamas
Telex: 20-423 indbank
Telephone: (809) 32-52859

Overseas
Union Bank

(Bahamas) Limited

Bolam House, George Street
P.O. Box N-8184
Nassau, Bahamas
Telex: 20 399
Cable: UNISEAS
Tel: (809) 32-2-2476/2-8078

person under the provisions of this Act or to the affairs of, or of any policyholder of, that person which the Registrar or such other official has acquired in the carrying out of their respective functions under this Act.

(2) Any person who contravenes sub-section (1) shall be guilty of an offense and is liable on summary conviction to a fine of five thousand dollars or imprisonment for six months or to both such fine and imprisonment.

Sec. 22. Notwithstanding the provisions of any other Act every external insurer registered under this Act shall be exempt from the payment of any tax, fee, duty or impost other than those in force at the commencement of, or payable in respect of registration under, this Act, for a period of fifteen years from the date of the first such registration of the insurer.

This new Act is a giant step toward restoring confidence in the Bahamas as a base for captive insurance companies — a position it once held prior to the introduction of the Insurance Act 1969 which, among other elements, resulted in the precipitous exodus of more than 80 per cent of the captives then in existence.

Buttressed by an ever-expanding force of locally based insur-

ance experts, and a vibrant and accommodative banking climate, the influx of captives to the Bahamas has been dramatic.

Domestic captive management concerns all indicate that they now have to cope with an increasing volume of inquiries, but predict that the inquiries will further intensify when the External Insurance Act is given international media exposure. There has already been an increase of between 20 to 25 captive companies registered in the Bahamas since the Act was introduced, and it is understood that there are approximately 13 others now "in the pipeline".

Two points should be emphasized. Firstly, that captives can accommodate unorthodox insurance needs and, secondly, that captives can also be used effectively by individuals and in estate planning. There is much diversity in the industry, and the flexibility, which is a germane feature of captives, facilitates adaptability to a vast spectrum of fiscal and economic objectives.

Oliver Gibson, the author of this article on captive insurance companies in the Bahamas, serves as consultant to Trans-World Management Corporation, P.O. Box N-3907, Nassau. He is an accountant by profession, and has contributed articles to leading international tax and financial publications.

Above: Dignitaries at Nassau's International Banking Conference in March 1983, included (l. to r.) Bahamas Central Bank Governor William Allen; Suzanne Black; Bahamas Prime Minister Sir Lynden Pindling; Jean-Pierre Fraysse. Below: Canadian Imperial Bank of Commerce's Nassau headquarters being constructed.

The Broad Scope of

International Banking in the Bahamas

O ffshore banking has grown phenomenally over the past quarter of a century, and has played a vital catalytic role in international trade and finance. "Offshore Banking" is evocative of the genetic term, "Eurodollar", which is simply defined as a United States dollar deposit held at a bank outside the U.S. A broader term, "eurocurrency", encompasses all currencies which are expatriated in the cycle of trade and commerce.

In 1960 the Federal Reserve Bank of New York estimated the size of the eurodollar market slightly in excess of $1 billion. The estimate for 1981 by most leading sources places the market in excess of $825 billion, with prospects for future growth of better than 20 per cent per annum. This proliferation of entrepôt banking was precipitated by a series of political and legislative events in the U.S. (and to a lesser extent in Europe) and collateral fiscal liberalization in several developing countries.

World War II produced in Europe ethnic cadres of wealthy political refugees who traded in dollars for both safety and anonymity. Thus, a European market for dollars was established outside of the U.S. Almost simultaneously, American banks began following their customers in pursuing Marshall Aid dollars (for reconstruc-

Why not get better financial advice?

That's what we're here for!

A Bank should not be simply a place to save money in, or borrow money from. A good bank should help you plan, help you earn the most from your savings, help you take advantage of experience and good financial advice. That's what makes the Bank of Commerce the better choice. Why not talk to the Commerce now. A better tomorrow can start today at the Commerce—**The "Why Not" Bank.**

**CANADIAN IMPERIAL
BANK OF COMMERCE**

tion of war-torn Europe) and opened offices on the continent and elsewhere. The momentum intensified in the early 1960s. The U.S. imposed the Interest Equalization Tax (IET); increased credit controls were introduced and a web of rules were enforced, the most notable of which were: (a) the Voluntary Foreign Credit Restraint Program (VFCR) in 1965, and (b) the Offices of Foreign Direct Investment (OFDI) Regulations, which require U.S. persons investing abroad to borrow abroad.

Under such regulations, U.S. banks were subjected to certain lending ceilings, rather high reserve requirements, interest rate ceilings and premium payments to the Federal Deposit Insurance Corp. The smaller banks without existent foreign branches and wishing to engage in the lucrative eurocurrency business (lending and deposit-taking) were forced to establish "limited service" branches offshore. The Federal Reserve Board formally agreed to permit the establishment of offshore limited service branches so that smaller banks could compete in the international financial market in 1969. The Bahamas was the major beneficiary of this movement offshore, and is today, next to London, the leading offshore financial centre in the world.

The eurodollar market in the Bahamas is currently running anywhere between $120 billion and $150 billion. All of the prime banks have offices in the Bahamas to engage in this market. These institutions are able to pay competitive rates of interest on deposits in the absence of Federal Reserve requirements and to make loans without interest rate and credit ceilings. **The money creation process is thus enhanced and profit margins are higher than onshore banking.** Excellent communications between the Bahamas and the U.S., proximity of the two countries and the fact that the Bahamas is in the same time zone as New York facilitate orderly parent/branch administrative functions. Circumvention of restrictions and regulations in the U.S. is not the only advantage, however, when using a tax haven as an offshore banking base; exceptional fiscal liberalities can also be exploited. In the Bahamas they include: no personal income tax; no corporate income tax; no sales tax; no tax on the accumulation of profits; no estate tax (inheritance tax nor death duty); no double-tax treaties; and strict bank secrecy enforced by law.

Within the spectrum of such supplemental benefits, many institutions have expanded into trust operations and other client financial services. It is not at all strange, therefore, to find banks within banks and/or eurodollar business being conducted on

behalf of and with in-house clientele. These activities give rise to an array of other business functions which are germane to clients' business requirements (i.e. mutual funds, stock trading, insurance, nominee services, etc.).

In the Bahamas there are over 330 banks, 230 of which also carry out trust business in some form. These institutions are kept to the fore of the international banking industry and are innovative in an ever-changing capital market. Citibank and Morgan Guaranty Trust launched a programme geared to attract large depositors to their Nassau branches. This programme involves large Certificates of Deposits issued in Nassau to be actively traded in the New York money markets. There isn't a secondary, or re-sale, market in CDs in Nassau – this medium is often used by banks to raise funds for lending and investment. These CDs are also more attractive to banks, corporations and other institutions with large amounts of cash to invest. Under the scheme, the CDs remain in safekeeping in Nassau, but upon that asset the bank would issue the owner's negotiable receipts in New York, which could be traded in the short-term money market. These CD receipts are offered through leading brokerage houses.

The Bahamas has a good reputation for efficient and sound regulation of its banking industry. Clearly, the chance of sustaining a dubious banking operation of any duration is remote, indeed. Regulation rules in themselves are not excessive, but the country values its banking reputation so much that the rules are enforced rather zealously. Requirements for obtaining a banking licence are not stringent; generally a good reputation, banking experience, a resident agent and the required paid-in capital suffices. Broadly, there are five classifications of banking licences obtainable in the Bahamas; they range from no restrictions to various degrees of restrictions, and annual fees assessed by the government range from $45,000 to $900. For any foreign corporation or individual wishing to engage in just the eurodollar market and other offshore public banking, the appropriate licence fee is $9,000 per annum. There are minimum paid-in capital requirements for banks and trust companies of $1,000,000 scaling down to $10,000; the paid-in capital level which applies to offshore eurodollar operations is $100,000.

The eurodollar industry has grown so rapidly and become so vast that it has expanded its traditional ambiance and the door has been opened to the heretofore passive observers. Many cities and states, New York the most notable, have passed legislation designed

170

to compete with traditional offshore financial centres for eurodollar business. In addition, the "regional banking syndrome" has given way to international banking initiatives. This metamorphosis has strengthened the international content of the U.S. banking system and has given rise to the prospect of a degree of dominance in the global banking community, especially since the dollar will continue to be the dominant medium of exchange for the foreseeable future.

During October 1981 U.S. banks were allowed to operate "International Banking Facilities" (IBF) under the aegis of the Federal Reserve Board, which allows the establishment of a "free trade zone" for international banking. IBFs needn't be separate offices—just a separate set of books for assets and liabilities related thereto. Deposits at IBFs are not subject to U.S. interest rate ceilings, and the facilities are exempted from state and local income tax. IBFs are not allowed to accept deposits from or make loans to U.S. residents, nor can they be used to finance activities in the U.S. The most damaging restriction, however, is the prohibition of IBFs issuing negotiable instruments and a "tentative" (because of the prospect of removal by pending legislation) requirement to insure deposits with the FDIC. Unmistakably, this free-zone concept was designed to compete for offshore eurocurrency business. To date, New York has been quite successful in attracting IBFs; it is understood that there are now over 110 in the city, and there some reports of banks in Caribbean centres shifting their eurocurrency lending operations to New York under the umbrella of IBFs. And so, practitioners in Caribbean offshore financial centres (like the Bahamas) are watching the activities in New York with considerable interest, cognizant of the possibility of New York gaining at their expense.

Despite New York's impressive progress, however, established offshore centres (tax havens) still have a competitive edge. IBFs are not exempt from federal income tax, and reserve requirements, though lowered, are still material. Moreover, investors take into account other elements as well, the most notable of which are: political stability; bank secrecy; and fiscal guarantees.

While it is easy to make out a "prima facie" case for the political stability of the U.S. and its commitment to democracy, the practical aspects become somewhat muddled to the foreign investor. The freezing of Iranian assets during the hostage crisis and the threat by courts to freeze the assets of New York-based branches of Swiss banks in insider trading investigations are viewed with much

Handelsbank N.W. (Overseas) Limited
Nassau, Bahamas

A wholly owned subsidiary of Handelsbank N.W., Zurich, Switzerland
♻ A member of the National Westminster Bank Group

Current and time deposits and savings accounts in
all major currencies.

Certificates of deposit.

Active in international lending operations.

Participating in international underwritings
of bonds and notes in various currencies.

Company management.

Incorporation and/or administration of
Bahamian corporations.

**RoyWest Building
P.O. Box N-4214
Nassau, Bahamas**

**Telephone: (809) 32-55534/28663
Telex: 20 525
Cables: Handelsbank, Nassau, Bahamas**

disdain by the investor whose paramount requirement is safety of capital. The Bahamas enjoys over 250 years of uninterrupted parliamentary democracy, and nationalization is constitutionally prohibited.

Bank secrecy is the cornerstone of most tax havens. Recent events, however (particularly surrounding the cases cited above), have shaken the resolve of Switzerland (considered the bastion of secrecy) to enforce it. The Bahamas has recently strenghtened its bank secrecy laws, and has resisted U.S. attempts to undermine bank secrecy via a proposed disclosure agreement as early as 1978.

There are no guarantees that the Federal Reserve Board will allow free zone banking indefinitely, or that all the benefits will be sustained throughout the life of IBFs. The fear is always that economic policies can change in the U.S. to the extent that severe credit controls and tighter grips on the money supply can be imposed; IBFs would not be sheltered from such adversities. Conversely, however, tax havens are generally committed to maintaining their status, and offshore banking is so significant to their economies that it is unlikely that they would engage in self-destructive moves against the industry. Established offshore centres like the Bahamas have demonstrated over and over their *savoir-faire* for maintaining the kind of attractions and conditions in which offshore banking can flourish.

The competitive edge in the New York versus offshore centres battle for eurocurrency business still seems decidedly in favour of the overseas centres. The cost of operating in New York is very high, and it is not difficult to undercut such costs substantially in most offshore centres. Additionally, the three per cent cash reserve requirement in New York translates to a margin of approximately 0.625 per cent at interest rates prevailing in 1982. During the month of October 1982 alone some shopping around to place $100,000 on 30-day deposit in New York produced a rate of 8.31 per cent. Placing the same amount in Nassau for a shorter term (seven days), an interest rate of 8.9375 per cent was obtainable.

Access to the IBFs is limited to individual non-U.S. residents, foreign corporations, foreign banks and foreign subsidiaries of U.S. corporations. However, residents (corporate and individual) of the U.S. can establish offshore banking facilities in overseas tax havens like the Bahamas to engage in the eurodollar market. As a matter of fact, this is implicitly encouraged by the U.S. tax code. Passive income, such as interest, is generally regarded as Sub-part F income, thereby bringing such income under the full weight of

The world's a smaller place when you bank with us

The Hongkong Bank Group today has over 900 offices in 53 countries, providing a full range of international financial services including commercial and merchant banking, insurance, finance and investment management, and trustee services.

Backed by more than a century of continuous service our offices in Asia, Europe, the Middle East and North America have developed special expertise in linking the business centres of the world.

For complete information please contact any of our following offices:

Equator Bank Ltd.
P.O. Box N-9925
1st Floor, Norfolk House
Frederick Street, Nassau.

Hang Seng Bank (Bahamas) Limited
P.O. Box N-4917
2nd Floor, Harrison Building
Marlborough Street, Nassau.

**The Hongkong and Shanghai
Banking Corporation
Hongkong Shanghai (Shipping) Limited
The British Bank of the Middle East**
all of which are located at:
P.O. Box N-4917
Claughton House,
Shirley/Charlotte Streets, Nassau.

The Hongkong Bank

The Hongkong and Shanghai Banking Corporation
Marine Midland Bank
The British Bank of the Middle East
Hang Seng Bank Limited
Wardley Limited
Antony Gibbs & Sons Limited
Mercantile Bank Limited

174

taxation. However, broadly speaking, if active banking business or financing is carried out, income from unrelated parties will be excluded from the scope of Sub-part F. This exclusion is found in S.954 of the Internal Revenue Code (IRC) under which dividends, interest and gains from the sale or exchange of stocks or securities derived in the conduct of a banking, financing or similar business may not constitute Sub-part F income – but only if this income is received from unrelated persons. However, if such income is received by a banking company from a related banking company it will not be considered Sub-part F income. It is obvious, therefore, that the idea of a U.S. person or corporation establishing an offshore bank in the Bahamas holds exciting possibilities for international business and exceptional tax benefits, both of a banking and non-banking nature. Closer scrutiny of the IRC's definition of what banking operations qualify as such are as follows:

An entity would be deemed to be conducting a banking, financing or similar business if it derives more than 50 per cent of its gross income from a business consisting of one or more of the following activities: receiving deposits of money from the public; making loans to the public; purchasing, or purchasing and discounting, accounts, notes or instalment contracts receivables; or

THE
INTERNATIONAL
NAME
IN
SWISS BANKING

PARIBAS SUISSE

Geneva
Basle · Lugano · Zurich · Nassau

Banque de Paris et des Pays-Bas (Suisse) S.A.

purchasing stock or debt obligations from the issuer or obligor (or connected person) thereof for the purpose of distributing such stock or obligations through re-sale to the public. From that it can be seen that the business mix can be flexible, i.e. 51 per cent banking, 49 per cent other.

The importance the eurodollar market played in fuelling the short-term credit needs of industry within the U.S. economy cannot be over-emphasized. The market has been equally accommodative in meeting the longterm credit needs of industry through the creation of the "eurobond". This instrument has been extremely helpful to big energy companies during the current recession in the energy market as such companies have been able to incur longterm debt in eurobonds at very competitive rates of interest. Some indications are also that the strength of the company's balance sheet is not an overwhelming consideration, as may be the case in the onshore U.S. banking market. Galveston Houston (a company supplying equipment and technical services to the oil industry) was able to raise $20 million in 15-year convertible debt carrying a coupon of 8¾ per cent in the eurobond market back in 1980. The company's balance sheet was not impres-

PORTFOLIO MANAGEMENT SERVICES LTD.

For offshore:
- Company Management
- Office Facilities
  (including reinvoicing)
- Stock & Bond Trading
- International Investment
- Advisory Service
- Commodity Futures Trading
- Buying, Selling & Warehousing of
  Gold & Silver bullion and coins
- International Tax Planning

"El Patio"
(Griffin House)
Fort Charlotte
P.O. Box N-8402, Nassau, Bahamas
Tel: (809) 32-57403/22740
Telex: 20 404 METAL

sive: equity of $25 million against longterm debt of $47 million, and assets of $34.8 million against liabilities of $15.3 million at the time.

Offshore eurodollars have also been used to hedge against adverse policy shifts in the U.S. An example of this is the move by banks during the October 1979 credit-tightening by the Federal Reserve Board. In anticipation of the move, U.S banks borrowed huge amounts in the eurodollar market which many observers felt ran as high as $8.5 billion; the ensuing credit constraints were thereby successfully hedged against.

The "offshore funds" market is currently running in the region of $1.7 trillion and within this enormous sphere are tremendous opportunities for both individual and corporate entrepreneurs, particularly those with international operations. There is a school of thought which subscribes to the view that there will be a significant slowdown in the movement of funds offshore as more and more economic giants like the U.S. establish domestic financial centres for offshore capital of their own. However, as these centres are for the most part off-limits to residents, interested individuals and corporations would have to seek out foreign centres to which access is readily available. This fact, coupled with the favourable tax treatment mentioned previously, would give impetus to the exploration and exploitation of tax haven centres by such parties.

Conventionally, offshore banks would be established by other banks, insurance and other financially oriented institutions. However, the formation of a tax haven offshore bank can be a key element in good tax planning in the affairs of both the individual and the corporation.

Having regard to the "banking test" outlined previously, the following examples are advanced:

A U.S. resident who has $1 million in cash on deposit in the U.S. would pay tax on the passive income (which is Sub-part F) at a very high rate. However, should that individual form a bank in the Bahamas with the $1 million and use the funds to discount trade notes for non-related U.S. corporations, or have the bank carry on other non-related banking business (51 per cent or more) such business will be excluded from Sub-part F treatment.

There can be many variations using offshore banks to promote tax avoidance in individual and corporate tax planning once it is recognized that banks are an ideal vehicle for U.S. entities to take funds offshore.

179

Escaping the U.K. Tax Net

Advice for Expatriates

The thought of higher income completely free of United Kingdom tax is, in most cases, the biggest attraction of working abroad. However, not everyone who leaves Britain for employment overseas will qualify for this privileged tax status, and we will examine here the most important considerations of residence overseas.

Whether you have just arrived in the Bahamas, are planning a visit to relatives in the U.K. or are considering returning to the U.K. for retirement or further employment, the importance of seeking professional advice at all stages cannot be overstressed.

There is no doubt that there are considerable financial benefits in working abroad — particularly the opportunity to escape the U.K. tax net, at least for a time. It's rather ironic, therefore, but nevertheless understandable, that financial motives are sometimes forgotten when making final arrangements for departure, with the result that the most fundamental tax aspects are often ignored.

Complicated tax laws may often mean that the new expatriate's financial resources need to be re-arranged to achieve the greatest reward, and the exact tax position will depend on the length of time to be spent working abroad.

Basically, there are two categories under which overseas employees will be assessed for U.K. tax. The Inland Revenue will continue to treat the British expatriate as resident and ordinarily resident for tax purposes unless the period of absence covers at least one complete fiscal year (i.e. April 6 to April 5). In planning the tour abroad, therefore, the objective must be, wherever possible, to spend at least one complete tax year overseas to achieve complete exemption from U.K. tax on all overseas earnings.

With the following exceptions, U.K. tax is levied on all of the resident's worldwide income:

(a) A deduction of 25 per cent may be made from the earnings attributable to the overseas employment before they are assessed for U.K. tax, provided that a total of at least 30 days is spent abroad in any tax year (either continuously or in total).

Clearly, this is a favourable concession — particularly to anyone subject to tax at the higher rates, where the resultant tax saving can be considerable. Furthermore, it's an allowance that encompasses a large number of U.K. residents who are continually travelling abroad on short trips. Anyone having a separate overseas appointment with a foreign employer is entitled to this deduction regardless of the period of his absence abroad.

(b) There is a much more valuable concession for people who spend more than 365 days abroad (although the period involved need not cover a complete tax year). In these cases, provided that no more than 62 intervening consecutive days (or one-sixth of the total period spent abroad) are spent in the U.K., all overseas earnings will be wholly exempt from U.K. tax.

The rule is a complicated one and anyone falling into this category should seek professional advice to ensure that any intended U.K. visit does not contravene this ruling, and thus invalidate his eligibility for this considerable benefit.

ESTABLISHING NON-RESIDENCE STATUS

Anyone working abroad for a complete tax year will normally be treated as non-resident for tax purposes, even if it is intended to maintain a home in the U.K. This, the most privileged tax status, carries complete exemption from U.K. income tax on all overseas income, as well as various concessions on investment income arising in the U.K.

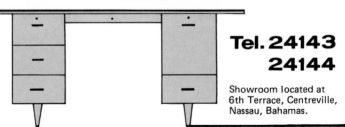

In practice, if someone leaves the U.K. for fulltime service overseas under a contract of employment covering a period of at least one complete tax year, he may establish non-residence status for U.K. tax purposes from the date of departure. U.K. income tax will, therefore, only be payable on pre-departure earnings, and overseas earnings will be exempt from the start.

To obtain this treatment from the time of leaving the U.K., it is necessary to show the U.K. tax authorities that you have entered into a specific contract with the employer abroad for a period which covers at least one complete tax year. Without such a contract, non-resident status cannot be determined in advance, and will only be granted retrospectively once the overseas employment pattern is established.

A U.K. non-resident is still liable to tax on income arising in the U.K., with the exception of interest from tax-exempt British Government Stock and, in certain circumstances — and by concession — interest paid on bank deposits. It is, therefore, important to review the sources of U.K. income and reduce these as far as possible in order to minimize the liability to U.K. tax. With the removal of exchange control, capital assets are now freely

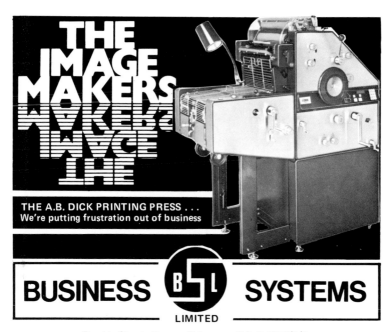

Bahamas International Trust Company Limited.

Incorporated under the laws of the Bahama Islands with an authorized capital of B$3,000,000. Paid up capital B$1,000,000.

The company acts as international financial adviser, investment manager, company manager, registrar and transfer agent, and as executor and trustee.

Correspondents:

THE BANK OF NEW YORK
BARCLAYS BANK INTERNATIONAL LIMITED
N.M. ROTHSCHILD AND SONS LIMITED
THE ROYAL TRUST COMPANY
THE ROYAL TRUST COMPANY OF CANADA

Enquiries will be welcomed, and may be addressed to any one of our Correspondents listed above, or directly to:

The General Manager

Bahamas International Trust Company Limited

Post Office Box N-7768, Nassau, Bahamas. Telex: 20 143 or 20 359
Cables: BITRUSTCO, NASSAU, Area Code: 809-32. Telephone: 2-1161

184

transferable to tax-exempt funds outside the U.K. which are, in any case, likely to produce a higher return than U.K. gilts or bank deposits over the longer term.

If you are a British subject, or fulfil certain other conditions, the Inland Revenue will allow part of your normal personal allowances to be set against your U.K. taxable income. Basically, the part for which you will qualify will be in direct proportion to the percentage of total income which arises in the U.K., but whether or not you can turn this to your advantage will depend on your personal circumstances.

The non-resident, by re-arranging his financial affairs, can realistically expect to escape any liability to U.K. taxation for the whole of the time spent abroad, except, perhaps, if a home is maintained in the U.K. from which the rent exceeds the entitlement to allowances and expenses, such as mortgage interest.

As can be seen, anything short of emigration may result in a liability to U.K. tax in one form or another. The British expatriate, however, is in a privileged tax situation — but it pays to find out just what liability exists before leaving.

In nearly every case, where non-resident status can be established, a refund of tax will be due on departure, since the authorities grant the full personal allowances for the year of departure for offset against pre-departure earnings. Repayment of the tax overpaid must be claimed from the Inland Revenue. The need to claim tax rebates also applies to anyone who cannot establish non-resident status, but who does qualify for the 25 per cent or 100 per cent tax exemption in respect of his overseas earnings.

This article began by suggesting that it is advisable to obtain professional advice before leaving. But, even after departure, there is always likely to be a continuing tax liability which, for the non-resident spending short periods visiting the U.K., can be a cumbersome and certainly confusing matter. However, specialist tax advisers exist in the U.K. who can undertake dealings with the tax authorities for you.

ONCE YOU'RE NON-RESIDENT — STAY THAT WAY AND MAKE THE MOST OF IT

The cost of a prolonged visit to any country is not necessarily dependent on a comparison of prices alone. The complex tax structures of most countries present problems to the visiting expatriate and to the foreign national entering the country to work.

Britain is no exception.

It is, therefore, important that the British expatriate planning a trip home on leave and the foreign national entering Britain to work for the first time fully understand the tax treatment they can expect if they stay too long.

The visiting rules are not defined in U.K. tax law, but court rulings over the years have provided the basis of current Inland Revenue practice. Depending on the time spent in the U.K. and the frequency of visits, the Inland Revenue may regard the visitor as resident and/or ordinarily resident. The basic premise is that the non-resident pays tax only on income which arises within the U.K., whereas the U.K. resident is potentially liable on worldwide income.

The status of "not ordinarily resident" will, in certain circumstances, govern the extent of U.K. liability, but the category of resident and ordinarily resident is the one under which the large majority of the U.K. population are assessed for tax. To the foreign visitor working in Britain, or to the visiting expatriate, it is the category to be avoided at all costs. It can result in paying tax not only on U.K. earnings, but on total worldwide income.

"Non-resident" status for tax purposes will be lost if:

(a) In any one tax year, six months, i.e. 183 days, or more are spent in the U.K. In calculating the time actually spent in the U.K., it is normal practice to deduct both the day of arrival and the day of departure. If and when the tax rules on visiting are contravened, non-resident status will be lost immediately, and the individual will be regarded as resident for tax purposes.

(b) Visits become "habitual and substantial", i.e. exceeding three months (90 days) annual average over any four consecutive tax years.

(c) A property is maintained in the U.K. which is available for occupation during the visit. In considering this rule, the availability of a property in the U.K. is ignored where the visitor is working fulltime overseas and all his duties are performed outside the U.K. Where this is not the case, the visitor will immediately be regarded as a resident for tax purposes for the whole year, notwithstanding the duration of the visit. It is not, however, the practice to regard unfurnished accommodation rented for a year or less, or furnished accommodation rented for two years or less as a place of residence for this purpose.

(d) On arrival in the U.K. it is intended to remain either permanently or for at least three years.

Gotthard Bank

NASSAU BRANCH

IBM House	Telephone (809) 32-51531/2/3/4
P.O. Box 6312	Telex: 20 151
Nassau, Bahamas	Cable BDG

IBM House	Telephone: (809) 32-51533
P.O. Box 6052	Telex: 20 216
Nassau, Bahamas	Cable GBI

Gotthard Bank International Ltd.

"Ordinarily resident" status is less easy to define, since it implies a more permanent situation. A visitor will be regarded as ordinarily resident in the U.K. by exceeding the 90-day rule referred to above. The visitor who maintains a property available here who is not working overseas will be treated as ordinarily resident merely by brief visits in four consecutive years. The person arriving in the U.K. for prolonged or permanent residence is also treated as ordinarily resident, but only from the date of arrival.

RESIDENT WIVES — A BLESSING IN DISGUISE?

Unlike most areas of U.K. taxation where a married woman is normally assessed jointly with her husband, the residence rules for visitors must be applied to each separately. The result is that the wife will frequently be regarded as resident whereas the husband will retain his non-resident status. But this is often a blessing in disguise.

This situation arises where the family maintain a property in the U.K., but only the husband is engaged in fulltime work overseas. Often, too, the wife's visits are longer because of the need to look after children being educated at schools in Britain or, in the case of the British expatriate family, the need to care for elderly relatives.

However, a wife who is regarded as resident need not suffer tax unnecessarily. Any income she may receive can be offset against her full personal allowances before any charge to tax arises, which can often result in a refund of tax already deducted at source. If the property is in joint names and is rented out, tax on the letting profit will frequently be halved, since the wife's share can be covered by these allowances.

Despite continual inflation, the cost of living in Britain is still relatively cheap compared to many other countries. However, prices and the cost of living are only part of the overall equation. If visits are extended beyond the temporary residence limits, tax becomes an expensive and unwelcome 'extra' that can often be avoided. The British expatriate is, in most cases, restricted by his employer in the frequency and duration of trips home and, therefore, unlikely to contravene any of the residence rules. However, the foreign national temporarily working in the U.K. is in even greater danger, but, with careful planning, periods of residence in the U.K. can often be undertaken without having to surrender to the pressures of the Inland Revenue.

189

So far, we have only discussed tax on income. For non-residents the treatment of U.K. assets for capital taxes provides certain additional concessions.

Chargeable gains (less losses and the normal allowances and exemptions) that accrue on the disposal of assets during a given tax year are liable to Capital Gains Tax. This is payable by anyone who is either "resident or ordinarily resident" in the U.K. for any part of the tax year in which the disposal is made. By Inland Revenue concession, however, a person becoming "not resident and not ordinarily resident" will not face a Capital Gains Tax liability on disposals made after the departure date within the tax year he leaves the U.K.

Similarly, any realized losses over the same period will not qualify to be offset against any future taxable gains. It, therefore, makes sense to realize any losses before departure, while a liability to Capital Gains Tax remains.

However, it should be remembered that Capital Gains Tax does apply to gains realized during the complete tax year of return to the U.K. (even if realized before return), unless non-residence status has been continuous for at least 36 months, when only gains realized after arrival fall into charge.

There is a definite trap awaiting the unwary in that, with so many other things to think about, the expatriate will often leave his personal financial arrangements to be sorted out in a period of comparative leisure after returning home. Doing so, however, involves tax risks, and a number of doors slam shut immediately upon arrival.

Anyone arriving in the U.K. for permanent residence will be regarded as "resident" and "ordinarily resident" from the date of his arrival. The six months "free period" granted to temporary visitors is not applicable. He may already be domiciled in the U.K. but, if not, he will become so from that date. The timing of his arrival may be significant and — in the year of arrival — he may enjoy a relatively favourable position since a full year's allowance and reliefs will be due even though he may have been resident for only part of the year.

Not everyone, of course, can time his arrival to extract the maximum advantage from this generous tax treatment. However, for most people it will help to reduce the shock of returning to the U.K. tax structure. The final assessment for tax of the new "permanent resident" will, of course, depend on his sources of income and assets.

In most circumstances, earnings, i.e. salary, bonus, terminal gratuities — and even leave pay which continues after arrival in the U.K. — will escape the attention of the tax man altogether.

If on arrival in the U.K. a person states that it is not his intention to remain permanently — but he subsequently decides to stay — there are special rules for determining his residence status. Anyone who visits the U.K. with the intention of remaining for three years or more will be treated as resident and ordinarily resident from the date of his arrival.

We have seen how important timing can be in relation to the date of arrival in the U.K., the closure of overseas bank accounts, and the realization of capital gains and losses. The temptation is, of course, for the busy expatriate–perhaps returning to uncertain employment prospects – to defer all decisions until after he has returned home, when he hopes to know more or less where he stands. However logical this approach, the net result of adopting this course will probably be to trigger any number of unnecessary tax liabilities.

In no respect is this more significant than in the choice of investments to suit the new circumstances. It goes without saying that investments which may well have been entirely suited to a period of non-residence status may be utterly unsuitable if the owner changes his residence and the whole of that income is aggregated for income tax purposes. At this stage, there is probably no shortage of advice from all manner of advisers ready and willing to help. If one were to believe some of the less reputable, the choice is simple: either you put everything you have into some "offshore" scheme, or the tax man will clobber you when you get home.

The fact is, of course, that many people will benefit from setting aside some part of their assets in some form of offshore tax shelter, but the extent to which it is prudent to do this will vary enormously having regard to the circumstances and objectives of each individual. Again, timing is important, since in order to be effective, most of the highly advantageous arrangements need to be implemented before the loss of non-resident status occurs.

The most significant of these investment vehicles is the offshore Single Premium Bond which affords the non-resident a means of investing in a fund located outside the U.K. to which income and capital gains will accrue free of U.K. tax, irrespective of his own future residence status. When he chooses to withdraw an income from the Bond it is taxed as a partial cashment of a life policy, thus avoiding basic rate tax altogether, and producing sub-

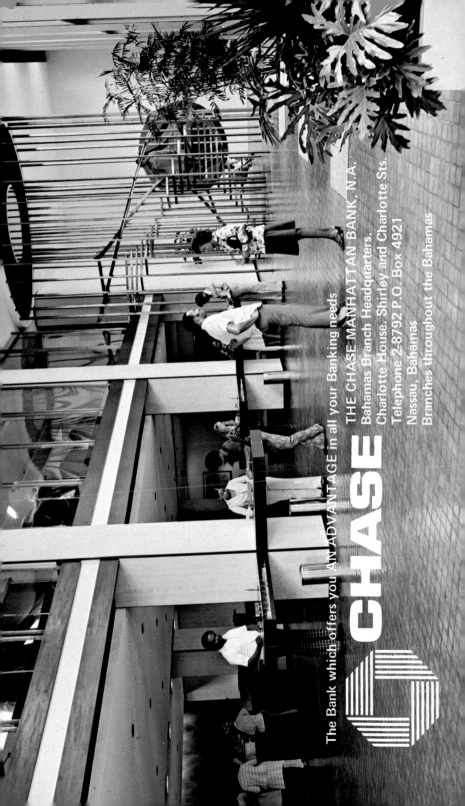

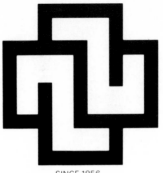

SINCE 1856

CREDIT SUISSE
YOUR BANK WORLDWIDE

Head Office: Paradeplatz 8, 8021 Zurich, Switzerland
With offices throughout Switzerland and in all major international
financial centres

CREDIT SUISSE
CS

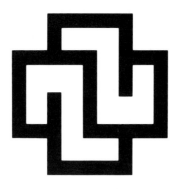

YOUR SWISS BANK
IN NASSAU, BAHAMAS

For first-class service in international banking

Deposits   Investments   Gold

Bahamian company and trust business

Credit Suisse Nassau Branch

P.O. Box N-4928, Rawson Square, Nassau, Bahamas.
Tel: (809) 32-28345 (direct line to Head Office), Telex: 20 178, Cables: Credsuisse

Credit Suisse (Bahamas) Limited

P.O. Box N-4928, Rawson Square, Nassau, Bahamas.
Tel: (809) 32-28345 (direct line to CS Zurich), Telex: 20 166, Cables: Credit

CREDIT SUISSE (BAHAMAS) LIMITED

THINK

Think
Very simple advice — yet incredibly important.
Because those who do, make it.
Those who don't, don't.
Think about it.

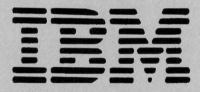

Church and East Bay Streets
P.M.B. 6400
Nassau, Bahamas
Telephone:
Area Code (809)-323-7350-1-2-3-4
Cable Address: Inbusmach

P. O. Box F 2502
Freeport, Grand Bahama
Telephone:
Area Code (809)-352-9751/2

stantial advantages even for the higher rate tax or investment income surcharge payer.

There are also 10-year "qualifying" policies written offshore which can be very useful – again, depending upon the period of overseas service, the resources available and the requirements of the individual. Having said this, in both cases the tax implications must be carefully considered, preferably with the help of a competent and impartial adviser. You will see that a period of non-residence is not quite as straightforward as it may appear. Tax is one of the most important considerations, and any failure to take into account U.K. taxation – at all stages – can prove very costly.

The author of this article on United Kingdom taxation and the expatriate, Christopher Hagues, heads the Caribbean Department of Wilfred T. Fry Ltd., a long established tax consultancy which has specialized in providing advice to British expatriates since the beginning of the century. The company's head office is located at Crescent House, Crescent Road, Worthing, Sussex BN11 1RN, England.

Old and new attractions for Nassau vacationers include the 143-year-old Christ Church Cathedral, where royalty worship when they visit here, and the almost-completed Cable Beach Hotel, on one of the island's finest beaches.

194

Local Investors Dominate

The Property Market

In recent years, Bahamian capital and not foreign investment has kept the Bahamas property market active, as increasing numbers of Bahamians who have moved into well-paying positions in the financial sector, the professions and in business have bought homes and building lots.

Having improved their economic status, they are now seeking to move up the social scale as well by purchasing or building homes in developed and developing areas such as Sea Breeze, Gleniston, Winton, Sans Souci and Westward Villas.

This has created a growing demand for houses costing between $60,000 and $100,000, and agents report that such properties have become scarce due to the fact that there has been very little speculative building in recent years. That condition has, inevitably, served to keep prices up.

Although building costs did not rise dramatically during 1982, prices for undeveloped properties did. That was due in part to increased demand, of course, but developers also reported that the cost of installing utilities increased from around $4,000 per average lot

195

THE GRAND HOTEL 1982

Industrial

Three- 1 million gal. water storage tanks - govt.	— Nassau
Borco desulfurization civil & foundations	— Freeport
Syntex addition	— Freeport
Grand Bahama Steel & Pipe (Turn-key)	— Freeport

Condominiums

Harbourside Cond.	— Paradise Is.
Conchrest Cond.	— Nassau
Chertsey Cond.	— Nassau
Windermere Beach Apts.	— Eleuthera

Resorts

Club Mediterranee	— Paradise Is.
Club Mediterranee	— Eleuthera
Loew's Harbour Cove Hotel	— Paradise Is.
Grand Hotel	— Paradise Is.
Britannia Hotel '80	— Paradise Is.
Cable Beach Hotel (joint-venture)	— Nassau
Ocean Club	— Paradise Is.
Treasure Cay Hotel	— Abaco
Peace & Plenty	— Exuma

Commercial

Claughton House
Charlotte House
Charlotte Car Park
50 Shirley St.
Banco Ambrosiano
British American Insurance
ED Sassoon Building
Chase Manhattan Bank
Golden Gates Shopping Center
P.M. Hospital Addition
   Ph. 1 - govt.
Seafloor Aquarium (turn-key)
St. John's College
P.D.S. facilities
Bank of Nova Scotia
Bahamas Telecomms. Corp.
St. Andrew's School
Royal Bank of Canada,
   Freeport

Custom Homes (Deluxe)

Edgar Kaiser Res. - Eleuthera
John A. McCone - Eleuthera
Henry McNeil - Eleuthera
William Simpson - Lyford Cay
J. Lehmkuhl - Lyford Cay
Constance Burrell - Lyford Cay
Weingart Res. - Lyford Cay

CAVALIER CONSTRUCTION

BUILDERS AND DEVELOPERS

GODFREY E. LIGHTBOURN
CHAIRMAN/CHIEF EXECUTIVE

EUGENE A. PYFROM
PRESIDENT

CRAWFORD ST., P.O. BOX N-8170, NASSAU, BAHAMAS
TEL: (809) 32-35171 — 32-55244 — 32-36011. TELEX: 20 299

198

to somewhere between $7,000 and $10,000.

Construction costs are figured at about $70 per square foot for a moderately well-furnished home, but for the type of residence which would blend into the surroundings in an upper class development, cost per square foot is reckoned to be between $75 and $90 — and up.

To illustrate how property values have escalated, one broker-developer related that in the early 1970s he and a partner bought up two miles of waterfront out east — an area particularly popular among Bahamians — at an average cost of $12,000 per lot. They sold off the lots for between $25,000 and $40,000 each, then re-purchased a lot for $60,000 and sold it for $120,000. Several lots were subsequently sold by their firm for original investors at $80,000 each to new clients.

Since there are now very few eastern waterfront lots available, and virtually no beachfront out west, Bahamians are looking for hilltop lots, and when they find them they are paying premium prices. In 1983 a new development in the Winton area (out east) was opened up, and large prime lots on a high ridge with sea views were priced from $90,000 to $120,000. Lots of 3,500 square feet on lower ground were being offered at between $30,000 and $45,000. Lots are available on time-purchase agreements to qualified buyers.

JACK ISAACS
REAL ESTATE CO. LTD.

- SALES
- RENTALS
- APPRAISALS
- MANAGEMENT
- BUILDING AND DEVELOPMENT

- HOMES AND SITES
- CONDOMINIUMS
- ACREAGE
- BUSINESSES
- FAMILY ISLAND PROPERTIES

WIR SPRECHEN DEUTSCH!

George Street (opposite Towne Hotel)
P.O. Box N-1458, Nassau, Bahamas
Tel: 2-1069/5-6326. (Evenings) 7-8129

In two other new eastern developments, Winton Meadows and Twynam Heights, lots are offered on a down-payment basis with the balance of the purchase price spread over a 10-year period with interest at 12 per cent. Lot sizes in Winton Meadows are 100 x 110 feet, and they sell $25,000 and up with a $500 down payment. In Twynam Heights, lots of 80 x 120 feet are offered from $25,000 to $50,000, with 10 per cent required as the down payment.

In Mount Vernon, on the south side of the Eastern Road, lot prices start at $25,000; those on high ground with sea views sell for $50,000. Lot sizes are 100 x 120 feet.

Out west, opposite Saunders Beach, in a new development called Vista Marina, lots of 100 x 150 feet are selling well at $25,000. The developer requires a 20 per cent deposit with the balance payable over five years at 12 per cent interest.

"It's the homes with six-figure and up price tags that are not moving at all," one realtor commented. "There's a canal property and home at Lyford Cay offered at $1.2 million that hasn't attracted a single bid, as far as I know. Another residence there is priced at $450,000, and I have listings in The Grove (off west Bay Street) for which the owners are asking $850,000 to $1 million — and they're not going to move

202

either unless we get the rich foreigners back."

It was evident, however, that there are growing numbers of Bahamians with a great deal of money to invest in real estate. Elaborate and costly Bahamian-owned homes have been built in areas such as Love Beach, Mount Vernon, Winton, and along the Eastern Road.

Lyford Cay is still the section well-to-do Bahamians aspire to, however, and brokers report that there is some speculative building going on there to cater for that expanding local market. Other new construction there in early 1983 included a residence for Prince and and Princess Guirey (she's the former Bobo Sigrist) near Lord and Lady Martonmere's winter home.

First class office and commercial accommodation has become difficult to locate in and near Nassau because, with the exception of the building constructed by Banco Ambrosiano, east of the city, and the Imperial Life Building in Centreville, there has been little major commercial construction since 1980.

"It's becoming economically feasible now," a developer says, "to take over second class office buildings and put them in first class condition. More and more companies are being established here, and there are more European — especially Swiss and Italian — banks mov-

BUILDERS
of the
LEADING HOMES
&COMMERCIAL
BUILDINGS

Bay View Mews, Paradise Island

In Nassau and the Out Islands

Estimates furnished without obligation.

CARL G.TRECO
CONTRACTORS LTD.

P.O. Box N-1587, Nassau, Bahamas.
Tel: Business 2-4996 or 5-8725

ing in. You can create good basic office accommodation in an existing building for between $15 and $20 per square foot, and let the tenant finish it. Rents are going up considerably, and in another two years we're going to be out of first class office space unless major new projects are started soon."

A prime problem is parking. The city's few commercial lots are already over-crowded, and it is practically impossible to find large enough properties in Nassau where adequate parking could be included in the design of a new construction project. Exterior parking facilities cost between $30 and $50 per space to provide, and underground or basement parking is costly.

"We had a new tenant recently," a developer says, "who needed four parking spaces for staff. We could only offer one, so the other three had to be found in three different locations in town."

Some three years ago Canadian Imperial Bank of Commerce acquired a large city property with about 200 feet fronting on Shirley Street, a main thoroughfare which runs parallel to Bay Street. In late 1982 the bank started construction of its corporate headquarters there, and completion date will be in the Spring of 1984. The building's four storeys will provide 40,000 square feet of space, and accord-

ing to G.S. Niesen, the bank's general manager, CIBC will use all but about 5,000 square feet, which will be rented out. Cost of the project will be in excess of $5 million. In this instance, the size of the property allows for the provision of staff and customer parking areas.

Construction began in late April 1983 of a new block of shops on Bay Street and the northeastern side of Frederick Street. Everette Sands, president of Butler and Sands, who are leading liquor merchants purchased the former El Toro restaurant and Savoy Theatre premises in 1982, and will develop the property in two stages.

In the first stage, to be completed by the end of 1983, five new shops will be created along the 102-foot Bay Street frontage, two of which, in the old theatre location, will be two-storied. Stage 2 will produce six more shops and a fast-food restaurant along Frederick Street north, where the property runs 245 feet. Sands's longterm planning calls for complete re-development of the site in about five years' time.

Early in 1983 Family Guardian Insurance Company, a Bahamian institution, purchased 9.2 acres from Sir Stafford Sands's estate at the junction of Shirley Street and the Eastern Road, opposite the Royal Nassau Sailing Club. "We may sell some of the property," says Roscow Pyfrom, the company's president, "but we'll keep about five

207

Universal Investment Realty

The most reputable full-service realty organization in the Bahamas.

BUILDERS · REAL ESTATE
ARCHITECTURE · DEVELOPERS
Renovation — Drafting Service

Corner of Madeira & Patton Streets, Palmdale,
P.O. Box N10386, Nassau, Bahamas. Tel: 2-8525/2-8168

acres and sometime within the next two or three years we plan to construct our corporate offices."

The 730-room Cable Beach Hotel, which is owned by the government's Hotel Corporation, was due to be completed before the end of 1983. "Because there's been so little investment building," one realtor pointed out, "there's going to be a serious problem when the hotel becomes operational—where is management going to house the expatriate staff they'll have to bring in to run it?"

The problem of attracting new foreign capital for real estate projects and residence acquisitions stemmed from the government's implementation of policies contained in the Immovable Property (Acquisition by Foreign Persons) Act.

Legislation to initiate a land policy had been foreshadowed by the Prime Minister, Sir Lynden Pindling, in October 1979, the year the property boom peaked. A Bill reached the House of Assembly in March 1981, and its passage by both chambers was obtained a few months later, but up to press time the Act had not been sent to the Governor General to be signed into law.

The principles it enunciates are conceded by all to be laudable. The government intends to preserve certain categories of properties

GLOBAL

REALTORS INVESTORS
DEVELOPERS & MARKETING CO.

"We Try To Make You Look Better"

We Provide Services Such As:

. Sale of Commercial and Residential land
. . Sale of Homes, Apartments, Restaurants and Hotels
. . . Property, Company and Investment Management
. . . . Counselling for Mortgage Financing
. . . . . Construction of Homes, Apartments and Offices
. . . . . . Drawing of Plans for all your needs
. . . . Land Surveying and Development
. . . . Rentals of Homes, Apartments and Offices
. . . . Renovations and Repairs
. . . . Sale of land within the entire Bahamas

" Nous travaillons pour vous"

Tout ce que nous vous fournissons

. Vente de terrain résidentiel et commercial
. . Vente des maisons, appartements, restaurants et hôtels
. . . La gestion des propriétés, compagnies et investissement
. . . . De conseil sur le financement hypothécaire
. . . . . La construction des maisons, appartements et bureaux
. . . . . . Un cabinet d'architectes pour tout vos besoins
. . . . Expertise de terrain et son developpement
. . . . Location des maisons, appartements et bureaux
. . . . Rénovations et réparations
. . . . Vente de terrain à travers toute les
        îles Bahamienne

Invest in "The Riviera of the New World" - The Bahamas
Investissez "sur la riviera du nouveau monde" les Bahamas

For all your real estate and investment needs, call or write
P.O. Box N-10004, Nassau, Bahamas. Tel: (809) 32-24167/42933

210

for acquisition by Bahamians, and to prevent future unproductive hoarding of properties by foreign speculators by requiring that development programmes start within a stipulated time-frame in instances where approval is given for land purchases by non-Bahamians.

But the unanimous complaint up to mid-1983 was that whatever machinery had been established to deal with purchase applications simply had not functioned effectively.

In the past, any foreigner who wanted to buy a Bahamian property had to apply to the Central Bank's Exchange Control Department to have the purchase registered as an "approved investment". The purpose of that was that if he later re-sold his investment he would be able to repatriate the proceeds of the sale in the currency used to make the original purchase.

Exchange Control approval was virtually routine. But now that the government has elected to enforce the provisions of the proposed Act, the decision as to whether or not a sale to a foreigner is approved (thus insuring currency repatriation protection) is no longer made by the Central Bank but by the Cabinet. The resultant delays have, not unexpectedly, caused some prospective foreign buyers to lose interest in proposed transactions and withdraw their offers.

ISLAND STEEL FIXER & BUILDING SUPPLY

Clifton Pier Power Station

Specializing in fabricated steel. All sizes
including bar joist, sheeting, lolly columns.
Wire mesh, joint compound tape, plywood, sheet
rock, felt, lumber, nails, shingles, etc.

East Street South
P.O. Box N-1882,
Nassau, Bahamas
Tel: 3-7760/5-3630

Mr. Stanley Bain, President
16 years experience

WE GUARANTEE PROMPT DELIVERY IN NASSAU AND THE FAMILY ISLANDS.

Several realtors were insisting that contracts foreign clients signed to purchase properties stipulate that the 10 per cent of the agreed sale price they deposited as a binder was to be refunded if the application to buy was refused. Others, having explained to the foreign purchaser that approval, if given, could take months or as long as a year or more in coming through, prescribed a three-months' closing date after acceptance of a deposit.

"If the answer wasn't received by completion date," said one agent, "then the client had obviously got a decision to make — either he went through with the purchase or he forfeited his deposit."

Provided the conveyance was properly drawn, the sale would, of course, still be perfectly legal even if government approval was ultimately denied. The disadvantage would be that if the purchaser subsequently sold his property for Bahamian dollars he would not be able to convert them to his own currency for repatriation.

Family Island property asking prices, particularly in the Abaco area, have risen over the last three years. A half-acre lot at Man-of-War Cay, Abaco, for instance, is listed at $85,000.

"One problem is that a lot of out island properties are owned by wealthy individuals who don't care whether they sell or not," an agent

213

Canadian Imperial Bank of Commerce, Shirley Street

Charbay Plaza, Bay Street

Complete Architectural & Engineering Services provided. Free Estimates.

Major projects: *Charbay Plaza *Silver Cay Club *Westwind I & II *Guanahani Village *Nassau International Bazaar *Mira Mar *Central Medical Centre * Canadian Imperial Bank of Commerce

SUNCO
Builders & Developers Ltd.

P.O. Box N-4829, Nassau, Bahamas
Tel: 3-4966 or 3-6255. Telex: 20 285 SUNCO BUILD

comments, "so they ask high prices just to see what happens."

At Double Bay, just south of Governor's Harbour, Eleuthera, beach frontage is offered at between $300 and $500 per beach foot. Several homes have already been built there, and about six acres remain for development. Lots vary in size from 100 to 200 feet on the beach, with depths of between 450 and 600 feet leading to high ground. A nearby property of 7.2 acres, with 600 feet of beach, is on the market for $1.2 million.

A leading agent states that he was only able to sell two lots in 1982 in fashionable Windermere Beach Estates, between Governor's Harbour and Rock Sound, where the Prince and Princess of Wales spent part of their honeymoon. Beach lots there were listed at $49,000 for 1.5 acres, and a half-acre lot inland, overlooking the Sound, cost $12,000.

"I got approval," the broker continued, "for a non-Bahamian to buy a lot in Windermere for $35,000, but the government insisted that he would have to build within two years, and he just wasn't ready to give that sort of guarantee, so the sale fell through." Most brokers agreed that a five-year time-frame would be equitable.

They are convinced, too, that the government should make

absolutely clear in a public statement what its priorities and objectives are in considering applications for property purchases and land development by foreigners. It is essential, they say, that some pattern be established which realtors and prospective investors can understand, of what projects are likely to be approved, and how long it is going to take for decisions to be made.

"Meanwhile," one broker concludes, "Bahamians who are buying good properties in their homeland are making sound investments which, historically, have always paid off in the longterm."

Below, the *Bahamas Handbook* gives a sampling of land offerings in the Bahamas, showing prices, sizes and other particulars.

(See also **Property Tax** on page 318).

NEW PROVIDENCE

CAVES LIMITED — West Bay Street. Approx. 1 mile from the airport. 30 acres of land available for hotels, condominiums and commercial development. Total cost $2.74 million. Will also sell six individual areas. Minimum 3.5 acres on waterfront $875,000 to maximum 8 acres with oceanview $675,000. All property is elevated. Contact Sloane Farrington Real Estate, Tel: 5-2353 or 4-1058.

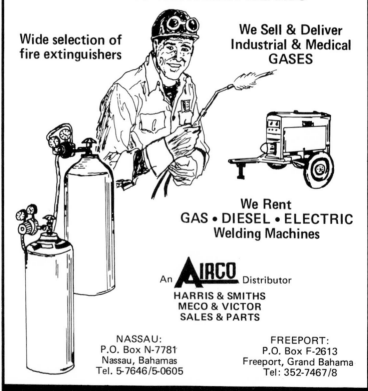 

LYFORD CAY — 17 miles from Nassau - 1,000 acres. The Lyford Cay Club, a private residential club. The Lyford Cay Company offers land for sale handled by Sales Department. Property around the Golf Course and on the ridge overlooking the golf course is $175,000. Canal lots $125,000. New Phase Three subdivision, two and three acres elevated $300,000; low $200,000. Water, telephone linkage, power and roads completed. Yacht harbour, golf course, shopping centre, skeet shooting. Lyford Cay Company Limited, P.O. Box N-7776, Nassau, Bahamas. Tel: Mrs. Roberta Hepburn or Fred Wanklyn, 7-4211; 7-4280.

MOUNT VERNON — Located on the Eastern Road. 4 miles from downtown. Approx. 50 acres. Residential lots are 100 x 120 and are priced from $25,000 to $33,000. Contact Brent Symonette, tel. 2-3041/2 or 2-3044.

SOUTH OCEAN VILLAGE — Southwest section of New Providence, 10 mins. from airport, 30 mins. from downtown Nassau. Development is adjacent to South Ocean Beach Hotel; 40 choice residential lots, many fronting on fairways of the championship South Ocean Golf Club course, several on high ground with magnificent ocean views. Lots priced from $16,900 - $25,000. Also acreage available for condominiums, townhouses, etc. New Providence Development Co. Ltd., P.O. Box N-4820, Nassau. Tel: 6-4177.

BIMINI

1,000 ft. first class beach property on South Bimini. Price on application to H.G. Christie Real Estate, P.O. Box N-8164, Nassau. Tel: 2-1041.

CAT ISLAND

PIGEON CAY — At the northwestern end of Cat Island. Approx. 4 miles of white sandy beach; approx. 100 acres. Excellent site for Marina and sub-division. Price is $600,000. H.G. Christie Real Estate, P.O. Box N-8164, Nassau. Tel: 2-1041.

ELEUTHERA

DOUBLE BAY - On the Atlantic side of Eleuthera just north of Windermere Island and near Governor's Harbour. About 1,000 acres, stretching from the Atlantic to the Caribbean side of the island. Main road bisects the property and there are roads extending into the property from the highway. Approx. 5,000 ft. Atlantic beach frontage and 5,000 ft. Caribbean frontage. Electricity and telephone are available to the whole area. Price is approx. $1,000,000. H.G. Christie Real Estate, P.O. Box N-8164, Nassau. Tel: 2-1041.

EXUMAS

BAHAMA SOUND - Great Exuma, developed by Bahama Acres Ltd. The company began Bahama Sound in the late 1950s and has developed over 8,000 acres, constructed over 250 miles of roads, invested millions of dollars and is presently 80% sold out and has over 14,000 deeded property owners. Standard homesites are 80' x 125' and start at $5,995 with a 40% discount offered to Bahamian buyers. Waterfront properties start at $35,000, minimum ½ acre. No discount is offered on waterfront properties. Sites include residential, business, multi-

221

222

dwelling, airport hangar space and hotel. More than 25 park and reserve areas have been set aside for recreational use of property owners. Contact Vernon T. Curtis, P.O. Box 8, Great Exuma, Bahamas. Tel: (809) 336-2055.

FLAMINGO BAY — Great Exuma, ½ mile from George Town and 130 miles from Nassau. Approx. 1,300 acres of rolling hills across the island from sea to sea. Properties start U.S. $25,000; and exclusive February Point offers fully serviced oceanfront properties ranging from $100,000 to $250,000. Hotel sites available. Seventeen miles of roads have been completed, 26 houses built and five efficiency villas; others under construction. Residents will have access to all beaches, tennis courts, marinas, Flamingo Bay Villa and all other facilities. Government 5,000-foot airstrip (to be extended) runs into part of the property. Development costs to date estimated over $10 million. Elizabeth Harbour Exuma Ltd., Nassau Beach Hotel Arcade, P.O. Box N-8727, Nassau. Tel: 7-8471. Also Flamingo Bay Villa, P.O. Box GT-90, George Town, Exuma. Tel: (809) 336-2661.

LONG ISLAND

BEVIS POINT — 150 miles southeast from Nassau. 600 acres of property for residential, commercial and multi-purpose development. Good elevation and beautiful beachfront property available. Price approx. $500 - $1000 per acre. For more information contact Levi Gibson and Associates, P.O. Box N-957, Nassau, Tel: 2-4654/5.

STELLA MARIS ESTATES AND INN AND MARINA/YACHT CLUB - 150 miles southeast from Nassau. 2,500 acres developed, approx. 70% sold. More than twenty million dollars in development to date. Residential, commercial, and multi-purpose lots from 11,700 sq. ft. to 1½ acres. Prices from $10,000 to

$35,000. Townhouses from $65,000; 2 bedroom, 2 bathroom new residences on hilltop or oceanfront lot from $75,000 to approx. $150,000. Full, tarred road, electricity and water services, internationally-known resort hotel with all resort services including full line of water sports - specialty SCUBA diving! Complete marina and yacht club with all repairs, parts, boat and onshore catering service. Out island-style shopping centre, own commercial and charter and hotel air transport-serviced airport; approx. 100 private homes, 20 to 30 under construction yearly. Also agents for superb beach property North End, Long Island. Long Island Estate Developers Limited, P.O. Box SM-30 1010, Stella Maris, Long Island, Bahamas. Tel: (809) 33-62106. Cable: Stellamar.

SAN SALVADOR

HIGH CAY — Just a half mile south of the historic island of San Salvador, almost 31½ acres. Good elevation; excellent beaches. The perfect spot to get away from it all. Price is $150,000. H.G. Christie Real Estate, P.O. Box N-8164, Nassau. Tel: 2-1041.

Prices and information are subject to change.

224

(Actual Photograph)
● 2-Bedroom villas completely furnished and maintained year-round from $175,000 US Please write for further information

● Time-sharing Interval Ownership
● Outright Ownership

DEVELOPMENT PROPERTY

RESIDENTIAL
COMMERCIAL
INDUSTRIAL
AGRICULTURAL

Tracts available within a total development
company which owns and is co-developing
5,200 acres on New Providence Island.
Featuring 16,000 linear footage of waterfront
and the ability to supply development infrastructure.

NEW PROVIDENCE DEVELOPMENT CO. LTD.

P.O. Box N-4820, Nassau, Bahamas
Tel: (809) 326-4177. Telex: 20 296

SLOW DOWN
AND STROLL INTO THE 18TH CENTURY.

In the Bahamas, you never run out of things to do. Until you want to. Enjoy antique elegance, Old World charm, gracious people. Dance under the stars, gamble, golf, sail, shop. Or slow down and catch up with yourself. All for so very few dollars — the most value at competitive prices. And it costs less to get here from most places in the USA.

For reservations or a brochure, including Nassau/Paradise Island, Freeport/Grand Bahama, The Abacos, Andros, Bimini, Eleuthera, and The Exumas, see your travel agent or call toll free in the USA, 800-327-0787. In Dade County, Florida, 443-3821.

It's Better In The Bahamas

Bahamas
Information

Accommodations

New Providence and Paradise Island accommodations range from plush suites and seaside cottages to bath-sharing guest rooms. In all, there are 69 hotels (totalling about 6,277 rooms) to choose from.

Enjoy breathtaking sea views, observe city activity or overlook a lush golf course — scenic views are as varied as the holiday facilities offered by larger hotels and resorts here. Golf courses, tennis courts, skin diving equipment and instruction, boat rental, beaches, swimming pools and night-clubs are usually available or arrangements can be made at nearby facilities.

During the high season, a three-room suite (two bedrooms and parlour), tastefully furnished, rents for $265-$540 per day on Paradise Island. Similar suites rent for about $295 per day in Nassau. Double room rates average $85 per day in Nassau and $125 on Paradise Island. Special package plans offered by tour operators in North America and Europe include accommodations, sightseeing and transfers, and rates vary according to package.

Modified American Plan (room, breakfast and dinner) or European Plan (room only) are offered at most hotels.

Guest houses are often less expensive and located near downtown Nassau. Many offer European Plan only, but restaurants are plentiful.

Family Island (out island) holiday living is generally in small hotels with a casual, homelike atmosphere. During the high season, double room rates average $50 per day. Larger resorts, comparable to those in Nassau, are found on several of the islands and room rental averages $90 per day. Both Modified American and European Plans are available, though American Plan (room, breakfast, lunch and dinner) can be found at a number of resorts. Dining facilities outside the hotel are limited so it is advisable to use MAP.

Scuba diving, swimming, fishing, shell-hunting and water-skiing are unsurpassed and most Family Island hotels are fully equipped to meet your preference.

The rates quoted above are EP winter rates (December-April); summer rates are slightly lower. There is a room occupancy tax of six per cent, three per cent of which is collected by the Government and three per cent is used by the hotels to fund their joint promotional and advertising budgets.

(See also **Accommodations**, Freeport/Lucaya section, page 386.)

Accounting Firms

Chartered Accountants

Alexander Grant Tansley Witt
Arthur Young & Co.
Atkinson, Ronald & Co.
Britchford, Donald E.
Butler, Taylor & Munroe
Clark, Hulland & Knowles
Cooper, Graham M. & Co.
*Coopers & Lybrand
Cross & Thomas
Deloitte, Haskins & Sells
Ernst & Whinney
Grant Thornton Intl.
*Klynveld Main Goerdeler
*Laventhol & Horwath
MacGregor Robertson & Co.
Mann Judd
*Michael Hepburn & Co.
*Pannell, Fitzpatrick & Co.
Pannell Kerr Forster
*Peat, Marwick, Mitchell & Co.
*Price Waterhouse
Pringle, R. H.
*Thorne, Riddell
*Touche Ross & Co.
Turquands, Barton, Mayhew & Co.
Williams & Co.
Wilson, F. R. & Co.

Accountant & Bookkeeping Services

Deal, Herbert A. & Co.
Mills, J. Tomlinson
Accounting & Computer Services Ltd.

*Freeport Branch also

Aerodromes

Below is a Civil Aviation Dept. list of civil and military airports and airstrips with runway specifications. Also included is basic information on the location and size of the facilities and whether they are designated as ports of entry for international flights.

Aircraft wishing to land at the U.S. military base in the Bahamas must have prior approval. Clearance to land at the Grand Bahama AAF (Gold Rock Creek) may be obtained from: H.Q., Eastern Space and Missile Centre, Patrick AFB, Florida, 32925.

Island/Aerodrome Location on Island	Co-ordinates	Port of Entry	Dimensions
ABACO			
Gorda Cay SW (Pvt.)	2605N 7732W	No	2,400 x 60
Marsh Harbour C (Gov.)	2631N 7705W	Yes	5,000 x 100
Mores Island S (Gov.)	2619N 7734W	No	2,640 x 140
Sandy Point S (Pvt.)	2600N 7724W	No	3,000 x 100
Scotland Cay CE (Pvt.)	2638N 7704W	No	2,700 x 100

Island/Aerodrome Location on Island	Co-ordinates	Port of Entry	Dimensions
Spanish Cay NE (Pvt.)	2657N 7732W	No	3,200 x 60
Treasure Cay NC (Gov.)	2645N 7724W	Yes	6,600 x 150
Walker's Cay N (Pvt.)	2716N 7824W	Yes	2,800 x 100
ACKLINS			
Spring Point C (Gov.)	2227N 7358W	No	5,000 x 150
ANDROS			
Andros Town C (Pvt.)	2442N 7748W	Yes	4,000 x 100
Congo Town SE (Gov.)	2409N 7735W	Yes	4,000 x 100
C. A. Bain Aerodrome SE (Gov.)	2417N 7741W	No	3,000 x 75
San Andros N (Gov.)	2503N 7803W	Yes	4,974 x 75
BERRY ISLANDS			
Chub Cay SW (Pvt.)	2525N 7753W	Yes	5,000 x 100
Cistern Cay N (Pvt.)	2547N 7752W	No	2,400 x 100
Great Harbour Cay N (Pvt.)	2545N 7751W	Yes	4,536 x 80
Little Whale Cay S (Pvt.)	2527N 7746W	No	2,000 x 50
Whale Cay SE (Pvt.)	2524N 7747W	No	2,600 x 60
BIMINI			
South Bimini S (Gov.)	2542N 7916W	Yes	5,000 x 100
CAT ISLAND			
Arthur's Town NW (Gov.)	2438N 7540W	No	7,000 x 150
Cutlass Bay SW (Pvt.)	2409N 7524W	No	2,450 x 60
Hawks Nest CW (Pvt.)	2409N 7531W	No	3,000 x 100
New Bight W (Gov.)	2419N 7527W	No	4,076 x 100
CAY SAL			
Cay Sal (Pvt.)	2342N 8025W	No	2,000 x 100
CROOKED ISLAND			
Colonel Hill C (Gov.)	2245N 7409W	No	3,500 x 60
Pitts Town N (Pvt.)	2250N 7421W	No	2,240 x 60

Island/Aerodrome Location on Island	Co-ordinates	Port of Entry	Dimensions
ELEUTHERA			
Cape Eleuthera S (Pvt.)	2447N 7618W	Yes	6,500 x 150
Governor's Harbour C (Gov.)	2517N 7620W	Yes	6,000 x 150
North Eleuthera N (Gov.)	2529N 7641W	Yes	4,500 x 100
Rock Sound S (Pvt.)	2454N 7610W	Yes	7,200 x 150
EXUMA			
George Town S (Gov.)	2328N 7546W	Yes	5,000 x 100
Hog Cay SE (Pvt.)	2324N 7628W	No	2,500 x 40
Lee Stocking Island S (Pvt.)	2347N 7606W	No	3,000 x 75
Norman's Cay N (Pvt.)	2436N 7649W	No	3,000 x 70
Rudder Cut Cay C (Pvt.)	2353N 7615W	No	2,700 x 100
Staniel Cay C (Pvt.)	2410N 7629W	No	3,030 x 75
GRAND BAHAMA			
Deep Water Cay E (Pvt.)	2638N 7757W	No	2,000 x 100
Freeport Int'l W (Pvt.)	2633N 7842W	Yes	11,000 x 150
Grand Bahama AAF C (USA)	2637N 7822W	No	7,200 x 200
West End W (Pvt.)	2641N 7859W	Yes	8,000 x 150
INAGUA			
Mathew Town W (Gov.)	2059N 7340W	Yes	5,000 x 100
LONG ISLAND			
Deadman's Cay C (Gov.)	2315N 7508W	No	4,000 x 100
Diamond Roads (Hard Bargain) S (Pvt.)	2302N 7453W	No	3,000 x 70
Hog Cay N (Pvt.)	2336N 7520W	No	1,800 x 50
Stella Maris N (Pvt.)	2323N 7516W	No	4,300 x 100
MAYAGUANA			
Mayaguana C (Gov.)	2223N 7302W	No	7,700 x 150
NEW PROVIDENCE			
Nassau Int'l W (Gov.)	2502N 7728W	Yes	4,750 x 150 8,240 x 150 11,000 x 150

Island/Aerodrome Location on Island	Co-ordinates	Port of Entry	Dimensions
RAGGED ISLAND			
Duncan Town S (Gov.)	2211N 7544W	No	2,500 x 75
RUM CAY			
Port Nelson C (Pvt.)	2339N 7451W	No	2,400 x 100
SAN SALVADOR			
Cockburn Town NW (Gov.)	2404N 7431W	Yes	4,500 x 150

Agriculture

Agricultural development continues to be a major part of the government's plans for economic expansion, and large investments in developing research, extension and marketing facilities have produced a continuous rate of growth, particularly in the production of winter vegetables, poultry and pork products.

The Department of Agriculture's principal drive in fruit and vegetable production is directed towards extending the season for these commodities so that summer imports can be greatly reduced and local processing increased.

Packing Houses are located in North Andros; Smith's Bay, Cat Island; Mt. Thompson, Exuma; North Long Island and three in Eleuthera (North, Hatchet Bay and Green Castle). There is also a wholesale Produce Exchange in Freeport, Grand Bahama.

The Government, through the department, has established grass roots agricultural services in the form of professionally trained resident agricultural extension officers at Grand Bahama, Andros, Eleuthera, Exuma and Long Island. Reliable sources of input supplies and a re-organized marketing infra-structure have created the environment needed to stimulate production.

Capital intensive agriculture on the pine islands continues to demonstrate longterm economic potential. The Key and Sawyer farms on Abaco have established over 3,000 acres of orchard (lime, avocadoes and grapefruit). Since the production season in the Bahamas is earlier than that of South Florida, the main competitor for the Bahamas' North American export market, Abaco crops have now established worthwhile markets in the United States and Canada.

On Grand Bahama Island, Parker Groves have established a plantation of over 1,000 acres and have developed markets in the United States for their crops of limes, avocadoes, zucchini and paw-paws.

As a result of test marketing of okras, avocadoes, mangoes, hot peppers and persian limes to identify markets in Western Europe, the marketing and extension divisions of the department have been able to develop the necessary production to supply new markets both in Europe and North America.

231

The department will continue to develop its Food Technology and Animal Feeds Unit, and the Bahamas Agricultural Research Centre on North Andros and the Central Agricultural Station on New Providence will continue to conduct research on agro-economic, horticultural and livestock problems affecting production in the sector. Development efforts in the south-eastern islands emphasize production of mutton, corn, sweet potatoes, cassavas, other staples and other storable crops.

Air Service
(The services listed below were in effect in February 1983, but may be subject to subsequent changes.)

BETWEEN NASSAU AND
Atlanta: Bahamasair, Delta, Eastern*; **Baltimore:** Eastern*; **Boston:** Delta; **Chicago:** Eastern*; **Dallas:** American; **Fort Lauderdale:** Bahamasair, Chalk's, Eastern; **Miami:** Eastern, Bahamasair, Chalk's (Paradise Island to downtown Miami); **Newark:** Bahamasair, Delta; **New York:** Delta, Eastern*, Pan Am; **Palm Beach:** Chalks; **Philadelphia:** Eastern*; **Tampa:** Bahamasair.
Montreal: Air Canada; **Toronto:** Air Canada.
Bermuda: British Airways.
Kingston: British Airways.
London: British Airways.

BETWEEN FREEPORT AND
Baltimore: Eastern*; **Fort Lauderdale:** Air Florida, Bahamasair, National Commuter Airlines; **Miami:** Air Florida, Bahamasair, Eastern, National Commuter Airlines; **New York:** Eastern*, Pan Am; **Orlando:** North American Airlines; **Philadelphia:** Eastern.

one stop-over and change of plane en route.

BETWEEN NASSAU AND
Freeport: Bahamasair.

Family Island Flights
Bahamasair, the national flagcarrier, links Nassau, in addition to Freeport, with various Family Island settlements, Miami and Ft. Lauderdale, via scheduled flights. Chalk's International operates daily Miami-Bimini and Miami-Nassau (Paradise Island) services.
Charter is available in Nassau through Trans-Island Airways, Pinder's Charter Service, Norman Nixon's Charter Service and M.D. Air

Services. Lucaya Beach Air Service provides charter service between Freeport, the islands and other destinations.

Air Florida operates scheduled flights from Ft. Lauderdale and Miami to Rock Sound and North Eleuthera, Treasure Cay and Marsh Harbour, Abaco, and George Town, Exuma.

There are charter operations based in some of the Family Islands such as Andros, Abaco, Eleuthera and Great Exuma.

Pompano Airways provides scheduled services from Ft. Lauderdale and Palm Beach to Bimini, Governor's Harbour and Treasure Cay.

Airline offices in Nassau

Air Canada . . . . Harrison Building (Tel. 2-1533)
Nassau Intl. Airport (Tel. 7-8411)
American Airlines . . . . Nassau Intl. Airport (Tel. 7-7001/4)
Bahamasair . . . . Nassau Intl. Airport (Tel. 7-8451/
7-8223)
British Airways . . . . Boyle Building (2-8600)
Nassau Intl. Airport (Tel. 7-8225/6)
Chalk's International . . . . Paradise Island (Tel. 5-2845)
Delta . . . . Harrison Building (Tel. 2-1911)
Nassau Intl. Airport (Tel. 7-7751)
Eastern . . . . Nassau Intl. Airport (Tel. 7-7441)

Air Florida's office is located at Freeport Intl. Airport (352-8371)

Airport Carpark, New Providence

Parking in a no-parking area at Nassau International Airport can mean a fine up to $60 or imprisonment up to three months. Also, the vehicle may be removed at the expense and risk of the owner.

The airport carpark rates are 30¢ for the first half-hour, 20¢ for the next half-hour and 10¢ for every hour or part thereof up to $2 a day. Cost for each additional day is $1.

Animals

An Import Permit is required from the Ministry of Agriculture and Fisheries for all animals being brought into the Commonwealth. Applications for such permits must be made in writing to the Ministry of Agriculture and Fisheries, P.O. Box N3028, Nassau, Bahamas. Telephone (809) 322-1277.

For the United States, Canada and the United Kingdom, following are the main provisions of the Import Permit as it applies to dogs and cats:

Dogs and cats over the age of six months arriving from the U.S. and Canada must be accompanied by a Veterinary Health Certificate issued within 24 hours of embarkation, and a certificate of Rabies Vaccination issued not less than 10 days nor more than nine months prior to arrival in the Bahamas.

Dogs and cats under six months old arriving from the U.S. and

Canada require a Veterinary Health Certificate only, but must be vaccinated against rabies on attaining the age of six months.

Dogs and cats brought from the U.K. may enter without having a rabies vaccination if accompanied by a Veterinary Health Certificate and a certificate stating that there have been no cases of rabies in the U.K. for the previous year.

Animals not meeting these conditions are not allowed to enter the Commonwealth.

Regulations for all other types of animals and relating to countries not mentioned above, may be obtained from the Director of Agriculture & Fisheries, P.O. Box N3028, Nassau, Bahamas. Applications should state: the kind of animal, breed, age, sex, and country of embarkation.

A duty for permanent entry of all animals into the Bahamas is levied based on a fixed charge plus 12½% of the value of the animal. For example, the duty on cats and dogs is $5 and 12%, while for horses it is $50 and 12½%.

Fees for dog licences in New Providence are: male or spayed female, $1.43; female $4.29. Family Island fees (including Freeport, Grand Bahama) are: male or spayed female, 26 cents; female 57 cents.

Architects

*Albury, Fred
**Alexiou & Assoc.
*Archer, Anthony
**Ar-Cop Limited
**Barratt, Peter
Bethel, Winston W. & Assoc.
*Braynen, Rodney & Assoc.
**Burnside, Jackson
**Cartwright, Donald
Clarke, David
*Colebrook, Arthur
*Davies, Daniel
*Ferguson, Amos
Hanna, Percy & Assoc.
*Isaacs, Michael
Johnson, Philip
**Jones, Winston
Lawrence & Asssoc.

LeFleur, Bruce
Melich & White
**Miller, Roston H. & Assoc.
Minns Architecture & Assoc.
†*Nairn, Beverly
**Nathaniels, Ray
Neill, Timothy
**Paine, Richard John
Pritchard, Jim
Proudfoot, Frank
Prydderch, Brian
**Rahming, Patrick
**Robertson Ward Assoc.
Robjohns, Clarke & Co.
*Rolle, Alvan K.
**The Architects Partnership
*Vanderpool, Barry

*Member of the Institute of Bahamian Architects
**Member of the Bahamas Association of Architects
†Interior Designer

Archives

A Public Records Office, Mackey Street, Nassau, serves as a repository for records and archives of the Government. Many private deposits, including the archives of the Anglican Church, have also been made.

Open to the public from 10 a.m. until 4:45 p.m. daily except holidays, the Archives include a microfilm collection of historical documents going back as far as 1700.

There is also a photograph collection, an oral history collection and some maps and plans. A Repair-Bindery Room exists where hand-paper repair of documents and book-binding are carried out. A small photographic laboratory has been established. Publications available at the Archives are the **Guide to the Records of the Bahamas**, Supplement to the Guide to the Records of the Bahamas and 10 booklets on past exhibitions, **Aspects of Slavery, The Sponging Industry, A Selection of Historical Buildings of the Bahamas, The Bahamian-American Connection, The Pineapple Industry of the Bahamas, Junkanoo, Constitutional Development in the Bahamas, The Salt Industry of the Bahamas, The Boat-Building Industry of the Bahamas, Settlements in New Providence,** and three mimeographed booklets containing transcripts from St. Matthew's Cemetery, Christ Church Cathedral Cemetery, and A Guide to African Villages in New Providence. Printed Annual Reports for 1977, 1978, 1979, 1980 and 1981 are also available and so is the booklet on **The First Ten Years 1969-1979 — A History of the Bahamian Archives**. Inquiries should be made to Mrs. Gail Saunders, the Chief Archivist, Department of Archives, P.O. Box SS6341, Nassau, Bahamas. Tel: (809) 322-3045.

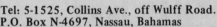

Balance of Payments
Balance of Payments of the Bahamas
B$ Millions
(Figures are supplied by The Central Bank and are
subject to subsequent up-dating.)

	1980 Credit	1980 Debit	1981 Credit	1981 Debit
Goods & Services	1,160.1	1,173.4	1,160.6	1,232.1
*Oil Trade	—	303.4	—	277.1
Other Merchandise	200.5	497.5	176.2	510.3
Travel	595.5	70.7	639.1	91.2
Other Current Items	364.1	301.8	345.3	353.5
Transfers	19.5	21.4	13.3	16.1
Public Capital	14.7	12.1	67.3	13.4
Private Capital	79.9	72.3	141.8	54.5
Financial Institutions (Net)	—	2.9	15.2	—
Errors & Omissions (Net)	17.4	—	—	76.1
Official Reserves (Net)	—	—	—	—
(Increase = Debit = Surplus)	—	14.0	—	10.5
(Decrease = Credit = Deficit)	—	—	—	—

The Bahamas continues to enjoy a stable Balance of Payments position as witnessed by the level of international reserves. The surplus in reserves in 1981 of $10.5 million was a result of continued improvements in both the current and capital account.

*Oil Trade excludes oil imported for refining and re-exported and trans-shipped oil.

Banking

At December 31, 1982, there were 346 institutions licensed to carry on banking and/or trust business under the Banks and Trust Companies Regulation Act, either within or from the Commonwealth of the Bahamas. Of these 346 institutions, 250 were permitted to deal with the public, 85 had licences restricting their activities to dealing only with or on behalf of certain specified persons, or to doing specific things, and 11 had non-active licences.

Of the 250 public institutions, 10 were designated by the Exchange Control Department to deal in Bahamian and foreign currencies and gold. There were eight trust companies designated by the Exchange Control Department to act as custodians and dealers in foreign securities. Of the remaining 232 public institutions, there were 130 Eurocurrency branches of banks based in the U.S.A., the U.K., South America, Hong Kong and Europe. Of the remaining 102, 72 were subsidiaries of banks or other institutions based outside the Bahamas, and the remaining 30 were Bahamian-based banks and/or trust companies.

Interest Rates

Interest rates on deposits vary from approximately 4.5% to 6.5% for savings deposits, up to 8% for fixed deposits. Rates on fixed deposits vary according to the amounts involved and the length of time of the deposit.

Rates charged for loans in the past have been slightly higher than in the U.S. However, at December 31, 1982, the rate was between 10 and 11% and rates on personal and mortgage loans ranged from about 12 to 18%.*

*In April 1980 legislation was enacted to exempt banks and trust companies from the provision of the Rate of Interest Act which prohibits interest rates in excess of 20% per annum. This amendment facilitates the worldwide dealings of licensed financial institutions in the Bahamas in view of prevailing international monetary conditions. The 20% ceiling still applies to non-licensed lending institutions and individuals.

Banking Hours

Banks are open Monday through Thursday from 9:30 a.m. to 3 p.m. and from 9:30 a.m. to 5 p.m. on Fridays. Some savings and loan institutions remain open from 9:30 a.m. to 4 p.m. Monday through Friday.

Central Bank

The central financial institution in the Bahamas is the Central Bank of the Bahamas. It was established in June 1974 by an act of parliament as successor to the Bahamas Monetary Authority. Its responsibilities include
Safeguarding the value of the Bahamian dollar,
Credit Regulation, Note issue,
Administration of Exchange Control Regulations,
Administration of Banks and Trusts Legislation,
Compilation of financial statistics.

The Central Bank of the Bahamas, like most other central banks, does not accept deposits from, nor make loans to, the public, but acts as a banker to banks and to the Government.

Any queries relating to banking in the Bahamas may be directed to the Bank Supervision Department of the Central Bank on Frederick Street, P.O. Box N4868, Nassau, Bahamas, or telephone (809) 322-2193.

Birds

The birds of the Bahamas are from the United States, Cuba, and the Caribbean. The majority of birds in the northern Bahamas are of North American origin, while more Caribbean species are found in the south. Only a few species of bird are endemic to the Bahamas. These include the Bahamas Woodstar hummingbird and the Bahamas swallow. Inagua is ornithologically the richest island, with a flamingo rookery of approximately 30,000 to 40,000 birds, Roseate Spoonbills, and a large proportion of the world population of Reddish Egrets. These birds are under the protection of the Bahamas National Trust, which administers the 287-square-mile Inagua National Park.

The numerous lagoons and mangrove swamps of the Bahamas attract a wide variety of herons and egrets. Sea birds and waders abound along the coasts, and hummingbirds are common. At the other extreme of size is the Magnificent Frigate Bird, which pilots have encountered at 8,000 feet. There are many North American migrants.

The Wild Birds Protection Act is designed to ensure the survival of all bird species throughout the Bahamas. Hunters should obtain a copy of the Act from Government Publications Office, Bank Lane, Nassau.

1. Closed season on the following birds is from March 1 to September 15: Zenaida (Wood) dove and Mourning (Florida) dove.

2. Closed season on the following birds is from March 31 to September 15: All wild ducks and geese (except Whistling Ducks, or Bahama Duck or White Jaw and Ruddy Ducks), Bobwhite Quail, Chuckar Partridge, Wilson's or Jack Snipe and Coot, Ring-necked Pheasant, Guinea Fowl, Black-crowned Night Heron, Yellow-crowned Night Heron.

3. The season for White-crowned Pigeon is subject to change each year. It usually begins in late September or early October and hunters are advised to contact the Ministry of Agriculture and Fisheries before October of each year.

During the closed season on all these birds, it is an offence to kill or capture or have in your possession any such bird unless you can prove it was taken in season.

4. Totally protected species. All other birds except those listed in (1), (2) and (3) above may not be shot, killed or caught at any time.

5. Status of Hunters. Only Bahamian citizens, permanent residents and licensed foreigners or those who have resided in the Bahamas for a continuous 90-day period may hunt here.

6. Bag Limits. At present 50 wild birds may be taken by one person per day and the possession limit is 200 birds at any one time.

7. Wild Bird Reserves. It is an offence to hunt, kill or capture any wild bird in certain areas. A list of these places, condensed below, can be obtained from the Ministry of Agriculture and Fisheries, Nassau.

New Providence area: Paradise Island, Lake Cunningham, Waterloo, Adelaide Creek, Goulding Cay.

Exuma area: Big Galliot Cay, Channel Cays, and Flat Cay, Big Derby Island, Little Derby Island, Guana Cay, Goat Cay, Betty Cay, Pigeon Cay, Cistern Cay, Harvey Cay and Rocks in vicinity of Leaf Cay, Exuma Land and Sea Park area.

Andros area: High Cay, Grassy Creek Cays and Rocks, North Rocks and Small Rocks, Washerwoman's Cut Cays including Dolly Cay, Sister Rocks, Pigeon Cay, and Joulter Cays, Big Green Cay and Little Green Cay.

Berry Islands area: Crab Cay and Mammy Rhoda Cay.

Little San Salvador: Little Island or Little San Salvador and Goat Cay.

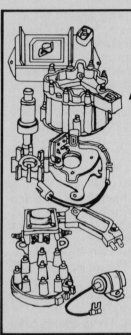
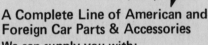

Eleuthera area: Wood Cay, Water Cay and Schooner Cays, Bottle Cay, Cedar Cay and Finley Cay.

Grand Bahama area: Peterson Cay.

Inagua area: National Trust areas have bye-laws which are in force.

8. Penalties. Any person who commits an offence against the Act is liable to a fine of up to $500 or one month imprisonment. Also the gun, ammunition, car, boat or plane and all equipment used on the hunting expedition is liable to be forfeited and auctioned. If the car, boat or plane is used by another person who commits an offence, the owner could still lose his property by forfeiture unless he **proves** he did not commit an offence and that he reported the incident to the police or game wardens.

9. The Act provides a reward of $500 or one-half the proceeds of the sale of forfeited articles, whichever is the greater amount, to persons who give information leading to the conviction of the offender.

Boating

The Bahamas is a boater's paradise. The waters are clear, teeming with fish; the climate allows almost year-round enjoyment.

Motor Boating

It is forbidden to drive a motor boat in the 200-ft. zone of water directly offshore any Bahama island — unless the boat is approaching or leaving a marina, jetty, dock, etc., at a speed not exceeding three knots.

It is illegal to drive a boat in a reckless manner, or while under the influence of drugs or alcohol. It is illegal for anyone under 16 years of age to drive a motor boat with an engine of more than 10 horsepower. However, a person aged 14-16 may operate a motor boat if supervised by someone 16 or over.

Water Skiing

Water skiing within the 200-ft. zone is also prohibited, unless the skier is being towed within a lane clearly marked off with buoys or ropes. All water skiers are required to wear an efficient flotation device. In the towing boat there must be a look-out (in addition to the driver) aged 16 or over. Skiing is forbidden in hours of darkness.

Boat Registration

The Water Skiing and Motor Boat Control (Amendment) Act 1980 requires the annual registration of all Bahamian motor boats with an engine rated over 10 h.p. Any person wishing to use such boats in the waters around the Bahamas must make application to either the Port

Director in Nassau or a commissioner in the Family Islands.

Initial registration fees are:

Motor boats less than 15 ft. in length ....$ 5
15 ft. or over, but less than 30 ft. ....$ 10
30 ft. or over, but less than 50 ft. ....$ 50
50 ft. or over, but less than 100 ft. $100
100 ft. or over $200
Fishing boats primarily designed to
navigate under sail, but having an
auxiliary engine of 10 hp or more ....   nil

Annual renewal fees are one-half of the above amounts.

The Port Director or commissioner where the boat is registered must be notified of any change of ownership or the fitting of a new engine to the registered boat.

The registration number must clearly show on both sides of the boat's bow. Failure to comply may result in a fine up to $75.

Any person using an unregistered motor boat to which the Act applies is liable to a fine up to $75 plus an additional fine equal to twice the appropriate registration fee.

Duty on Boats

If you are staying in the Commonwealth less than six months and are not employed here, duty is not levied on your boat. If your boat is imported for longer periods or permanently, import duty of 10% of the value and stamp tax of 1% are payable to Bahamas Customs. See page 284 for **Fishing Regulations.**

Broadcasting

Radio Bahamas, consisting of ZNS 1, 2 and 3, is Government-owned and operated by the Broadcasting Corporation of the Bahamas. It is exclusively financed by advertising, announcements, programmes and production services.

ZNS-1, in New Providence on a frequency of 1540 kilohertz (kHz) is powered by 20,000 watts and received throughout the Bahamas 24 hours per day. ZNS-2 covers New Providence on a frequency of 1240 kilohertz with 1,000 watts daily. Both stations are AM and FM; ZNS-1 FM at 107.1 megahertz (mHz), ZNS-2 FM at 107.9 megahertz.

ZNS studios are situated at Third Terrace (East), Centreville, Nassau, N.P.

The third station, Radio Bahamas Northern Service (ZNS-3), officially opened in Freeport, Grand Bahama in May 1973. ZNS-3 is on a frequency of 810 kilohertz and is powered by 1,000 watts. This station is designed to cover the northern Bahamas — Grand Bahama, Abaco and Bimini — and since September 1981 it operates 18 hours of separate local programming per day and networks with Radio Bahamas for the remainder of the day.

Radio Licences

An annual licence is required for operation of private radio stations, as well as ship radio stations, and stations in the land mobile service. No licence is required for radio and television receivers in private homes. For a "fixed private station," such as those on privately-owned cays in the Family Islands, the annual licence fee is $15. An amateur "ham" operator is charged $6 per annum.

Mobile stations (in cars and trucks) may be licensed for $15 annually. Cost of licences for marine radios ranges from $15 per annum for a pleasure boat to $30 for an ocean-going work vessel. "Citizen's band" equipment is limited to five watts and restricted to one to 23 channels and requires no licence.

Licensing is administered by the Bahamas Telecommunications Corporation, John F. Kennedy Drive, P.O. Box N3048, Nassau. Free application forms are available.

Budget

(See Public Finance.)

Building Permits

Floor Area	Cost of Permit
Up to 500 sq ft.	$ 7.50
500-1,000 sq. ft.	$ 4.00 per hundred sq. ft.
1,000-1,500 sq. ft.	$ 6.50 per hundred sq. ft.
1,500-10,000 sq. ft.	$ 8.00 per hundred sq. ft.
10,000 & up	$10.00 per hundred sq. ft.

To build a wall or fence (any boundary structure), $4.00 per hundred lineal feet. Removal of structures without demolition such as sheds, garages, etc., $7.50 minimum. Reclamation of land, $2.50 per hundred square feet. Building of small private docks and of any size swimming pool, $7.50 minimum.

Renewals

Where the gross area of the floor space is:
Less than 1,000 sq. ft. .... $ 5.00
Over 1,000 sq. ft. and up to 1,500 sq. ft. 15.00
Over 1,500 sq. ft. 25.00

Deposits: under 500 sq. ft., $5; 500 sq. ft. to 1,500 sq. ft., $10; 1,600 sq. ft., $12.80, with deposit increasing 80¢ per hundred sq. ft.

Building Permits Issued by the Ministry of Works in Nassau for New Providence.

Year	No. Permits Issued	Total Estimated Value (B$)
1978	1,529	51,516,000
1979	1,715	95,611,000
1980	1,734	168,662,000
1981	1,947	98,760,000
1982	2,061	187,941,000

Business Licence Tax

The Business Licence Act, which came into effect in September 1980, introduced for the first time in the Bahamas a tax on earnings in the form of fees payable to the government for a licence to operate a business. Annual licence renewal applications and payments are due every March 31.

Fees are based, in the case of most businesses, on their total gross profits less the "cost incurred in producing that turnover". They range from $1 for "a very small business with a low profit" to $180,000 for "a very large business with a very high profit".

Companies designated "non-resident" under the Exchange Control Regulations Act pay an annual fee of $100. The Business Licence Act authorizes inspection of any licensed business's books and records by agents of the Finance Ministry.

The Act's definition of "business" includes all types of manufacturing and commercial undertakings, and also covers the professions such as law, accounting and medicine. Where a business consists of separate and distinct undertakings, a separate licence must be obtained for each operation.

A Bahamian or Bahamian company (i.e., one with 100% Bahamian ownership) wishing to start a new business may commence operations as soon as application for a licence is submitted, and prior to the determination of the application. A non-Bahamian or a company not 100% Bahamian-owned must wait for approval of the licence application before starting the undertaking.

Similarly, the Act provides for automatic annual renewal for Bahamian businesses (provided other statutory requirements have been complied with), but renewal of a non-Bahamian business licence is at the discretion of the Minister of Finance, whose decision "shall not be called into question by any court".

Companies licensed under the Banks and Trust Companies Regulations Act 1965 (which imposes separate fees) are not required to pay for a Business Licence, and registered insurers pay a licence fee of 1% of gross premiums collected each quarter, or $25, whichever is the higher.

244

Chamber of Commerce

The Bahamas Chamber of Commerce is a non-profit, non-political corporate body of business houses and professional men and women. Its primary interest is promoting, fostering and protecting Bahamian commerce and industry in all its aspects. Also it provides Government with a responsibile vehicle for dialogue with the private sector.

Since the Chamber is concerned with all phases of the economy of the Bahamas, it maintains active standing committees which parallel the areas of responsibility of most of the Government's ministries. These committees meet at least monthly. Much of their routine business concerns pertinent recommendations to Government and requests from Government for private sector co-operation on various projects.

The Chamber also maintains trade division committees comprising representatives from every business sector of its membership. Its offices are located at Shirley Street and Collins Avenue, Nassau. Tel: (809) 322-2145, 322-3320. Mailing address: P.O. Box N665, Nassau, Bahamas.

Churches

Denominations include Anglican, Baptist, Christian Scientist, Church of God of Prophecy, Greek Orthodox, Jewish, Lutheran, Methodist, Plymouth Brethren, Presbyterian, Roman Catholic, Seventh-day Adventist, Jehovah's Witnesses and small sects. On New Providence, the three largest denominations are Baptist, Anglican and Roman Catholic. There are many churches throughout the islands.

Cinemas

Nassau has several good movie houses, offering everything from first-run Hollywood films to popular shoot-em-up re-runs. The Shirley Street Theatre is a modern motion picture theatre, located, as the name implies, on Shirley Street. The Capital is a small Over-the-Hill theatre.

Sunshine Twin Cinemas is an air conditioned twin theatre on Blue Hill Road, and the Sunshine Golden Gates Theatre is in the Golden Gates Shopping Centre. For an evening performance, seats in the various theatres range from $2.75-$4.00 downstairs and $2.75-$4.50 balcony.

There is one drive-in theatre, the Prince Charles, named for the highway on which it is situated. Admission is $3.00 per adult.

Citizenship

The Constitution of the Bahamas contains detailed provisions of who is, or who can become, a citizen. Other provisions affecting the

acquisition or loss of citizenship are contained in the Bahamas Nationality Act, 1973.

Under the Constitution, those who became, or were eligible to become citizens on the date of independence — July 10, 1973 — include:

1. A person born in the Bahamas.

2. A person born outside the Bahamas if his father did, or would have but for his death, become a citizen of the Bahamas, provided that this person is or was a citizen of the United Kingdom and Colonies.

3. A person who was registered as a citizen of the Bahamas under the British Nationality Act, 1948. Excepted from this provision are those persons registered or naturalized under the British Nationality Act, 1948, and who were not resident in the Bahamas on Dec. 31, 1972; or who were registered on or after Jan. 1, 1973, or who on July 9, 1973, possessed the nationality of some other country.

Other sections of the Constitution relate to those persons born since independence. They provide that:

4. A person born in the Bahamas after that date shall be a citizen if either of his parents is a citizen of the Bahamas.

5. A person born in the Bahamas, neither of whose parents is a citizen, shall be entitled to be registered as a citizen of the Bahamas, subject to such exceptions or qualifications as may be prescribed in the interests of national security or public policy, by making application within 12 months after his 18th birthday. Such persons, if they are citizens of another country, will be required to renounce that citizenship, take an oath of allegiance, and make a declaration of intent concerning residence.

6. A person born legitimately outside the Bahamas after July 9, 1973, if his mother is a citizen of the Bahamas, is entitled to make application between the ages of 18 and 21 years to be registered as a citizen, subject to national security and public policy considerations. He is required to renounce any other citizenship, take an oath of allegiance and make a declaration of intent concerning residence.

Any woman who is married to a person who is or becomes a citizen of the Bahamas is entitled to be registered as a citizen, provided she is still married to that person and subject to national security and public policy considerations.

In all cases (with the exception of 1, 2 and 3), registration as a citizen is subject to such exceptions or qualifications as may be prescribed in the interests of national security or public policy.

Prior to independence the designation of "Bahamian status" was given to some British subjects who met certain qualifications, including at least five years residence in the Bahamas, and to others who automatically acquired "Bahamian status" by marriage. Bahamian status conferred on them equal rights with Bahamians with regard to employment and business.

Foreign nationals who were not British subjects were able to qualify for Bahamian status by becoming British subjects naturalized in the Bahamas.

247

Bahamian status continued after independence but has been abolished in favour of full citizenship or permanent residence. The grant of citizenship to persons with Bahamian status is also subject to considerations of national security and public policy as well as residence qualification.

Aliens who are not entitled to be registered or naturalized by virtue of an existing status are nevertheless able to apply for citizenship in the Bahamas under the Nationality Act. Qualifications include residence for prescribed periods, knowledge of the English language and the intention to continue to reside in and to make the Bahamas their permanent home.*

*In the speech from the throne, delivered by H. M. The Queen at the official opening of the new legislative session on October 20, 1977, the Government foreshadowed its intention to hold a Referendum on a proposed change in the Constitution which would preclude the Courts from reviewing a ministerial decision to grant or refuse citizenship to any applicant. An Act to establish the statutory machinery for a Referendum was passed in late 1977 but it was unknown at press time when the referendum was to be held.

Climate

The Isles of June. This term has been aptly applied to all the Bahamas for the climate is mild. Having a tropical maritime wet-and-dry type climate with winter incursions of modified polar air, generally the Bahamas experiences neither frost, snow, sleet, hail nor extremes of temperatures. A unique exception to that occurred on January 19, 1977 when parts of the northern Bahamas experienced a brief flurry of light snow. Climatological data given below covers the 30-year period between 1951 and 1980, and shows the lowest recorded temperature as being 44.1 degrees. However, that record low was replaced on January 20, 1981 when the temperature dropped to 41.4 degrees.

In centrally-situated New Providence, winter temperatures seldom fall much below 60°F and usually reach about 75°F during the afternoon. In the summer, temperatures usually fall to 78°F or less at night and seldom rise above 90°F during the day. In the more northerly islands, winter temperatures are somewhat lower than in New Providence, and some five degrees higher in the southern islands, but in summer months temperatures tend to be similar all over the Bahamas.

Sea surface temperatures normally vary between 74°F in February and 83°F in August.

Humidity is fairly high, especially in the summer months, but there is usually a pleasant breeze which lessens the humid effect. Winds are predominantly easterly throughout the year, but with a tendency to become northeasterly from October to April and southeasterly from May to September. Wind speeds are on average below 10 knots in all seasons, but in the winter months periods of a day or two of north and northeast winds of about 25 knots may occur. The special case of hurricanes is discussed below.

There is more than seven hours of bright sunshine in Nassau on the average in all months except October, when it is marginally less.

Nevertheless, periods of a day or two of cloudy weather can occur at any time of the year. The length of day, the interval between sunrise and sunset, varies from 10 hours and 35 minutes in late December to 13 hours and 41 minutes in late June.

Rain showers can occur at any time of the year, but the rainy months are May to October. As a rough guide, at Nassau rainfall averages two inches a month from November to April and six inches a month from May to October. In the northern islands it is up to 20% more, and in the southern islands only half the Nassau total. Rainfall is mainly in the form of heavy showers or thundershowers, which clear quickly.

Nassau can be affected by hurricanes or tropical storms between June and November, the greatest risk being in August, September and October. The most recent hurricane experience occurred in 1979 when Hurricane David affected all the islands with either gale or hurricane force winds during September 1 to 3. Based on figures compiled for the past 90 year period, Nassau may expect to experience hurricane conditions on the average of once in nine years. An efficient warning system gives ample notice for necessary precautions to be taken.

Following are climatological data for Nassau International Airport, based on the 30-year period 1951-1980.

Temperature

Highest temperature recorded (°F)

JAN.	FEB.	MAR.	APR.	MAY	JUN.	JUL.	AUG.	SEP.	OCT.	NOV.	DEC.
85.6	86.9	88.5	90.3	91.3	93.0	93.4	94.4	93.2	91.0	89.0	86.7

Mean of daily maximum temperature

76.7	77.0	79.7	81.7	84.4	86.9	88.7	89.1	88.0	85.0	80.9	78.0

Mean temperature

69.6	69.5	71.8	74.4	77.4	80.1	81.9	81.9	80.8	78.2	74.4	70.9

Mean of daily minimum temperature

62.2	62.4	64.7	67.5	70.6	73.6	74.9	75.1	74.2	72.1	67.8	63.8

Lowest temperature recorded

44.1	45.8	47.2	49.6	55.6	60.2	68.0	67.6	59.5	56.0	51.0	46.0

Humidity

Mean relative humidity(%)

77	76	75	75	78	80	78	79	82	81	79	78

Mean dew point (°F)

61.7	61.3	63.7	64.9	69.8	73.6	74.5	74.6	74.9	72.1	66.7	63.3

Wind

Mean wind speed in knots

8.3	8.8	8.7	8.9	8.3	7.4	7.6	7.0	6.8	7.5	8.2	8.2

Sunshine

Mean hours of bright sunshine

7.3	7.8	8.5	9.0	8.6	7.6	8.9	8.6	7.1	6.8	7.5	7.1

Mean length of day — hours

10.3	11.3	12.0	12.7	13.3	13.7	13.5	13.0	12.3	11.6	11.0	10.6

Rainfall

Mean rainfall in inches

1.72	1.62	1.20	2.16	4.60	8.79	6.36	7.36	6.94	8.07	2.70	1.61

Company Formation

A Bahamian company (e.g., a subsidiary of a foreign company) can be organized in a few days by a Bahamas lawyer. It is not necessary to file or publish any financial information other than details of its issued capital unless it is a banking company. But the proposed company's name should be reserved in the office of the Registrar General (P.O. Box N532, Nassau) before the memorandum and articles of association are sent for registration.

Companies registered in foreign countries need not form a Bahamian company to do business in the Commonwealth. They must register here, though, under the Foreign Companies Act, if they plan to own Bahamas land.

A Bahamian company doing business outside the islands may adopt an official seal, under The Companies Seals Act, for use in any area where its business is conducted.

Five persons or more must subscribe for at least one share each in any Bahamian company to be incorporated. If nominee shareholders are used, the shares can be endorsed, together with a declaration of trust, and held by the beneficial owners. If desired, the beneficial owners' names need never appear at all, as all shares may be held in nominees' names.

Under current practice, the identity of the beneficial owners of foreign companies which are incorporated and administered by authorized agents need not be disclosed to Exchange Control except by specific request of the Bahamas Central Bank.

While the Act does not provide for the company director or officer to reside in the Bahamas, the company must have a local registered office.

Companies without staffed offices in the Bahamas usually locate their registered office in the chambers of the Bahamas lawyer who handles the incorporation, the office of a chartered accountant (called "certified public accountant" in the U.S.) or in a trust company office.

FILING WITH REGISTRAR GENERAL

The first steps in formation of a company include filing with the Registrar General, along with a fee of $290, a memorandum giving the company's name, its objects and authorized capital, the articles of association covering rights of members and embodying all internal regulations not provided for by the Bahamas Companies Act; and copies of all special resolutions with names and full postal addresses of officers, directors, managers and registered office location (any subsequent changes must be filed as well).

A Bahamas company should also keep a register of members with their names, addresses, occupations and amount of shares; a register of charges showing all mortgages and charges affecting the company's property; and a register of directors and managers.

Fees (stamp duty) paid to the Public Treasury on formation of a Bahamas company are based on an escalating scale. They begin at $60 for companies with a capital of $5,000 or under, but for instance, a company with $60,000 capital pays a stamp duty of $225. If the authorized capital is increased after incorporation, the fee rises accordingly.

A company in which not less than 60% of its shares are beneficially owned by Bahamians is charged an annual tax of $250. A company in which less than 60% of its shares are beneficially owned by Bahamians is charged an annual fee of $1,000. There is no annual fee chargeable on a non-profit company. A company formed on or after July 1 of any year is not liable to pay the fee through the subsequent year.

Every company formed under the Bahamas Companies Act must file at the Registry an annual return prepared on the 14th day succeeding the company's annual general meeting. The annual return must be authenticated by the signature of the secretary or manager or one of the directors of the company and must bear the seal of the company. It discloses the following:

(a) a list of company members stating the names, addresses and occupations of all members mentioned and the number of shares held by each;

(b) amount of the company's capital and number of shares into which it is divided;

(c) number of shares taken from the formation of the company up to the date of summary;

(d) amount of calls made on shares;

(e) amount of calls received;

(f) amount of calls unpaid;

(g) amount of shares forfeited;

(h) names, addresses and occupations of persons who have ceased to be members since the last list was compiled and number of shares held by each;

(i) the registration number of the company;

(j) the names, addresses and occupations of officers or managers of the company.

EXCHANGE CONTROL PERMISSION

Any company to be incorporated for non-residents of the Bahamas must first have the permission of Exchange Control. For the purposes of Exchange Control, such companies are classified as "resident" and "non-resident."

A "resident" company is one which carries on business in the Bahamas, or is owned by Bahamas residents, or owns property in the Bahamas. It must convert all its foreign currency earnings into Bahamian dollars unless special permission is given. It cannot without Exchange Control permission maintain a foreign currency bank account. Approved status is normally granted in respect of the shares issued provided they are paid for in a foreign currency (e.g., U.S. dollars) and converted into Bahamian dollars.

The company cannot borrow in the Bahamas without prior permission of Exchange Control and any further issue or transfer of shares requires the prior permission of Exchange Control.

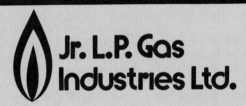

"NON-RESIDENT" COMPANY

In a "non-resident" company, there must be no Bahamian share-holders. It may not conduct its operations in the Bahamas nor deal in Bahamian currency or securities without prior permission of Exchange Control but may operate foreign currency accounts in and outside the Bahamas.

It also may operate an external account in the Bahamas to meet local expenses but such an account must be fed entirely with foreign currency. Any further issue or transfer of shares other than those outlined in the initial application require prior permission of Exchange Control. A certificate of validation may be issued if shares have been transferred without prior Exchange Control approval.

Constitution

When independence from Great Britain was achieved on July 10, 1973, a new Constitution representing the supreme law of the land went into effect for the Commonwealth of the Bahamas.

The Constitution proclaims the Bahamas as a sovereign democratic state, sets forth requirements for citizenship and guarantees fundamental human rights such as freedom of conscience, expression and assembly. It also protects the privacy of the home and prohibits deprivation of property without compensation and due process of law.

The Bahamas retains its ties with the Commonwealth of Nations (formerly the British Commonwealth) and also retains the British monarch as its head of state. The Queen is represented in the Bahamas by a Governor General who is appointed and serves at Her Majesty's pleasure.

There is a bicameral parliament consisting of a Senate and a House of Assembly. The Senate has 16 members, nine appointed by the Governor General on the advice of the Prime Minister, four on the advice of the Leader of the Opposition and three on the advice of the Prime Minister after consultation with the Leader of the Opposition. This arrangement provides for the Opposition to have no less than four members in the Senate and to claim up to three more based on its numerical strength in the House of Assembly.

The House of Assembly must have at least 38 elected members. This number may be increased on the recommendation of the Constituencies Commission, which is charged with reviewing electoral boundaries at least every five years. The present membership was increased in 1982 to 43.

The executive branch consists of a Cabinet of at least nine members, including the Prime Minister and the Attorney General. All Ministers must be members of parliament and the Prime Minister and the Minister of Finance must be members of the House of Assembly. Up to three Ministers can be appointed from among the Senators.

An independent judiciary including a Supreme Court and a Court

of Appeal is provided for, along with the right of appeal to Her Majesty's Privy Council.

Also provided under the Constitution are a Public Service Commission, Public Service Board of Appeal, a Judicial and Legal Service Commission and a Police Service Commission.

The Constitution can be amended by Act of Parliament but there are two categories of provisions — entrenched and specially entrenched — which can be amended only by a prescribed voting formula and with approval by the electorate in a referendum.

The entrenched provisions include those relating to the establishment of the Public Service and qualifications for members of parliament. These provisions can be amended only by a two-thirds majority vote in both houses of parliament and by referendum.

The specially entrenched provisions relate to citizenship*, fundamental rights, establishment and powers of parliament, the Cabinet and the judiciary. These can be amended only by a three-quarters majority vote in parliament and by referendum.

*In the Speech from the Throne, delivered by H.M. The Queen at the official opening of the new legislative session on October 20, 1977, the Government foreshadowed its intention to hold a Referendum on a proposed change in the Constitution which would preclude the Courts from reviewing a ministerial decision to grant or refuse citizenship to any applicant. An Act to establish the statutory machinery for a Referendum was passed in late 1977 but no further steps have been taken to implement the law, or to hold a referendum.

Cost of Living, Nassau

Freight and Customs duties result in comparatively expensive food, rent, automobiles and some items of clothing.

Medical care and dentistry can be less costly than in the United States. An out patients clinic at Princess Margaret Hospital in Nassau is available at $1 per visit — but you may wait several hours for treatment.

Doctor's office calls average $20-$30. A Princess Margaret Hospital room is $10.50-$31. Private duty nurses are recommended. Their cost — $50 per shift, three shifts each day.

Electricity and water charges are billed quarterly for residential accounts, but may be billed monthly on request. Telephone rental is on a monthly basis. The average deposit for electrical service varies with a home's size and location. It ranges from $35 to more than $1,000, with about $100 as average. Telephone deposit is $50 for landlords, or $150 for tenants. A $30 water deposit is required for buildings with one water closet or bathroom and $80 for those with two or more.

Virtually all homes and apartments for rent or sale here are furnished down to china and cookware. Rents vary according to location and season. Summer is the best time for apartment hunting.

In general, an efficiency apartment rents monthly on a one-year lease from $150-$650; one bedroom, $250-$750; two bedrooms, $350 up. A two bedroom detached house can rent from $450 to

$1,500. Short-term leases usually include utilities.

Building cost for an average three-bedroom house — living room, dining room, kitchen, bath and patio — is a minimum of $45 per square foot. That is $67,500 for 1,500 square foot home. A more elaborate three-bedroom home with maid's quarters may range from $60 to $75 per square foot. The house would cost $132,000 to $165,000 but could go considerably higher.

New Providence has well-stocked supermarkets. In addition to U.S. brands, they carry a range of name brands from other countries.

NEW PROVIDENCE PRICES IN 1983 (January)

Food

1 lb. butter	$ 1.84
½ gal. milk	$ 1.99
1 doz. large eggs	$ 1.13
1 loaf sliced bread	$ .99
4.4 lbs. sugar	$ 1.49
5 lbs. flour	$ 1.79
5 oz. bar bath soap	$ .85
1 lb. bacon	$ 2.39
1 lb. T-bone steak	$ 5.99
1 lb. ground beef	$ 1.99
1 lb. frying fish	$ 1.69
10 ozs. instant coffee	$ 6.39
1 lb. regular ground coffee	$ 3.29
100 tea bags	$ 3.99
16 oz. can green beans	$ .89
32 oz. mayonnaise	$ 2.69
6-pack sodas	$ 2.70
5 lbs. potatoes	$ 1.79
1 head lettuce	$ .99
3 lbs. onions	$ 1.39
1 lb. tomatoes	$ .89
½ gal. ice cream	$ 2.69

Other Items and Services

1 pack filter cigarettes	$ 1.50
New York Times	$ 1.15
1 pt. gin	$ 4.80
1 pt. scotch	$ 4.85
1 pt. rum	$ 2.85
1 pt. Drambuie	$ 6.15
1 case (24 bottles or cans) beer	$17.75
Shampoo and set	$14.00
Manicure	$ 6.00
Men's haircut	$ 5.00
1 gal. high test gasoline	$ 1.52
Dry cleaning: 1 dress	$ 3.75
1 man's suit	$ 3.75

Currency

The currency of the Bahamas is the Bahamian dollar, which is the only legally acceptable currency. Nevertheless, the U.S. dollar is normally accepted throughout the islands (stores, hotels, etc.). The Bahamian dollar is presently at par with the U.S. dollar.

In January 1972, the rate of exchange for the Bahamian dollar against the U.S. dollar was B$0.97 to U.S. $1. The rate of exchange of the Bahamian dollar against the pound sterling was B$2.5275 to £1; and the Bahamian dollar was fixed against the pound sterling.

On June 23, 1972, the United Kingdom Government allowed sterling to float. As a result, the Bahamian dollar was fixed against the U.S. dollar (instead of sterling) at B$0.97 to U.S. $1.00 on June 28, 1972. This rate of exchange prevailed throughout the remainder of the year. When the U.S. dollar was devalued in February 1973, the value of the Bahamian dollar was adjusted so that it was at par with the U.S. dollar.

The Canadian dollar was worth approx. B$0.79 as at January 28, 1983.

Customs

Generally, the ad valorem (of the value) tariff for imported goods is 32½%, clothing 22½%.

Some items have a higher tariff, examples of these being: tobacco 120%, pool tables 100%, sparkling wine 50%, room air conditioners 52½%, automobiles 45%, TV receivers and record players 42½%, satellites and accessories 62½%.

Some staple food items have a low tariff, examples of these are: condensed milk 10%, evaporated milk 10%, and potatoes 5¢ per 100 lbs., cooking oil (vegetable) 22½%.

The 1978 Budget abolished duties on practically all medicines, tinned corned beef and raffia (artificial straw). Other tariff changes announced at the same time reduced the duty on fine crystal to 12½%; on china to 12½%; on cameras and photographic accessories to 2½%; on watches to 12½%; on cashmere, angora and woollen sweaters, cardigans and pullovers to 5%.

There is a 1½% stamp tax on the value of imported goods with the exception of inexpensive gifts (up to $100) arriving by post.

For Customs purposes the value includes the cost of the goods, ocean or air freight and all other charges incidental to their importation.

There is also a ½% stamp tax on exports based on the f.o.b. value of the goods.

Duty Exemptions

Certain items may be imported exempt from Customs duty. They include:

1. All goods imported with the prior approval of the Minister of Finance by a charitable organization to be used exclusively for charitable purposes.

2. Models, teaching aids, sound recordings, scientific apparatus and materials to be used exclusively for the purpose of scientific or cultural institutions, if approved by the Minister of Finance.

Additional information on Customs duty and exemptions may be found in the Tariff Act of 1975 and its amendments. In 1976, the Customs Management Act of August 1976, came into effect. This replaced the former Customs Regulations Chapter 97. Copies may be obtained from the Publications Office, Parliament Square, Nassau.

Duty-Free Importation

Certain items are basically duty-free and these include:
1. Orthopaedic appliances, surgical belts, trusses and the like; splints and other fracture appliances; artificial limbs, eyes, teeth and other artificial parts of the body; hearing aids and other appliances which are worn, carried or implanted in the body to compensate for a defect or disability.
2. Paintings, drawings and pastels executed entirely by hand other than industrial drawings or hand-printed manufactured articles.
3. Antiques of an age exceeding 100 years.
4. Baby formulae and tea.

Temporary Importation

Certain goods may be imported conditionally on a temporary basis against a security bond or a deposit which is refundable on their re-exportation. They include:
1. Any fine jewellery, approved as such by the Comptroller of Customs, imported on consignment, and upon executing a security bond, if satisfactory proof be given:
   (a) for the exportation thereof to the exporter and country from whom and from where it was imported within a period of six months, and
   (b) for the payment of duty on any such jewellery not exported from the Bahamas within the six-month period.
2. Goods for business meetings or conventions for a period up to one month after the meeting or convention is over.
3. Travelling Salesman's Samples. Goods must not be for sale, they must be approved by the Comptroller of Customs and the sales person must have a valid immigration permit. A refundable deposit is required equal to the prescribed duty on the goods, and is refunded upon re-exportation of the goods within three months of arrival.
4. Automobiles or motor cycles brought into the country by a bona fide visitor for not more than six months. A refundable deposit equal to the prescribed duties (46½%) is required and is refunded upon re-exportation provided the vehicle has not been used for commercial purposes while in the Bahamas. Only one such permit per family may be issued during any calendar year.
5. Photographic and cinematographic equipment belonging to members of the foreign press, radio, TV or motion picture ser-

vices, as well as clothes and props belonging to actors and actresses accompanying these services are allowed temporary importation up to 90 days upon the approval of the Ministry of Tourism and Ministry of Finance. Extra time is normally allowed provided application is made in advance to the Ministry of Tourism or Bahamas News Bureau.

6. Any goods such as special tools for repair work or testing equipment can be imported on the payment of 2½% duty of the C.I.F. value (cost/insurance/freight). Also a refundable deposit equal to what the prescribed duty would be on a regular import is required. Prior approval for this must be obtained from the Minister of Finance, for which application should be made to the Comptroller of Customs, P.O. Box N-155, Nassau, Bahamas.

Import Entry Forms

Entry forms are required for goods coming to the Commonwealth by sea, air or post.

Imports arriving by sea are released to the importer on presentation of forms processed at the Customs House, Arawak Cay. For goods sent by air, entry forms are presented to the Customs Officer in the Air Express building at Nassau International Airport. Similar facilities also exist at Family Island ports of entry. Entries are required for goods sent via parcel post, either sea or air, only if the goods are of a commercial nature or of a value in excess of $100.

Goods may be cleared through Customs without proper invoices by provisional entry. The importer leaves a deposit sufficient to cover duty (usually double the estimated duty of the imports), with the understanding that when the invoices arrive, the provisional entry must be adjusted. The residue of the deposit made is refunded after payment of the proper duty amount. Payment in a foreign currency for goods imported to the Bahamas may be arranged by a Bahamas bank after presentation of an Exchange Control approval.

Importing Possessions

A person settling in the Bahamas as a resident pays duty on household effects, e.g., furniture, china and appliances. Most personal effects such as clothing and articles of personal adornment already in use and possession are not dutiable.

Duty-free Quotas for Bona Fide Visitors to the Bahamas

In the case of bona fide visitors arriving in the Bahamas, certain items may be brought in duty-free. They include:

1. Wearing apparel, toilet articles and similar personal affects.
2. 1 quart of alcoholic beverage; 1 quart of wine; 1 lb. in weight of tobacco or 200 cigarettes or 50 cigars. These items apply to adults only.
3. Any other gift items up to the value of $25.

Duty-Free Quotas for Returning Bahamians and Residents

A Bahamian through birth or naturalization, or a person granted permission by the Immigration Department to reside in the Bahamas and who has been in residence for over one year, may bring back with him into the Bahamas duty-free goods worth up to $25 and returning residents who have been abroad for over one year, up to $240.

Duty-Free Quotas for Bahamas Residents Going Abroad

UNITED STATES — According to U.S. regulations, Bahamians and Bahamas residents visiting the U.S. may take with them duty-free gifts worth up to U.S. $100. These gifts may not include alcoholic beverages or cigarettes. To take advantage of this $100 gift exemption, the visitor must remain in the U.S. at least 72 hours. He may use this exemption once every six months.

Visitors to the U.S. are also entitled to bring in duty-and tax-free one litre of alcoholic beverages for their own use, provided they are at least 21 years old. Also allowed duty-and tax-free besides personal effects are 200 cigarettes, for personal use.

If the individual is not entitled to or does not qualify for the $100 gift exemption, he may take with him duty-free articles up to $25 in value for personal or household use. Neither $100 gift exemption nor the $25 exemption may be grouped together for members of a family.

CANADA — Bahamians or Bahamas residents may take with them on a visit to Canada duty-free, apart from personal effects, any number of gifts valued up to $25 (Canadian) provided these gifts are not advertising matter. For personal use, persons 16 years of age or older may take in 200 cigarettes, 50 cigars and 2 lbs. of tobacco. Persons 18 years of age or older may take in for their personal use 40 ozs. of liquor.

UNITED KINGDOM — Those visiting the United Kingdom from the Bahamas may take in free of duty and tax 400 cigarettes or 200 cigarillos or 100 cigars or 500 grammes of tobacco. Alcohol allowance is two litres of still table wine and either one litre of drink over 22% proof or two litres of not over 22% proof, fortified or sparkling wine. These allowances are not for persons under the age of 17. The allowance for perfume is 50 grammes (two fluid ozs.), nine fluid ozs. of toilet water and £28 worth of other goods.

Rates of duty and tax are complicated and change from time to time so it is advisable to check with your airline or travel agent for current regulations when making reservations.

Duty-Free Quotas for Visitors to Bahamas

UNITED STATES RESIDENTS — Each U.S. resident (including a minor) may take home duty-free purchases up to U.S. $400 in retail value if he has been outside the U.S. more than 48 hours and has not taken the exemption in 30 days. A family may pool exemptions, i.e., a family of four may take home $1,600 worth of goods, but see below for age limit on liquor and cigarettes.

The exemption may include up to one litre (33.8 oz.) of liquor per person over 21, and 100 cigars (Cuban cigars not allowed) per person regardless of age.

Articles accompanying the traveller, in excess of the $400 duty-free allowance, up to $1,000 are assessed at a flat rate of 10 per cent of the fair retail value. Members of a family travelling together may

group articles for application of the flat duty rate. For example, a family of four could have their purchases grouped for a total of $4,000 fair retail value for entry at the flat rate of duty.

If the returning U.S. resident is not entitled to the $400 duty exemption due to the 30-day or 48-hour minimum limitations, he may still import duty-free $25 worth of personal or household items. This exemption may not be pooled.

Antiques are admitted to the U.S. duty-free provided they are over 100 years old. The Bahamas store selling an antique should provide the buyer with a form indicating the value and certifying the age of the object. The buyer must present this form to U.S. Customs.

An antique must be sent through an antique port designated by the U.S. Customs Service if it is worth more than the individual's exemption or the pooled family exemption. At the antique port, the object is passed by an appraiser at the importer's expense. If classed as antique, it is admitted to the U.S. duty-free.

Importation of fruits, plants, meats, poultry and dairy products is generally prohibited. There are some exceptions. Consult the U.S. Dept. of Agriculture (Tel: (809) 327-7127) for further information.

Certain items carrying a trade-mark or trade name may be brought into the U.S. in specified amounts only, or not at all. For example, one bottle only of Chanel No. 5 may be imported per person. Importation of Bahamian tortoise-or turtle-shell goods is prohibited. Consult U.S. Customs (Tel: (809) 327-7126) at Nassau International Airport or obtain a copy of **Know Before You Go** from the Bureau of Customs, Washington, D.C. 20229, for further information.

CANADIAN RESIDENTS — A Canadian may take advantage of one of three categories of duty-free exemptions. If he has been out of Canada for 48 hours, he may make a verbal declaration to claim a $10 duty-free allowance any number of times per year, which would not include alcohol or tobacco. If he has been out of the country for 48 hours, once every quarter, he may choose to make a verbal declaration and claim a $50 allowance which could include up to 200 cigarettes and 50 cigars, and two lbs. tobacco and 1.1 litres (40 ozs.) alcoholic beverage. These exemptions may each be claimed quarterly per calendar year.

If the person has been out of Canada for seven days or more, he may make a written declaration and claim $150 exemption including the amounts of alcohol and tobacco indicated above. This exemption may be claimed once a year.

Goods claimed under the exemptions may be gifts or items for personal use but not items for sale or for household or general family use. All persons, including infants, are entitled to the exemptions and parents or guardians may sign for those children who are unable to sign for themselves.

For the importation of tobacco, the claimant must be over 16 years of age. In case of liquor, wine or beer, the person must have attained the age prescribed by the provincial or territorial authority at the point of entry.

Goods acquired in the Bahamas, or elsewhere outside continental

North America, may be shipped or mailed separately if they are declared at the first port of entry.

UNITED KINGDOM RESIDENTS — Duty-free allowance for tobacco goods is half that allowed for Bahamian visitors to the U.K. However, for alcoholic drinks, perfume, toilet water and other goods, the same allowances are available to U.K. residents as to visitors. See page 261.

Sending Gifts from the Bahamas

TO THE U.S. — Any number of gifts may be sent to the U.S. from the Bahamas. Recipient pays no U.S. duty if the gift he receives is worth U.S. $50 or less. If the gift is worth more than $50, he pays duty on the full value. According to U.S. regulations, the duty-free status applies under the following conditions:

1. Only $50 worth of gifts may be received by the U.S. addressee in one day.
2. Value of the gifts must be clearly written on the package, as well as the words "Gift Enclosed."
3. No cigars, cigarettes or liquor may be sent as gifts. Perfumes valued at more than $1 may not be sent.
4. Persons in the U.S. are not permitted to send money to the Bahamas for gifts to be shipped to them duty-free. Gifts must be unsolicited.
5. Shops and commercial firms may wrap and mail the duty-free gifts for customers who pay for them personally in the Bahamas.
6. Persons may not mail a gift addressed to themselves.

TO THE U.K. — Bona fide unsolicited gifts sent to the United Kingdom are subject to Customs charges at their destination with the exception of:

1. Postal packages of small value which are not gifts of cigarettes, cigars, tobacco, snuff, spirits or wine.
2. Packages not more than 22 lbs. gross weight, not exceeding £5 in value, marked "Gift," containing only foodstuffs (other than caviar), consumable medical supplies, soap or well-used clothing.

TO CANADA — Bona fide unsolicited gifts sent to Canada are subject to Customs charges at their destination except for:

1. Presents worth $25 or less each and containing no advertising matter, tobacco or alcoholic beverages. There is no restriction on the number of gifts that may be sent.

Defence Force

The Royal Bahamas Defence Force came into existence officially on March 31, 1980. Prior to that, since 1977, the Force had worked in close co-operation with the now disbanded Marine Division of the

Royal Bahamas Police Force, many of whose officers transferred to the Defence Force.

The Ministry of Defence is in the portfolio of the Prime Minister. The RBDF has a seagoing fleet of one 103-foot patrol craft, five 60-foot craft and several high speed craft for shallow water patrol duties in the Family Islands. The Air Wing at present has one Aero-Commander. The Force consists of 45 officers and 357 marines, headquartered at Coral Harbour. Expansion and development over the next four years call for the enlistment of some 700 officers and marines, possibly including females.

Dentists

Nassau

Dr. E. Paul Albury
Dr. R. E. Bailey
Dr. J. L. Burnside
Dr. Norman Cove
Dr. A. P. Davis
Dr. C. W. Eneas
Dr. C. W. Eneas, Jr.
Dr. Sparkman Ferguson

Dr. John Godet
Dr. Nigel Lewis
Dr. Hal E. Leyland
Dr. John H. Louis, Jr.
Dr. Veronica McIver
Dr. R. W. Sawyer, C. B. E.
Dr. Sidney Sweeting
Dr. C. O Vanderpool

Princess Margaret Hospital

Dr. Vincent Dames
Dr. Emmanuel Francis
Dr. S. Kalamuddin
Dr. Arturo Rodriguez
Dr. Hayward Romer
Dr. Munir Ahmed Rachad (Oral Surgeon)

Family Islands

Abaco (Marsh Harbour), Dr. N. H. Cove
Abaco (Treasure Cay), Dr. J. R. Robinson
Eleuthera (Governor's Harbour), Dr. Olga Bacchus
Freeport, Grand Bahama, Dr. Kenneth Alleyne, Dr. Albert Antoni, Dr. Larry Bain, Dr. E. L. Colson, Dr. G. Michael Newton

Departure Tax

There is a departure tax of $5 for adults and $2.50 for children * leaving the Bahamas for a foreign destination. Children under three are exempt, but this tax applies to anyone else departing from the islands, by air or ship, whether vacationer or resident.

There is also a tax of $2 on every ship or plane ticket issued in the Bahamas for international travel.

Three through 11 years of age

Divorce

In the Bahamas, a husband may file for divorce on the ground of adultery only, but a wife may file for divorce on the grounds of adultery, rape, sodomy, or bestiality. A petition for divorce may be filed any time after the marriage. Three months after a **Decree Nisi** is granted, the divorce may become final and a **Decree Absolute** may be issued. In special cases, this period may be reduced to six weeks. Marriages not consummated may be annulled.

Any couple, regardless of nationality, may obtain a divorce in the Bahamas if it can be established that the husband is domiciled here. A wife may file for a Bahamian divorce for any of the above mentioned reasons even though her husband is not domiciled in the islands if she can establish that (1) she and her husband have lived three years of their married life here and that these years directly preceded commencement of the suit and (2) her husband has deserted her and has gone abroad. Desertion is never grounds for divorce, nor is physical or mental cruelty. In 1982, 166 divorces were granted in the Bahamas.

A divorce obtained abroad will be recognized in the Bahamas if it can be shown, to the satisfaction of the Court, that the party obtaining the divorce had a real and substantial connection with the country in which the divorce was obtained.

Doctors & Hospitals

Princess Margaret Hospital, on Shirley St., Nassau, is government-operated and accommodates 450 patients. Departments: medical, surgical, maternity, intensive care, eye wing, chest wing, private wing, ambulatory care facility, including accident and emergency, general practice and specialty clinics, laboratory (including blood bank), X-ray, pediatrics, physiotherapy, pharmacy, public health, nurses training school and administration.

Rassin Hospital, on the corner of Shirley St. and Collins Ave., is an acute care, privately operated hospital with 22 patient beds. Medical specialties: General Surgery, Orthopaedic Surgery, Obstetrics and Gynaecology, Ophthalmology, Internal Medicine, Family Medicine and Pediatrics. Ancillary Departments: Clinical Laboratory, Radiology (X-Ray and Ultrasound), Pharmacy, Respiratory Therapy, and Physical Therapy. The Medical Staff consists of numerous physicians who are in private practice in New Providence. President - Dr. Meyer Rassin. Administrator - Mr. Barry Rassin.

Sandilands Rehabilitation Centre, in Sandilands Village on the Island of New Providence, comprises a 150-bed Geriatric Hospital, and a 210-bed Psychiatric Hospital, including a Maximum Security Unit and Child and Family Guidance Centre. The hospitals are known as the Geriatric Hospital and Sandilands Hospital, respectively.

Western Medical Centre, in Lyford Cay, is a 14-bed medical care facility with a 4-bed intensive care unit. Full X-ray, laboratory, and diagnostic facilities. Also employing 3 doctors.

DOCTORS, NEW PROVIDENCE
General Practitioners

Dr. F. E. Adderley
Dr. Timothy Barrett
Dr. P. J. Bennetts
Dr. V. Bowe
Dr. H. S. Cash
Dr. R. E. Crawford
Dr. K. R. Culmer
Dr. L. W. Culmer
Dr. E. L. Donaldson
Dr. N. R. Gay
Dr. R. Van Tooren

Dr. M. Gerassimos
Dr. M. I. Hale
Dr. L. C. Huggins
Dr. T. P. Jupp
Dr. E. Laidlaw-Thompson
Dr. L. J. McCarroll
Dr. W. H. P. Poad
Dr. M. Ritchie
Dr. B. E. A. Rolle
Dr. G. P. Syme-Thomson
Dr. G. White

Obstetrics and Gynaecology
Dr. E. M. Achara
Dr. A. Donaldson
Dr. B. J. Nottage
Dr. C. J. B. Orr
Dr. G. Sherman

Surgery
Dr. W. Campbell (ENT)
Dr. I. E. Farrington
Dr. M. Rassin
Dr. S. Soni

Psychiatry
Dr. D. Allen
Dr. B. Humblestone
Dr. H. Podlewski

Ophthalmology
Dr. K. W. Knowles

Orthopaedics
Dr. G. C. Bain
Dr. W. Chutkan

Psychology
Dr. T. McCartney

Anaesthetics
Dr. Yutuk Angole
Dr. H. A. Graham

Pathology
Dr. A. Hanna

Dermatology
Dr. Q. M. S. Richmond

Pediatrics
Dr. P. McNeil
Dr. P. Roberts
Dr. D. C. Sands
Dr. G. Sands
Dr. Y. Skeffrey
Dr. M. Stevenson
Dr. J. Wershing

Internal Medicine
Dr. T. R. Allen
Dr. C. W. M. Bethel
Dr. P. Gomez
Dr. J. A. Johnson
Dr. R. Knowles
Dr. J. A. Lunn
Dr. A. M. Thompson-Hepburn

Radiology
Dr. L. Carroll
Dr. S. Kisumbi
Dr. N. J. Lim

Some of the above doctors have a general practice in addition to specialization.

Family Island Clinics
There are about 50 clinics throughout the islands. The facilities and staff vary somewhat with the clinic. In cases where more medical assistance is needed, the patient is flown to Princess Margaret Hospital in Nassau.

268

Medical Officers — Family Islands (Government)
Abaco (Cooper's Town), Dr. P. Pai
Abaco (Marsh Harbour), Dr. L. Cleare
Acklins (Spring Point), Dr. P. Gunabe
Andros (Fresh Creek), Dr. V. K. Diwan
Andros (Kemp's Bay), Dr. R. Casino
Bimini (Alice Town), Dr. P. Duncombe
Cat Island (Smith's Bay), Dr. K. Vaklev
Eleuthera (Rock Sound), Dr. R. Guina
Eleuthera (Harbour Island), Dr. F. Biney
Eleuthera (Governor's Harbour), Dr. N. Bacchus
Exuma (George Town), Dr. E. Patlak
Grand Bahama (Eight Mile Rock), Dr. H. N. Patel
Grand Bahama (West End), Dr. R. Fernandez
Grand Bahama (East End), Dr. K. Nehru
Great Harbour Cay, Dr. E. F. Huffman
Inagua (Mathew Town), Dr. J. Ebarle
Long Island (Deadman's Cay), Dr. J. Pedroche
Long Island (Stella Maris), Dr. O. Gaida

Private Practitioners—Family Islands
Abaco (Green Turtle Cay), Dr. C. Mendelson
Abaco (Marsh Harbour), Dr. E. F. Gottlieb, Dr. J. S. Fifer
Abaco (Treasure Cay), Dr. D. Rodgers
Eleuthera (Rock Sound), Dr. N. Kerr
Grand Bahama (Freeport), Dr. A. Antoni
Grand Bahama (Freeport), Dr. A. Antoni
Grand Bahama (Freeport), Dr. R. Antoni
Grand Bahama (Freeport), Dr. R. Bailey
Grand Bahama (Freeport), Dr. M. Bethel
Grand Bahama (Freeport), Dr. V. Burell
Grand Bahama (Freeport), Dr. R. J. Clement
Grand Bahama (Freeport), Dr. I. Horsfall
Grand Bahama (Freeport), Dr. R. Philip
Grand Bahama (Freeport), Dr. R. Roop
Grand Bahama (Freeport), Dr. P. Bethel-Etuk
Grand Bahama (Freeport), Dr. W. Pratt
Grand Bahama (Freeport), Dr. J. Turnquest
Grand Bahama (Freeport), Dr. D. Jenkins
Grand Bahama (Freeport), Dr. W. Campbell
Grand Bahama (Freeport), Dr. R. McKeage
Grand Bahama (Freeport), Dr. G. Bain
Grand Bahama (Freeport), Dr. L. Burton
Grand Bahama (Freeport), Dr. F. Weinberg

Driver's Licence and Vehicle Information

There are three types of drivers' licences in the Bahamas: for all
motor vehicles with standard shift or automatic transmission; for two-
wheels (motorcycles, scooters and the like); and for commercial or

public service vehicles. The Road Traffic Department, including the Driving Test Centre, is in the Clarence A. Bain Building, Moss Road and Thompson Boulevard. All applications for driving permits and licences are processed there.

Licence Requirements

Applicants must be at least 17 years of age to qualify to drive a motor car or motorcycle. Applicants must be at least 15 years old in the case of motor assisted cycles equipped with pedals. First-time applicants must secure a learner's permit for $5 and then take a combined oral and driving test when they feel they are ready to drive unaccompanied. The oral test concerns highway code (traffic regulations). Appointments are made for the tests at the Road Traffic Dept. and must be kept promptly. A fee of $5 is charged for each driving test. If for some reason an applicant finds that after making an appointment for a test he is unable to attend as scheduled, he should inform the Road Traffic Dept. at least 24 hours beforehand. Failure to do so will result in the forfeiture of the $5 fee.

A period of 45 minutes is allowed for each applicant's test, and a late-comer will be rescheduled for a later date, possibly as much as three months later.

Licensed drivers may apply to the Road Traffic Dept. and upon presentation of the old licence and completion of a records form, will be issued a licence. Cost is $10 and the old licence is retained by the licensee if it is other than Bahamian in origin. A separate application for a separate permit must be made to receive a public service (chauffeur's) licence. This is required to operate commercial vehicles. There is an additional fee of $25.

Tourists or persons staying but not working in the Bahamas may drive on their foreign licence for up to three months. Expatriates must have a licence "when they start to work," according to a Road Traffic spokesman. Periods of settling in are not considered; only when employment actually begins is the licence necessary.

Driving in the Bahamas is on the left side of the road. Motorcyclists (drivers and passengers) are required by law to wear a protective helmet.

Vehicle Ownership

A vehicle ownership fee is paid annually, from March. The fee, which ranges from $40 to $280, depends on the size of the vehicle. There is a $5 annual fee for licence plates or a $50 fee to reserve the same plate number each year. When any vehicle is licensed for the first time in the Bahamas, the initial fee for licence plates is $12. There is a fee of $10 for transfer of a vehicle already licensed. The new owner must also present a bill of sale, the registration card with his name entered in the space provided, and proof that the vehicle is covered by Road Act Insurance.

Importing an Automobile

Owners of cars imported to the Bahamas should contact the Road Traffic Department to provide a description of the vehicle and receive a licence number. It is suggested that insurance be obtained before moving the car from the dock. The car should be driven directly to the Road Traffic Department for registration. The car must also be inspected as soon as possible after arrival. Also, all cars from right-hand drive countries must have their headlights adjusted to dip left. Cars are inspected annually and a $10 fee is charged. The import duty on motor cars and public service vehicles is 45% plus 1½% stamp tax.

1981
Licensed Drivers

Private	41,476
Provisional	10,316
Public Service	5,123
International	1,675
	58,590

1981
Vehicles Registered

	New Providence (Dec. 31, 1981)	Family Islands (Dec. 31, 1981)
Private cars	32,384	15,058
Government-owned cars	180	85
Private trucks	4,596	3,353
Government-owned trucks	287	162
Private motorcycles	1,250	1,240
Government-owned motorcycles	124	11
Private miscellaneous vehicles	327	103
Taxi-cabs	518	596
Self-drive cars	617	682
Self-drive scooters	522	273
Tour cars	126	10
Buses	628	300
Government buses	39	4
Livery cars	20	—
Total:	41,618	21,877

Drugs

The Dangerous Drugs Act, Chapter 223, makes it an offence for an unauthorized person to import, export or be in possession of Indian hemp (marijuana), cocaine, morphine, opium or lysergic acid (LSD) in the Bahamas. The only exception to this is for a qualified person (registered medical practitioner, registered dentist, licensed veterinary surgeon or licensed pharmacist) to whom special permission is granted for medical or scientific purposes.

The provisions of the Act are stringently enforced and visitors from countries where drug laws are less strict should be aware of Bahamian law in this respect.

The Act as amended in May 1980 provides the following penalties for contravention of its provisions:

(a) On conviction on an indictable charge, a fine of up to $200,000 or to imprisonment for up to 10 years or to both such fine and imprisonment, and (b) on summary conviction, a fine of up to $5,000 or to imprisonment for up to five years, or both such fine and imprisonment.

Economy

Tourism accounts for the major portion of the gross national product and generated about $639.1 million in foreign currency in 1981.

Banking and finance, which produced an estimated $92.8 million in 1981, are listed as the second largest source of income of the Bahamas.

Industrial development is of ever-increasing importance to the economy. Greatest industrial activity is at Grand Bahama, where there is an oil refinery and a petroleum trans-shipment terminal.

Drug manufacturing, light assembly, aragonite mining and salt production by solar evaporation are other major industrial undertakings in the Bahamas.

In 1981/82 domestic export of fruits and vegetables totalled $3.5 million; fish and fish products totalled $11.5 million (1982 declared value).

(Figures were provided by The Central Bank of the Bahamas and the Ministry of Agriculture and Fisheries, and are subject to revision.)

Education

Bahamian education is under the jurisdiction of the Ministry of Education. The Ministry has responsibility for all educational institutions in the islands. Two hundred and twenty-five schools exist in the Commonwealth of the Bahamas. Of these, 187 (83.1%) are fully maintained by Government, whereas 38 (16.9%) are independent schools.

There are 38 government-owned schools in New Providence and 149 on the Family Islands.

Twenty-six independent schools are located on New Providence and 12 on the Family Islands.

Libraries are in the portfolio of the Ministry.

Schools in the Bahamas are categorized as follows: Primary ages 5-11+; Junior High 11-14+; Junior-Senior High 11-16+; Senior High 14-16+. There are also all-age schools. Special Schools (all-age) cater to students having severe learning disabilities.

Free education is available in Ministry schools in New Providence and the Family Islands. Courses lead to the Bahamas Junior Certificate (B.J.C.) usually after 9-10 years, the General Certificate of Education (G.C.E.) of London University Ordinary Level and Royal Society of Arts Certificates after 11-12 years.

Independent schools provide education at Primary, Secondary

and Higher Levels. The term "college" in their names does not mean a university-type school, but in English usage connotes a fee-paying school.

Several schools of continuing education offer secretarial and academic courses.

The government-operated Princess Margaret Hospital offers a Nursing Course at two levels.

The College of the Bahamas was established in 1974. It provides a two or three year programme leading to an Associate Degree in any of the seven academic divisions. Several college degree programmes are offered in conjunction with the University of the West Indies, Florida International University and University of Miami.

Additionally, the Bahamas has been affiliated with the University of the West Indies since the early 1960s. This institution is a regional one which serves the English Caribbean countries. Students may seek admission through the Extra Mural Department of the University. The University of the West Indies also offers a Hotel Management programme leading to a Bachelor's Degree.

The Hotel Training College offers a wide range of subjects up to middle management level in aspects of Hotel Work. Enrolment in this institution includes Bahamian as well as regional and international students.

The Ministry of Education provided the following breakdown of the Bahamas school population for 1982.

Primary	Government	Independent	Total
New Providence	14,734	3,803	18,537
Family Islands	4,912	247	5,159
All-Age			
New Providence	56	1,948	2,004
Family Islands	8,736	2,636	11,372
Junior High			
New Providence	5,940	—	5,940
Family Islands	243	—	243
Junior/Senior High			
New Providence	1,018	3,996	5,014
Family Islands	4,731	442	5,173
Senior High			
New Providence	5,681	—	5,681
Family Islands	930	365	1,295
Special Schools	—	235	235
Totals	46,981	13,672	60,653

New Providence Schools

The following is a sampling of New Providence schools. For a complete list (including Family Island schools), contact the Ministry of Education, P.O. Box N3913, Nassau, Bahamas.

NURSERY SCHOOLS, KINDERGARTEN

Dame Doris Johnson Christian Pre-school — Blue Hill Road. For children 2 to 5 years old. Sessions 7:30 a.m. to 6 p.m. For further information call: 2-1565.

Infant Education Centre — 8th Terrace East, Collins Avenue. For children toilet-trained to five years. Four terms per year, fees $145 per term. Sessions 8 a.m. to 3:30 p.m. After-school care until 6 p.m. (extra). Modern methods used by qualified staff. Branch #2 located in Tropical Gardens (near airport). P.O. Box N10576, Nassau, Bahamas, Tel. 5-8567 or 7-8533.

International Pre-school — Eastern Road. For children 2½ to five. Three terms. $200 per term. Sessions 8:30 a.m. to 12:30 p.m. Three teachers. Operated by Mrs. M. Hall, P.O. Box SS5705, Nassau, Bahamas. Tel. 4-1485.

Jack and Jill Nursery School — Dowdeswell Street. For children three to five. Three terms. $120 per term. Sessions 9 a.m. to 1 p.m. Operated by Mrs. Dot Symonette, P.O. Box SS5653, Nassau, Bahamas. Tel. 5-3711.

Munro School — Williams Court. For children 2½ to five. Three teachers. Three terms, $200 per term. Sessions 8:30 a.m. to 12:30 p.m. Nursery and Kindergarten classes. Operated by Mrs. Charles Munro, P.O. Box N134, Nassau, Bahamas. Tel. 5-4967.

Wee Wisdom School — Collins Avenue, Centreville. For children three to five. Three terms $610 per year. Sessions 9 a.m. to 1 p.m. A division of Nassau Christian Schools, operated by Baptist International Missions, P.O. Box N3923, Nassau, Bahamas. Tel. 2-1586/3-2641.

PRIVATE PRIMARY SCHOOLS

Xavier's Lower School — West Bay Street, Roman Catholic. Co-educational. Students four to 11. Three terms, $685 per year plus $20 book fee for first term only. Kindergarten through sixth grade. Enrolment: approx. 450. Teachers: 21 lay teachers, one priest. Apply to Headmistress, Sr. Genevieve Brown, Xavier's Lower School, P.O. Box N7076, Nassau, Bahamas, Tel. 2-3077.

PRIVATE PRIMARY-SECONDARY SCHOOLS

Kingsway Academy — Bernard Road. Kindergarten to Grade 11. Co-educational, evangelical, interdenominational. Three terms a year. Fees: $290 per term K-6; $300 per term Grades 7-11. Anticipated 10% increase for September 1983. Classes; Monday through Friday, 9 a.m. to 3 p.m. K-6; 8:30 a.m. to 3:00 p.m. Grades 7-12. Accommodates 650 children. Apply to Mrs. Carol Harrison, Principal, P.O. Box N4378, Nassau, Bahamas, Tel. 4-2158.

Queen's College — Village Road. Methodist. Co-educational for children 3½ to 11 (primary school) and 11 to 19 (high school). Three terms. Fees, which are subject to change, are as follows: $340 per term for Early Learning Centre, $380 per term for primary school students. Grades 7-9, $430 per term; Grades 10-11 $450; Grade 12, $500. The school maintains a Sixth Form ($600 per term) where students pursue A-level studies in selected subjects. Incidental fees include uniforms, materials for practical subjects and selected workbooks. Included in the fee is the rental cost for textbooks and the cost of exercise books. Students may take the Bahamas Junior Certificate and the G.C.E. of London University, Ordinary and Advanced Levels. Enrolment, approx. 1,400. Teachers: 87. Apply to Charles Sweeting, Principal, Queen's College, P.O. Box N7127, Nassau, Bahamas, Tel. 3-2153, 3-1666 or 3-2646.

St. Andrews School — Yamacraw Road. Non-denominational. Co-educational, for students three to 17. Three terms. $380 to $860 per term depending on class and age. Incidental fees: uniforms. Students take G.C.E. examinations of London University and the SSAT, PSAT, SAT, and AP tests. Enrolment: approx. 850. Teachers: 46. Apply to Headmaster, St. Andrew's School, P.O. Box N750, Nassau, Bahamas, Tel. 4-2621.

St. Anne's School — Fox Hill. Anglican. Co-educational, for students five to 18. Three terms per year; Preparatory Department $260 per term; Senior Department $320 per term. Incidental fees: uniforms, books, equipment. St. Anne's students have the advantage of taking horseback riding lessons, at a reduced rate, at St. Anne's Riding School which is adjacent to the School. Students take the Bahamas Junior Certificate Examinations, the G.C.E. 'O' Levels of London University, Pitman's English, French, Spanish, Pitmanscript, Typewriting and Accounts, R.S.A. Arithmetic and Mathematics, American P.S.A.T. and S.A.T. Admission to the Senior Department is by examination. Enrolment: approx. 728. Teachers: 27, Senior Department; 9, Preparatory Department. Principal, Father Patrick Adderley; Deputy Headteacher Preparatory Department, Mrs. Paula Small. For admission, apply to the Principal, St. Anne's School, P.O. Box SS6256, Nassau, Bahamas, Tel. 4-1203 (Senior Department), 4-1481 (Preparatory Department).

St. John's College — John F. Kennedy Drive. Co-educational, for students five to 19. Three terms; Preparatory Department $260 per term; Senior Department $320 per term. Incidental fees: uniforms, books, equipment. Students take the G.C.E. of London University at Ordinary Level, RSA and Pitmans examinations. Admission to the Senior Department is by examination. Enrolment approx. 1,000. Teachers: 34 full-time in Senior Department, 14 full-time in Preparatory Department. Apply to Principal, St. John's College, P.O. Box N4858, Nassau, Bahamas, Tel. 2-3783.

Jordan-Prince Williams School — Cowpen Road. For children four to 18 years. Three terms a year; Primary section $185 per term; Senior section $265 per term. Incidentals: uniforms, text books. Senior section students may take B.J.C., R.S.A., and G.C.E. of London University at Ordinary Level. Commercial subjects and Physics also offered. Enrolment:600.Apply to Principal, Jordan-Prince Williams School, P.O. Box GT2198, Nassau, Bahamas, Tel. 5-5546-7.

PRIVATE SECONDARY SCHOOLS

St. Augustine's College — Bernard Road. Roman Catholic. Co-educational. Ages 11 to 18. Education equivalent to British comprehensive schools, incorporating elements of American junior and senior high schools. Three terms per year, $930 per year. Students may take examination for G.C.E. of London University at Ordinary Level. In addition, the SAT is taken in the final year for admission to American colleges and universities. Entrance examinations are held in February each year. Enrolment: 997. Teachers: three priests, one deacon, one brother, three nuns and 56 lay teachers. Apply Principal, St. Augustine's College, P.O. Box N3940, Nassau, Bahamas, Tel. 4-1511.

GOVERNMENT SECONDARY SCHOOL

Government High School — Yellow Elder Gardens. Co-educational for students 14 and older. Three terms per year, no tuition fees. Incidental expenses: uniforms and book deposit. Students may take the G.C.E. of London University and RSA Pitmans examinations. They may also take College Entrance Board examinations for American colleges. For admission, apply to Principal, P.O. Box N726, Nassau, Bahamas, Tel. 5-6492.

HIGHER EDUCATION

College of the Bahamas — Government-sponsored college built on the community college concept. The institution, which is housed on two campuses, Oakes Field and Soldier Road, in Nassau, offers a wide range of programmes leading to Advanced Level G.C.E. (London), the Associate Degree, College Diplomas and Certificates. The academic programmes of the College are the responsibility of the six academic divisions: Business and Administrative Studies, Education, Humanities, Natural Science, Social Science and Division of Technology. The College in co-operation with two foreign universities, offers degree programmes in Education, Business and Technology: University of Miami, Bachelor of Business Administration; University of the West Indies, Bachelor of Education and Diploma in Education

The new Division of Continuing Education also has academic programmes as a part of its responsibility.

The College operates on a semester system with two semesters, September-December and January-April, and one summer session May-June. Tuition fees are currently $25 per credit hour per semester for Bahamians, and $50 for non-Bahamians. Enrolment for the Spring of 1983 was 1,546 students. Enquiries and applications should be sent to Registrar, College of the Bahamas, P.O. Box N-4912, Nassau, Bahamas.

SCHOOLS FOR THE HANDICAPPED

Red Cross Centre for Deaf Children — Horseshoe Drive. Government-assisted. Pre-school through 18, some in special classes in government primary and senior high schools. Help also given to hard of hearing children in ordinary classes. No tuition fees. Co-educational. General studies with the help of modern hearing aid equipment. Classes from 9 a.m. to 3 p.m. Ten specialist teachers. Enrolment: 49. Also parental guidance and testing facilities. Apply to Mrs. Paulamae Darcy, Red Cross Centre for Deaf Children, P.O. Box N91, Nassau, Bahamas, Tel. 3-6767.

School for the Blind and Visually Handicapped — Mackey Street, The Salvation Army. Co-educational for school-aged children daily. Special adult classes. Cassette service programme for home use provided in Nassau and the Family Islands. Instruction: general knowledge, reading Braille, elementary subjects and Scripture. Also, mobility, group discussion, music and techniques of daily living. Apply to Captain Henry L. Arrowood, P.O. Box N1980, Nassau, Bahamas, Tel. 5-2445 or 5-4889.

Stapledon School — Situated on Dolphin Drive, is co-sponsored by the Bahamas Association for the Mentally Retarded and the Ministry of Education. It is co-educational for educable and trainable mentally retarded. 9 a.m. to 3 p.m. Enrolment is 165 and there are 22 teachers. Tuition is $40 per term and bus fees are $5 weekly. Apply to Headmistress, Stapledon School, P.O. Box N4270, Nassau, Bahamas, Tel. 3-4669 or 3-6000.

Electricity

In New Providence, electricity is generated by the Bahamas Electricity Corporation at three locations: Clifton Pier, Blue Hills and Soldier Road. Three steam turbines and one diesel-driven alternator are used at Clifton Pier (three additional diesel generators are presently being installed), one combined cycle unit and four gas turbines at Blue Hills and two diesel alternators at Soldier Road

The Corporation is active in the Family Islands, generating and distributing electricity in North and South Bimini; North and Central Andros; Cooper's Town, Abaco; Great Exuma; San Salvador and Great Harbour Cay.

NEW PROVIDENCE/PARADISE AND FAMILY ISLANDS
Total annual units (kwh) generated by BEC:

1977-78	366,000,000
1978-79	386,000,000
1979-80	390,000,000
1980-81	383,000,000
1981-82	414,000,000

Each year's figure refers to the 12-month period ending September 30, i.e., the 1977-78 figure reflects from October 1, 1977 to September 30, 1978.

Total electricity consumers connected by BEC on New Providence, Paradise Island and the Family Islands as of September 30, 1982 was 36,217.

Total Installed Capacity — 127.2 MW
Maximum Demand 1982 — 67 MW
Supply Voltages and Frequency
> 3 phase, 4 wire, 208/120 volts, 60 cycles.
> 1 phase, 3 wire, 240/120 volts, 60 cycles.

Tariffs in New Providence & Paradise Island:
The principal rates are:

(a) **Residential** (Quarterly)
For each unit of electricity — 8.36¢
Minimum charge of $7.87 per quarter.

Residential (Monthly)
For each unit of electricity — 8.36¢
Minimum charge of $2.62 per month

(b) **Commercial**
Maximum demand not exceeding 10 KVA:

1. Quarterly

First 180 units per quarter	— 11.75¢ per unit
Next 6420 units per quarter	— 9.25¢ per unit
Remaining units per quarter	— 7.25¢ per unit

Minimum charge of $15.75 per quarter

2. Monthly

First 60 units per month	— 11.75¢ per unit
Next 2140 units per month	— 9.25¢ per unit
Remaining units per month	— 7.25¢ per unit

Minimum charge of $5.25 per month

3. Maximum demand exceeding 10 KVA:

First 200 KVA	— $54.60 per KVA per annum
Next 400 KVA	— $49.80 per KVA per annum
Remainder	— $45.00 per KVA per annum
Unit charge up to 100,000	— 7.25¢ per unit per month
Excess of 100,000	5.95¢ per unit per month

Minimum charge of $4.55 per month x KVA demand

(c) Surcharge Provisions

The basic rates and charges are increased by a surcharge of 4.00 cents for each unit of electricity consumed in each billing period.

That surcharge is increased or decreased by 0.03 cents per unit for each increase or decrease of $1.00 above or below $126.00 per long ton in the weighted average price paid by the Corporation for automotive diesel oil during the three months prior to the month of billing; and by 0.01 cents per unit for each increase or decrease of $1.00 above or below $80.00 per long ton paid by the Corporation for bunker 'c' fuel oil during the three months prior to the month of billing.

No variation in the surcharge exceeding 10% of the surcharge of 4.00 cents per unit can take effect in any month without the approval of the Minister of Works and Utilities.

Temporary Supplies
For electricity supplied for service of a temporary nature:

(a) 11.75¢ per unit consumed
(b) $10 connection fee
(c) Meter rental, $5 per month
(d) Cost of installing the connection

The service may be disconnected without notice should it be used to supply any part of a permanent electrical installation which has not been inspected and passed by the Ministry of Works' inspector, or if the premises are being used for residential or business purposes.

Other charges
- (a) Special Reading — $2.50
- (b) Connection or disconnection other than on occasion of change of consumer — $2.50
- (c) Meter Test — minimum — $5.00
- (d) Replacement of consumer's fuses — $2.50
- (e) Visit with intent to disconnect — $10.00
- (f) Reconnection after disconnection for non-payment — $15.00

FAMILY ISLANDS

Rates and charges to consumers in the Family Islands vary with the different utility companies and the size of their operations. In general, the rates and charges are higher than in New Providence and Freeport.

In the Family Islands all consumers are billed monthly.

- (a) **Residential**
  For each unit of electricity — 13.00¢
  Minimum charge of $2.40 per month

- (b) **Commercial**
  Maximum Demand exceeding 10 KVA:
  ALL KVA — $48.00 per KVA per annum

First 20,000 units per month	— 11.50¢
Next 20,000 units per month	— 11.00¢
Next 20,000 units per month	— 10.50¢
Remaining units per month	— 10.00¢

  Minimum charge — $4.00 x KVA per month

- (c) **Surcharge Provisions**
  1. The basic rates and charges made by reference to units of electricity consumed (however expressed), are increased by a surcharge of 9.15¢ for each unit of electricity consumed in every billing period.
  2. The surcharge of 9.15¢ for each unit of electricity consumed referred to above shall be increased or decreased in respect of units of electricity consumed by the amount of 0.034 cents per unit for each increase or decrease, as the case may require, of $1.00 above or below $275.10 per long ton in the weighted average price paid by the Corporation for automotive diesel oil delivered at Clifton Pier on the Island of New Providence during the month prior to the month of billing; provided that no variation in the

surcharge exceeding 10% of the surcharge mentioned in (a) above shall take effect in any month without prior approval in writing from the Minister.

Employers' Organizations

Bahamas Assn. of Land Surveyors, P.O. Box N7782, Nassau.
Bahamas Assn. of Social Workers, P.O. Box GT2699, Nassau.
Bahamas Beauticians & Cosmetologists Employers Assn.
Bahamas Boatmens' Assn., P.O. Box N552, Nassau.
Bahamas Employers Confederation, P.O. Box N166, Nassau.
Bahamas Employers Confederation, P.O. Box F650, Freeport, Grand Bahama.
Bahamas Glass Bottom Boat Assn., P.O. Box N552, Nassau.
Bahamas Hotel Employers' Assn., P.O. Box N7799, Nassau.
Bahamas Manufacturers Agents and Wholesalers Assn., P.O. Box N272, Nassau.
Bahamas Mechanical Contractors Assn., P.O. Box N14316, Nassau.
Bahamas Motor Dealers Assn., P.O. Box N4177, Nassau.
Bahamas Professional Photographers Assn., P.O. Box N586, Nassau.
Bahamas Real Estate Dealers Assn., P.O. Box N4051, Nassau.
Bahamas Soft Drink Bottlers Assn., P.O. Box N272, Nassau.
Bahamas Supermarket Operators Assn., P.O. Box N4206, Nassau.
Bahamas Contractors Assn., P.O. Box N4632, Nassau.
Bahamas Welding Contractors Assn., P.O. Box N1283, Nassau.
Corporation of Accountants & Auditors, P.O. Box N1669, Nassau.
Freeport Hotels and Restaurants Employers' Assn., P.O. Box F2623, Freeport, Grand Bahama.
Nassau Assn. of Shipping Agents, P.O. Box N1451, Nassau.
Professional Photographers Assn., P.O. Box N7458, Nassau.

Engineering Firms

*Anthony B. Dean & Associates Ltd.
*George V. Cox & Partners
*Paul Hanna & Associates
*O'Brien Engineering Co. Ltd.
*Coburn E. Sands

*The Bahamas Institution of Professional Engineers was formed in 1972 and at least one staff member of each firm listed above is a member of the institution.

Exchange Control

Exchange Control is the imposition of rules and regulations on transactions whereby a country conserves its foreign currency resources. In The Bahamas, Exchange Control is administered by The Central Bank of the Bahamas. The Central Bank is, therefore, responsible for the control and regulation of gold and foreign currency under the Exchange Control Act 1952 and the Exchange Control Regulations 1956.

Legal Tender. The Bahamian dollar is legal tender in the Commonwealth of the Bahamas; all other currencies are foreign.

Residential Status. For Exchange Control purposes in the Bahamas, the countries of the world have been divided into two categories — the Bahamas and the rest of the world. The Central Bank has the authority to determine residential status of all persons (including legal entities). Resident individuals are either citizens of the Bahamas or citizens of other countries who have been so designated by the Bank. Residents are subject to many, although, in most instances, liberal Exchange Control Regulations. For example, residents in the Bahamas may not purchase foreign currency, maintain foreign currency accounts or remit foreign currency abroad without the prior permission of the Central Bank.

Non-resident individuals are citizens of a country outside the Bahamas who may reside in the Bahamas but are not gainfully employed in the Bahamas. These persons are subject to minimal currency regulations. Foreign currency deposits held by non-residents are exempt from Exchange Control regulations.

Foreign citizens who are gainfully employed within the Bahamas for one year or longer are regarded as "temporary residents". Such persons may be eligible for certain exemptions which permit them to retain all existing non-Bahamian assets, to operate foreign currency accounts and to repatriate Bahamian assets on leaving the Bahamas.

Investment Currency. This is a pool of foreign currency which is available for capital investment abroad by residents. Central Bank permission is required for the acquisition and disposition of investment currency. Investment currency changes hands at a premium, and the premium is determined by the demand and supply for the foreign currency.

Authorized Agents/Dealers. The Central Bank appoints Authorized Agents for the purpose of dealing in Bahamian and foreign currency securities and receiving securities into deposit. Authorized Dealers are banks that are permitted to deal in all foreign currencies, and are also appointed by the Central Bank to approve certain Exchange Control applications under delegated authority. This authority is laid out in the Exchange Control Notices. Presently there are 11 Authorized Agents and 10 Authorized Dealers.

Direct Investment. This works two ways — by non-residents inward and residents outward.
1. The prior permission of the Central Bank is required for a non-resident to invest (i.e. business, property, etc.) in the Bahamas. If the non-resident investment in the Bahamas is made with foreign currency which is converted to Bahamian dollars, it is accorded "approved status". "Approved status" facilitates the investor's repatriation of income and capital gains which may accrue from his investment.
2. Permission for resident companies in the Bahamas to extend their business outside the Bahamas depends largely on the

probability of a good return to the Bahamas via increased income of foreign currency and/or increased exports. Direct investment outside the Bahamas must be an extension of an existing business within the Bahamas. Foreign currency to finance direct outward investments is normally purchased through the investment currency market.

Purchase of Property Outside The Bahamas. Residents of the Bahamas are permitted to purchase property outside the Bahamas for use by the family. If the application is approved by the Central Bank, the foreign currency necessary to acquire the property must be purchased through the investment currency market.

Loans. Resident companies which are owned wholly or partially by a non-resident require the prior permission of Exchange Control to borrow Bahamian dollars and foreign currency. Resident companies wholly owned by residents, and resident individuals require Exchange Control permission to borrow foreign currency.

Dollar Cards. Residents may submit application to the Central Bank for a Dollar Card. This card permits the resident to purchase foreign currency drafts up to $1,000. The card is used to purchase personal items and to pay credit card bills.

Payment for Imports. The prior permission of Exchange Control is required for the purchase of foreign currency for payment of imports. The Authorized Dealers in the Family Islands, however, have been authorized by the Central Bank to sell foreign currency for imports without prior Central Bank permission. Application for the purchase of foreign currency to pay for imports must be accompanied by a relevant invoice.

Allowances. Residents of the Bahamas are normally permitted to convert $1,000 into foreign currency per year for personal and holiday travel purposes. Foreign currency may also be obtained for business travel, medical, educational and other purposes.

Emigration. A resident leaving the Bahamas must apply to the Central Bank to convert his Bahamian assets. Currently he is permitted to convert up to B$25,000 into foreign currency at the official rate of exchange. His remaining assets are blocked for a period of four years. If he wishes to convert his blocked assets within the four-year period, he has to go through the investment currency market, which involves paying a premium on all foreign currency purchased. However, immediately after leaving, the emigrant is permitted to convert all income accruing from his Bahamian assets at the official rate of exchange. Temporary residents are permitted to repatriate all of their Bahamian dollar balances.

Export Entry

An Export Entry Form is required for goods being exported from the Bahamas. Forms are available at several Nassau book shops and office supply stores. The completed forms should be taken to the Central Bank, between Frederick and Market Sts., Nassau, for authorization; then to Customs.

Ordinary parcels, clothing, gifts, tourist items, etc., to be sent through Post Offices or Parcel Post do not require an Export Entry Form. See also **Customs.**

Fishing

The beautiful and tranquil waters of the Bahamas produce a great variety of game- and food-fish, and anglers from many other parts of the world come here to test their skill. Modern facilities to accommodate sports fishermen are available throughout most of the Bahamas.

Following is a list of some of the game species found in Bahamian waters, with a guide to seasons and locations when and where they can be caught.

Allison tuna: Best months are June, July and August, though season runs off and on throughout the year. Best place — all deepwater areas of the Bahamas.

Amberjack: November through May. Look for it near all reef areas and around old wrecks throughout the islands.

Barracuda: Year round. Found throughout the Bahamas, especially near reefs. Also in shallow water, and occasionally offshore.

Blackfin tuna: May through September. Very plentiful in vicinity of Nassau.

Bluefin (Giant) tuna: May 7 to June 15. Bimini, Cat Cay and West End, Grand Bahama.

Blue marlin: Off and on throughout the year but the best months are June and July. It's found all along the western side of the Bahamas, from Bimini and Cat Cay to Walker's Cay; off Andros, at the Berry Islands near Chub Cay; both sides of Exuma Sound and in the Atlantic Ocean from Eleuthera north to Green Turtle Cay, Abaco.

Bonefish: Year-round. This king of the shallow waters can be found in quantity throughout the islands. Three world record bonefish were caught in the Bahamas.

Dolphin: Winter and spring. All deepwater areas.

Grouper: Year-round. All reefs throughout the Bahamas.

Kingfish: May, June and July. Good fishing all over, but Berry Islands and western Abaco are among the best spots.

Sailfish: Summer and fall. Berry Islands, Chub Cay, Bimini, Cat Cay, West End, Walker's Cay and Exuma Sound.

Tarpon: Year-round. Best bets are Andros and Bimini.

Wahoo: November through April, with best months January and February. Most plentiful in Exuma Sound around the cays and at the lower end of Eleuthera. Other good areas — Northeast Providence Channel from Nassau to Spanish Wells and in the Northwest Providence Channel around the Berry Islands and off Sandy Point, Abaco.

White marlin: Winter and spring. From Bimini, east to Eleuthera, and from Walker's Cay south to Exuma Sound in the ocean, or the deep channels nearby.

Licences: Legislation still in the drafting stage may require sports fishermen to obtain licences to fish in Bahamian waters. Direct inquiries to the Ministry of Agriculture and Fisheries (see address at end of section). All foreign sports fishing vessels must make an official entry at a Port of Entry in the Bahamas, before starting to fish. See page 314.

It is an offence against the Bahamas' penal code for foreign vessels to engage in commercial fishing in Bahamian waters. No permits are granted to foreign vessels to fish, except for scientific research operations carried out by bona fide institutions of higher learning.

Licences are required for the export of fish and all other marine products from the Bahamas. This includes the export of live fish for aquarium purposes, and in this case licences are issued strictly to a few scientific institutions.

Underwater Fishing (Spearfishing). It is ILLEGAL:
  (a) To use underwater breathing apparatus, other than a snorkel, to capture any fish or marine product.
  (b) To use any device, other than a Hawaiian Sling, for the discharge of a missile under water. (The Hawaiian Sling is identified as a device — usually made of wood or plastic — for the discharge of a missile under water by the force of a rubber spring.)

It is prohibited to take, capture, or kill any kind of marine product by spearfishing within certain areas around New Providence, including The Narrows, lying between Paradise Island and Athol Island, and the Sea Gardens, while using underwater apparatus.

In the words of the Ministry of Agriculture and Fisheries:

"It is prohibited to take, capture or kill any marine product whilst using underwater apparatus (including the Hawaiian Sling) in the inshore waters on the eastern, northern and western sides of New Providence Island (Nassau) in that body of water extending Northwardly from the coast line of New Providence Island between East End Point and Clifton Point and bounded: on the East, by an imaginary line drawn from East End Point to the eastern end of Athol Island; on the North, by an imaginary line joining Athol Island, Paradise Island, Silver Cay, Long Cay and North Cay (Balmoral Island), thence to an imaginary point one mile due North of Northwest Point (New Providence) and thence to another imaginary point one mile due west of Goulding Cay; and, on the Southwest, by an imaginary line drawn from the said point one mile due West of Goulding Cay to Clifton Point. It includes the waters lying between Paradise Island and Athol Island known as The Narrows and which comprises the area known as The Sea Gardens."

Prohibited Areas. It is unlawful to remove, by any means, any marine product from the bottom of the seas in the area referred to above as the Sea Gardens. Also, it is unlawful to take, capture, kill, uproot or destroy any marine product other than fish or crawfish within a half-mile of the coast (at low water mark) of Balmoral Island (North Cay). Capture of fish or crawfish with underwater apparatus is prohibited in the southern half of this area.

Sponges. No person other than a Bahamian may fish for, take or gather any sponge. The use of dredges for taking sponges is prohibited, as is the use of any diving apparatus except for scientific investigation under permit.

Bonefish. Legislation for bonefish is concerned mainly with prohibition of netting in the interests of sport fishing for this species. It is an offence to buy or sell bonefish in, or within, three miles of New Providence.

Turtles. Strict regulations cover the landing of turtles for sale, both in New Providence and the Family Islands. Main laws are:
    (a)   It is an offence to take or capture turtles on any beach.
    (b)   The taking, buying and selling of turtles' eggs is an offence.
    (c)   From April 1 to June 30, inclusive, it is **closed season** on the taking of Loggerhead turtles.
    (d)   Minimum size limit for the Hawksbill turtle is 17 inches from neck scales to tail pieces. For the Green turtle, it is 15 inches from neck scales to tail pieces.

Crawfish (Spiny Lobster). Closed season for crawfish is from April 1 to July 31, inclusive. During this period, it is an offence to fish for, or to possess, live or fresh crawfish.

The minimum size limits for crawfish are: — a carapace length of 3⅜ inches from the base of the horns to the end of the jacket, or an overall weight of one pound or a tail weight of five ounces.

No person shall have in his possession, sell, expose or offer for sale any egg-bearing crawfish or any crawfish from which eggs have been clipped or otherwise removed.

The use of anything other than a Hawaiian Sling or Pole Spear is prohibited for the taking of crawfish as fresh food. Traps for the capture of crawfish may only be used by persons who have obtained the necessary permit from the Ministry of Agriculture & Fisheries, P.O. Box N3028, Nassau.

Bahamian fishermen must make application for licences for export of crawfish prior to July 10 of each year. Applications should be made in writing to the Ministry of Agriculture and Fisheries.

Stone Crab. It is an offence to take, kill or be in possession of stone crabs within two miles of the coast of the Biminis and of Grand Bahama.

Conch (Strombus gigas). In the interest of dietary requirements in the Bahamas, there is a total prohibition on the export of edible conch meat, and/or shells, except that, under licence, permission may be given for the export of cut shell-lip for cameo manufacture or crushed shell for terrazzo manufacture, and conch products that consist of 40% or less of edible conch.

The Ministry of Agriculture and Fisheries, P.O. Box N3028, Nassau, may be consulted for further information.

Flora

Listed below are some flora found in the Bahamas.

TREES: African Tulip (*Spathodea campanulata*), Australian Pine (*Casuarina*), Bead Tree (*Adenanthera pavonina*), Black Mangrove (*Avicennia germinans*), Bottle Brush (*Callistemon*), Buttercup Tree (*Cochlospermum vitifolii*), Butterfly Flower (*Bauhinia*), Buttonwood (*Conocarpus erectus*), Calabash (*Crescentia cujete*), Cancer Tree (*Jacaranda coerulea*), Cedar (*Cedrela odorata*), Cork Tree (*Thespesia populnea*), Dogwood (*Piscidia piscipula*), Dutchman's Pipe (*Ilex cassine*), Ficus (Rubber Tree) (*Ficus elastica*), Five Fingers (Poui) (*Tabebouia bahamensis*), Frangipani (*Plumeria*), Golden Shower (*Cassia fistula*), Gumelemi (Gumbo-Limbo)(*Bursera simaruba*), Horseflesh (*Caesalpinia vesicaria*), Horse Radish (*Moringa oleifera*), Humming-Bird Trumpet (*Tabebuia*), Jerusalem Thorn (*Parkinsonia aculeata*), Jumbie Bean (Jumbay) (*Leucaena glauca*), Lignum Vitae (*Guaiacum sanctum*) (National tree), Manchioneel (*Iley cassine*), Mangrove (*Rhyzophora mangle*), Milkberry (Wild Saffron) (*Bumelia americana*), Monkey Fiddle (*Araucaria*), Shaving Brush Tree (*Pachira insignis*), Palms — Coconut, Date, Fan, Fishtail, Pond Top, Royal, Silver Thatch (*Palmae*); Pain in Back (*Trema lamarckiana*), Pine — Norfolk Island, Yellow (*Pinus caribea*); Poison Wood (*Metopium toxiferum*), Poor Man's Orchid (*Bauhinia*), Pride of India (*Lagerstroemia speciosa*), Quick Silver (*Thouinia discolor*), Rose of Venezuela (*Brownea grandiceps*), Royal Poinciana (*Delonix regia*), Sandbox (*Hura crepitans*), Satin Leaf (*Chrysophyllum oliviforme*), Sea Hibiscus (*Mahoe thespesia*), Wild Mammee (*Clusia rosea*), Woman's Tongue (*Albizzia lebbek*), Yellow Elder (National Flower of the Bahamas) (*Stenolobium stans*).

SHRUBS: Angel's Trumpet (*Datura arborea*), Aralia (*Polyscias balfouriana*), Bahamas Blue Pea (*Clitorea ternata*), Crepe Myrtle (*Lagerstroemia indica*), Croton (*Codiaeum*), Four O'Clock (*Mirabilis jalapa*), Gardenia (*Gardenia augusta*), Governor Bailey (*Clerodendrum splendens*), Hibiscus (*Hibiscus*), Jasmine (Madagascar) (*Stephanotis floribunda*), Joe Bush (*Jacquinia*), Lucky Seed (*Thevetiana peruviana*), Match-Me-If-You-Can (*Acalypha*), Natal Plum (*Carissa grandiflora*), Oleander (*Nerium oleander*), Pearl Necklace (*Sophora tomentosa*), Pigeon Berry (*Duranta excelsa*), Plumbago (*Plumbago capensis*), Poinsettia (*Euphorbia pulcherrima*),Pride of Barbados (*Caesalpinia pulcherrima*), Saga (*Lantana*), Show Berry (*Chiococca pinetorum*), Sea Lavender (*Statice latifolia*), Shell Ginger (*Alpinia speciosa*), Strong Back (*Bourreria ovata*), Snakeroot (Bitter Bush) (*Picrodendron baccatum*), Sweet Margaret (Guanaberry) (*Drypetes diversifolia*), Turk's Cap (*Malvaviscus arboreus*), Wild Guava (*Catesbaea spinosa*).

CLIMBERS & VINES: Allamanda (*Allamanda cathartica*), Bleeding Heart (*Clerodendrum thomsonae*), Cereus (Night Blooming) (*Hylocereus undatus*), Chalice Flower (*Solandra guttata*), Christmas Flower (*Turbina corymbosa*), Dipladenia (*Dipladenia amoena*), Honeysuckle (*Tecomaria capensis*), Love Vine (*Cuscuta*), Mexican Flame Vine (*Senecio confusus*), Moon Flower (*Calonyction aculeatum*), Pandora Vine (*Podranea ricasoliana*), Paper Flower (*Bougainvillea*), Passion Flower (*Passiflora*), Potato Vine (*Solanum jasminum*), Queen's Wreath (*Petrea*), Rangoon Creeper (*Quis qualis indica*), Sky Blue Flower (*Thunbergia*), Stephanotis (*Stephanotis floribunda*), Virginia

Creeper (*Parthenosissus quinquefolia*), Coral Vine (*Antigonon leptopus*), Easter Lily Vine (*Beaumontia grandiflora*).

GRASSES: Bamboo (*Bambusa*), Guinea Grass (*Panicum maximum*), Sugar Cane (*Saccharum officinarum*).

LILIES: Aloe (*Aloe vera*), Century Plant (*Agave americana*), Spanish Bayonet (*Yucca aloifolia*).

TUBEROUS PLANTS: Elephant's Ear (*Caladium*).

SUCCULENTS: Humming-Bird Cactus (*Pedilanthus tithymaloides*), Life-Leaf (*Bryophyllum*).

CACTUS: Queen of the Night (*Selenicereus grandiflorus*).

FRUIT TREES: Avocado pear (*Persea americana*), Banana (*Musa spp.*), Barbados cherry (*Malpighia glabra*), Beach almond (*Terminalia catappa*), Breadfruit (*Artocarpus communis*), Cashew (*Anacardium occidentale*), Coconut (*Cocos nucifera*), Date (*Phoenix dactylifera*), Fig (*Ficus carica*), Genip (*Melicocca bijuga*), Governor's plum (*Flacourtia indica*), Grapes (*Vitis spp.*), Guava (*Psidium guajava*), Grapefruit, tangerine, orange, sour orange, lime, lemon, shaddock, calamondin (*citrus spp.*), Kumquat (*Fortunella spp.*), Longan (*Euphoria longan*), Loquat (*Eriobotrya japonica*), Lychee (*Litchi chinensis*), Mamey (*Mammea spp.*), Mango (*Mangifera indica*), Natal plum (*Carissa grandiflora*), Papaya (*Carica papaya*), Passion fruit, granadilla (*Passiflora spp.*), Peach (*Prunus persica*), Pineapple (*Ananas comosus*), Plantain (*Musa paradisiaca*), Sapodilla (*Achras zapota*), Sea grape (*Coccoloba uvifera*), Strawberry (*Fragaria spp.*), Surinam cherry (*Eugenia uniflora*), Soursop, custard apple, sugar apple (*Annona spp.*), Tamarind (*Tamarindus indica*), Tung oil (*Aleurities fordii*), Pomegranate (*Punica granatum*).

FRUIT VINES: Cantaloup, cucumber, musk melon, watermelon (*Cucumis*).

VEGETABLES: Beans — Red, Lima, White (*Legumes*); Beetroot (*Beta vulgaris*), Breadfruit (*Artocarpus incisus*), Broccoli (*Brassica olerace*), Brussel Sprouts (*Brassica olerace*), Cabbage (*Brassica olerace*), Carrot (*Daucus carota*), Cauliflower (*Brassica olerace botrytis*), Celery (*Apium graveiens*), Cho-Cho (*Sechium edule*), Corn (*Zea mays*), Eddoe (*Colocasia esculenta*), Eggplant (*Solanum melongena*), Lettuce (*Lactuca sativa*), Okra (*Hibiscus esculentus*), Onion (*Allium cepa*), Peas — Pigeon (*Cajanus indicus*), Sweet (*Pisum sativum*), Peppers — Sweet, Hot (*Capsicum*), Potato — Irish (*Solanum tuberosum*), Sweet (*Ipomoea batatas*); Pumpkin (*Cucurbita pepo*), Radish (*Raphanus sativus*), Shallot (*Allium*), Spinach (*Amaranthus caudatus*), Squash (*Cucurbita pepo*), Swiss Chard (*Lactuca*), Tomato (*Lycopersicon esculentum*), Turnip (*Brassica rapa*), Watercress (*Lepidium sativum*), Yam (*Dioscorea*).

HERBS: Basil (*Ocimum basilicum*), Chives (*Allium schoenoprasum*), Dill (*Peucedanum graveolens*), Parsley (*Petroselinum crispum*), Sage (*Salvia officinalis*), Thyme (*Thymus vulgaris*).

Freight Services

Goods to be sent air freight from New Providence should be taken to Nassau International Airport for handling by the airlines which will transport them — or to a forwarding agent.

Goods to be sent via ship should be taken to the shipping company office or to the dock, depending on company policy. Or delivery can be handled through a forwarding agent.

Incoming Freight

There is a $5 minimum overstay charge by all Nassau-operating airlines for shipments under 100 pounds left at air cargo sections beyond 48 hours, plus $1 per 100 pounds or part thereof for each additional day.

Freight not claimed at the dock within five days is sent to a government warehouse for holding. There is a charge for transporting the goods to the warehouse as well as a storage fee.

Gambling

Casino gambling is legal in the Bahamas. At present, there are three casinos — at New Providence, at Paradise Island and at Freeport, Grand Bahama. All are owned by the Government's Hotel Corporation. A third government-owned casino, the Monte Carlo at Freeport/ Lucaya, was still under construction early in 1983, but was scheduled to be completed in the latter half of that year.

The casinos at Paradise Island and Freeport are operated by subsidiary companies of Resorts International Inc., viz, Paradise Enterprises Limited and G.B. Management Limited, respectively. At press time it was not known who would operate the Corporation's projected casino to be located in a convention complex planned for the Cable Beach, New Providence, area. Meanwhile, Playboy Clubs operates, on behalf of the Corporation, a casino* located in The Ambassador Beach Hotel, Cable Beach.

Visitors have a choice of games, including roulette, black-jack, baccarat, dice, slot machines and the wheel of fortune commonly known as the 'big six'. **Bahamians and Bahamas residents are prohibited from gambling in the casinos under a maximum penalty of a $500 fine.**

Hobby Horse Hall racetrack was closed in 1977. Since then a number of reports have circulated relative to the construction of a new racetrack in the Gladstone Road area for both horse and dog racing. At press time, no official announcement had been made by the Government to confirm such proposals.

Geography

The Bahamas, an independent state within the Commonwealth of Nations, comprises a 100,000 square mile archipelago that extends for over 500 miles between southeast Florida and northern Hispaniola; between longitudes 72°40'W and 80°45'W and latitudes 20°45'N and 28°N.

The waters surrounding the Bahamas are virtually free of pollution and silt, making them among the clearest and most colourful in the world. Bordered on the west by the great "ocean river" known as the Gulf Stream, the islands have a near-perfect climate. Other geographical features are land elevations up to 206 feet. Some of the deepest water in the world is in the Tongue of the Ocean east of Andros Island. Approximately one mile deep, these waters off Andros are utilized for oceanographic research by scientists of the Atlantic Undersea Testing and Evaluation Centre (AUTEC), a multi-million dollar joint U.S.-U.K. research base. Tongue of the Ocean is flanked by one of the world's longest barrier reefs.

* *Closed August, 1983.*

The estimated land area of the Bahamas has been listed as 5,358 square miles by the Department of Lands and Surveys. (Figures are subject to change as more accurate surveys and maps are completed.) Land area of islands, as well as their highest point, is as follows:

Islands	Highest Point (Feet)	Area (Sq. Mi.)
Abaco	120	649
Acklins	142	150
Andros	102	2,300
Berry Is.	80	12
Bimini	20	9
Cat Is.	206	150
Cay Sal Bank	10	2
Conception Is.	66	4
Crooked Is.	155	92
Eleuthera	168	200
Exuma (Gt. & Lt.)	125	72
Exuma Cays	130	40
Grand Bahama	68	530
Inagua (Gt.)	120	596
Inagua (Lt.)	99	49
Little San Salvador	93	8
Long Cay	108	9
Long Is.	178	173
Mayaguana	131	110
New Providence	123	80
Plana Cays	63	6
Ragged Is.	116	9
Rum Cay	130	30
San Salvador	123	63
Samana Cay	80	15

Total: 5,358

Grand Total including small, uninhabited rocks and islets, **about 5,400 square miles.**

Gun Permits

The Firearms Act, 1969 (amended 1974) sets out Government policy toward firearms, establishes comprehensive procedures for the control of their possession by private individuals and states fees payable.

Under the Act, there are three licensable categories: revolvers; rifles and other firearms and ammunition; and guns. The revolvers include all handguns, such as magazine-fed selfloaders, commonly called automatics, as well as cylinder-fed revolvers. Rifles are defined as including air rifles declared to be dangerous, but specifically applying to rimfire and centrefire shoulder arms. Guns mean smoothbore guns such as shotguns with barrels not less than 20 inches in length, and air guns not defined as specially dangerous.

Completely forbidden are tear-gas pens, military arms such as artillery, flame-throwers, machine guns and automatic carbines. Exempted from any licensing requirements are toy guns, dummy firearms, spear guns designed for underwater use.

Licensing procedures for each of the three legal firearms categories are as follows:

Revolvers

A special licence, granted very sparingly, is issued only by the Commissioner of Police. A person wishing to import or possess a revolver must fill out an application form. What the police consider a good reason must be given for the handgun's possession and must be verified by police investigation before the special licence is issued. The licence is then carried to Customs or Parcel Post, if the revolver is being imported, or to the dealer, if it is being purchased locally. Pistols being imported are subject to a Customs charge of $50 plus 12½ per cent of their value.

Rifles and other Firearms and Ammunition

An application form for the issue of a firearm certificate must be completed and handed in to the Commissioner of Police. A separate application must be made for each firearm and for each quantity of ammunition. Presentation of the certificate and payment of duty, if an import, will bring the rifle, firearm or ammunition into possession.

Guns

An application for a gun licence shall be made in New Providence to the Commissioner of Police and in any Family Island district to the commissioner of that district. A separate application must be made for each gun. Presentation of the gun licence, and payment of duty, if an import, will bring the gun into possession.

Fees

Gun licences issued under the Act are purchased for $10. Rifle licences cost $20. A revolver requires a special licence costing $20; and a dealer's licence sells for $50. All must be renewed annually. Licences and firearms certificates expire on the yearly anniversary of the date of issue.

Temporary Importation

Temporary importation of guns (excluding handguns) must be authorized by the Commissioner of Police. Presentation of the permit and a deposit for approximately double the amount of duty will bring the gun into possession. The deposit is returned when the gun is taken from the Commonwealth.

Exemption

Non-residents of the Bahamas visiting the islands aboard a foreign vessel are not required to obtain permits nor pay any fees or duty on firearms during a visit to the islands. This exemption is limited to three months following the arrival of the vessel at her first port of call. Three conditions are attached: Possession of firearms aboard the vessel must be declared to a Customs officer or a commissioner within 48 hours after the arrival of the vessel; the firearms are not used in the territorial waters of the Bahamas; and, they are not brought ashore.

A Note of Caution

If in any doubt as to proper procedure in importing a firearm into the Bahamas, it is suggested that it be left where it is, with arrangements made to send it along later after personal inquiries with the Police Commissioner's office.

Harbour Control

Nassau Harbour Control went into operation in 1974. This office controls and gives clearance to all ships entering and leaving the Harbour of Nassau. Also, permission must be obtained from Harbour Control for the movement from one berth to another while in the harbour. The office is in operation at all hours.

Small fishing boats or small pleasure craft should telephone Nassau Harbour Control at 2-1596 before leaving the harbour, so the whereabouts of these vessels can be ascertained in case they are later overdue.

The VHF radio frequencies of Harbour Control are: Channels 06, 09, 14, 16, 12, 68, 73, 74, 79, 20, 65 and 66. Bahamas Telecommunications Corporation maintains a constant watch on VHF Channel 16, the emergency frequency. For commercial traffic, VHF Channel 27 should be used through Nassau Marine Operator.

AM radio ship-to-ship frequencies are 2182, 2638 and 2738 kcs, however, 2638 and 2738 have been phased out, and cannot be re-licensed. They should be used only in emergencies. The international emergency frequency, 2182 kcs, is controlled by Bahamas Telecommunications Corporation. For commercial traffic, AM frequency 2198 should be used.

Single side band frequencies are 3300.0, 4139.5, 5057.0, 8100.0.

History

The history of the New World began here — with Christopher Columbus landing in 1492 on an island called Guanahani by the natives but which he renamed San Salvador.

The people he met he called "Indians." They called themselves **Lukku-cairi,** or "island people." Consequently, the surrounding islands were known by early Spanish explorers as the Lucayan Islands.

That name did not endure, as more notice was taken of the shallow water — **bajamar** in Spanish. Now, these 700 islands, set in shallow turquoise waters, are known as the **Bahamas.**

The Bahamas remained in Spanish hands for more than a century. But it took the Spaniards less than 20 years to annihilate the first inhabitants of the islands. The formerly happy "Indians" were shipped off to work the gold mines and to die in Hispaniola. Those first Bahamians are thought to have been Arawaks, a gentle people who arrived in the islands about 800 or 900 A.D. fleeing the fierce and cannibalistic Caribs from South America through the Antilles.

The Spanish took little interest in the islands after the potential for slave labour was gone. They moved on in their quest for gold and the Fountain of Youth.

In 1629, England's Charles I granted the Bahamas to Sir Robert Heath, his Attorney General. But Sir Robert was unable to meet the conditions of his charter. The Eleutherian Adventurers, a party of Englishmen hoping to found a new land of religious freedom, set out from Bermuda in 1647. They gave their name (Eleuthera, derived from the Greek word for "freedom") to the Bahamian island which they colonized.

The islands became a lair for notorious pirates for the next 70 years. Woodes Rogers, an ex-privateer appointed first Royal Governor, quelled the pirates in 1718.

Nassau was captured by yet another country during the American Revolution, when the fledgling United States Navy took the island with a comic no-shots-fired battle. The invaders relinquished their claim after two weeks.

Many Loyalist fled the U.S., however, moving even the stones of their American homes to the Bahamas.

In 1782 the Bahamas fell to Spain again, but the islands were returned to the British a year later and remained a British colony.

During the American Civil War, the Bahamas was a haven for Confederate blockade-runners. Later, the islands blossomed as a base for rum-runners who brought prosperity while illegally supplying liquor during the American prohibition era.

In the 1950s, a campaign began to make tourism the islands' major industry. There were 45,371 visitors in 1950; by 1960, that total had grown to 341,977. In 1982, the Bahamas welcomed over 1.94 million visitors.

In 1964, a new constitution gave the colony internal self-government. Sir Roland Symonette, leader of the United Bahamian Party, was appointed Premier. Lynden O. Pindling, head of the Progressive Liberal Party, was appointed Leader of the Opposition.

The majority of the House of Assembly seats went to the PLP in the 1967 general election and Mr. Pindling became Premier.

The Constitution was revised in 1969 to give the Bahamas Government more responsibility for its own affairs. It changed the status from British Colony to Commonwealth, with Mr. Pindling becoming the Prime Minister. In the New Year's Honours List, 1983, he was created a Knight Commander of the Most Excellent Order of St. Michael and St. George (K.C.M.G.).

In December 1972, a Constitutional Conference was held in London to draft an independence constitution. On July 10, 1973, The Commonwealth of the Bahamas became independent within the Commonwealth of Nations.

The general election held on June 10, 1982 returned the PLP as the government for the next five years when they won 32 of the 43 House of Assembly seats. The Free National Movement won the other 11 seats, and is the Official Opposition.

Tourism is still the Commonwealth's chief industry but over the last two decades banking has become a major part of the economic pattern. Other industries are oil refining, trans-shipment and bunk-

294

ering; farming; fishing; aragonite mining; and production of salt by the evaporation process.

Holidays

The following public holidays are observed in the Bahamas:
New Year's Day
Good Friday
Easter Monday
Whit Monday (seven weeks after Easter)
Labour Day (first Friday in June)
Independence Day (July 10)
Emancipation Day (first Monday in August)
Discovery Day (October 12)
Christmas Day
Boxing Day (the day after Christmas).

Holidays which fall on Saturday or Sunday are usually observed on the following Monday.

Stores in New Providence and most Family Islands are closed on holidays. Some stores close at noon Friday but open Saturday. Others close half day Saturday.

Hotel Encouragement

With tourism as its main industry, the Bahamas has given special encouragement to private capital for the building of hotels and resorts throughout the country.

Refunds of Customs duties paid on materials imported to construct and equip hotels, several tax guarantees, and concessions for improving these guest facilities are granted by the Hotels Encouragement Act.

A hotel (including residential club) promoter applies in writing to the Ministry of Tourism, Nassau, citing full particulars on the proposed guest facilities, its amenities, estimated cost, and proposed plans for location and building(s).

The Government then may enter into an agreement with the promoter to refund all Customs duties paid for materials, imported and purchased locally, to construct, extend, equip, furnish or complete the hotel.

Upon approval, the promoter may also import duty-free, the construction plant required to construct, extend, equip, furnish and complete the new facility, and the refund active dates are decided upon by the Government.

The new facility is exempt from real property taxes and any other taxes hereafter imposed on real property for 10 years from the date the new hotel opens. There is further exemption from real property taxes in excess of $14.29 for every bedroom in the hotel for the second 10 years of operation.

Hotel earnings, or rental paid for lease or sub-lease, are exempt from direct taxation for 20 years from the opening date. If the promoter or operator is a company, there is an exemption from direct tax "on or against dividends declared in respect of its indebtedness" for the same 20-year period.

Existing hotels and new hotels may be rehabilitated, remodelled, air conditioned or extended and Customs duty refunds may be obtained on materials imported for such alterations by applying in writing to the Permanent Secretary, Ministry of Tourism, stating nature, extent and estimated cost of the alterations in order to obtain approval in principle from government. This approval in principle must be obtained prior to purchases if the promoter wishes to receive Customs duty refunds.

To obtain these concessions, a new hotel located in New Providence must have at least 20 bedrooms together with suitable public rooms for the accommodation and entertainment of guests. A new hotel on the other islands must have at least 10 bedrooms.

These concessions apply to all amenities offered in conjunction with the hotel, e.g. golf courses, marinas, harbours, roads, air fields, landscaping, etc.

For further information, contact the Ministry of Tourism, P.O. Box N3701, Nassau.

Immigration

Each person entering the Bahamas must fill out, upon entry, an embarkation-disembarkation card, prepared in duplicate. In the case of non-residents, the duplicate is retained and must be surrendered upon departure from the country.

Passports and Visas

British subjects from the United Kingdom and colonies and Canadian citizens may enter the Bahamas as visitors without passports or visas for periods not exceeding three weeks. For longer stays, passports are required. For direct travel between the U.K. and the Bahamas, British passports that have expired within the past five years will be accepted.

U.S. citizens entering the Bahamas as visitors are not required to have passports or visas, provided they are in possession of adequate identification and proof of citizenship (e.g. birth certificate, voter registration card, draft card, selective service card), onward or return tickets and sufficient funds to maintain them during their stay.

The following categories of persons may enter the Bahamas without visas for a single visit for a period not exceeding 30 days:

(a) Landed immigrants of Canada who upon arrival in the Bahamas are in possession of the Canadian Immigration Record and Visa (Form IMM. 1000);

(b) Alien residents of the United States of America who upon arrival in the Bahamas are in possession of the United States Alien Registration Card (also referred to as a "Green Card"), with the exception of South African nationals who fall in either of the above mentioned categories and always need a passport and visa even when in transit.

Transit without visas is now allowed to nationals of the Dominican Republic.

Citizens of the following countries require passports but no visas: Belgium, Greece, Iceland, Italy, Liechtenstein, Luxembourg, Netherlands, Norway, San Marino, Spain, Switzerland and Turkey.

Citizens of the following countries require passports but no visas for stays of three months or less: Austria, France, the Federal Republic of Germany, Denmark, Finland, Sweden, Republic of Ireland, Israel and Japan. For longer stays, visas are required.

Citizens of the following countries require passports but no visas for stays not exceeding 14 days: Argentina, Bolivia, Chile, Colombia, Costa Rica, Ecuador, Guatemala, Republic of Honduras, Mexico, Nicaragua, Panama, Paraguay, Peru, El Salvador, Uruguay, Venezuela. For longer stays, visas are required.

However, citizens of Colombia entering the Bahamas from the U.S. must supply proof of sufficient funds for their stay, hold onward or return tickets to a country to which they have proof of entry rights, and meet any health requirement as may be stipulated from time to time. If they are in transit through ports of the U.S., they are required to have a Bahamian visa, but are exempt from the above-noted requirements.

Citizens of the following countries require passports and visas to enter the Bahamas for any purpose: Dominican Republic (except in transit), Haiti, South Africa, all Communist countries. Nationals of all other countries are advised to check entry requirements with the Immigration Department, P.O. Box N831, Nassau, Bahamas.

Smallpox vaccination certificates are not required of visitors from the following countries: U.S.A., Bermuda, Canada, Jamaica, Greenland, Iceland, Panama Canal Zone, Australia and New Zealand.

A visitor with proper documents (these include evidence of financial support and a return ticket) may be landed by a Bahamas immigration official for a maximum period of eight months. Should he wish to stay longer he must apply to the Director of Immigration, P.O. Box N831, Nassau, who will consider him for temporary residence on an annual basis. (Visitors and temporary residents cannot engage in gainful occupation while in the Bahamas.)

Permits

Permits issued by the Immigration Department are required for the following categories of persons:
1)   Those wishing to reside on an annual basis
2)   Those wishing to take up employment
3)   Those wishing to engage in business
4)   Those visiting the islands to engage in the business of selling.
Permits are not required by:
1)   Bona fide visitors
2)   Those enjoying diplomatic, consular or similar privileges in the Bahamas
3)   Those employed in the Service of the Bahamas or of the

United Nations or any of its agencies or any inter-Governmental organization in which the Bahamas participates, coming to the Bahamas to carry out official duties.

Application for a permit in each case should be supported by the following documents:

A.   Two full-face photographs carrying the signature of the applicant on the reverse thereof. Minimum picture size 2 x 2 inches; maximum 3 x 3 inches.

B.   A police certificate from the applicant's place (or places) of residence for the past five years. Since United Kingdom authorities do not issue police certificates, applicants from the U.K. may substitute a sworn affidavit of good character, which may be obtained by appearing before any justice of the peace or notary public.

C.   Two written character references signed by responsible persons in the applicant's home country, or if the applicant is known in the Bahamas, local persons may be used as references.

D.   A valid health certificate issued not more than 30 days preceding application for permit.

In the case of annual residents, at least one financial reference must be submitted in addition to character references. In the case of those wishing to engage in business, one financial reference must be submitted in addition to character references.

The Director of Immigration, subject to general and specific directions of the Immigration Board, is empowered to issue permits. Under the Immigration (Fees) Regulations, a sliding scale, according to occupation, allows work permit fees from $25 (for a farm worker) to $1,000 (for secretaries) to $5,000 (for senior professional people such as managing directors) to be collected when the permit is granted. The same fee is collected upon renewal of the permit annually.

For an annual residence permit, a head-of-household pays $1,000 and each dependent, $20. However, if the male spouse is married to a Bahamian citizen, the permit will cost $100, with no charge for permits for dependents. Renewal fee is the same amount. (See also **Permanent Residence,** page 300.)

Travelling Salesman's Permit

Travelling salesmen planning to do business in the Bahamas must obtain work permits from the Department of Immigration, and a licence from the Licensing Authority.

The requirements for such a permit are:

A.   Completed Immigration Department Form I, with two passport size photographs signed on the reverse, and a police certificate.

B.   Two letters of character reference.

C.   Passport or other travel document.

D.   A letter from salesman's company stating he is travelling to the Bahamas to sell on their behalf. (Letter should be addressed to: Director of Immigration, P.O. Box N831, Nassau.)

E. Two letters sponsoring him as a salesman from two sponsors in the Bahamas in the type of business on which he plans to call.

F. A complete list of accounts on which he will call.

G. Payment of an annual fee of $1,500. (A permit can be obtained for three months at a cost of $375.)

The licence is issued when the approved work permit is presented at the Licensing Authority office.

Permission to Work

As in many other countries, the Government of the Bahamas attempts to ensure that immigrants do not create unfair competition for employment. No expatriate may be offered employment in a post for which a suitably qualified Bahamian is available. A permit application will not be considered if the prospective employee is already in the country, having entered as a visitor.

The Immigration Board will consider employment of a non-Bahamian, provided it is thought that the prospective employee will be an asset to the Bahamas, only after:

1) The employer has advertised and interviewed locally, having found no suitably qualified Bahamian to fill the post.

2) The employer has obtained from the Labour Exchange a certificate stating that no qualified Bahamian is registered who might fill the post.

Ordinarily, the employer submits the permit application for the prospective employee (including documents listed under **Permits** A., B., C., D.) along with a copy of his local advertisement, applications of applicants attracted by this advertisement, the results of interviews with local applicants, and the certificate issued by the Labour Exchange.

Employers may obtain permits for longer periods than the standard one-year period in respect to certain key personnel on contract. Such contracts should indicate that their renewal would be subject to obtaining the necessary Immigration permission, and they may be endorsed to the effect that the employer is expected to train or find a suitable Bahamian replacement within a stipulated period.

Each permit issued by the Immigration Board relates to a specific post. Permits are not altered by the Director of Immigration to reflect change of employment or residence. However, a person holding a work permit may make application for a new one (his new employer having been unsuccessful in recruiting a qualified Bahamian to fill the post) without having to leave the islands.

The renewal of a permit on expiry is not automatic. Generally, no expatriate may be continually employed in the country in any capacity for more than five years. However, there are likely to be cases where hardship will be caused by rigid implementation of this policy; according to Government, this factor will be kept in mind in applying the regulations.

An employer must inform Immigration within 30 days that a non-

Bahamian employee is no longer employed or be liable to a fine not exceeding $150.

A non-Bahamian who ceases to be employed must take his permit to Immigration for cancellation within seven days of his ceasing to be employed. The permit shall be deemed cancelled with effect from expiration of that seven-day period. An employee failing to comply with this regulation is liable to prosecution and may, if convicted, be liable to a fine not exceeding $100.

Opening a Business

Permanent residents (and others) wishing to open a business or a local branch are required to submit full, specific details of their project to the Director of Immigration. Each applicant will be considered on its own merits, with special emphasis on financial standing; on the number of Bahamians to be employed and whether or not it is necessary to bring in expatriate managerial or specialist staff.

The Immigration Department will pass on its recommendations to the Bahamas Licensing Authority for consideration. (Note: Even though a businessman is granted a licence by the Licensing Authority, he must still apply for a work permit.)

Professional and Technical Skills

While it is necessary to safeguard the interests of Bahamians, particularly in the years ahead when improved educational opportunities will increase the availability of trained and qualified Bahamians, the Government presently welcomes people with specialist qualifications and skills not immediately available, particularly when the employment of such persons would increase the employment prospects of Bahamians. This applies particularly to qualified professional and technical skills and certain specialized occupations in the hotel trade.

Enquiries should be addressed to the appropriate Ministry of Government, or to professional associations, where these exist:

Medicine, Dentistry, Nursing ...... Ministry of Health
Box N3729, Nassau
Teaching .... Ministry of Education
Box N3913, Nassau
Engineering .... Bahamas Institution of
Professional Engineers
Box N7838, Nassau
Hotel Executives .... Bahamas Hotel Association
Box N7799, Nassau

Bonding

A bond is required for each person granted a work permit, if necessary, to repatriate the employee and his dependents and to pay any public charges, including medical expenses, incurred by the employee.

Permanent Residence

An application for permanent residence may be made at any time.

This status is usually accorded to those who wish to put down roots in the Bahamas by investing in property or in a business or who are retirees. Persons coming to the Bahamas who wish to take up permanent residence must apply to the Permanent Secretary, Ministry of Labour and Home Affairs, who then forwards the application to the Immigration Board.

Applications for this status of residency must (1) be of good character and (2) be prepared to show evidence of financial support. Such an applicant must also state that he intends to reside permanently in the Bahamas.

A person holding a certificate of permanent residence who wishes to include his wife, or dependent child under the age of 18 and ordinarily resident in his household, may have them endorsed on the certificate at the time of his original application or at a subsequent date, subject to such conditions as might be laid down by the Board.

Persons who held valid certificates of permanent residence prior to the Immigration Act (1975) continue to hold such status automatically.

Spouses of Bahamians may be issued a certificate of Permanent Residence with the right to engage in gainful employment. In the case of males, such application may only be made after five years of marriage to his Bahamian wife. Females married to Bahamians may apply at any time after the marriage.

A certificate of permanent residence may be revoked by the Board should the person holding the certificate (1) have been ordinarily resident outside the Bahamas continuously for a period of three years, (2) is or was imprisoned for a criminal offence for one year or more, (3) has so conducted himself that in the opinion of the Board it is not in the public interest that he should continue to enjoy the privileges conferred by the certificate, and (4) being the wife of a holder of a permanent residence certificate, she becomes legally separated from her husband or the marriage is dissolved or annulled.

Cost of a permanent residence certificate is $5,000. Endorsements are free.

Persons holding these certificates require work permits if they wish to take up employment.

Persons who formerly possessed Bahamian Status (Belongers) whose applications for citizenship were not determined by Aug. 1, 1976, should have also applied for permanent residence. Belongers who failed to make such application prior to Aug. 1, 1976, ceased to enjoy at that date any immigration status.

Persons in this category, on acquiring a Permanent Residence Certificate, would continue to enjoy the same rights and privileges they had known under the old Bahamian Status, with the exception of the right to vote in a parliamentary election.

Permanent Residents who were formerly Belongers enjoy the new status for a lifetime. The certificate is issued free of charge and it contains no restriction regarding the right of the holder to engage in gainful employment.

(See also **Citizenship,** page 245.)

Import Entry

The agency responsible for approving applications for the purchase of foreign currency for payment of goods imported into the Bahamas is the Exchange Control Department of the Central Bank of the Bahamas, situated between Frederick and Market Streets, Nassau. Exchange Control forms are available at several Nassau book shops and office supply stores. The forms should be filled out by the individual or company importing goods and taken to Exchange Control, together with supporting documents and invoices, for authorization. See also **Customs** and **Exchange Control.**

Industries Encouragement

In an effort to broaden the base of the Bahamian economy, the Government has adopted a policy of diversification, which means, in effect, the encouragement of industries other than tourism. In 1970 the Industries Encouragement Act was passed, providing incentives for manufacturers of approved products. These incentives include duty-free importation of machinery and raw materials as well as tax exemptions.

The Minister of Economic Affairs may declare that a manufactured product is an "approved product" if such a declaration is in the public interest and the manufacture of such a product will benefit the Bahamas, "both economic and social considerations being taken into account".

Every "approved manufacturer" is entitled to import into the Bahamas duty-free:
1. Machinery and raw material necessary to manufacture the approved product;
2. Any "scheduled article" for the purpose of constructing, reconstructing, altering or extending, but not repairing, the factory premises. Scheduled articles include all building materials, tools, plant, equipment, pipes, pumps, conveyor belts or other materials or appliances necessary. In New Providence, this excludes equipment used to manufacture wooden door frames, moulding, cement tiles or cement blocks.

The manufacturer is guaranteed no export taxes on the approved product, no income tax in respect of any profits or gains from the product's manufacture, and no real property tax on factory premises — for the "statutory period". If the manufacturer's date of production was prior to Jan. 1, 1976, the statutory period extends through Dec. 31, 1989. Otherwise, it lasts 15 years from the date agreed to be production date.

Applications for approval of a product or manufacturer must be addressed to the Minister of Economic Affairs, P.O. Box N4596, Nassau.

For specific requirements and restrictions, consult the Industries Encouragement Act, 1970, or the Minister of Economic Affairs.

Industrial Relations Act

The Industrial Relations Act, 1970, called for registration of trade unions. The Act makes it unlawful for a trade union to operate in the Bahamas — or for any person to take part in its activities — unless the union is registered.

Applications to register a trade union should be made to the Registrar of Trade Unions, Labour Department, P.O. Box N-1586, Nassau.

The Registrar shall refuse to register a trade union if the union's principal objects are unlawful or contrary to statutory objects, or if its name is misleading or so similar to an existing name as to deceive the public, or if there is failure to comply to specified balloting procedures.

Upon registration, the trade union is issued a certificate as evidence of that registration.

Every trade union is required to have a registered office. Unions may own or lease land, but all real and personal property is vested in the trustees of the union.

No person under the age of 16 may be a member of a trade union. A union may not have foreign connections without a proper licence in writing from the Minister of Labour & Home Affairs.

An employer is required to recognize a union as bargaining agent if more than 50% of his employees are members. An employer has 14 days to accept or reject a union claim for recognition. No employee can be dismissed or adversely treated as a result of his union involvement.

All industrial agreements between employer and union must be sent in writing to both the Industrial Relations Board and the Minister of Labour and Home Affairs, according to the Act. The Minister has 14 days to make comments to the Board. After taking these comments into consideration, the Board may register the agreement if it does not contain any illegality. Properly registered industrial agreements are considered binding.

Any strike is illegal that has a purpose other than the furtherance of a trade dispute, or if designed to coerce the Government. The same applies to a lockout. A picket must be able to produce on his person written authorization by a trade union official, and he must picket peacefully, near a place or building where a party to the dispute works, with no more than 14 other individual pickets.

For specific information, contact the Registrar of Trade Unions.

Industry

Tourism is the major industry in the Bahamas. Visitors now total nearly two million a year, accounting for two-thirds of the country's employment.

A diversification policy has added new industries and the biggest of these is oil. The Bahamas Oil Refining Company in Freeport produces low-sulphur fuel. Total exports of petroleum products in 1982 for the Bahamas were over $2.24 billion, according to The Central Bank of the Bahamas.

Also at Freeport is a giant trans-shipment complex owned by the Bahamas Government and Burmah Oil Company in London.

In addition, the Franklin Chemicals Company recently opened its $30 million petro-chemical plant in Grand Bahama.

Crude oil is imported mainly from the Middle East. There has been no oil discovered in the Bahamas from previous exploration activities, which were terminated in the 1960s. In the interim, the government has enacted the Petroleum Act 1971 and the Petroleum Regulations 1978.

To date three licences to explore and prospect for oil have been issued to Getty Oil, Natomas B.P. Petroleum Development Limited and Arco along with four permits to conduct seismic and other geological surveys. Other applications are under active consideration.

Bearing in mind the rate of improvement in the technology being used in the petroleum industry, there is guarded optimism for the success of the new programme. Marine geologists believe that plant and animal sediment built up under Florida and the Bahamas 30 million years ago may have produced vast deposits of oil and gas.

New Providence is the home of Bacardi & Co. This is one of the largest producers of rum, with sales of approximately 1.3 million cases in 1982.

The merging of the Bahamas Development Corporation and the Agricultural Corporation into The Bahamas Agricultural and Industrial Corporation is geared to actively promote industrial undertakings. The concept of Free Trade Zones is also being examined and active discussions are being held for the development of time-sharing resorts in the Bahamas.

Near Bimini is Ocean Industries' multi-million-dollar aragonite mining operation, a comparatively new major industry for the Bahamas. That firm, which has been given sole rights to mine aragonite by the Bahamas Government, estimates reserves in the billions of tons.

Morton Salt Company at Inagua produces over 700,000 tons of salt a year.

See also **Agriculture,** page 231, and **Freeport Industry,** page 405.

Insurance
The Act of 1970 which regulates insurance in the Bahamas is administered by the Registry of Insurance Companies, a Department of the Ministry of Finance with offices in the Churchill Building, Nassau. The function of this office is to regulate, inspect, license and control insurance companies, agents, brokers and salesmen.

Application to do any kind of insurance business in or from the Bahamas must be made to the Registrar of Insurance Companies.

As of December 1981, there were 70 registered insurance companies in the Bahamas, 22 of which were non-resident insurers, 35 registered agents and 30 registered brokers. According to the Registrar, gross premium income for the years 1977 through 1981 was as follows:

Year	Millions (B$)
1977	40.
1978	45.3
1979	50.7
1980	62.5
1981	75.7

In addition to legislation concerning Insurance companies, there is a Road Traffic Act making insurance on all motor vehicles mandatory. There are sections of the Act applicable to Public Service vehicles and private passenger cars, commercial vehicles and motor cycles. Under the terms of the present Act, it is compulsory to carry insurance against bodily injury or death to any person arising out of the use of a vehicle; this applies to passengers in certain vehicles, such as buses, taxis, tour cars and jitneys. The penalties for operating a vehicle without valid insurance are laid out in the Act.

The present Act requires that insurance be carried only to provide indemnity against claims for bodily injury or death and not against property damage. This results in two types of insurance policy being available for what is commonly known as "Third Party" insurance. The minimum requirement by law is provided under what is defined as an "Act" policy whereas the "Third Party" policy extends to include damage to property arising out of the use of a vehicle, such as damage caused to another car.

Marine insurance is written in respect of Cargo and Hull policies. Also available are Protection and Indemnity covers, which can be extended to include Oil Pollution liabilities imposed under the Merchant Shipping (Oil Pollution) Act.

Insurance Companies, Agents and Brokers dealing with general insurance business are members of the Bahamas General Insurance Association. Those insurers handling Life and Health business belong to the Bahamas Association of Life and Health Insurers.

Captive Insurance Companies

The Bahamas Government is committed to a policy of encouraging and developing an expanded captive insurance business here. The Government has introduced a Bill which amends previous legislation so as to make the Bahamas fully competitive with other captive insurance centres, but up to press time it had not been dealt with by Parliament.*

In support of that commitment, the assurance has been given that captive insurance companies established here will receive the co-operation of all government agencies, including the granting of work permits in areas where there are no Bahamians suitable for the job, and

* The Act came into effect during August 1983.

opportunities for captive insurance firms to acquire housing for their expatriate staff.

Nassau's extensive financial sector includes institutions which provide expert banking, custodianship and investment management facilities, as well as sophisticated management company, legal, accounting and audit services.

See also **National Insurance,** page 310.

Judicial System

British Common Law is the basis of the Bahamas judicial system, though there is a large volume of Bahamian Statute Law. The highest tribunal in the country is the Court of Appeal. This is presided over by three judges appointed by the Governor General. In practice, they are usually leading jurists of England or West Indian nations, and they need have no former ties with the Bahamas.

A Chief Justice and four Justices who are appointed by the Governor General preside over the Supreme Court, which has general civil and criminal jurisdiction. The court hears civil matters throughout the year. There are four sessions a year for criminal matters, beginning on the second Wednesday of January and the first Wednesday in April, July and October.

New Providence has four Magistrates' Courts and Freeport has one. These courts are presided over by Stipendiary and Circuit Magistrates who exercise summary jurisdiction in criminal matters and in civil matters involving amounts not exceeding $571. In addition, all Family Island Commissioners exercise summary jurisdiction in criminal matters of a less serious nature and in civil matters involving amounts not exceeding $286.

Appeal from a decision of a Family Island Commissioner acting in his capacity as a magistrate goes to the Stipendiary and Circuit Magistrate, and an appeal from a decision by an S. and C. Magistrate goes to the Supreme Court. An appeal from a Supreme Court decision lies to the Bahamas Court of Appeal, and an appeal from the Bahamas Court of Appeal lies to the Privy Council in England.

Junkanoo

Junkanoo is a festive Bahamian parade which takes place traditionally in the early hours of Boxing Day (December 26) and New Year's Day, winding up after sunrise.

Individuals and groups in colourful crepe-paper costumes parade through the centre of Nassau, and West End (Dec. 26 only) and Freeport (Jan. 1 only) to the tune of cowbells, goatskin drums, whistles and horns. The movement is a slow, dancing march which Bahamians call "rushing".

During the past 10 years Junkanoo has expanded to some of the Family Islands and is now celebrated each year at Mathew Town, Inagua; George Town, Exuma; Governor's Harbour, Eleuthera; and Harbour Island.

It is said that Junkanoo originated during the days of slavery when the slaves were given time off to celebrate the holidays with African dance, music and costume. Today, the groups and individuals compete for prizes of up to $3,000 in various categories. They are judged on the basis of performance, music and originality of costumes.

The Masquerade Committee in Nassau, which organizes the Junkanoo festivals, also contributes prize funds to the Family Islands parades.

The origin of the word Junkanoo is obscure. Some say it comes from the French **gens inconnus** meaning "the unknown" in reference to the masks worn by the paradėrs; **junk enoo,** Scottish settlers' appellation for the parades meaning "junk enough", and **John Conuu** or **Conny,** the name of an early 18th century African prince from the former Gold Coast, now Ghana, who demanded the right to celebrate with his people even after being brought to the West Indies in slavery.

Law Firms
Nassau
P.O. Box

Adderley, Malcolm	N1342
Adderley, Neville K. & Co.	N8199
Adderley, Paul L. & Co.	N4
Albury, Harrington	N1699
Alexiou, Knowles & Co.	N4805
Allen, Gomez & Co.	N10205
Barnwell, V.C.A.	N4759
Benjamin, Allan J.	N102
Bethell, David C.	SS5873
Bodie, Ortland H., Jr.	N9559
* Bostwick & Bostwick	N1605
Bowe & Mackay	N4839
Butler, Russell & Co.	N4916
* Callenders, Orr & Co.	N7117
* Carson, Lawson, Klonaris, Sawyer & Knowles	N4645
Cash, Fountain & Co.	N476
* Christie, Ingraham & Co.	N7940
** Clark, Foster (Abaco)	445 **
Curry, Richard J.B.	SS5349
Dean, Michael	N3114
* Dupuch & Turnquest	N8181
Edwards, Desmond	N3334
Fawkes, Sir Randol F.	N7625
* Gomez, Dennis & Co.	N9843
Graham, Thompson & Co.	N272
Green, Terence Newton	N685
Hall, Rosalie	SS5393
Hanna, Arthur D. & Co.	N4877
Harris-Smith & Harris-Smith	N4255
Henderson, Sir Guy McL.	N1447
Henderson, Bowe & Co.	N7101
Higgs & Johnson	N3247
Higgs & Kelly	N1113

Hilton, Cecil I. & Co. N7050
Hilton, Langton T. N4616
Hollingsworth & McKinney N9306
Horton, Michael N3822
Isaacs, Bethell, Barnett & Co. N1372
Knowles, Sir Leonard J. N862
Lockhart, McDonald & Co. N8615
Maillis & Maillis N4014
Martin, Carlton N4535
* McKinney, Bancroft & Hughes N3937
* Nottage, Miller & Co. N4691
Parker, Cedric L. N1953
Pinder, Godfrey W. & Co. N3715
Pritchard, Artemas P. N514
Pyfrom & Roberts N3950
* Roberts, E. Dawson, Higgs & Co. N918
Rolle, Knowles & Co. N8680
Sands, Harry B. N624
Seligman, Maynard & Co. N7525
Stewart-Coakley, Alva M. N685
Thompson, Jeanne I. N4375
Thompson & Thompson N4206
Toothe, Paton & Co. N9306
Turner, Maxwell S.A. N1147
* Wallace Whitfield, Cecil N753
Wells, Campbell & Co. N9665
Zervos, Nicholas J. N763

* Freeport office also.
** Abaco office.

Libraries

Nassau Public Library, Shirley Street:
    Mon., Tues., Wed., 10 a.m. to 8 p.m.
    Thurs. and Fri., 10 a.m. to 5 p.m.
    Sat., 10 a.m. to 2 p.m.
Fox Hill Public Library, Bernard Road:
    Mon.-Fri., 10 a.m. to 8 p.m.
    Sat., 10 a.m. to 1 p.m.
Eastern Public Library, Mackey Street:
    Mon.-Fri., 10 a.m. to 9 p.m.
    Sat., 10 a.m. to 4 p.m.
Southern Public Library, Blue Hill Road:
    Mon.-Fri., 10 a.m. to 9 p.m.
    Sat., 10 a.m. to 5 p.m.

Ranfurly Out Island Library

The Ranfurly Out Island Library was initiated by Lady Ranfurly, wife of the Earl of Ranfurly, Governor of the Bahamas, in 1953. From 1956 to 1978 the late Lt.-Gen. Sir Dudley Russell was Chairman. The work was carried on until 1980 by the late Lady Russell, and is now continued by a Chairman with a committee and other volunteer workers.

The Government has made buildings available in the compound of the Learning Resources Unit on Mackey Street, and provides a small allowance for expenses.

Books are donated and contributions come from the Ranfurly Library Service in London, the Toronto and Ottawa Overseas Book Centres in Canada, the American Women's Club in the Bahamas, Barclays Bank International Limited, Nassau residents and other friends.

Books, magazines and periodicals are distributed to schools in the Family Islands and some educational institutions in Nassau.

Marriage Licences

Marriage licences cost $5.71 and are obtained in New Providence at the Registrar General's office, Post Office Building, East Hill Street, P.O. Box N532, Nassau. No blood test is required. Minimum age without parental consent is 18.

Minors may be married with both parents' consent if they have reached the age of 15. However, under special circumstances, those between the ages of 13 and 15 may apply to the Supreme Court for special permission to marry. Consent forms for minors are available at the Registrar General's office.

Applications for marriage licences and consent forms must be filled out in the presence of the Registrar General or a magistrate, justice of the peace, notary public, Registrar of Marriages or a marriage officer of the Bahamas. One party of the couple desiring to be married must have resided in the Bahamas for a period of at least 15 days immediately prior to the date of application for a marriage licence, but the Registrar General can exempt any applicant from this requirement.

A divorced person is required to provide a certified copy of his or her final divorce decree, and a person whose former spouse has died must provide a certified copy of the death certificate.

In 1982, there were 1,313 marriages in the Bahamas, compared with 1,282 in the previous year.

National Anthem

Lift up your head to the rising sun, Bahamaland;
March on to glory, your bright banners waving high.
See how the world marks the manner of your bearing!
Pledge to excel thro' love and unity.
Pressing onward, march together to a common
*   loftier goal;*
Steady sunward, tho' the weather hide the wide
*   and treach'rous shoal.*
Lift up your head to the rising sun, Bahamaland;
'Til the road you've trod lead unto your God,
March on, Bahamaland!

—by Timothy Gibson, C.B.E.
(1903-1978)

National Insurance

The National Insurance Act of 1972 established a national insurance scheme which provides benefits to qualifying persons in respect of retirement, invalidity, sickness, maternity, funeral expenses and industrial benefits. Upon the death of the breadwinner of a family, payments are also made to his or her surviving dependents.

Non-contributory assistance programmes were introduced by the National Insurance Regulations, 1974. Qualification for assistance is by a prescribed test of an individual's resources, and benefits include old age non-contributory pensions, invalidity assistance, survivor's assistance and sickness assistance.

The contributory programme also began in 1974, and coverage was extended to self-employed persons in 1976. Sickness benefits came into effect in April 1975, and maternity and funeral benefits were added in September of that year.

Three other benefits to which employed and voluntarily insured persons became entitled in 1977 are retirement, survivor's and invalidity. Self-employed persons also became eligible for these benefits in 1979.

Retirement benefit is paid to an insured person who is 65 years or older, has retired from gainful occupation and has paid the required minimum amount of contributions to the scheme. Survivor's benefit is paid to the surviving dependents of a deceased insured person who had paid the required minimum contributions to the scheme. Invalidity benefit is paid to an insured person between the ages of 16 years to 65 years, who has paid the required minimum number of contributions to the scheme and is unable to continue gainful employment due to some permanent illness.

The rates of contributions vary according to the income received of both the employed and the self-employed persons. In each case there are six wage groups ranging from Group 1 with income up to $19.99 per week to Group 6 with income of $100 per week and upwards. The weekly contribution for employed persons ranges from $1.35 in Group 1 to $9.75 for those in Group 6. This amount includes both employer and employee contributions. The weekly contributions of self-employed persons range from $1.05 in Group 1 to $7.55 in Group 6.

Sickness and maternity benefits range from $23 per week for insured persons in Group 1 to $66 per week for persons in Group 6. Sickness benefit is payable for up to 156 days in a continuous period of incapacity and maternity benefit is paid for up to 13 weeks starting six weeks before the expected confinement. Funeral benefit in the form of a $1,000 grant is paid on the death of an insured person or the spouse of an insured person.

The National Insurance Act provides that a previously insured person, upon cessation of employment, may opt to become a Voluntarily Insured Person who is entitled to retirement, invalidity, survivor's and funeral benefits only. Contributions in this category range from $0.75 per week in wage Group 1 to $5.45 in Group 6, and the wage group is determined by the wage group in which a person has paid the greatest number of contributions during the period of two years immediately preceding the date on which he last ceased to be employed.

Industrial Benefits were introduced into the scheme in late 1980. The benefits are paid to, or in respect of, employed persons above or below the upper limit of compulsory school age, who suffer injury, disability or death as a result of an accident arising out of, or in the course of his employment, or as a result of a prescribed disease developed because of the nature of his employment.

These benefits replace the provisions of the repealed Workmen's Compensation Act, and include: Injury Benefit, which is paid for a continuous period, or in spells, for up to 156 days from the date of the accident, or the date of the development of a prescribed disease; Disablement Benefit, which is paid according to the degree of disablement which the person suffers as a result of the accident or prescribed disease; Death Benefit, which is paid to surviving dependents, when the death is a result of the accident or prescribed disease.

Injury Benefit ranges from $24 per week in Group 1 to $73 per week in Group 6. Disablement ranges from $50 for 1% disablement to $1,200 for 24%, paid in the form of a grant; for 25% and up to 100%, payment is made by a pension, for life or for a specified period, according to the Group in which Injury Benefit was paid. Death Benefit is paid according to the Group in which the Injury Benefit was paid or was payable.

The National Insurance Scheme is administered by a tripartite Board consisting of 11 members. Five members are appointed at the discretion of the Minister responsible for National Insurance; three members represent employers, and three members represent the insured persons.

The Board has its headquarters in Farrington Road and a local office in Citibank Building, Thompson Boulevard. There are other local offices in Freeport, Grand Bahama and in most of the Family Islands.

National Symbols

THE FLAG

The design of the Bahamas flag is a black equilateral triangle on a background of three equal horizontal stripes: aquamarine, gold and aquamarine.

Symbolism of the flag's colours and design was officially described as: Black, a strong colour, represents the vigour and force of a united people; the triangle pointing towards the body of the flag represents the enterprise and determination of the Bahamian people to develop and possess the rich resources of land and sea symbolized by

311

gold and aquamarine respectively; the colours of the flag are symbolic of our bright tropical region, of our land of sea and sun.

COAT OF ARMS

By royal warrant dated December 7, 1971, the Bahamas was granted a new coat of arms, the description of which, in heraldic terms, is as follows:

"Argent a representation of the Santa Maria on a base barry wavy of four Azure on a Chief Azure a demi Sun Or And for the Crest upon a representation of Our Royal Helmet mantled Azure doubled Argent On a Wreath Or and Azure A Conch Shell proper in front of a Panache of Palm Fronds proper And for Supporters On the dexter a Marlin Proper on the sinister a Flamingo proper; And upon a Compartment Per pale Waves of the Sea and Swampland proper together with the motto: FORWARD, UPWARD, ONWARD, TOGETHER."

NATIONAL FLOWER

The Yellow Elder (Tecoma stans or Stenolobium stans), a tubular-shaped yellow flower with delicate red stripes on each petal, is the national flower of the Bahamas.

NATIONAL TREE

The Lignum Vitae, or Tree of Life, is the national tree. It is the heaviest of all woods with clusters of small blue flowers at the branch tips.

NATIONAL BIRD

The national bird is the flamingo, a pink long-legged wader, of the genus phoenicopterus. See **Birds,** page 238.

Newspapers

The **Nassau Guardian,** a morning paper, and **The Tribune,** an afternoon paper, are the two national dailies (Mon.-Sat). They are printed in Nassau and widely circulated in Nassau and Freeport with delayed and limited circulation in the Family Islands. Both sell for 30¢ in Nassau. The Tribune costs 35¢ and The Guardian 30¢ in the Family Islands.

The **Freeport News** is published daily, Monday-Friday, in Freeport, and sells for 25¢.

Foreign newspapers, including the **New York Times,** the **Wall Street Journal, The Times,** and the **Daily Telegraph,** are usually available in Nassau one day after publication.

Paradise Island

This international playground lies across the harbour from Nassau, connected by a $2 (per car) toll bridge. The Paradise Island development is principally owned by Resorts International, Inc., a U.S. firm traded on the American Exchange. Paradise Island offers 14 hotels with a total of 3,030 rooms, numerous restaurants featuring international cuisine, top-calibre entertainment in its Cabaret Theatre, one of the world's largest casinos, an 18-hole golf course, Cloisters and surrounding gardens, Hurricane Hole Marina and Paradise Beach.

Population

Following the last Census, which was taken in May 1980, a projection estimate placed the population at 210,066 for all the Bahamas. No subsequent estimate was available at press time.

Following is an island-by-island breakdown of the 1980 census:

Island	1980 Population
Abaco	7,324
Acklins	616
Andros	8,397
Berry Islands	509
Bimini	1,432
Cat Island	2,143
Crooked Island	517
Eleuthera, Harbour Island and Spanish Wells	10,600
Exumas	3,672
Grand Bahama	33,102
Inagua	939
Long Cay	33
Long Island	3,358
Mayaguana	476
New Providence	135,437
Ragged Island	146
Rum Cay and San Salvador	804
Total:	209,505

	Boats	Ports of Entry Land Planes	Sea Planes
Abaco			
Grand Cay	Yes	No	Yes
Treasure Cay	Yes	Yes	Yes
Marsh Harbour	Yes	Yes	Yes
Sandy Point	Yes	No	Yes
Snake Cay	Yes	No	Yes
Spanish Cay	Yes	Yes	Yes
Andros			
Congo Town	No	Yes	No
Fresh Creek	Yes	Yes	Yes
San Andros	No	Yes	No
Berry Islands			
Chub Cay	Yes	Yes	Yes
Great Harbour Cay	Yes	Yes	Yes
Bimini			
Alice Town	Yes	No	Yes
South Bimini	No	Yes	No
Cat Cay	Yes	No	Yes
Eleuthera			
Governor's Harbour	Yes	Yes	Yes
Hatchet Bay	Yes	No	Yes
North Eleuthera	No	Yes	No
Rock Sound	Yes	Yes	Yes
Exuma			
George Town	Yes	Yes	Yes
Grand Bahama			
Bell Channel Bay, Lucaya	Yes	No	No
Freeport	Yes	Yes	Yes
Gold Rock Creek	Yes	Yes	Yes
South Riding Point	Yes	No	Yes
West End	Yes	Yes	Yes
Harbour Island	Yes	No	Yes
Inagua			
Mathew Town	Yes	Yes	Yes
Mayaguana			
Abraham's Bay	Yes	Yes	Yes
New Providence			
East Bay Yacht Basin	Yes	No	No
John Alfred Dock	Yes	No	No
Kelly's Dock	Yes	No	No
Nassau Harbour Club Marina ..	Yes	No	No
Nassau Int'l Airport	No	Yes	No
Nassau Yacht Haven	Yes	No	No
Prince George Dock	Yes	No	No
Union Dock	Yes	No	No

	Boats	Land Planes	Sea Planes
*Paradise Island	Yes	No	Yes (Private)
Ragged Island	Yes	Yes	No
San Salvador			
Cockburn Town	Yes	Yes	Yes

*For aircraft of Chalk Airlines only

Postal Information

N.B. Only **Bahamian postage stamps** are valid.

AIR MAIL

Destination	Letters	Air Letter Forms	Post Cards	Second Class
Inter-Island	10¢ per 1 oz. or fraction thereof	—	8¢	—
United States (incl. Alaska, Hawaii, U.S. Virgin Islands, Puerto Rico), Canada	31¢ per ½ oz.	25¢	25¢	20¢ per ½ oz.
West Indies	31¢ per ½ oz.	25¢	25¢	30¢ per ½ oz.
Central and South America, Bermuda, Falkland Islands, U.K., Irish Repub., all countries in Europe, the Azores, Iceland, islands of the Mediterranean	35¢ per ½ oz.	25¢	25¢	20¢ per ½ oz.
All countries in Africa, Australia, New Zealand and islands of the Pacific and Indian Oceans, Soviet Union, Turkey	50¢ per ½ oz.	25¢	25¢	30¢ per ½ oz.

Consult Post Office about mailing small packets abroad via second class.

SPEEDMAIL

As of January 1, 1983 a new service known as SPEEDMAIL was inaugurated. For a fee of $1, in addition to regular postage, items posted for this service will be delivered to the addressee's postal box at the General Post Office within one hour of posting, within three hours to any other post office in New Providence, and within 24 hours to Freeport. **Items must be handed over the stamp counter for processing.** Efforts are being made to extend the Speedmail service later to the U.S., Canada and the U.K.

REGISTRATION FEE

The fee for registration of mail inside the Bahamas is 40¢; for all other destinations 80¢.

EXPRESS FEE

There is an express (special delivery) fee of 80¢ to all participating countries.

PARCEL POST INFORMATION, NEW PROVIDENCE

Size, weight limits — Weight limit is 22 lbs. Size limit for packages sent Parcel Post is 3½ feet in length. No package may exceed 6 feet, 7 inches in combined length and girth. Parcels exceeding this size should be sent by air or sea freight.

Incoming Parcels from abroad are charged at the rate of 30¢ per item and are subject to Customs examination and assessment. Where possible, the assessment of duty is included in the notice of arrival sent to the addressee. In other cases the addressee may be asked to supply invoices or to attend while the Customs examination is made. Parcels are delivered at Parcel Post after any Customs and/or other charges have been paid.

POSTAL SERVICE FROM NASSAU

Approximate times of posting at the General Post Office to connect with outgoing mails:

Foreign Air Mail

U.S.A., Central and South America, Asia, Australia, Africa:
  Mon.-Sat. 10 a.m., 3 p.m.

Bermuda:
Jamaica:
Europe: { *The Postmaster General advises that new schedules affecting these destinations are announced from time to time. Check with any post office for new mailing times.*
Haiti:
Canada:
Turks and Caicos:

Foreign Surface Mail

Via the U.S., Mon. and Wed. 10 a.m.; via the United Kingdom, Fri. 10 a.m.

HOURS OF SERVICE, NASSAU

General Post Office	8:30 a.m.-5:30 p.m., Mon.-Fri.;
	8:30 a.m.-12:30 p.m., Sat.
Postal Savings Bank	9 a.m.-5:30 p.m., Mon.-Fri.
Grant's Town Branch	9 a.m.-5 p.m. Mon.-Fri.;
	9 a.m.-Noon, Sat. (Mail only)
Shirley Street Branch	8:30 a.m.-5:30 p.m., Mon.-Fri.;
	9 a.m.-Noon, Sat. (Mail only)
Parcel Post	9 a.m.-5 p.m., Mon.-Fri.;
	9 a.m.-Noon, Sat.

WAREHOUSE CHARGE

Parcels remaining in any Post Office (including
  Parcel Post) in the Bahamas more than 30 days
  after notice of arrival has been dispatched .... 30¢ per day

SURFACE (REGULAR) MAIL LETTERS

Inter-Island	All Other Destinations			
5¢ per 1 oz.	1 oz.	25¢	1 lb.	$2.30
or fraction	2 ozs.	30¢	2 lbs.	$4.00
thereof	4 ozs.	60¢	4 lbs.	$6.50
	8 ozs.	$1.20		

POST CARDS

Inter-Island	All Other Destinations
3¢	20¢

PRINTED PAPERS

(Includes newspapers; books; magazines; Christmas and greeting cards.)

Inter-Island	All Other Countries	
3¢ for 1 oz. or part thereof	1 oz.	12¢
	2 ozs.	15¢
	4 ozs.	28¢
	8 ozs.	50¢
	1 lb.	90¢
	2 lbs.	$1.50
	4 lbs.	$2.10

SMALL PACKETS (UP TO 2 LBS.)

Inter-Island	Overseas Countries	
Parcel Post rates	4 ozs.	28¢
	8 ozs.	50¢
	1 lb.	90¢
	2 lbs.	$1.50

Note: All countries participate in the small packet service, but some limit the weight to 1 lb.

PARCEL POST RATES

Parcel Post rates to overseas destinations vary considerably and information can be obtained at any Post Office. Examples of rates are:

	Air		Surface	
	Up to one lb.	Each extra lb.	Up to one lb.	Each extra lb.
Canada	$2.10	$2.10	$1.15	$1.15
Great Britain	6.00	2.75	5.00	1.25
United States ...	1.85	1.85	1.00	1.00

PARCELS — INSURANCE & COMPENSATION

Destination	Rate	Insurance	Compensation
Canada	$1.00	$50 or part thereof Maximum $200	Maximum $200
United States	$2.00	$50 or part thereof Maximum $100	Maximum $100
UPU (Parcel Agreement Countries)	40¢	$80 or part thereof Maximum $1,970	Maximum $1,970 (General)

Property Tax

Under the provisions of the Real Property Tax Act, real property tax is imposed on:

(a) all developed properties in New Providence (the island on which Nassau, the capital, is located), except those ex-

318

empted by the provisions of Section 37, viz: churches, schools, etc.;

(b) all developed properties in the Family Islands which are owned by non-Bahamians or non-Bahamian companies (Bahamian companies being as defined in the Companies Act);

(c) all undeveloped properties in New Providence and the Family Islands which are owned by non-Bahamians or non-Bahamian companies, except those which the Minister of Finance is satisfied are being used exclusively for commercial farming.

The rates of the tax are as follows:

(a) on the first $20,000 of assessed value, $\frac{1}{2}$ of 1% per annum;

(b) on the next $30,000 of assessed value, 1% per annum;

(c) on assessed value in excess of $50,000, $1\frac{1}{2}$% per annum.

Owners who live in their homes for an aggregate of nine months of each year prior to the tax year, which expires on October 15 each year, may claim and be allowed an exemption from the tax on the first $20,000 of the assessed value. Persons who rent their properties may not claim the exemption on the first $20,000 of the assessed value.

The Act requires that all persons declare their property to the Chief Valuation Officer annually and forms for this purpose may be obtained from the Valuation Office in Nassau and Commissioners' offices in the Family Islands.

Persons not declaring their property to the Chief Valuation Officer are liable to a fine of $3,000 and shall be required to pay the back taxes for a period of up to 10 years without benefit of the owner-occupier exemption of $100 per annum. Persons who do not pay their tax when it is due are also liable to a surcharge of up to 10% of such tax per annum.

Persons purchasing taxable property should satisfy themselves that the tax has been paid up to date, as otherwise the purchaser will be liable for the outstanding tax which is a first charge on the property.

Property Transactions

Real estate agents charge a commission of 6% of the price paid for developed properties anywhere in the Bahamas. This is in line with the practice in the United States and Canada.

Sales of undeveloped properties throughout the Bahamas entail payment of an agent's commission of 10%, which is some 2% lower than the U.S. commission rate on similar transactions. The Government Stamp Tax on property conveyances is graded as follows:

From	Up to and including	Stamp Tax (%)
$0	$6,000	$\frac{3}{4}$ of 1%
$6,000.01	$20,000	1%
$20,000.01	$30,000	2%
$30,000.01	$50,000	$3\frac{1}{2}$%
$50,000.01	$100,000	$4\frac{1}{2}$%
Over $100,000		5%

In the case of property sales to non-Bahamians, the Stamp Tax is doubled. It may be agreed in such instances that the vendor and the purchaser each pay half of the tax.

The fee charged by the lawyer who prepares the conveyance is normally 2% of the sale price.

Generally, payment of commission, tax and legal fees falls upon the seller. Sometimes property owners will list a net sales figure, in which case the agent must add those charges to the price he quotes to a prospective buyer.

Public Finance

Totals for 1981-1983 are as follows:

Year	Revenue (B$)	Expenditure (B$)
1981	293,134,787	278,790,504
1982	305,109,400 (Est.)	304,130,584 (Est.)
1983	327,074,600 (Est.)	325,875,403 (Est.)

Revenue of the Bahamas for the years 1981-83 derives from the following sources:

Description TAX REVENUE	Actual Revenue 1981 $	Estimated Revenue 1982 $	Estimated Revenue 1983 $
Import & Export Duty	150,127,698	156,800,000	165,800,000
Property Tax	6,314,666	8,500,000	12,000,000
Motor Vehicle Tax	4,176,312	4,470,000	7,330,000
Gaming Taxes	12,052,361	14,500,000	14,500,000
Tourism Tax	11,113,399	12,200,000	15,030,000
Stamp Tax	16,213,653	16,300,000	19,400,000
Other Taxes	11,727,995	13,835,000	15,650,000
TAX REVENUE SUB TOTAL	211,726,084	226,605,000	249,710,000
NON-TAX REVENUE			
Fees & Service Charges	55,893,602	42,261,000	44,475,500
Revenue from Govt. Property .	8,073,931	12,313,000	13,483,000
Interest & Dividends	11,123,239	5,600,000	7,600,000
Reimbursement & Loan Repayment	868,916	11,710,000	5,055,000
Services of a Commercial Nature	5,449,015	6,620,400	6,751,100
NON-TAX REV. SUB TOTAL	81,408,703	78,504,400	77,364,600
Tax Revenue Grand Total ...	211,726,084	226,605,000	249,710,000
Non-Tax Revenue Grand Total	81,408,703	78,504,400	77,364,600
FINAL TOTAL ALL REVENUE	293,134,787	305,109,400	327,074,600

Expenditures of the Bahamas Government, 1981-83:

Ministry/Department	Actual Expenditure 1981 $	Estimate 1982 $	Estimate 1983 $
Governor General and Staff . .	376,500	421,760	428,774
The Senate	133,102	144,950	140,510
House of Assembly	848,312	1,203,600	928,195
Audit Dept.	632,936	668,880	677,067
Court of Appeal	108,799	120,000	123,700
Judicial Dept. — Supreme Court	1,152,009	1,354,340	1,332,010
Dept. of Legal Affairs	597,059	788,800	754,790
The Service Commissions . . .	260,262	262,150	256,977
Police Dept.	19,396,185	18,007,780	18,388,862
Bahamas Information Services Dept.	138,861	239,300	148,524
Office of the Prime Minister . .	833,494	1,050,000	1,050,948
Ministry of External Affairs . .	2,041,186	3,352,770	3,487,188
Dept. of Statistics	652,743	781,000	705,167
Ministry of Defence	6,631,405	9,244,150	7,197,638
Dept. of Public Personnel . . .	1,133,397	1,265,700	1,223,809
Gaming Board	640,595	753,000	687,663
Dept. of Local Government . .	4,227,883	4,708,500	4,843,076
Dept. of Fisheries	—	727,250	601,900
Ministry of Economic Affairs .	252,177	334,820	378,729
Ministry of Finance	5,949,663	5,841,540	17,605,813
Treasury Dept.	7,912,326	6,970,700	7,095,030
Customs Dept.	6,603,383	4,912,780	6,647,812
Registrar General's Dept. . . .	439,768	435,785	465,930
Public Debt Servicing	45,819,831	64,524,069	61,676,497
Ministry of Home Affairs	1,054,207	1,167,650	1,211,827
Immigration Dept.	3,739,364	4,318,950	4,459,754
Prison Dept.	3,346,955	3,731,400	3,674,546
Parliamentary Registration . .	456,424	650,790	238,241
Lands & Surveys Dept.	759,171	884,980	907,716
Dept. of Agriculture	—	2,223,460	2,384,618
Dept. of Housing	197,236	325,600	323,289
Dept. of Physical Planning . .	252,569	501,140	279,869
Ministry of Education & Culture	57,056,726	55,563,580	58,383,475
College of the Bahamas	4,546,488	5,239,100	4,911,300
Ministry of Youth, Sports/ Community Affairs	1,610,816	2,084,040	1,796,206
Ministry of Health	40,852,819	42,703,070	45,024,138
Ministry of Housing & National Insurance	—	—	985,435
Social Services Dept.	3,212,383	4,991,100	5,183,883
Boys' Industrial School	364,474	490,560	459,169

321

	Actual Expenditure 1981 $	Estimate 1982 $	Estimate 1983 $
Girls' Industrial School	181,480	224,740	214,432
Labour Dept.	557,062	952,300	709,551
Ministry of Agriculture & Fisheries	4,307,523	1,358,200	1,170,742
Ministry of Works & Utilities	9,735,875	10,653,750	10,953,934
Ministry of Transport	2,480,967	2,635,000	2,806,560
Post Office Dept.	3,380,006	3,248,000	3,304,340
Aviation Dept.	4,170,259	4,690,250	4,686,809
Port & Marine Dept.	2,635,920	2,863,600	2,431,230
Road Traffic Dept.	1,126,592	1,311,200	1,176,350
Ministry of Tourism	24,149,190	21,152,600	29,304,846
Meteorological Dept.	878,847	950,000	940,282
Dept. of Archives	223,022	280,700	289,234
Printing Dept.	732,253	821,200	817,018
TOTAL	278,790,504	304,130,584	325,875,403

Service Clubs in Nassau

A.H.E.P.A.
Canadian Men's Club
Canadian Women's Club
Delta Sigma Theta
   Sorority, Inc.
Innerwheel Club of Nassau
Innerwheel Club of East Nassau
Innerwheel Club of South-East
   Nassau
Kiwanis Club of Cable Beach
Kiwanis Club of Fort Montagu
Kiwanis Club of Nassau

Kiwanis Club of Over the Hill
Lions Club
Nassau Jaycees
Pilot Club of Nassau
Rotary Club of Nassau
Rotary Club of East Nassau
Rotary Club of South-East
   Nassau
Rotary Club of West Nassau
Toastmasters International
Women's Corona Society

Ship Services

Passenger ships calling year round in Nassau:—
Emerald Seas — twice weekly to and from Miami
Flavia — twice weekly to and from Miami
Mardi Gras — once weekly to and from Miami
Oceanic — once weekly from New York
Starward — once weekly to and from Miami
Sunward II — twice weekly to and from Miami

The following are additional passenger and cruise ships which call at Nassau:

Carnavale, Eugenio C, Fairwind, Nordic Prince, Oriana, Queen Elizabeth II, Skyward, Song of Norway, Southward, Sun Viking, Song of America, Festivale, Rotterdam, Federico C, Volendam, Amerikanis, Dolphin, Caribe, Astor.

Nearly all shipments of cargo coming to the Bahamas from Europe, parts of the Orient and the West Indies are trans-shipped through ports in Florida, mainly by container storage. An exception to this is the importation of cars which are shipped here directly from Japan. Nassau also has direct passenger connections with the United States.

Sports

As a result of the cultural cross-mixture of the country, a variety of European and American sports are participated in by Bahamians. In total some 39 different types of sports are played. Of these, the number one sport appears to be softball — the fast-pitch and the slow-pitch versions.

Under the direction of the Bahamas Softball Federation, affiliated with the World Softball Congress, there is a broad spectrum of competitive and recreational leagues for men and women in New Providence and several Family Islands. Largely because of such a wide base, the Bahamian men's and women's national teams have been rated high in the world. The Bahamas national teams are currently top rated in Central America and the Caribbean region.

In 1983 the 48-member Bahamas track and field team won the 12th annual Carifta Games, held in Martinique, with a total of 41 medals, including 14 gold, 18 silver and nine bronze. Local teams had previously captured the top spot in the Games in 1980 and 1981.

The Bahamas Olympic Association is concerned with international amateur sports events, and is affiliated with the International Olympic Committee. In fact, during early 1983 IOS's president, Juan Samaranch, spent three days in Nassau appraising the sports potential of these islands.

Bahamian track and field stars have performed at a high level in a number of international competitions. Highlighting the recent list of accomplishments was the outstanding performance of the seven-member squad which competed in the 1982 Commonwealth Games in Brisbane, Australia. The team earned six medals and members were responsible for establishing three Commonwealth Games records.

Track and field teams from the Bahamas compete regularly in the Olympic Games, Pan American Games, Central American and Caribbean Games, Commonwealth Games and Carifta Games. During 1980 and 1981, the Bahamas junior (under 20 years) track and field teams won the Carifta (Caribbean Region) and the Central American and Caribbean (CAC) Championships.

Basketball is also a very popular sport in the Bahamas. Under the auspices of the Bahamas Amateur Basketball Association, in affiliation with Federation Internationale de Basketball, it is played throughout the Family Islands. The sport has grown in recent years to such a high level that many Bahamian student-athletes are offered athletic scholarships to study at universities and colleges in the United States.

It is not uncommon, in fact, to find a number of Bahamian male and female student-athletes participating on college campuses across the length and breadth of the U.S. Among the most notable during the past few years has been Mychal Thompson, the National Basketball Association's number one draft choice, currently starring for the Portland Trail Blazers.

Sailing, which includes Olympic-type events and local work-boat sailing, is a favourite recreation. Bahamian yachtsmen compete regularly in local and international sailing events. In fact, the single Olympic gold medal won by the Bahamas was in sailing when Captain Durward Knowles and the late Cecil Cooke won the Star Class event at the 1964 Games in Tokyo.

Many local regattas are held for workboats, of which the annual Family Island Regatta in George Town, Exuma is the most outstanding. Famous as a year-round water sports haven, the Bahamas hosts international sailing, windsurfing and powerboat events.

Record-breaking fishing tournaments are held throughout the year. The waters surrounding the archipelago are acknowledged to be the clearest in the world, and offer superb diving. Swimming, snorkelling and water-skiing are favourites among Bahamians and visitors alike. Equipment is available from shops, hotels and marinas. (See Fishing Regulations, page 284, and Boating, page 241).

Tennis continues to boom, and most major hotels and resorts have excellent tennis facilities. In the Caribbean region, Bahamian players are rated among the top in both senior and junior play.

Golf is another popular dry-land sport. Nassau has four 18-hole courses, Paradise Island one, Grand Bahama boasts six and several of the Family Islands also have excellent courses.

Squash and bowling have also attracted a growing enthusiastic following in recent years, and national and international competitions are held in Nassau and Grand Bahama Island. Coaching is available and tourists are welcomed.

Professional boxing and wrestling matches are staged in Nassau and Freeport throughout the year, and Bahamian boxers are billed from time to time in international contests.

Horseback riding is increasing in popularity, both in Nassau and in Grand Bahama. Riding stables are located in Nassau and on Paradise Island. Shows and competitions are held periodically during the year before judges of international repute from England and the U.S.

Bahamas volleyball teams have dominated the Caribbean Championships and as is the case with baseball, basketball and track and field, this sport has allowed many Bahamian student-athletes to win athletic scholarships to universities in the U.S.

Soccer, swimming, netball, field hockey, American football, bad-

324

minton, table tennis, rugby and cricket also attract enthusiastic participants and spectators.

The government's interest in developing the high potential of Bahamian athletes was underlined by the appointment in 1977 of a Ministry of Youth, Sports and Community Affairs. The Ministry officially opened the new "Chevron 440" running track in Nassau during 1981, and it was named in honour of former Bahamian Olympic sprinter and world record-holder, Thomas A. Robinson.

Individual Bahamians are to be found in the top echelons of international sports in many areas. Among the most notable are Andre Rodgers, the first Bahamian major league baseball player; Elisha Obed, World Boxing Junior Middleweight Champion; Bradley Cooper, Shonel Ferguson and Stephen Wray, all Commonwealth Games record holders; Glenroy "Flo" Saunders, who placed third in the 1981 World Bowling Championships. Several Bahamians have played with major league baseball teams, and well-known Bahamians Osborne "Goose" Lockhart and Kendal "Tiny" Pinder are presently members of the famed Harlem Globetrotters Troupe.

Statistics

The Department of Statistics, established in 1969, falls within the portfolio of the Deputy Prime Minister. Its responsibility is to collect, collate and analyze information from all sectors of the country: economic and social, Government and private. Collated information is made available to all Government Departments to facilitate their planning as well as to the private sector. However, the Department undertakes to protect the confidentiality of specific information from individual and corporate sources.

There are two main areas. Economic statistics relate to imports, exports, prices, income, balance of payments, etc. Social statistics include population census, migration and vital statistics.

The Department puts out a number of publications which are available from the Government Publications Office in Parliament Square, Bay Street. These include:

External Trade Statistics (annually, $6)
External Trade Statistics (quarterly, $2)
Shipping Statistics (annually, $2)
Retail Price Index (monthly, $3 per annum)
Construction Statistics (quarterly, $1)
Immigration Statistics (annually, $2)
Vital Statistics (annually, $3)
Statistical Abstract (annually, $5)
Statistical Summary (quarterly, $2)
The Census Report 1970 ($10)
Agriculture and Fisheries (quarterly, $1.50)
Labour Force Report (bi-annually, $5)
Household Income in the Bahamas (bi-annually, $5)

Tax Benefits for Canadians
by H. Heward Stikeman, Q.C.

Despite the many restrictions which the Canadian income tax law has placed upon the use of "tax havens," the Bahamas retains its attractiveness for Canadians. The islands continue to prove a sound and durable base from which to invest in Canada or from which to conduct off-shore operations for the benefit of Canadians.

In fact the "new" tax law as it has been altered and adapted over the last years has increased the scope for the Bahamas as a locus for international activity and constructive tax planning.

The growing dependence of the Canadian tax system on a wide network of international tax treaties has further enhanced the useful-

---

Noted Canadian tax counsel H. Heward Stikeman, Q.C., B.C.L., D.S., discusses the advantages of the Bahamas as a sound, legitimate tax haven for Canadians.

He is a senior partner in the law firm of Stikeman, Elliott, Tamaki, Mercier & Robb of Montreal, London, England and Hong Kong, and of Stikeman, Elliott, Robarts & Browman of Toronto and Ottawa, and has practised law as a tax counsel in Montreal since 1946.

He is a director of the Mercantile Bank of Canada, CAE Industries Ltd., Fulcrum Investment Company Limited, ATICA International, and Rawson Trust Company, Nassau.

In the publishing sphere, he is Editor-in-Chief of the *Canada Tax Service*, the *Canada Tax Letter*, *Doing business in Canada* and the *Canada Tax Cases*, and also edits several Canadian tax manuals.

Mr. Stikeman was born in Montreal on July 8, 1913. He was educated at Chestnut Hill Academy, Philadelphia; Trinity College School, Port Hope, Ontario; McGill University, Montreal; and the University of Dijon, France.

ness of the Bahamas as a fiscal staging ground for entry into many other jurisdictions. In short, and for many reasons not related to tax, the Bahamas has today more rather than less to offer Canadians.

The Bahamas, by reason of not imposing income or estate taxes, has no tax treaties with any country. At first blush, it might appear that the consequences of residence in the Bahamas *vis à vis* Canadian investment could become a handicap when compared with residence in jurisdictions which do have tax treaties with Canada. To some extent this is true unless appropriate legal steps are taken to correct the situation.

The fact that in Canada residence remains the foundation of direct taxation, whereas, in many other countries, including the U.S., citizenship or the jurisdiction of incorporation of a company play predominant roles, is, in itself, of assistance to Canadians wishing to take advantage of the Bahamas.

Under the Canadian Federal income tax system, individuals resident in Canada are taxed on their world income whereas non-resident individuals are taxed only with respect to income from employment in Canada, a business carried on in Canada and from gains realized on the disposition of taxable Canadian property (discussed later). They are not taxed with any reference to the fact that they are or are not Canadian citizens. A non-resident corporation is subject to Canadian federal or provincial tax only on income derived from its business carried on in Canada and from gains realized on the disposition of taxable Canadian property. Like individuals, resident corporations are taxed on their worldwide income.

Canadian companies incorporated after April 26, 1965 are automatically deemed residents of Canada. Companies incorporated in Canada before April 27, 1965, which were non-residents of Canada, remain non-residents of Canada until they become Canadian residents by some change of fact, such as the carrying on of a business in Canada or the transfer of their effective management and control to Canada, whereupon they will forever be treated as such.

CANADIAN WITHHOLDING TAX

The basic Canadian withholding tax on investment income, certain pensions, dividends, interest (save on Canadian or Provincial government bonds), rent, certain types of royalties, income from a trust and certain other forms of revenue paid by Canadian residents to persons abroad, is 25 per cent. This tax must be withheld from the gross payment by the payor unless the recipient of the income lives in a country with which Canada has a tax treaty. In that event the withholding tax may be reduced to 15 per cent or less, depending on the terms of the treaty. As noted above, the Bahamas and Canada do not have a tax treaty between them since the Bahamas levies no tax equivalent to the Canadian income and capital gains taxes. However, pensioners residing outside of Canada may receive free of withholding tax, their full old age security payments and benefits under the Canada or Quebec Pension Plans.

Only non-residents of Canada who are recipients of interest on bonds of or guaranteed by a Canadian government or municipality will remain immune to this tax — there being no tax of any kind withheld from such income.

The Canadian branch tax levies a 25 per cent tax on the after-tax branch profits of non-resident corporations carrying on business in Canada to the extent such profits are not reinvested in certain capital assets used in the business in Canada.

The branch tax treats non-Canadian corporations that carry on business in Canada through a branch in a manner similar to those companies that carry on business through a subsidiary. If the branch belongs to a resident of a country with which Canada has a tax treaty, the rate may be reduced to 15 per cent.

SPECIFIC PROVISIONS

Increasingly non-residents and residents must take account of many useful or bothersome provisions of the Canadian law when entering into various forms of commercial or investment transactions.

THIN CAPITALIZATION PROVISIONS

The "thin capitalization" provisions contained in subsection 18(4) of the Income Tax Act relate to the deductibility of interest paid on money borrowed from abroad by Canadian resident corporations.

Interest payments made to non-residents with whom a Canadian company does not deal at arm's length (usually shareholders) are not always entirely deductible in computing taxable income in Canada. They will be disallowed to the extent that the ratio of the company's equity capital to the debt due to non-resident shareholders (who have a 25 per cent or more interest in the company) or related persons is less than one to three. After November 12, 1981, the calculation of shareholders' equity excludes capital invested by shareholders who have a less than 25 per cent interest in the company. While back-to-back loans are forbidden, guarantees given by a parent company on behalf of its subsidiary to foreign lenders will not result in a disallowance of any interest paid to the lender by the subsidiary of the parent.

SPECIAL EXEMPTION FROM WITHHOLDING TAX

One of the more significant relieving measures introduced by the Minister of Finance in his 1975 budget is that which exempts from Canadian withholding tax interest paid to arm's length non-resident creditors on certain corporate securities issued between June 23, 1975, and December 31, 1983. This measure has been extended to such securities issued before 1986. The exemption will be granted regardless of the currencies in which the borrowing is made or the interest is paid. The obligation itself may take any form and may be by way of bond, debenture, note or mortgage, secured or unsecured. Interestingly enough, there is no restriction preventing the guarantee of the debt by a non-resident person who is not at arm's length with the borrower. Thus Bahamians may lend to Canadians against the security of a guarantee by someone outside of Canada not at arm's length with the borrower, upon terms which may exempt the interest paid from Canadian withholding tax. Such a loan is limited to a debt of which the borrower is not obliged to repay more than 25 per cent of the principal amount within five years of the date of issue except in the event of a failure or default, or if terms of the obligation become unlawful or are changed by virtue of legislation or by a court. This will not disqualify a security which gives to the borrower a bona fide right of prepayment even if it is exercised before the five-year period ends. It is expected that this provision will encourage the refinancing of many corporate loans and open avenues to effectuate such refinancing through Bahamian and other appropriate tax-free areas.

NON-RESIDENT-OWNED INVESTMENT CORPORATION

A non-resident-owned investment corporation is a Canadian incorporated company wholly owned by persons resident abroad and having certain prescribed kinds of income. Prior to 1976 these companies were treated as corporate conduits for an investment portfolio or as a convenience in the conduct of a business entirely carried on outside Canada. The tax was paid by the N.R.O. internally and dividends paid out to non-residents were free of withholding tax.

Today N.R.O.'s are taxed at 25 per cent on their world income except that only capital gains from the disposition of "taxable Canadian property" are included in the computation of income. Also, no deduction is allowed for interest expenses.

Dividends out of ordinary income (e.g. income other than from capital gains) are subject to the normal withholding tax rates and give rise to a tax refund to the N.R.O. Dividends with respect to income from most capital gains are not subject to withholding tax.

Effectively an N.R.O. permits in most cases a non-resident to obtain, via the use of a Canadian resident corporation, the same tax treatment as would have been obtained had the non-resident invested directly. The "flow through" mechanism does not work in all instances and may lead to undesired results with respect to certain types of investments.

It is possible for an N.R.O. to be liquidated and its assets transferred to a Bahamian or a Panamanian company resident in Nassau and still have its portfolio effectively managed in Canada without thereby being taxed by Canada as a resident corporation. This would effectively place the shareholders of the Bahamian or Panamanian company in the same position as that of an individual who held his security portfolio directly. Similar benefits may be obtained by the use of companies established in Holland and/or the Netherlands Antilles.

BAHAMAS BENEFITS

Despite the restrictive and wide-ranging nature of the Canadian fiscal law, tax havens, tax shelters and tax sparing are continuing to play an important part in Canadian tax planning. In particular, the utilization of testamentary trusts and certain inter vivos trusts can yield rewards. Nevertheless, there is today less emphasis on a search for an absolute tax haven, in which no income tax whatever is imposed. Taxpayers are increasingly searching for tax shelter areas in

329

which low rates of tax are imposed but to which jurisdictions some appropriate international Tax Treaties also apply. Nevertheless, treaties may be used, on expert advice, by Bahamian residents by setting up suitable trusts or corporations in appropriate treaty jurisdictions.

Of the few remaining absolute tax havens, there are not many that offer benefits comparable to the Bahamas in terms of flexibility of corporate structure, good accounting and legal services, readily available first class financial and banking services, proximity to the world markets and good docking and harbourage facilities.

Quite apart from the corporate interest, however, a number of Canadian individuals look to the Bahamas as a place from which to conduct some of their business activities while reducing the strain upon their constitutions caused by the competitive struggles of the Canadian scene and its climate.

Some achieve this by becoming non-residents of Canada and setting up their homes in the Bahamas. Once they do this, they suffer no income tax in Canada, save the appropriate one on the profits from business done there or the 25 per cent withholding tax on certain kinds of income derived from residents of Canada.

CAPITAL GAINS TAX ON NON-RESIDENTS

Non-resident individuals pay income tax to Canada at applicable personal rates on $\frac{1}{2}$ of the capital gains realized by them on the disposition of certain specific kinds of property known as "taxable Canadian property." If, as the result of a large capital gain, such an individual becomes taxable at the top rate, he could lose as much as 30 per cent of his capital gain.

"Taxable Canadian Property" is defined in paragraph 115(1) (b) of the Income Tax Act and comprises the following:

a) Canadian real estate
b) Shares in a Canadian private corporation
c) Shares in a Canadian public corporation if during some part of the five-year period preceeding the disposition thereof ending after 1971 the shareholder and other persons with whom he did not deal at arm's length owned 25 per cent or more of the shares of that company
d) An interest in a partnership under certain conditions
e) A capital interest in a trust (other than a unit trust) resident in Canada
f) A unit of a unit trust (other than a mutual fund trust) resident in Canada
g) A unit of a mutual fund trust if at any time during the five years immediately preceeding the disposition thereof not less than 25 per cent of the issued units of the trust belonged to the non-resident person or to him and persons with whom he did not deal at arm's length

This means, therefore, that a non-resident who holds Canadian real estate or shares in family corporations qualifying as private corporations or any other of the above-listed items, will be taxable when he disposes of such property for a capital gain. All non-residents are supposed to report dispositions of such property to the Canadian fisc and to indicate the name of the person to whom the property is sold and pay the appropriate tax in Canada.

Upon payment of a tax, a "certificate" will be issued to the non-resident and this will protect a Canadian purchaser of the asset from having to pay some of the tax that might not have been paid by the non-resident.

The recourse of the Canadian Government against a non-resident who does not pay such a capital gains tax is shifted to the ultimate Canadian purchaser. He is required to withhold and pay to the Canadian Government 15 per cent of the purchase price paid by him to the non-resident. The Canadian resident purchaser may, however, avoid this burden by establishing to the satisfaction of the Minister that, after reasonable enquiry, he had no reason to believe that the "non-resident person" was not resident in Canada.

If a portfolio of taxable Canadian property could be transferred to a Bahamian Corporation owned by a non-resident of Canada, the disposition of the Bahamian corporation would not trigger Canadian capital gains tax. It should be noted, however, that under the provisions of the Canadian Foreign Investment Review Act, permission may have to be obtained from the Canadian Foreign Investment Review Agency to transfer control of a Canadian business to a non-Canadian.

THE EXIT TAX

Another problem which faces individuals who consider taking up residence in the Bahamas is the exit tax imposed by Canada upon capital gains deemed to arise from the notional realization of certain capital property at the time they give up Canadian residence.

However, an individual giving up Canadian residence is not required to pay a deemed capital gains tax on any property that would fall within the category of "taxable Canadian property" listed above. This is because, after he has left Canada and become a non-resident, he will remain taxable in respect of that property as already stated.

On the other hand, an individual leaving Canada who prefers not to pay a capital gains tax on ½ of all the unrealized capital gains from property other than "taxable Canadian property" may elect to postpone the tax until actual realization and give security therefor. By virtue of this election, he undertakes to be treated as a resident of Canada in the year in which he realizes any of the property in respect to which an unrealized capital gain would have been payable to Canada when he left.

Thus, even though he may become a non-resident and realize upon the taxable asset many years in the future, he will have to pay Canadian income tax not only on one-half of the capital gains that accrued to the time of departure but also on the portion of the capital gain accruing after departure. The penalty for the election therefore may be considerably higher than the payment of the unrealized capital gains tax upon leaving Canada. Several methods exist which enable someone in this situation to eliminate or reduce the Canadian capital gains tax on non-residents by the judicious utilization of tax treaties and their residence rules.

In order to take advantage of the benefits offered by the Canadian system and to achieve a minimum tax position under the law, a sound knowledge of the technical subtleties of residence and domicile is required.

For example, in the case of an individual, he would be held to be a resident of Canada if he maintains a home there to which he may return at any time and more particularly, if he leaves in the home his wife or children or servants ready to receive him or his family. Canadian residence would result even if he has another home in the Bahamas or somewhere else. A summer cottage in Canada, however, will not jeopardize his non-resident status.

Likewise, an individual who may be separated from his spouse and resident in the Bahamas may be surprised to find that the presence of his separated spouse in a home of his maintained in Canada would bring him within the Canadian jurisdiction as a resident, unless such separation is effected by a bone fide written agreement, or by a judgement of a court.

Residence is a question of fact and the object is to determine whether the individual's attachment to Canada is so strong in a geographical sense that it can be said that there he has a permanent abode. This is not to be confused with domicile, which will be dealt with later.

One means of reducing the impact of the exit tax is for a Canadian resident to roll over his non-taxable Canadian property (on which he would otherwise pay the exit tax) into a Canadian holding company before he changes his residence. The roll-over may be accomplished without tax incidence and, upon the change of residence, because the Canadian holding company will be taxable Canadian property, there will be no capital gains tax payable at that time.

BECOMING A NON-RESIDENT OF CANADA

In order to become a non-resident of Canada, an individual must give up his home and all attachments within Canada such as major directorships, clubs, apartments and the like, and acquire a residence in another jurisdiction by purchasing a home or renting an apartment in which he lives as his central family headquarters.

Nevertheless once a former Canadian resident has become a non-resident, he may return to Canada each year for temporary visits without being taxed provided he does not sojourn in Canada for periods which in the aggregate exceed 182 days in any calendar year.

Thus, purely on an individual basis, because the Bahamas imposes no income tax of any kind, a non-resident Canadian citizen may reside there and remain outside Canada for at least six months in the year, without losing his contacts with his home country and with the advantage of paying to Canada only 25 per cent on certain kinds of investment income derived from Canadian sources and no withholding tax on certain kinds of interest.

He will, however, suffer a withholding tax of 30 per cent on U.S. source investment income, and, of course, will have to pay Canadian income tax on half the profits from the disposition of "taxable Canadian property," as already mentioned.

The same individual, if he wishes to continue his business activities in Canada, may do so as a non-resident and pay tax at the appropriate personal graduated rates in Canada on the profit derived from the business there carried on by him if it is a sole proprietorship or a partnership. Should he elect to use a company, whether Bahamian, Canadian or of some other jurisdiction, to conduct his Canadian business, the situation will be somewhat different. If the company is managed in Canada, it may be fully taxed there as a resident and the non-resident shareholder would thus pay withholding tax on any dividends or interest he received from it.

There have been recent cases before the Canadian Courts in which attacks made by the Revenue on offshore subsidiaries of Canadian corporations have been tested. The income of the subsidiaries has been added to the income of the Canadian parent on the footing that the subsidiary was itself a sham and served no business purpose other than the reduction of tax. Some of these cases involve fairly substantial numbers of employees and large investment in such jurisdictions as the Bahamas, Bermuda and the like. Much will depend upon the outcome of this litigation as to whether offshore subsidiaries continue to be suitable vehicles for offshore business income, quite apart from the hazards which they always pose under FAPI.

These cases stand on their own facts and need not pose a threat to normal activities carried on bone fide in the Bahamas provided management and control of the Bahamian corporation is not in Canada.

SUCCESSION DUTY AND ESTATE TAX ADVANTAGES

One of the main advantages to an individual who has achieved non-residence and settled in the Bahamas used to be the fact that, with a very few mere formal legal steps accomplished, he could almost entirely eliminate provincial succession duty and federal estate tax. This involved giving up his Canadian domicile and acquiring a Bahamian domicile of choice and the utilization of an appropriate trust or holding company framework.

In future, effects of giving up Canadian domicile may not be quite so beneficial as before, but may still be useful.

Such a step should be accomplished with the guidance of attorneys in the Bahamas and Canada, and is really a conversion of the non-resident status by certain formal acts and statements into a permanent abandonment of any intention to return to Canada. As already mentioned, both non-resident status and domicile outside Canada can be acquired without giving up Canadian citizenship.

The Federal Government has abandoned both estate and gift taxes, but has imposed in their place a capital gains tax on the death of a non-resident in respect to his taxable Canadian property. He may, however, legally avoid these taxes by judicious use of a non-Canadian, non-resident holding corporation or trust.

In the Provincial succession duty field, the picture is becoming simpler. With the abandonment of the estate and gift tax field by Ottawa many of the provinces face reduced revenues. All the provinces have accepted this loss and have given up estate taxes save the province of Quebec, which retains substantial rates of succession duties and gift tax. The exemption for widows is without limitation.

Since the advent of the Parti Quebecois government in Quebec in 1976 that province has revamped its succession duty laws and increased the rates of tax substantially in both the succession duty and gift tax field, the top succession duty rate of 35 per cent being reached on estates of over $2 million. The top gift tax rate is 20 per cent.

As a general rule, Quebec now seeks to impose succession duty on property situated in the province passing on death. Beneficiaries resident or domiciled in Quebec receiving property situated outside of Quebec are also subject to duty. However, moveable property situated in Quebec passing from a person not domiciled or resident in Quebec to a beneficiary not domiciled or resident in Quebec is not subject to duty.

Thus, property situated anywhere in the world passing to persons domiciled or resident in the province and immovable property situated in Quebec will be subject to duty. This is, in effect, an "accession duty" and means that if a person is domiciled in the Bahamas and dies leaving property anywhere in the world to an heir who is resident or domiciled in the province, that heir will pay provincial duty on the value of the amount left to him.

Thus, it will be necessary for persons resident or domiciled in the Bahamas and having prospective heirs living in Quebec, to provide in other directions and in particular by the removal of the legal situs of assets from Quebec and by the provision of an heir other than a person resident or domiciled in Quebec. This may be done by a number of fairly simple corporate or trust devices that require professional assistance.

CORPORATE USES OF BAHAMAS BY CANADIANS

This brings us to the consideration of corporate uses of the Bahamas by Canadians. Under Canadian tax law, a company, no matter where incorporated, is resident where its seat of management and control is found (subject to recent restrictions on Canadian companies set out above). This is usually held to be the place where the directors meet or from which the day to day management instructions emanate or are carried out; **Unit Construction Company Limited v. Bullock** (1959) 3 All E.R. 831. In this case, the House of Lords established that management and control are matters of fact, not necessarily only matters of law.

This means that if a non-Canadian company has a board of directors which meets in Nassau and which there decides its affairs and manages its business, but in reality it receives instructions from Canada by, say, telephone or letter, or by the personal visitation of a Canadian resident, such a company could well be held to be a resident in Canada, with serious tax consequences.

In order to prevent a company from being legally resident in Canada and thereby paying tax at corporate rates which range from 25 per cent to 50 per cent, management and control must be exercised, bona fide and in fact, outside of Canada. This may be difficult to achieve in many instances.

Notwithstanding all this, many businesses are able to use either non-resident Canadian companies, if one can still be acquired, or a non-Canadian company resident in the Bahamas, which is so qualified by having competent and responsible staff running it in that jurisdiction for the purpose of carrying on the offshore business of a Canadian operation.

When used in this context, such a company is usually wholly owned or at least controlled by Canadian individual shareholders or by another Canadian corporation which carries on the Canadian portion of the business. There is allocated to the non-resident company the offshore business which can be more economically or beneficially effected by a non-Canadian company.

The non-resident company could perform legitimate functions of an extraterritorial nature such as world advertising, world-wide selling, the financing and organizing of sales abroad, the management and servicing of the facilities needed to maintain the products sold abroad and the operation of ships or self-insurance activities.

FOREIGN AFFILIATE TREATMENT AFTER 1975

Since 1975, the treatment of profits earned in an offshore subsidiary under the new Canadian law has been radically different from that previously in existence.

The foreign affiliate rules affect any foreign corporation which a Canadian resident controls alone or together with a related group, or with four or less persons resident in Canada.

When a foreign corporation qualifies as a "controlled foreign affiliate" the dividends which pass upstream to the Canadian shareholder are tax free when paid out of surplus earned before 1976. Dividends from surpluses composed of active business income earned after 1975, paid by foreign affiliates to Canadian shareholder companies, continue to be received tax free if they are derived from business operations carried on in a country with which Canada has a treaty.

However, after 1975, dividends paid by a foreign affiliate from active business profits earned in a non-treaty country are included in full in the income of a Canadian corporate shareholder subject to the deduction from that income of taxes paid to the jurisdiction where the profits were earned. Passive income is treated quite differently from active business income.

The concept of Foreign Accrual Property Income or FAPI is Canada's scheme to tax the passive earnings of foreign corporations controlled by Canadian taxpayers. In many ways it is not unlike its American counterpart, "Subpart F," of the Internal Revenue code. Foreign accrual property income is income from property or from a business other than an active business. Each year an appropriate share of the

FAPI of a controlled foreign corporation (and certain trusts), if it exceeds $5,000 in amount, is included in the income of Canadian taxpayers controlling the foreign corporation in the taxation year in which the foreign corporation's taxation year has terminated.

FAPI is computed in accordance with the rules of the Canadian Income Tax Act, and in its computation there will be allowed all deductions permitted under the Canadian law. Furthermore, the FAPI of the foreign corporation may be reduced by its losses for the year from property or from businesses other than active businesses and by its active business losses to an extent permitted by regulations.

FAPI does not include interaffiliate dividends, taxable dividends received from taxable Canadian corporations, active business income, income pertaining to an active business, amounts received from other affiliates and deductible by them in computing their active business income and capital gains from dispositions of property used principally in an active business. Recent changes to the Income Tax Act exclude from FAPI capital gains from the disposition of "excluded property," the most important element of which consists of shares of foreign affiliates carrying on an active business.

On the other hand, FAPI does include income from property and from businesses other than active businesses, one-half of all capital gains other than gains from dispositions of "excluded property," payments for services deductible by a related Canadian taxpayer (including Canadian insurance premium income for the insurance of Canadian risks) and service income, if the services are performed by a related individual resident in Canada.

NON-RESIDENT TRUSTS

It is perhaps significant that the changes in the Canadian budget which became law in 1975 permit non-residents of Canada to establish inter vivos trusts outside of Canada for the benefit of Canadian beneficiaries in certain circumstances. The advantage of this is that the trust may receive income which, even though it may be from Canadian assets, will not be taxable in the hands of the beneficiaries until it is actually distributed to them, i.e. there will be no attribution. Similarly trusts set up under Wills of persons who did not reside in Canada at any time in the 18 months prior to their death may dam up income for the benefit of Canadian-resident beneficiaries without any attribution to them before it is actually received.

The residence of these trusts is important and must be outside Canada since Canadian-resident trusts are liable to capital gains tax and other adverse tax consequences and would not serve the purpose of estate planning. This requires that the majority if not all trustees having legal and actual control of the trust assets be non-residents of Canada.

A recent and important decision in the courts has helped those who would use other jurisdictions to be certain about where their trusts are resident. In 'Thibodeau Family Trust v. Q.' (1978) C.T.C. 539 the Federal Court of Canada decided that a trust is resident where the majority of the trustees reside and where it is provided in the trust document that all matters of trustees' discretion may be settled by a majority of them.

It is more difficult in the case of a corporate trustee which may reside in several jurisdictions. In such case Revenue Canada's position is that the trust will be resident where its affairs are effectively managed and controlled. In all cases, as was held by the Privy Council in the Canadian case of **'Holden v. M.N.R.'** (1928-34) C.T.C. 129, it seems the residence of the beneficiaries is irrelevant in determining liability for Canadian tax of a trust.

Accordingly trusts and their uses are more beneficial to Canadians going off-shore or to non-residents having Canadian investments than they were before tax reform in 1972. Expert professional advice in this area is essential but the utilization of trusts, particularly those established in the Bahamas, can pay substantial dividends.

CURRENT ATTITUDES TOWARDS TAX PLANNING

While the Canadian law contains a number of technical provisions which narrow the field of manoeuvre for the taxpayer, the general principles continue to apply.

In the case of **C.I.R. v. Fisher's Executors** (1962) A.C. 395 at page 412; 10 T.C. 302 at pages 327 and 340, Lord Sumner said:

"My Lords, the highest authorities have always recognized that the subject is entitled so to arrange his affairs as not to attract taxes imposed by the Crown, so far as he can do so within the law, and that he may legitimately claim the advantage of any express terms or any omissions that he can find in his favour in taxing Acts. In so doing, he neither comes under the liability nor incurs blame."

In **Duke of Westminster v. C.I.R.** (1936) A.C. 1 at pages 7-8, Lord Atkin said:

"It was not, I think, denied — at any rate it is incontrovertable — that the deeds were brought into existence as a device by which the respondent might avoid some of the burden of surtax. I do not use the word 'device' in any sinister sense, for it has to be recognized that the subject, whether poor and humble or wealthy and noble, has the legal right so to dispose of his capital and income as to attract upon himself the least amount of tax."

In the course of the same case, Lord Tomlin said:

"Every man is entitled if he can to order his affairs so that the tax attaching under the appropriate Acts is less than it otherwise would be. If he succeeds in ordering them so as to secure this result, then, however unappreciative the Commissioners of Inland Revenue or his fellow taxpayers may be of his ingenuity, he cannot be compelled to pay an increased tax."

While these cases set a well-accepted legal principle, there is in Canada a growing tendency to look to the substance of a transaction, rather than to its strictly legal form. In furtherance of this philosophy, Revenue Canada has a special unit which investigates the activities of off-shore operations by Canadian residents. Thus, the uses made by Canadians of Bahamian corporations must be limited to commercially defensible activities and should not be employed merely to hide or artificially minimize truly Canadian income. In this whole field, the area of manoeuvre is narrowing and a conservative approach should be the watchword.

As will be noted from the foregoing, the achievement of a safe, viable and defensible offshore operation in the Bahamas is dependent upon the observance of a number of strictly technical points of law, in both Canadian and Bahamian jurisdictions, and the ability to establish all the facts needed to support such points of law.

Tax Benefits for U.S. Companies

By Sidney R. Pine

A United States individual or company can start international operations with relatively small amounts of capital and then expand with tax-free or low-taxed accumulations of earnings instead of net-tax dollars earned in the U.S. Thus, expansion abroad can be more rapidly accomplished with 100¢ tax-free dollars, instead of less than 50¢ dollars (which is net after approximately 50% U.S. tax).

The tax advantages or tax deferrals are available by reason of the foreign taxation provisions of the Internal Revenue Code (IRC), which set forth the conditions under which the U.S. will exempt or defer foreign income from U.S. taxation.

What types of business venture, suitable for the Bahamas, can enjoy U.S. tax advantages? In the first place, it should be recognized that a company is usually the best method of operating a business in the Bahamas. The reason for this is that companies, even though controlled by U.S. persons, are granted certain tax advantages and concessions under U.S. tax laws which are not available to U.S. individuals.

New York tax attorney Sidney R. Pine examines the U.S. tax position of American business interests investing in the Bahamas.

Counsel to the firm of Trubin, Sillcocks, Edelman & Knapp of Park Avenue, New York, he authored the original *Tax and Business Benefits of the Bahamas,* and subsequent editions, for Prentice-Hall, Inc. He has since then revised that article in collaboration with several co-authors.

More than a theorist in the field of tax advantages and international financing for American business interests abroad, Mr. Pine helped pioneer use of the islands as a base for such foreign operations.

His articles have appeared in such publications as *Journal of Commerce* and *American Banker.*

Mr. Pine was educated at Columbia University. He and his wife, Lee, maintain a home at Governor's Harbour, Eleuthera, as well as in New York City.

If a Bahamas or other foreign company is at least 50% controlled by non-U.S. persons, U.S. tax laws do not apply to its foreign income and only in rare instances will there be any U.S. income tax. Accordingly, if U.S. persons own 50% or less of a Bahamas company none of its foreign income will be subject to U.S. taxation unless and until dividends are paid to U.S. shareholders, or they sell their shares, or the assets are distributed.

Where a Bahamian or other foreign company is more than 50% controlled by U.S. shareholders, it is known under U.S. tax laws as a "Controlled Foreign Corporation" (CFC). U.S. shareholders who own at least 10% of the voting control of a CFC are taxable each year on their proportionate share of only certain kinds of income of the corporation.

The kinds of income which are thus currently taxable are, generally, income from the insurance or reinsurance of U.S. risks, passive income such as dividends, interest, capital gains, royalties and the like, sales income where the goods are either purchased from or sold to a related person, income from services if rendered to a related person, increases in investments in U.S. property, foreign aircraft and shipping income but only to the extent that it is not reinvested in foreign aircraft and shipping operations, income attributable to international boycotts, income attributable to the bribery of foreign government officials and income which is foreign oil or gas related.

Even as to these kinds of income there are many exceptions and exclusions.

Every other kind of foreign income, however, is free of current U.S. taxation. In other words, even if the Bahamas company is U.S. controlled, its U.S. shareholders are not required to include such foreign earnings in their annual taxable income.

The types of U.S. controlled foreign companies particularly suitable for operations in the Bahamas and having these U.S. tax advantages include, among others, the following:

MANUFACTURING PRODUCTION

Income from the sale of products or goods manufactured or produced in the Bahamas is not subject to current U.S. taxation even though purchases and sales involve the parent corporation or other related persons.

The same result applies to rental income where such products or goods are leased instead of sold.

Likewise, income from services rendered before a sale or in connection with an effort to sell such products or goods is not currently taxable.

SALES OF PRODUCTS AND GOODS

If the parent corporation or other related person is not involved in the purchase of products or goods, then income from such sales is not subject to current U.S. taxation no matter where or by whom the products or goods were manufactured or where the sales are made or where such products or goods are used or consumed.

Even if a related person is involved, part of all the sales income is free of current tax if the products or goods are manufactured, produced, grown or extracted in the Bahamas, or if they are for use, consumption or disposition in the Bahamas, or if the Bahamas company qualifies as an Export Trade Corporation.

INSURANCE

Income derived by a Bahamas insurance company from the insurance or reinsurance of risks anywhere in the world except the U.S. is not subject to current U.S. taxation.

Even underwriting income from the insurance or reinsurance of U.S. risks is exempt from current U.S. taxation if the premiums relating to such U.S. risks do not exceed 5% of all premiums.

The Bahamas Government has recently amended its Regulations applicable to insurance so that there are now advantages and incentives for an insurance company insuring or reinsuring non-Bahamian risks.

BANKS AND FINANCE COMPANIES

Dividends, interest and capital gains received in the conduct of a banking or financing business in the Bahamas from persons not related are exempt from current U.S. taxation.

Interest from even a related person is exempt, under certain conditions, if the related person is primarily engaged in the banking business.

Similar to foreign banking companies, dividends, interest and capital gains received in the conduct of a financing business from persons not related are exempt from current U.S. taxation.

Also, interest from a related person is so exempt under certain conditions, if the related person is primarily engaged in the financing business.

SERVICE COMPANIES

This is a broad category and includes any Bahamas corporation rendering services which are technical, managerial, engineering, architectural, scientific, skilled, industrial, commercial or the like.

Many types of companies in the Bahamas would fall into this category. A partial list would include engineering, sales promotion, sales engineering, merchandising, advertising, consulting, etc. With reference to such companies, income from such services, performed for persons who are not related, is exempt from current U.S. taxation.

Income from services rendered within the Bahamas is also exempt even though such services are rendered for or on behalf of a related person.

Income from services rendered by a foreign company in the Bahamas before a sale or in connection with an effort to sell products or goods manufactured, produced, grown or extracted by it are also exempt from current U.S. tax even though such income is received from a related person.

If the Bahamas company qualifies as an Export Trade Corporation, then, subject to statutory limitations and qualifications, part or all of services income rendered in connection with the sale of U.S. goods is currently exempt from U.S. tax even though such income may be from a related person.

LEASING AND ROYALTIES

Rents derived in the active conduct of a trade or business in the Bahamas and received from persons not related are not subject to current U.S. taxation.

Rents are also so exempt even when received from a related person if such rents are for use of property located in the Bahamas.

Royalties, as, for example, payments in connection with patents, copyrights, inventions, models, designs, secret formulas or processes, are currently exempt from U.S. taxation when derived in the active conduct of a trade or business in the Bahamas and received from persons who are not related.

Royalties are also so exempt even when received from a related person if such royalties are for the use of property or property rights within the Bahamas.

SHIPS AND AIRCRAFT

Income is exempt from current U.S. tax when received for the use or hiring or leasing or for services related to the use of any vessel in foreign commerce even though received from a related person.

Income is also currently exempt from U.S. tax when received for the use or hiring or leasing or for services related to the use of any aircraft in foreign commerce even though received from a related person.

However, such shipping and aircraft income is currently exempt from U.S. tax only to the extent that such income is reinvested in shipping and aircraft operations.

CERTAIN INVESTMENT INCOME EXEMPT

Dividend and interest from a related foreign corporation is exempt from current tax if both payer and payee are incorporated in the Bahamas and the payer has a substantial part of its assets used in the business in the Bahamas.

Even if the foreign company is "controlled," the current taxation provisions of the Act do not apply to U.S. shareholders who own less than 10% of the voting power.

If less than 10% of the annual gross income of a Bahamas company is foreign base company income, then none of the income is considered foreign base company income within the Act.

Telephone-Telegraph

The Bahamas Telecommunications Corporation (BaTelCo) has jurisdiction over commercial telephone, telegraph and teletype services. It also licenses all private radio-telephone stations.

Nassau and Grand Bahama's Freeport and Eight Mile Rock have 24-hour telephone and telegraph service to every part of the globe. Family Island telephone service generally is a daytime service. Major centres are open until 9 p.m. and on an emergency basis thereafter.

Nassau Forward Scatter Station and the Florida/Bahamas Submarine Cable provide excellent reception, eliminating problems of atmospheric interference.

In 1971, Direct Distance Dialling (DDD) was introduced between Nassau and the U.S.A.; in 1973 to Canada; in 1976 to Bermuda; and in 1979 to Mexico City, Mexicali and Tijuana, Mexico; Hawaii, Puerto Rico and the Virgin Islands. Freeport (Grand Bahama), Andros, Abaco, Exuma, Eleuthera and Harbour Island can receive calls, but cannot originate them. Eight Mile Rock (Grand Bahama), Bimini and North Andros have two-way DDD service.

Telephone rental rates in Nassau: $9.50 per residential phone per month and $20 per business phone per month. Rates cover all local calls made. An extension phone costs $1.50 for residential and $2 for business per month. Switchboard systems have different rate structures.

Automatic telephones are available in Eight Mile Rock, West End, Freeport, Pinder's Point, Hunters, Mather Town, Lewis Yard, Williams' Town and Smith's Point, Grand Bahama; Governor's Harbour, Harbour Island, Rock Sound and Tarpum Bay, Eleuthera; Fresh Creek and North Andros; George Town, Exuma; Alice Town and Bailey Town, Bimini; Bullocks Harbour, Berry Islands. The rates are the same as in Nassau.

TELEGRAPH RATES TO PRINCIPAL POINTS FROM BAHAMAS

In general, telegrams are via Cable & Wireless (CW) sent through the British Commonwealth; Tropical Radio Telegraph Co. (TRT) or International Telephone & Telegraph Co. (ITT) sent through the U.S. and other countries.

TELEGRAPH RATES

	Full Rate per word B$	Night Letter 22 words min. B$	add. word B$
Australia	.30	3.30	.15
Austria	.48	5.28	.24
Barbados	.26	2.86	.13
Bermuda	.26	2.86	.13
Canada	.26	2.86	.13
Germany	.43	4.73	.21½
Grand Cayman	.26	2.86	.13
Great Britain, Channel Islands and the Irish Republic	.42	4.62	.21
Jamaica	.26	2.86	.13
Japan	.83	9.13	.41½
Mexico	.48	5.28	.24
Puerto Rico	.30	3.30	.15
Spain	.53	—	—
Sweden	.49	—	—
Trinidad	.26	2.86	.13
Turks Islands	.26	2.86	.13
United States	.24	2.64	.12
Hawaii	.30	3.30	.15

Special greetings (GLT) rate to U.K., Canada, British territories via Cable & Wireless: $1.30 for 10-word minimum; 13¢ each additional word. There is no special greeting rate to the U.S.

Telegraph rates to and from Nassau and the Family Islands are 21¢ for minimum message of six words (addressee and address are counted and charged for) and 3½¢ for each additional word.

Telegraph messages to freighters, tankers, liners, and other vessels on the high seas are 18¢ per word for a minimum message of seven words.

TELEX RATES TO PRINCIPAL POINTS FROM THE BAHAMAS

	3 mins. B$	add. min. B$
Australia	12.00	4.00
Austria	12.00	4.00
Barbados	12.00	4.00
Bermuda	9.00	3.00
Canada	10.50	3.50
Germany	12.00	4.00
Grand Cayman	12.00	4.00
Jamaica	12.00	4.00
Japan	9.00	3.00
Mexico	12.00	4.00
Puerto Rico	9.00	3.00
Spain	12.00	4.00
Sweden	12.00	4.00
Switzerland	12.00	4.00
Trinidad & Tobago	12.00	4.00
Hawaii	12.00	4.00
United States	7.50	2.50
United Kingdom	12.00	4.00

TELEPHONE RATES TO PRINCIPAL POINTS FROM BAHAMAS (PERSON TO PERSON)

	Weekday		Sunday	
	3 mins. B$	add. min. B$	3 mins. B$	add. min. B$
Antigua	9.00	3.00	9.00	3.00
Barbados	9.00	3.00	9.00	3.00
Bermuda	10.00	2.50	10.00	2.50
Bermuda (DDD)	7.50	2.50	7.50	2.50
Canada (see Bahamas Rates to Canada)				
Germany	15.00	5.00	15.00	5.00
Grand Cayman	9.00	3.00	9.00	3.00
Great Britain	15.00	5.00	12.00	4.00
Haiti	9.00	3.00	7.50	2.50
Italy	15.00	5.00	15.00	5.00
Jamaica	9.00	3.00	7.50	2.50

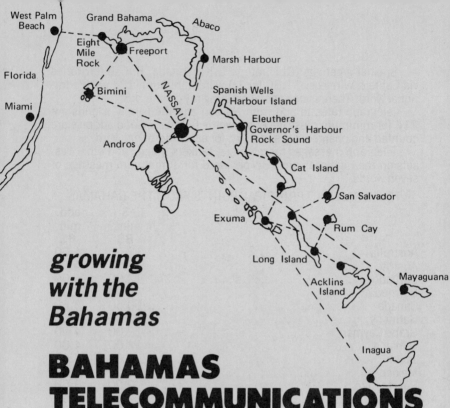

growing with the Bahamas

BAHAMAS TELECOMMUNICATIONS CORPORATION

GRAND BAHAMA: EIGHT MILE ROCK — WEST END — FREEPORT — PINDER'S POINT — HUNTERS — MATHER TOWN — LEWIS YARD — WILLIAMS' TOWN — SMITH'S POINT; ELEUTHERA: GOVERNOR'S HARBOUR — HARBOUR ISLAND — ROCK SOUND — TARPUM BAY; ANDROS: FRESH CREEK — NORTH ANDROS; EXUMA: GEORGE TOWN; BIMINI: ALICE TOWN — BAILEY TOWN; BERRY ISLANDS: BULLOCKS HARBOUR.
Now Have Automatic Telephone Facilities

While all automatic facilities can receive DDD calls, only subscribers in New Providence, Grand Bahama, Bimini and North Andros can initiate them. **Direct Distance Dialling** is available to the U.S.A., Canada, Bermuda, Jamaica, Mexico City, Mexicali and Tijuana, Mexico; Hawaii, Puerto Rico, the Virgin Islands, Trinidad and Tobago.

AUTOMATIC INTERNATIONAL TELEX SERVICE IS ALSO AVAILABLE

Save Time & Money USE D.D.D.

		Weekday		Sunday	
		3 mins. B$	add. min. B$	3 mins. B$	add. min. B$
Japan (Honshu, Shikouk Island, Hokkaido, Kyushu)		15.00	5.00	12.00	4.00
Puerto Rico		9.00	3.00	7.50	2.50
Sweden		15.00	5.00	12.00	4.00
United States:					
Alaska, Hawaii		15.00	5.00	12.00	4.00
(other states, see below)					

BAHAMAS RATES TO U.S.A.*

		DDD			Person to Person**
		Day	Night***	Sun.	
ZONE 1 (0-500 Miles)					
Alabama, Florida, Georgia,	3 Min.	$2.40	$1.80	$1.80	$4.50
South Carolina	Add. Min.	.80	.60	.60	1.50
ZONE 2 (501-1000 Miles)					
Delaware, District of Columbia, Kentucky, Maryland, Mississippi, North Carolina, Tennessee,	3 Min.	$3.15	$2.40	$2.40	$6.00
Virginia, West Virginia	Add. Min.	1.05	.80	.80	2.00
ZONE 3 (1001-2000 Miles)					
Arkansas, Colorado, Connecticut, Illinois, Indiana, Iowa, Kansas, Louisiana, Maine, Massachusetts, Michigan, Minnesota, Missouri, Nebraska, New Hampshire, New Jersey, New Mexico, New York, North Dakota, Ohio, Oklahoma, Pennsylvania, Rhode Island, South Dakota, Texas, Vermont,	3 Min.	$3.90	$2.85	$2.85	$7.50
Wisconsin	Add. Min.	1.30	.95	.95	2.50
ZONE 4 (2001-3000 Miles)					
Arizona, California, Idaho, Montana, Nevada, Oregon, Utah, Washington,	3 Min.	$4.65	$3.45	$3.45	$8.25
Wyoming	Add. Min.	1.55	1.15	1.15	2.75

*Except Alaska, Hawaii.
**All operator assisted calls are billed at person-to-person rates. Station rates are available only for calls billable abroad.
***6 p.m. to 7 a.m. Monday through Sat.; 6 p.m. to Midnight Sat.; Midnight Sun. to 7 a.m. Mon.

BAHAMAS RATES TO CANADA

Direct Distance Dialling facilities exist between Canada and Nassau (both ways).

City	Person to Person		DDD		
	Weekday	Sun.	Day	Night	Sun.
Calgary	9.00	6.00	7.20	6.00	4.80
Vancouver	11.25	7.50	9.00	7.50	6.00
Winnipeg	9.00	6.00	7.20	6.00	4.80
Moncton	7.50	5.25	6.00	4.95	3.90
St. John's	7.50	5.25	6.00	4.95	3.90

	Person to Person		DDD		
	Weekday	Sun.	Day	Night	Sun.
District of MacKenzie	7.50	5.25	6.00	4.95	3.90
Halifax	7.50	5.25	6.00	4.95	3.90
Ottawa	7.50	5.25	6.00	4.95	3.90
Toronto	7.50	5.25	6.00	4.95	3.90
Charlottetown	7.50	5.25	6.00	4.95	3.90
Quebec City	7.50	5.25	6.00	4.95	3.90
Montreal	7.50	5.25	6.00	4.95	3.90
Saskatoon	9.00	6.00	7.20	6.00	4.80
Whitehorse	12.00	9.00	9.60	8.40	7.20

Rates shown are for first 3 mins.

TELEPHONE RATES, NASSAU-FAMILY ISLANDS

Telephone rates to and from Nassau and the Family Islands are $1.80 for three minutes and 60¢ each additional minute.

Radio telephone service to ships-at-sea via Nassau radio telephone: $4.92 minimum to ocean-going vessels for three minutes and $1.64 each additional minute. To private yachts: $1.26 minimum for three minutes, 42¢ each additional minute.

Television

ZNS TV transmitter power is 50,000 watts E.R.P. on Channel 13, and operates in full colour. Channel 13 is seen 130 miles from Nassau and operates six hours per day Monday through Friday, 16 hours on Saturday and 12 hours on Sunday. ZNS TV began Test Transmission on July 4, 1977, with its official programming commencing July 10, 1977. On October 20, 1977, Her Majesty Queen Elizabeth II officially opened ZNS TV-13.

Channel 13 is autonomous of any external Television network; its programming being chosen by the programming staff of the Bahamas Broadcasting Corporation to serve the national interest.

In January 1983, the station installed a facility to receive satellite transmission for re-broadcast.

Time

The Bahamas operates on Eastern Standard Time, which is five hours behind Greenwich Mean Time. The islands are on Eastern Daylight Time (four hours behind GMT) from the last Sunday in April to the last Sunday in October.

Tourism Information

In 1982 there were 1,947,740 foreign arrivals in the Bahamas. Of those, 1,121,070 came by air and 826,680 came by sea.

This represents an increase of 10% from the 1981 figure of 1,763,320.

Total visitor spending in 1981 was $639,116,638. No estimate for 1982 was available at press time.

The two main tourist centres are New Providence and Grand Bahama. New Providence (Nassau and Paradise Island) offers 6,277 hotel rooms and Grand Bahama (Freeport and West End) has 3,421. Family Island hotel rooms total 2,088.

The Ministry of Tourism tabulates the visitor arrivals to the Bahamas as follows:

Year	Nassau	Grand Bahama & Family Islands	Total
1978	1,024,760	682,180	1,705,280
1979	1,060,550	728,870	1,789,420
1980	1,090,900	813,660	1,904,560
1981	989,800	773,520	1,763,320
1982	983,320	964,420	1,947,740

(These figures include transits.)
Components may not add up to totals due to rounding.

The Bahamas Ministry of Tourism maintains 17 overseas sales offices abroad. Information about the Bahamas can be obtained from:

UNITED STATES
Atlanta: 1950 Century Blvd., N.E., Suite 26, Atlanta, Ga. 30345
Boston: 1027 Statler Office Building, Boston, Mass. 02116
Chicago: 875 North Michigan Ave., Suite 1816, Chicago, Ill. 60611
Dallas: 2825 Southland Center, Dallas, Texas 75201
Houston: 5177 Richmond Avenue, Suite 755, Houston, Texas, 77056
Los Angeles: 3450 Wilshire Blvd., #208, Los Angeles, Ca. 90010
Miami: 255 Alhambra Circle, Coral Gables, Fla. 33134
New York: (General Sales Office) 30 Rockefeller Plaza, Room 52, New York, N.Y. 10020
Philadelphia: 42 S. 15th St., Philadelphia, Pa.
San Francisco: 44 Montgomery St., San Francisco, Ca. 94104
Washington, D.C.: 1730 Rhode Island Ave., N.W. Washington, D.C. 20036

CANADA
Montreal: 1255 Phillips Square, Suite 1105, Montreal, Quebec, Canada, H3B 3G1
Toronto: 85 Richmond Street West, Toronto, Ontario, Canada M5H 2C9
Vancouver: 470 Granville St., #129, Vancouver, B.C. V6C 1V5

ENGLAND
London: 23 Old Bond Street, London W1X 4PQ, England

FRANCE
Paris: 9 Boulevard de la Madeleine, Paris, France

GERMANY
Frankfurt: 6000 Frankfurt AM Main, Zimmerweg 10, Second Floor, West Germany

Trade Unions
Airport, Airline and Allied Workers Union
Bahamas Brewery Distillers Workers Union
Bahamas Communications and Public Officers Union
Bahamas Construction & Civil Engineering Trade Union
Bahamas Doctors Union

Bahamas Electrical Workers Union
Bahamas Electrical Utility Employee Managerial Union
Bahamas Hotel Catering and Allied Workers Union
Bahamas Hotel Managerial Association
Bahamas Housekeepers Union
Bahamas Musicians & Entertainers Association
Bahamas Public Services Union
Bahamas Taxi-Cab Union
Bahamas Telecommunications Management Association
Bahamas Transport Distributive and Allied Workers Union
Bahamas Union of Teachers
Bahamas Utilities Services & Allied Workers Union
East Side Stevedores Union
Grand Bahama Commercial, Clerical and Allied Workers Union
Grand Bahama Public Service Drivers & Allied Workers Union
Grand Bahama Telephone & Communications Workers Union
Oil & Fuel Services Workers Union
Tourism Service & Allied Workers Union
United Brotherhood of Longshoremen's Union
Bahamas Construction & Maintenance Workers Union
Bahamas Electrical Utility Managerial Union
Commonwealth Cement & Construction Workers Union
Grand Bahama Entertainers Association
Bahamas Maritime Port & Allied Workers Union
Commonwealth Transport Union
Commonwealth Wholesale Retail & Allied Workers Union
Commonwealth Electrical Workers Union
Bahamas Professional Pilots Association
Bahamas Merchandising Workers Union
Commonwealth Union of Hotels Services & Allied Workers

Transportation

Taxis on New Providence are plentiful and all have meters. The rates are Government-controlled. The first one-fifth mile costs $1.20 for one or two passengers, with each additional one-quarter mile adding 20¢. Additional passengers after the first two pay $1.50 per person. Accompanied children under three ride free.

Cabs hired by the hour have a maximum rate of $12 per hour for five-passenger cabs; each additional half hour $6. Larger cabs for seven or more passengers are $15; each additional half hour $7.50.

Car rental prices are competitive, with Hertz and Avis represented at airport and downtown offices. Pick up from your hotel anywhere in New Providence (including Paradise Island) is free of charge. There is, however, a charge for delivery to West End, Grand Bahama, from Freeport. Prices go from $44 per day ($308 per week) for a standard Volkswagen, to $75 per day ($448 per week) for a large station wagon and include free unlimited mileage. Off season rates are slightly less.

Visitors may use their home driver's licences here for three months. Traffic moves on the left side of the road.

Motor scooters are $25 per 9 a.m.-5 p.m. day, including gas. Insurance is $2, but a deposit of $25 is required. It is wise for a novice to practise scooter skills in light traffic before attempting Bay Street. There is a law which requires drivers and riders of motor scooters and motor bikes to wear crash helmets. These helmets are available at no extra charge from the rental companies.

Bicycles rent at $8 per day. A $20 deposit is required.

The jitney (small bus) provides inexpensive touring and a close view of local life. Fare is 50¢ a ticket that can take you the length of the island. Service is from 6:30 a.m. to 7:30 p.m. Bus stops are marked. However, both the routes and time schedules may be unpredictable and at press time it was foreshadowed that bus fares might be increased in the near future.

Paradise Island guests may utilize the 50¢ bus service around Paradise Island. It stops at every hotel front door at about 30 minute intervals from 8:30 a.m. to 1:30 a.m. the following morning. These buses are very distinctively marked with blue and white stripes and "Paradise Island" in large letters on the sides. A ferry service operates from the end of Casuarina Drive, Paradise Island, across the harbour to Rawson Square and back at $1 per person one way. This is a daytime service, 9 a.m. to 5:30 p.m. with departures from both sides of the harbour about every twenty minutes.

A horse-drawn surrey ride costs $8 for a half-hour trip for two passengers and a personalized tour of Nassau's downtown area. Rates for additional passengers and extended trips should be negotiated with the driver beforehand. The surrey ranks are in Rawson Square, downtown Bay Street and north Frederick Street.

Power or sail boats are available by the hour, half-day, day, week, or month.

To visit any of the Family Islands on a budget try a mail boat. More than 20 of these motor vessels leave Nassau each week carrying mail and provisions to the Family Islands. Passengers share the same food and shelter as the crew for $16 to $25 one way.

For example, the **Bahamaland** sails to Exuma every Tuesday at 2:00 p.m. and returns to Nassau by the end of the week. One-way passage is $25.

Arrangements for passage on the mail boats are made through the boat captains at Potters Cay — the area underneath the Paradise Island Bridge — and some of the boats have booking offices on Bay Street.

It is not luxury travel, so taking a blanket and some non-perishable food and drink would be a good idea. However, some have sleeping quarters and food services at extra charge.

Scheduled inter-island air service is provided by Bahamasair. Round trip fares (from Nassau) include $90 to George Town, Exuma; or $96 to Freeport.

Charter planes are available, too. A five-passenger Piper Aztec, for example, costs $170 per flying hour, while the cost of chartering a nine-passenger Islander is $210 per flying hour.

Voting

To register in the Bahamas, a prospective voter must:

1. Be a citizen of the Bahamas, either by birth or naturalization, and be 18 years or older.

2. Be subject to no legal incapacity (e.g. in prison or a mental institution).

3. Have been a resident of a constituency for three months previous to registration.

To register, application should be made to the Parliamentary Registrar's Office, The Mosko Building, Hawkins Hill (Mt. Royal Ave), Nassau, or to a revising officer, or to a Commissioner in the Family Islands.

To vote, one must be duly registered and must have been ordinarily resident in his constituency for some period during the six months immediately preceding the day of election.

If the voter has moved to a new constituency and has lived there for less than six months, he is entitled to vote in his old constituency if he was registered there.

In 1982 five new constituencies were added to the previous 38; three in New Providence — Holy Cross, Blue Hills and Yamacraw — and two in the Family Islands — Marco City in Grand Bahama and Bimini. There are now 23 constituencies in New Providence, and 20 in the Family Islands.

The last general election in the Bahamas was held June 10, 1982 when nearly 90 percent (75,604) of those registered to vote cast their ballots. In accordance with the Constitution, the next general election will be in 1987.

Wages

Wages for housemaids range from $50 to $60 per week, with uniforms and meals left to the employer's discretion. Gardeners earn between $60 and $100. Restaurants and hotel cooks (short-order, not chefs) earn about $85 to $100.

A cocktail waitress at a large, oceanfront hotel makes about $50 weekly and a bartender about $70 to $100, excluding gratuities. Uniforms and meals usually are furnished by the employer.

An executive secretary with five to 10 years' experience earns about $250 to $275; a stenographer-secretary between $250 and $285; a junior secretary $100.

The following is a cross-section of types of jobs, with wage ranges and averages in the Bahamas in 1983:

Type of Job	Wage Average B$/week
Stenographer Secretary	250-285
Hotel & Restaurant Manager	450-500
Head Cook	250-300
Cook, except private services	175-200
House Maids	70- 90
Janitor	100
Farm Helpers	60
Truck Drivers	200
Fork Lift Operator	140-175
Labourers and Handyman	100-110

These wage scales were provided by the Ministry of Labour.

Water Rates

Current **New Providence** water charges are based on the following quarterly rates:

—A minimum charge (including the first 2,000 gals. or part thereof) per meter per quarter in accordance with schedule given below.

—For every 1,000 gals. (or part thereof) in excess of 2,000 gals. but not exceeding 15,000 gals. per meter per quarter, $6.80 per 1,000 gals.

—For every 1,000 gals. (or part thereof) in excess of 15,000 gals. per meter per quarter, $12.40 per 1,000 gals. And, in each case, a proportionate sum for periods other than thirteen weeks.

Minimum Charge Schedule

Meter size (in inches)	Per Quarter	Meter Size (in inches)	Per Quarter
(a) ½-⅝ inch	$21.00	(f) 2 inches	$ 126.00
(b) ¾ inch	$31.20	(g) 3 inches	$ 210.00
(c) 1 inch	$48.00	(h) 4 inches	$ 420.00
(d) 1¼ inch	$66.00	(i) 6 inches	$ 735.00
(e) 1½ inch	$84.00	(j) 8 inches	$1,050.00

A charge of $10 is made for meter readings other than the normal ones. Reconnection charge after disconnection due to non-payment of water charge is $15.

A deposit of $20 is required for dwelling-houses with one water closet or bathroom and $50 for those with two or more. For commercial establishments the deposit is not less than $20.

Notice of customer's discontinuance of the service should be sent to General Manager, Water & Sewerage Corp., P.O. Box N3905, Nassau in writing at least "seven clear days" before such discontinuance.

Family Island water rates are as follows:

—$1.15 every 1,000 gals. (or part thereof) not exceeding 13,000 gals. per meter per quarter.

—$1.45 every 1,000 gals. (or part thereof) in excess of 13,000 gals. but not exceeding 26,000 gals. per meter per quarter.

—$2 every 1,000 gals. (or part thereof) in excess of 26,000 gals. per meter per quarter.

Grand Bahama water rates are as follows (see also **Water Supply** in Freeport Blue Pages for Freeport/Lucaya rates):

—$2.50 every 1,000 gals. (or part thereof) not exceeding 13,000 gals. per meter per quarter.

—$3.50 every 1,000 gals. (or part thereof) in excess of 13,000 gals. but not exceeding 26,000 gals. per meter per quarter.

—$5.00 every 1,000 gals. (or part thereof) in excess of 26,000 gals. per meter per quarter.

Wildlife Preserves

The Exuma Cays Land and Sea Park, one of the areas under the protection of the Bahamas National Trust, is about 40 nautical miles from Nassau. The ocean voyage through the park is brief but exciting — with fine anchorages scattered among small islands in a 176-square-mile area set aside for yachting, skin-diving, hiking and observation of unique Bahama flora and fauna.

A full-time warden for the Park was appointed on January 1, 1982, with the common law authority of a constable.

In brief, the Park Rules provide that:

1. Plants, animals and marine life may not be disturbed or removed.

2. No garbage or waste may be deposited in the water or on the land.

3. No boat may take each day more than six crawfish, 12 conchs, four scalefish (however, not more than one each of rockfish, grouper, muttonfish and hogfish), 48 whelks, provided always that no spearfishing equipment other than a hand-held spear or Hawaiian sling may be used for the purpose of the aforesaid.

4. Every person who offends against these bye-laws shall be liable to a fine not exceeding $2,500, and any boat or equipment used may be forfeited.

According to the Trust, the park's bird life includes 42 species of nesting land birds, several of which are endemic to the Bahamas, and many migrants.

Other parks maintained by the Trust include the Inagua Park, nearly 300 miles of flamingo nesting area; the Pelican Cays (off Abaco); Peterson Cay (off Grand Bahama). One protected area of natural woodland in southeast Abaco facilitates the breeding of the Bahamian parrot—an endangered species. The 40-acre Lucayan National Park on Grand Bahama Island contains the Lucayan Cavern, the longest underwater cave system in the world. It has presently been explored to a distance of 33,000 feet. Conception Island, north of Rum Cay, is a station for migrating birds and a turtle-breeding ground.

The purpose of the National Trust is to help perpetuate conservation, science and education, aesthetic values, and outstanding recreational areas. The Trust is a non-profit organization, supported entirely by donations and the annual subscriptions of its members. Membership applications may be obtained from Bahamas National Trust, P.O. Box N4105, Nassau, Tel: (809) 322-8333.

The Ministry of Agriculture also maintains protected areas on land and in the sea.

ZNS

ZNS are the call letters for Radio Bahamas, the national broadcasting system. These letters were assigned in May 1936 when the fledgling radio station was recognized and accredited by the American Federal Communications Commission.

The letter Z was assigned to all British stations in the Caribbean and Atlantic islands, including Bermuda. The words attached to the call letters are Zephyr (balmy breeze) Nassau Sunshine.

In the early 1950s ZNS became a 1A station under the North American Regional Broadcasting Agreement. That meant that ZNS became a Clear Channel station with the same protection given to high-powered United States stations so that no other station may broadcast on ZNS's frequency (1540kHz) within approximately 1,000 miles. See also **Broadcasting**, page 242.

ZNS - I	1540 KHz	20,000 WATTS	RADIO BAHAMAS
ZNS - II	1240 KHz	1,000 WATTS	NEW PROVIDENCE
ZNS - III	810 KHz	1,000 WATTS	NORTHERN SERVICE
ZNS - TV 13		50,000 WATTS	THE BAHAMAS

ZNS-TV COLOUR 13

THE BROADCASTING CORPORATION OF
THE BAHAMAS, THIRD TERRACE EAST, CENTREVILLE
P.O. BOX N-1347, NASSAU, BAHAMAS. TELEX: 20 253
TELEPHONE: (809) 322-4623. CABLES: ZNS, NASSAU

INVESTIGATE COMMERCIAL OPPORTUNITIES IN TAX FREE FREEPORT
What A Climate To Do Business

Everyone in the know knows that Grand Bahama is one of the most popular sub-tropical resort islands in the world. No great wonder! Six great championship golf courses, big game fishing, tennis everywhere, the largest marina in the Bahamas, fabulous El Casino, superb restaurants, luxury hotels, beautiful apartments, homes and condominiums are available. Did we forget to mention 80 miles of glorious sand beaches, great ocean bathing and the most glorious weather? An altogether ideal setting for work and play.

Now ask Syntex, Standard Oil of California, Charter Oil, Smith-Kline Beckman Corporation, Cooper Laboratories, Barclays Bank International, Royal Bank of Canada, Bank of Nova Scotia and Chase Manhattan Bank (among other major financial institutions and companies) about some other friendly Freeport facts like:

• Tax advantages that provide exceptional incentives for commercial and industrial development • No income tax • No personal property tax • A stable government • Sound economy • Facilities to operate under bond with no customs and excise duties • Duty free entry to the U.S.A., Canada, Japan and E.E.C. countries for a large range of goods manufactured in the Bahamas.

Or, ask us for all the facts on why

IT'S A PLEASURE TO DO BUSINESS IN FREEPORT

THE GRAND BAHAMA PORT AUTHORITY
Group of Companies

Freeport, Grand Bahama Island • Cable: Portauth • (809) 352-6711

Churchill & Jones
Real Estate Limited

The way we figure it any real estate salesman can sell you a plot of land, home or apartment. But that would be that.

At Churchill & Jones, we're the Number One Full Service Real Estate Broker on Grand Bahama Island, and still trying harder.

We can boast of specializing in real estate consulting, sales, re-sales, tax appraisals, listings from West End to MacLean's Town, Walker's Cay to Inagua and everywhere in between. But we won't.

We can tell you about our property management division, which includes collection, maintenance, storage facilities, renovations, and the like. But we won't mention that either.

We can also tell you that we're the on-site brokers for the Grand Bahama Development Company Ltd. (Developers of Freeport) and important parcels of land in Bahamia, Lucayan Beach West, and Fortune Bay.

And that we're the exclusive agents for Silver Sands, Casa Bahama, Colindale, Gleneagles Investments, Forestview and numerous other condominium apartments in Lucayan Towers and Kings Bay.

But we'd really like to suggest that you give us a call when you're thinking about an important investment like Real Estate. It costs nothing to talk.

Our number is listed below and our names are Hilary V. E. Jones, David P.L. Hunter and Harold L. Rodgers, Jr.

FULL SERVICE REAL ESTATE BROKERS

Number One
Queen's Highway

PHONE

352-7305

P.O. Box F-2480
Freeport, Bahamas

Consult us on development plans, design, decoration

Freeport/ Lucaya

Right Under our Feet...
the World's Largest
Underwater Cavern

The first question asked by well-travelled visitors to Freeport is: "What is the history of the island?" "Scarcely any!" one used to reply. "There were a few scattered settlements from the 1800s onwards. The people lived peacefully – fishing, sponging, or farming. A few lived wickedly over different periods as wreckers, gun-runners or bootleggers. The city of Freeport itself was only founded in the mid-1950s. Really, you want to visit Nassau to get any historical atmosphere ... " If asked about flora and fauna, it could only be said that, although to the residents these were most attractive, there was nothing exceptional to remark upon.

However, gradually over the past 10 years, a handful of dedicated people have enabled us to change our tune, for history has been uncovered before our very eyes, or rather, under our very feet. By the discovery of the bones of some Lucayan Indians, it has been confirmed that there *is* a previous history to Grand Bahama. Added to this, the island turns out to be the proud possessor of the longest known underwater cavern in the world, and also of a most exceptional one-inch crustacean, so unrelated to anything else that not only has a new name been invented for it, but also a new class.

But like all the best stories, this should begin at the beginning. To comprehend why this cave, and those subsequently discovered, are here, one has to understand a little about the formation of the Bahamian islands as a whole. Geologists tell us that the islands of the Bahamas were once joined together as a great underwater mountain range, of which the present islands and banks are flattened peaks (it is known that around us are channels, or valleys, some 10,000 ft. deep). Jacques Cousteau remarked that the islands

354

Marine biologist Jill Yager investigates an underwater stalactite.

were formed like a limestone sponge, and it is thought that the present formation came about during the four glacial and inter-glacial periods. Every time giant glaciers built up during the Ice Ages, the level of water dropped; each time they melted, the ocean levels rose until they were some 25 ft. above the present level. So perhaps the Bahamas was, some 25,000 years ago, all one big island, with the sea lapping some 400 ft. lower than it does now.

Because of Grand Bahama's "sponge-like" structure, it has long been known that "ocean holes" – little lakes connected underground to the sea—are common here, and that they are often far inland. People had known about a cave at Gold Rock for a considerable time; the Abaco Lumber Company had felled trees near it, and the local villagers had for many years grown pigeon peas around it. Gold Rock is very close to the United States Missile Base where, between 1966 and 1970, a young electrical engineer named Dennis Williams was working on the Apollo programme. When manned expeditions to the moon ceased, Williams worked for a time for the Grand Bahama Port Authority, and at the same time was becoming a highly-qualified instructor in those things he loved best—flying, scuba-diving, and the much more specialized art of cave-diving.

Flying low over the island, Williams used to look with some interest at the number of blue holes and cave mouths which were visible from the air. He became friendly with Ben Rose who, in 1970, although not himself a cave-diver, had bravely taken a plunge into the cave at Gold Rock (now known as Ben's Cave) and told him about it. Various other divers had also gone a little way into it, and a nearby cave, being fascinated by the mysterious domed roof, with a small window of light at the peak of the dome, now known as the Skylight Cave. Under the dome was found a heap of stones, the top of which was just below the surface of the water, so that divers were able to stand on it in order to admire the formation of the cavern, and the "eye" directly above.

In September 1973, Dr. Warren Duncan, who was diving with his family, was astonished to discover a human shin bone standing upright in about six feet of water. He returned the following weekend, and this time found part of a human skull under a pile of rocks in about 12 feet of water. The skull having been examined and found to be definitely not Negroid or Aryan, excitement mounted, and U.C.L.A. was contacted with a view to having it carbon-dated. But this would have been expensive, and would have spoiled part of the skull, so it was decided to rely on visual examination by other experts. Due to the flatness of the skull, it was pronounced by the Smithsonian Institution to be definitely Lucayan. Later, parts of seven or eight more skeletons were discovered, and pulled out of what is now thought to have been a ritual burial mound. Perhaps hoping to find gold ornaments, or else just for the kick of having a human skull to show off at home, various visitors to the cave desecrated this mound before there was a chance of experts examining, photographing, or properly measuring the rock on which people had so casually been standing.

Williams by this time had dived further inside the cave and realized its uniqueness, and for the past dozen years, with a handful of other keen cave-divers, he has pioneered techniques and developed equipment to explore extensively the labyrinthine tunnels of what has now been named The Lucayan Cavern.* So far, he has used some 33,000 feet of exploration line, weaving an underground cobweb of surveyed tunnels for no less than six miles. We will come to his great contribution to this adventure story later on, and deal first with the discovery of our earliest Bahamian settlers.

Architect and town planner Peter Barratt, who was largely responsible for the attractive layout of Freeport, is not only a diver who has found some of the Indian bones himself, but is also a keen archaeologist, and it is he who sent the carefully-packed bones and

---

*On March 1, 1983 the Bahamas National Trust closed the cavern to the public after if was discovered that "irreparable damage has been caused by souvenir hunters, and by persons who did not conduct their diving expeditions in a scientifically professional manner". On June 20 it was announced that the cavern will be closed for two years.

356

Archaeologist Peter Barratt at the Ben's Cave entrance to Lucayan Cavern.

skulls hither and yon for expert appraisal. He has catalogued the finds and has also, financed by Mrs. Wallace Groves, wife of the founder of Freeport, started a small museum at the Garden of the Groves to show them off. Like Williams, he believes that there are yet many miles of cave to explore, and in his most informative book, *Grand Bahama*, he observes that there are several large voids open to the surface of the island known as "ocean holes" or "sink holes" (the same phenomenon in the sea being called a "blue hole", "solution hole" or "boiling hole"). Fresh water, in this land of oolithic limestone, lies close to the surface on top of the underlying salt water, so he feels it would have been natural for the Lucayans to settle themselves near the cavern and also close to the sea, just like the recent Gold Rock small-holders planting their pigeon peas around a sort of open fresh-water well where they would only have needed to sink a bucket on the end of a rope for irrigation purposes.

Who were the Lucayans? They were a branch of the Arawak Indian tribe who migrated from the eastern slopes of the Andes in South America, settling the Caribbean between 800 and 1492 A.D. They were close cousins of the Arawaks found in Cuba, Jamaica and Haiti, who developed the Tainan culture. It is known that the second wave of the strange island-hopping migration landed our Arawaks in the southern Bahamas; they were now calling themselves "Lukku-cairi" or "island people". They were a gentle race, forced to flee ever northwards, savagely hunted by the fierce Caribs who slaughtered the men and made slaves of the women.

The first sign of human life ever recorded on Grand Bahama was an old crone seen by Ponce de Leon in 1513. He called her "La Vieja" and noted that he saw her on a tiny cay off West End. She may have been left behind when other Indians left the island, or she could have been some sort of shepherdess, put there to tend a herd of domestic animals, perhaps the yellow dogs. That islet has been named Indian Cay, but this appears to be the only instance of the sighting of an Indian, either living or dead, on Grand Bahama up to Dr. Duncan's discovery on that famous day in September 1973.

One of the skulls found in the burial mound was that of a 12-year-old girl, now named "Lucy", and beside it was a greenish nephrite bead, but there have been no other artefacts found here. Many experts have speculated about this strange collection of bodies, heaped together with flat rocks on top of them. Could the mound initially have been *above* water—in which case over the last 400-odd years the sea must have subsided? Or did the Lucayans go in for some form of underwater burial? Perhaps over future years, exploration will produce more of these mounds to satisfy our curiosity.

Let us return to Dennis Williams and the exciting discoveries he has made with his regular diving companions, Gene Melton, an engineer on the U.S. space shuttle at Cape Canaveral; film-maker Paul Mockler, and marine biologist Jill Yager, who teaches at St. Paul's School in Freeport. It was with Melton in 1976 that Williams did his longest exploratory swim of 33,000 ft., and they have established definitely that even though they have "only" mapped a total of six miles so far, the Lucayan Cavern is already the longest known underwater cavern in the world. Jill Yager has found with him not only her unique crustacean, but also other rare specimens of underwater life, and together Dennis and Paul made a film showing the discoveries.

The easiest way to describe the cavern is to relate some of the sequences of this excellent film. First one sees Williams piloting his own plane over a large circular hole set in a wilderness of palmetto bushes, wild pigeon peas, and pines. He and Miss Yager are pointing out the cavern to Professor John Holsinger from the Old Dominion University of Virginia, a cave explorer and world authority on cave crustaceans. One of the objects of the trip is to try and collect for the professor a specimen of this totally new crusta-

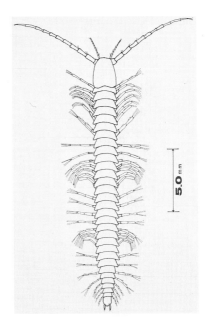

Most primitive living crustacean in the world today was discovered in the Cavern. (Drawing by Dennis Williams).

cean, one inch long, which Miss Yager discovered and subsequently named for posterity as *Speleonecies lucayensis* (Greek for "Lucayan cave-swimmer"). Not a diver himself, the professor has to sit for hours at the mouth of the cave while Williams and Miss Yager don enormously heavy twin air tanks weighing 140 lbs., a stomach tank (50 lbs.), and other back-up gear weighing some 40 lbs., which they will take to enter the most extensive system of submerged caverns anywhere on earth.

As they descend the long ladder into the water, one sees that they carry with them survey reels (1,000 ft. of nylon line) which they will tie to a stalactite as they leave the first cavern, then fasten the other end round a handy "pillar" when they reach their destination. Each diver carries a primary light, plus spares, and Williams also clutches a specially-designed bank of 1200-watt floodlights. The twin tanks carry more air than that normally used by a scuba-diver, enabling them to stay down for three to four hours. They risk their lives every time they embark upon these dives – there is no one to rescue them if they get lost, run out of air, or lose their lights.

Unexpectedly in the film, we see another form of extreme danger: after swimming some distance, the beautiful forest of orange, red, green and blue "mites and tites" turns into an area of crumbling rock which can break away at the slightest touch. Jill, in the lead, touches a piece of such rock, to find sections of wall and ceiling dropping all around her. The noise, echoing through the camera sound-system, is hollow and frightening; to those experiencing the actual fall and the beating of the resulting waves around them, it must be nerve-shattering. Explorers and cameraman alike turn around and head for a safer area, knowing well that their exit as well as the chamber ahead of them could have been blocked.

Now they proceed through another cave-mouth in their search. In a huge, vaulted cavern, they point out an interesting vertebrate – a blind cave-fish, floating vertically, pink and sadlooking. His eyes covered by thick translucent membranes, he has got used through centuries of darkness to living without using his eyes, and employs other senses instead. *Lucifuga spelaectes*, as he is called, was first found in the Bahamas (in Nassau) as recently as 1969.

Later, they meet a tiny cave-dweller, an undetermined species of *Thermosbaenacean* called *Stygiomysis spelaeotes*. At last, with a beaming smile, Miss Yager finds what she is looking for, *Speleonectes lucayensis* himself (or "The Little Creature", as they call him). She opens a specimen jar, and in goes the most primitive living crustacean in the world today, his nearest relative, a fossil found in Texas, being 250 to 300 million years old! In over three years of searching, the divers have only seen this crustacean twelve times, and they have taken four for scientific research. It is interesting that all the specimens found have been collected in total darkness in salt water, and at a depth of at least 45 feet. The Little Creature fits into no other class of crustacean apparently, so he has been awarded not only a name but a class all on his own, i.e. *Remipedia*, from the Latin word *remipedes*, meaning oar-footed.

Satisfied, the divers turn and swim back towards the entrance hole, from which, as they emerge from total darkness, one sees a glorious translucent turquoise ray of light beaming downwards from the "skylight" hole above. But they cannot shoot triumphantly up to show their find to Professor Holsinger. Experience dictates that, for fear of getting "the bends", they must let their bodies adjust gradually by staying just below the surface for a frustrating 20 minutes. At last they emerge, and the professor gloats admiringly over the bottle in which The Little Creature churns anxiously round and round, using his remarkable oar-like swimming technique.

Later in the film, one sees Miss Yager in a laboratory at the Florida Institute of Technology, where she wrote a most erudite

This stalagmite has been christened "The Wedding Cake".

paper on the find, happily dissecting her new pet and recording every aspect of the strange body for posterity. And back home, with his computer, Williams shows how copious records have been kept of the geology, the history and the denizens of the Lucayan Cavern.

Seeing this film, and talking to these courageous divers later, one realizes what a great contribution they have made to Grand Bahama's history, and, by the very nature of their researches and their solicitude for the environment, to its future as well. A three-year grant has been awarded by the American National Science Foundation for research on The Little Creature, but, apart from Mrs. Groves's assistance in creating the museum, all other research has been done at the personal expense of Jill Yager, Dennis Williams and Peter Barratt. One may be sure that they will go on digging, diving and researching until the island has given up many more of its secrets in the way of Ice-Age underwater caverns, prehistoric crustaceans and pre-Columbian Indians. If you are reading this in a comfortable chair somewhere in the middle of Grand Bahama Island, it is quite likely that they may be swimming underneath you, right now! An intriguing thought – but then they do some intriguing things here. As Williams noted in his log-book: "Grand Bahama is hollow – we have seen her insides!"

Freeport's Investment Opportunities

The sun, the sand, the sea, the blue skies—and no taxes! This has been the Bahamian theme song to attract new investors for nearly half a century. Perhaps 30 or 40 years ago, taxation abroad was the main hazard, but today this has been joined by inflation, recession and unemployment. These are not confined to any one country but seem to be a general malaise.

One recipe endorsed by all investment consultants is to diversify your portfolio with funds allocated to domestic investment, precious metals, and foreign real estate. The Bahamas has many advantages—the islands are close to the United States mainland; there are excellent air and sea communications, and a good quality of life. Read all about it in *The International Man** by Douglas Casey.

Possibly the over-riding concern of any foreign investor is the stability of the local government and of the economy, and the answers here are reassuring. There are no natural resources and the government is exploiting tourism and foreign investment to the full to create new jobs for the growing population. The same government has been in power since 1967, and has developed a policy for Bahamianization of retail and other trading businesses, leaving the field open for foreign investment in tourist-oriented real estate development, in light or heavy industry, as well as for the retiree who can prove financial independence and who demonstrates a good character and background.

Freeport is a planned community with superb infrastructure, miles of paved highways, city power and water, CATV or Satellite TV with numerous channels, plus miles of white, sandy beach, fine championship golf courses, more than 5,000 resort hotel rooms, a casino, International Bazaar, Underwater Explorers Society, two U.S. supermarkets, government hospital and two private clinics, and many schools. There is no Real Property Tax, nor are there any personal or corporate taxes in Freeport.

The Grand Bahama Port Authority is anxious to see more investors coming in who will create the maximum activity in Freeport. The city was planned, less than 30 years ago, to be neatly

---

*Published by Kephart Communications Inc., 901 North Washington Street, Alexandria, Va. 22301, the book examines in detail the comparative advantages of very nearly every known country on the face of the globe. The Bahamas rates high marks, and comes out top of the field for a second home or as an off-shore investment centre.

divided into areas for heavy industry, light industry, offices and shops—all, of course, separate from the residential districts.

There are already several successful industries here: an oil refinery, an oil trans-shipment company, a cement company, four pharmaceutical plants and vacant buildings for another, a perfume factory, an electric auto corporation, a liquor blending company, jewellery manufacturers, three shipping companies, and a cancer immunology research centre.

There are also numerous international banks, hotels with huge conference rooms, and–most important to the potential investor–excellent architects and construction companies. But in its short life, Freeport has not yet come anywhere near being fully exploited. There are still 100,000 acres available which can either be bought outright, or else leased to anyone whose application is approved by the Port Authority and the government.

And how does a business become eligible for approval? "We need people with expertise, who will employ and train Bahamians, and who will be active in the way of import/export, thus creating waves of further employment and prosperity on the island," says Jack Hayward, O.B.E., chairman of the Grand Bahama Development Company, one of the Port Authority Group of Companies. "They must of course undertake to do nothing to spoil the environment, and we would prefer to *lease* the land longterm rather than sell it outright, but we will certainly consider every application on its merits. We need good businesses here, which will fully integrate into the Bahamian scene, so we lean over backwards to help the right people with finding the perfect site.

"We are also very accommodating, when necessary, in the matter of service charges and licence fees. Although we would like to do so, we do not ask companies to contribute towards upkeep of the harbour and the airport, both owned by the Port Authority and both of which, with their respective accommodation of ocean-going freighters, tankers and jumbo jets, are essential to business on Grand Bahama. We are also enthusiastically encouraging agricultural development on the island, which has the advantage over Florida for growing citrus fruits in that it is totally frost-free."

Freeport has always had a cosmopolitan and transient population, and as owners move frequently, you will find many large and well-furnished houses for sale at prices which are extremely attractive in the international real estate field. There must be nearly 60,000 plots in Freeport–the majority of which were sold over 15 years ago to foreign investors.

But 15 years is a long time and death, divorce, disenchantment and disappearance are taking their toll. The majority of the original buyers are trying to "disinvest", and as a result, there are many superb opportunities. Location is still the prime criterion in buying real estate, and the prospective purchaser should survey the market and look for property with attractive features–located on or near a beach, on a waterway or near a golf course, and preferably fully serviced and ready to build. Buying a small lot with no special features may be cheap, but it's a sure way of making a bad investment.

If you want to go into business in Freeport you should apply for a licence from the Port Authority, which must also be approved by the Bahamas Government. They are looking for solid financial references and the capacity to sustain a growing business during its early years. They also want evidence of your professional expertise and personal probity. In a tax-free society, the government can't afford to get saddled with failures, either personal or business.

In addition to the immediate tax freedoms, the government offers a wide range of incentives under the Industries Encouragement Act, and is also a signatory of the Lomé Convention which permits the export of goods to the European Economic Community nations without payment of tax or customs duty if these items have been partly or wholly manufactured in the Bahamas. Similar concessions permit goods to be shipped into the U.S. under the General System of Preferences. There are daily roll-on/roll-off ships from nearby Florida ports, and an ample supply of semi-skilled and unskilled labour available at very competitive rates.

You should weigh up the advantages of doing business or establishing an off-shore second home in Freeport, and if you are prudent you will make sure that your proposal meets the stated requirements of the government. Every transaction must be a two-way street, and if you are looking for a tax-free profit or a good quality of life in a tax-free area, the government in its turn is looking for a source of employment and training for Bahamians so that they can move into management positions and prosper. If your business requires particular skills which cannot be found in the Bahamas, you can apply for a limited number of work permits to employ non-Bahamian staff until local replacements can be trained. If you plan to retire in Freeport you'd be expected to apply for permission to build or buy a permanent home.

Once you have decided on your own personal Freeport investment programme and know the type of property you need, you should get in touch with one of the many firms of full-service real

estate agents on the island. These are firms which not only sell real estate (and are not tied to any particular subdivision or development) but which also manage property, for you may want to rent before you buy, or rent out the house or condominium apartment you have just bought.

Many of these firms can also supply appraisals, carry out project analysis and collect mortgages or other payments as well as giving competent advice and purchasing assistance in interior design and furnishing.

There are no real estate licensing laws in the Bahamas, and it is recommended that you contact a member of the Grand Bahama Real Estate Association, which maintains high professional standards and is backed by a strong code of ethics.

If you are planning retirement in the Bahamas, there are a number of possible alternatives, including:

a. A Time-Sharing Resort: For a small investment, you can secure the right to use the accommodation you want for a limited period of time. When evaluating a time-share resort, look at the amenities and facilities offered, check that the maintenance charges can't be escalated rapidly, that there are sound management teams which are likely to be in existence for the term of your investment, and that they are affiliated with one of the major time-share exchange organizations.

b. A Condominium: Location is always a predominant feature, as well as the amenity of the apartment you are buying. You should also check the solvency of the condominium association, and enquire if there are pending assessments or capital levies.

c. A Second Home: The substantial retiree, or the retiree whose special skills can make a contribution to the community, is the person whom the government really wants to attract. With the rising cost of new construction, plus high interest rates, there are many advantages to buying a previously-owned house. Location in a good residential district, adjacent to the amenities you enjoy, is obviously a "must". In addition, you will almost certainly find a fully-furnished home, completely equipped with a full range of modern appliances. There are competent architects and contractors who can build to your plans and specifications.

Most of the land and buildings in the Freeport area of Grand Bahama have a clear root of title, usually from a direct Crown Grant or from the Grand Bahama Development Company, recorded in the Registry of Records in Nassau. Attorneys can quickly establish by search in the Registry that the title is good, and you are protected

by your attorney and his professional insurance. Title insurance is also available, but is frequently a duplication of something you have already paid for.

Nearly all the homes and condominium apartments in Freeport are sold fully furnished, and although you may plan to change the decoration scheme to meet your personal taste, you don't have to do it right away. In most cases a tooth-brush is all you need to move into your new home!

It is difficult to be precise about costs, but the following yard-stick figures apply:

A half-acre lot in a good area, fully serviced, $8,000 to $15,000; canal-front lots, fully serviced, $15,000 to $30,000; oceanfronts lots, $75,000 to $100,000; 2-bed/2½-bath condominium townhouse, $85,000; and a large single-family home on a half-acre lot, $175,000 and upwards.

The Bahamas Bar Association has established a minimum scale of fees, at present two per cent of the negotiated/agreed sales price.

Stamp Duty is a fee paid to the government at closing, and is on a sliding scale related to the price of the house. Your real estate broker can advise you in advance of the amount involved in your transac-

A limited number of single family canal-front and golf course lots are available for building purposes within Tamarind — a mature development in the heart of Freeport/Lucaya.

Other land throughout the development is available on attractive terms for commercial development and housing estates.

Please address enquiries to:
The General Manager,
Tamarind Developments (Grand Bahama) Limited,
P.O. Box F-614, Freeport, Grand Bahama, Bahamas.
Tel: (809) 373-4100/3. Telex 30 074 Tamluc
or visit our office situated on Midshipman Road in Freeport/Lucaya.

TAMARIND DEVELOPMENTS
(Grand Bahama) LIMITED

370

tion, and in addition to perfecting a good title, your attorney will apply for Exchange Control approval to register your investment in foreign currency. This ensures that at some future date you can repatriate the proceeds of a sale or rental of your property in the currency of your choice.

Commissions are almost invariably paid by the seller—about eight per cent to 10 per cent on a house or condominium.

Many properties are owned by resident Bahamian corporations, and by purchasing the shares you acquire title to the assets, and your attorney will make sure there are no undisclosed liabilities. If you want to form a Bahamian corporation, your attorney will take detailed instructions from you, and can arrange for nominee officers, directors and shareholders if you wish to preserve anonymity.

A new corporation usually costs about $1,500 to form, and there is an annual Registration Fee of $1,000 payable to the government. Some existing corporations with very favourable builder/investor licences can also be bought.

If you visit the Bahamas planning to purchase real estate, it would pay you to come prepared with both character and financial references, as well as a police certificate. This is a very normal safeguard, with similar procedures in Switzerland, the Channel Islands and most other sophisticated tax haven areas. It ensures that foreign investors are of known good character, and capable of carrying out their development programmes. Remember, you are likely to live in close proximity to other foreign investors, and this screening process will be your protection and reassurance in the future.

You won't find much finance available in Freeport, except on short (five-year) terms, and at interest rates about three per cent above the U.S. prime rate. Longterm mortgage finance is not available in Bahamian currency to non-Bahamians. This policy has successfully channelled the majority of low- and medium-cost houses into Bahamian hands. Some sellers will give back mortgages.

You should allow 90 to 120 days from the date of acceptance of your offer to the date of completion. This makes it possible to carry out all the title searches, to obtain the necessary approvals, and to transfer money. Once again, it will minimize the delays if you give your attorney a power-of-attorney so that he can act for you at closing and you do not have to come back unless you want to.

On average, it takes five to six weeks to clear a personal cheque presented for payment in the Bahamas. Even certified or cashier's cheques may require authentication by tested telex or telephone

372

conversation, unless the cashing bank in the Bahamas is able to recognize the signature on a draft or cashier's cheque from the drawing bank. Possibly the quickest and most satisfactory method of transferring funds for completion is by telex transfer from your home bank to an account you will previously have opened in one of the numerous Freeport banks.

At the time that you get the acceptance, the broker should supply you with an inventory of the furniture and contents, and you should check this schedule on receipt, and again on the day of closing. Most houses are sold in "as is and as seen" condition, but it still pays to test-run any appliances and establish their state, so that you can make allowance in the price, and arrange to buy and install replacements.

Enjoy a leisured vacation in Freeport/Lucaya, but while you are here it takes very little effort on your part to investigate the offshore investment opportunities available on the island. What Freeport has to offer can well turn out to be exactly what you have been looking for to expand or diversify your business activities, or to provide a tax shelter and hedge against inflation for your personal investments.

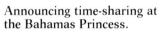

New Cruise Schedules Provide

A Boost for Tourism

—BY SUZANNE TWISTON-DAVIES

Bringing the ships of Scandinavian World Cruises to Grand Bahama, thus turning the island into one point of a triangle with New York City and Florida, has given a welcome boost to tourism in the Bahamas.

The cruise line is a division of an old-established Copenhagen company, called D.F.D.S., which is the largest car/passenger-carrying concern in the world to-day. The chairman of E. H. Mundy & Co., Kenneth Golding, knew the late managing director of D.F.D.S. in London, and it was their joint planning over a decade which, since February 1982, has resulted in three very sophisticated, comfortable, Bahamian-registered ships sailing regularly to and from Grand Bahama on cruises to suit almost every pocket.

All three vessels are car-ferries as well as cruisers, which brings a new dimension to tourism in the Bahamas, for now tourists can be independent on arrival. Imagine leaving New York with your own car, and having a pleasant cruise to Grand Bahama; after a few days of trying out beaches and restaurants all over the island, you cruise on to Miami or Port Canaveral, explore part of Florida or visit Disneyland, and then drive back to New York. Or else you can return to Freeport and sail northwards, driving off in New York City, still with your own car.

Every five days throughout the year, the M/S *Scandinavia*

374

leaves New York City on a two-and-a-half-day cruise to Freeport, carrying up to 1,600 passengers and 400 cars. On arrival in Freeport, 84 of those cars can be taken on by the 11,000-ton M/S *Scandinavian Sea*, which arrives at 10 a.m., two hours after the New York ship. The *Sea* is at the end of a midnight cruise from Port Canaveral, during which her passengers will have enjoyed the casino facilities, a midnight buffet and a discotheque. This ship now sails (perhaps with some of the transferred New York passengers and cars) at 12:30 p.m. on her return voyage to Port Canaveral, arriving there at 10:30 p.m.

One-way passengers pay $59, plus $15 for full-day meal charges, and $6 port charges (or round-trip $89, plus $10), and they may have a cabin for $25 extra. On the other five days that the *Scandinavian Sea* does not connect with the *Scandinavia* in Freeport, she makes 11-hour "Cruises to Nowhere" out of Port Canaveral at $35 per person, with $7 port charges, plus $15 for two meals (and $10 for children under 12, who incidentally *only* pay for meals, not travel). Therefore, for a total of $57, an adult can enjoy two meals, movies, revues, cabaret, casino, swimming-pool and deep-sea fishing, if weather permits—all packed into 11 "get-away-from-it-all" hours.

The alternative trip, if one has brought a car from New York and then wishes to gravitate over to south, instead of central,

Florida is to sail on the third ship, the M/S *Scandinavian Sun*, which leaves Freeport daily at 5:30 p.m., arriving in Miami at 11:30 p.m. With its efficient organization, added to the easy roll-on/roll-off system of all three ships, this 11,000-ton cruiser can have 150 cars and up to 1,000 passengers neatly deposited at Terminal No. 7, near Biscayne Boulevard, in a very short space of time. The round trip, meals included, costs $89 (one way $59) plus port charges of $12 (or $6). A two-berth cabin costs an extra $60, but unless you strike bad weather, you will not need one.

I took my car over to Miami recently after driving it easily up the ramp onto the ship at Freeport Harbour at 3 p.m., one hour before the embarkation time for passengers without cars. For a while I relaxed in the sun beside the swimming pool and then–the *Scandinavian Sun* having sailed at 5:30 p.m. –I went off for a tour of the ship's amusements. The boutique had some attractive clothes and gifts at reasonable prices; spread over her seven decks, the ship also offered a discotheque, games room, movie theatre, casino-style gambling with British croupiers, plus a large amount of hungry slot machines which were being fed huge meals by hopeful coin-pushers, and occasionally responded with a generous hic-cough.

We docked at 11:30 p.m., and after brief immigration and customs formalities, my car and I rolled off onto the Miami Pier, and I was very soon checking into my hotel. Very reasonable packages can be obtained through the shipping company for stays of one or two nights at any of five Miami hotels, or, for those coming in the opposite direction, there are six Grand Bahama hotels offering packages which include golf, scuba-diving and snorkelling. Yet another alternative is for Floridians to make a full-day return trip (leaving at 8 a.m. and getting home at about 11:30 p.m.) with a chance to visit one of Grand Bahama's beautiful beaches and explore the fascinating International Bazaar.

Now we come to the most exciting cruise of all, to be equally appreciated by tired tycoons, by monotony-bound mothers, or by adventurous adolescents. The M/S *Scandinavia* has something for every taste, and it offers a brief but really refreshing break.

On a windy day in February, I embarked at 2 p.m. on this magnificent 30,000-ton vessel, built in Nantes, France at a cost of $100 million. She is 607 feet long and 88 feet wide, with a maximum speed of 20.9 knots (24 m.p.h.). I was a little apprehensive that, being eight decks high (183 feet from keel to funnel wing), she might roll a lot, but during the whole two-and-a-half-day cruise, which included a stretch of rough sea, I never heard of a seasick passenger. This was due to her stabilisers, oar-like extensions 14 feet under water which, controlled from the bridge, act like the wings of a plane, tilting against the waves so the ship does not pitch about.

Scandinavian World Cruises wisely judges their passengers to be interested people, and I jotted down some statistical notes which I found on information posters hung by the lifts on various decks. The ship having sailed punctually at 3 p.m., I sat on deck in glorious sunshine while we slipped out of Freeport Harbour, past the four-masted schooner which plies between Florida and the Bahamas, and which obligingly spread her sails to add to the romantic ambiance, and then I started to digest these notes.

I learned that it took 193,548 square feet of carpet to cover the inside of the ship (very nice it is, too, in a dull pink) and 107,526 square feet to cover the outside decks with "green lawn", which, unfortunately, got rather soggy when there was sea-spray around. It took 135 tons of paint to make the *Scandinavia* a dazzling white with deep blue trimming, and it had been necessary for marine architects to make 5,000 drawings for the ship to be built.

Soon it was time to take a shower in my cabin and change for dinner (men wore ties and jackets, and there were plenty of attractive long skirts). I discovered that the television which is in every cabin showed not only the news twice a day, plus feature films, but also gave a constant time-table of ship's events. Later, I explored the shops with their Pringle sweaters, Otagiri china, swim suits and cotton dresses, and met some friends for a drink in the John Paul Jones Pub, where a pianist played nostalgic music. Then I went in to dinner.

The waiters – among them British, Bahamians, Malays, Indians, Chinese and Italians – all worked briskly and with much good humour as they served an excellent selection of food and wine, took endless photographs of honeymoon couples, sang "Happy Birthday" to some lucky person for whom the kitchens had made a cake, and wore fancy clothes as they did a sort of "conga" round the dining room when bringing in the dessert. After dinner we proceeded to the Blue Riband Room for a "Caribbean Evening" of calypsos, dancing and limbo contests.

My bed was comfortable, and after a good sleep I breakfasted at 8:45 – the first sitting is at 7:30 – on coffee and a huge choice of fruit juices, cereals, home-made croissants, kippers, bacon, eggs, pancakes, sausages, French bread. The two girl college students who

(Continued on pg. 416)

Freeport/Lucaya is Poised for an
Economic Upswing

During the early part of 1983, there was an incredible mushrooming of new buildings on Grand Bahama. Wherever you drove, along main roads or in the "backwoods", men could be seen hammering happily at the roof of a half-finished building while a cement-mixer churned away below. Many single family homes, a few duplexes, and several apartment buildings were in the course of construction.

It is revealing to read the actual statistics of this progress. In 1976, 51 building permits were issued by the Port Authority, construction costs being $1,152,429. In 1979, there were 141 permits, costs amounting to $10,652,147. But 1982 hit an all-time high of 222 permits at an overall construction cost of $24,527,581.

A $1 million apartment complex of 20 units is being built in Bahama Terrace, which will eventually increase to 150 units, and a smaller apartment building is growing at Silver Cove. In the Discovery Bay area, a group of Norwegian investors has completed the first phase (48 units) of a new $100 million resort complex, spread over 24 acres, which should, before the end of the decade, comprise a 72-unit time-sharing property, a large hotel and a townhouse development. They expect by then to employ 600 people.

The Grand Bahama Development Company has donated to the Ministry of Housing 120 acres, in scattered lots, for both low- and medium-cost housing, as well as property on some good-sized lots for multi-family housing.

Reasonably-priced Bahamian straw items, like hats and handbags, lure buyers to the International Bazaar.

There is also plenty of commercial building: a new mini-mall of seven stores is being built, and a large department store and an office/shops complex is being erected. Sunco Builders and Developers, Ltd., from Nassau, are building their own new offices near Portion Control so they may more easily involve themselves in adding to the architectural beauties of the island. One of their first jobs was a considerable expansion to the premises of the Bank of Nova Scotia. The Bank of Montreal is completely rebuilding, and a service station and convenience store are planned at Coral Road/ East Sunrise.

Electric Auto Corporation (Bahamas), Ltd., has had considerable success since settling in Freeport, in spite of being unable to introduce the largescale operation, employing many Bahamians, which they at first hoped to do. They assembled 10 electric cars in

"IN THE BAHAMAS, IT'S ALWAYS PRINCESS."

BAHAMAS PRINCESS: Grand Bahama Island, Bahamas.
P.O. Box F-207
Tel: (809) 352-6721

LOCATION: One of the largest resorts in the world, located at the heart of the island's celebrated attractions. Set in 100 acres of lush gardens.

ACCOMMODATIONS: 585 rooms, suites, and villas. Two PGA golf courses, 6 tennis courts, day/night play. Two pools. Shops. Private beach club. Superb restaurants. Nightly entertainment.

PRINCESS TOWER: Grand Bahama Island, Bahamas.
P.O. Box F-2623
Tel: (809) 352-9661

LOCATION: Luxury tower in a fairytale Moorish design, adjacent to the famous El Casino and the exciting 12-acre International Bazaar.

ACCOMMODATIONS: 400 rooms and suites. Largest freshwater pool on the island. Six tennis courts for day/night play. Shops. Two PGA 18-hole golf courses available at its sister hotel, the Bahamas Princess. Private beach club. Superb restaurants. Nightly entertainment.

Bahamas Princess

Princess Tower

1982, and hope to complete 50 in 1983. The bodies of ordinary cars are imported, the engines removed and large batteries are substituted. Testers then take the completed vehicles out on the Grand Bahama Highway, where, with police co-operation, they can "let them rip" to test performance.

The Bahamas Oil Refining Company in 1982 refined only about 100,000 barrels of crude oil a day when their capacity is 500,000 barrels. This was caused by the world's depressed oil situation, but they hoped that refining output would increase to 180,000 barrels during 1983.

Todhunter Mitchell & Co., Ltd., is the only company on the island to blend, bottle and distribute alcoholic beverages. They turn out between 1,000 and 1,200 cases a day of 35 different products including gin, vodka, whisky, rum and liqueurs, employing 35 people. They obtain raw materials from Scotland, the U.S., Jamaica and Canada, and sell to the U.S., Canada, Germany and Central and South America.

Syntex Corporation, established since 1967, employs 218 people in the manufacture of chemical products such as unguents, birth control pills and prescription aspirin.

Freeport is fortunate that Franklin Chemicals, Ltd., a pharmaceutical company, chose to come here rather than Singapore, which was the other alternative. Franklin produces a first-rate product – Cimetidine, the active ingredient of the ulcer-pacifying drug, Tagamet. The company has accomplished what it promised to do – not only is it bringing money into the island, providing employment and training for 16 (soon to be 32) young Bahamians who have a basic grasp of maths and chemistry. They have 130 employees, and later there will be 160 on the payroll.

The plant stands on 22.5 acres of land in the heavy industry area, and was officially opened by the Prime Minister on October 1, 1982.

The company has already established an Industrial Education Fund, has given a bus for the use of Hawksbill Primary and High Schools, and has also made a generous donation to the scholarship fund of the Freeport Friends of the Arts. The plant is run as a very efficient, clean operation and the company spent $9 million on environmental protection equipment. Every facet is carefully planned – from the main gate, a tanker carrying 4,000 to 5,000 gallons of solvents will be directed to containers one way, and dry goods into the warehouse another way. A storage shed holds sodium bricks which go into the "third step" reactor: Franklin

makes the third, fourth, fifth and sixth steps in the Tagamet process, the "second step" being the dry bulk powder which comes to them from Mexico or Switzerland for mixing with other chemicals. The end product is packed in kegs and shipped to Canada, Peru and Venezuela for final tableting, packaging and sale.

Farming on the island is coming into its own, particularly in the realm of fruit- and vegetable-growing. Grand Bahama's terrain is the same as that of south Florida, and the same fruits can be grown here, but Grand Bahama has the advantage of being frost-free.

Veterinarian Peter Bizzell runs the Bahamian Mariculture Research Institute in conjunction with the Institute of Marine Science of Florida. Between them, they have put together a floating field station at Fortune Bay, and a "grow-out area" for the cage culture of groupers, snappers, crawfish, conch and tilapia. The latter, originally fresh-water fish from Africa, breed successfully, since the female keeps the young in her mouth, safe from predators, after hatching. Dr. Bizzell takes varieties of small fish and grows them in cages of varying size, length, and mesh-type in the Grand Lucayan Waterway to establish what food they will eat, and how fast they will grow.

The most exciting thing to happen to tourism in 1982-83 on the island was the advent of Scandinavian World Cruises (see page 374). Two more airlines are bringing people in – Air Canada has recommenced flying to the island on a seasonal basis, and Pan American has a daily flight between Freeport and New York. The airport facilities have been greatly improved at a cost of $2 million, which makes the first impact upon tourists very inviting.

The two Princess Hotels, owned by Lonrho Ltd., also the Xanadu Hotel have had structural improvements, and the 16-year-old Holiday Inn has had a $2½ million face-lift, and will have another $1½ million spent on it in 1984. The Grand Bahama Hotel and Country Club, at West End, which closed during 1982, re-opened in January 1983 after being renovated to the tune of some $2 million.

The hotel, which has its own jet-length airstrip, has been turned into a village concept, and re-christened Jack Tar Village with everything from golf, big-game fishing and moonlight cruises outside, to shops and a night-club inside. The guests pay $1,000 a head per week "all-in". It has been repeated for some years that the once-famous Lucayan Beach Hotel would "re-open before Christmas". Renovations in early 1983 were almost completely finished, and it appeared then that the hotel would, in fact, be in full swing before the end of 1983. Princess Hotels International have expressed interest in running the adjoining Monte Carlo Casino.

Tourists are becoming increasingly involved in scuba-diving, and the Silver Sands Sea Lodge and the Lucayan Bay Hotel both offer packages with the Underwater Explorers' Club.

Something is always going on in Freeport, such as the annual Michelob 200 race, featuring some of the biggest powerboats in the world. With the wonderful shopping facilities offered by the International Bazaar and the Straw Market, with excellent restaurants and golf courses, with glorious beaches, snorkelling, sailing, wind-surfing, and para-sailing, no tourist need ever be bored on Grand Bahama Island.

Suzanne Twiston-Davies, who contributed all the preceding reports on Grand Bahama developments, was born in Wales and educated in England and at the University of Lausanne, Switzerland, where she read French, German and Philosophy. She has travelled extensively, particularly in Europe, Australia and the West Indies, and spent 15 years in BBC Television. She worked for some time in Trinidad and the United States before becoming a freelance journalist.

384

Freeport
Information

Accommodations

A variety of facilities is available for visitors to Freeport/Lucaya. These range from luxury beachfront properties to apartment complexes that do not offer the services available in major hotels, but are cheaper to rent.

The apartment rental properties are booked through local real estate agencies. They usually include maid service and television hookup. A kitchen is included. They are available in a variety of locations and in efficiency, one, two and three bedrooms. Most have swimming pools and are within easy access of the beaches. Many have coin-operated washers and dryers.

Freeport's smaller hotel rates start at about $55 per day double occupancy in summer and $75 in winter. They all have dining facilities, swimming pools and cocktail lounges.

The larger hotels offer a full range of activities and facilities for visitors. Rates start at approximately $59 per day double occupancy in summer and $79 in winter, exclusive of government tax of 6% per day (divided equally between Government and hotel promotion and advertising), energy charge of $1 per day, and daily maid service of $1.50 per day, which is common to all hotels.

Some are located on the beach and all have swimming pools. Live entertainment featuring island groups playing goombay-calypso music is found at all hotels, some of which also have a weekly beach barbecue or moonlight cruise. All hotels have access to golf courses and tennis courts. Silver Sands and Lucayan Bay Hotel also have a special scuba-diving package with the Underwater Explorers' Society.

Accounting Firms

Andreae & Fingland
Certified General Accountants of the Bahamas
Coopers & Lybrand
Deloitte Haskins & Sells
Michael Hepburn & Co.
Klynveld, Main, Goerdeler
Pannell, Fitzpatrick & Co.
Price, Waterhouse & Co.
Peat, Marwick, Mitchell & Co.
Thorne Riddell

Agriculture

Grand Bahama Farms grows lettuces, tomatoes, cabbages, peppers, some citrus, watermelons and cucumbers. On occasion, a small surplus of peppers, cucumbers and cherry tomatoes is exported to the U.S. Parker Groves plantation produces mainly limes, but also avocadoes, zucchini and paw-paws which they are already exporting. Bahamas Poultry Co. Ltd. runs about 45,000 birds from day-old chicks. The Produce Exchange deals only with locally-grown fruits and vegetables. Two groups have begun experimenting with mariculture research for the breeding of more conch, lobster, dolphin, grouper, stone crabs and tilapia.

The Department of Agriculture has an office in Freeport (tel: 352-2144), and encourages small farmers to develop. With loans from the Development Bank in Nassau, plus water testing facilities supplied by Syntex, and with agricultural supplies allowed in duty free, smallholdings are developing all over the Island.

Air Services

Six scheduled airlines serve Freeport/Lucaya. They include Air Florida, serving Miami, Orlando, Tampa, Pensacola, Fort Lauderdale, West Palm Beach and New York (La Guardia); Bahamasair, offering Miami, Fort Lauderdale, Nassau (and thence connecting inter-island services); Eastern Airlines to Miami; North American to West Palm Beach, Orlando, Fort Lauderdale. Air Canada now flies on a seasonal basis between early November and late April, with one weekly flight to Toronto and two weekly flights to Montreal (Mirabelle). Pan American has a daily non-stop flight to New York.

Lucaya Beach Air Service and Helda Air Holdings provide charter services between Freeport, the islands and Florida. Both companies also provide an air ambulance.

Numerous charter flights also visit Freeport.

The airport runway is 11,000 feet long and 150 feet wide, and is paved with asphaltic concrete. Taxiways are 75 feet wide. A new six-storey Control Tower has been built by the Grand Bahama Port Authority Group of Companies at a cost of about $2,000,000. Terminal space includes a 6,000-sq-ft in-transit lounge. The new tower is equipped with improved Direction Finding equipment, weather radar, weather satellite receiving equipment and a lighted beacon. Freeport's is the largest privately-owned international airport in the world. There is a long-term car park and the exit barrier is operated by four 25¢ pieces.

Animal Clinic

Two veterinarians, Dr. Alan Bater and Dr. Peter Bizzell, run the Freeport Animal Clinic on the Queen's Highway (352-6521), and also provide an emergency service.

Architects

Architects, Incorporated
Architects Partnership
Architectural Consultants & Associates
Griffiths & Hodgkins
Montgomery A. Pratt Associates

Banking

There are six major clearing banks in Freeport/Lucaya — the Bank of Montreal, Bank of Nova Scotia, Barclays Bank International Ltd., Canadian Imperial Bank of Commerce, Chase Manhattan and 'Royal Bank of Canada.

There are also the Commonwealth Industrial Bank, Ltd., The Finance Corporation of the Bahamas, Ltd., and First Home Savings and Loan, Ltd.

Commercial banking hours are 9:30 a.m. to 3 p.m. Monday to Thursday, and 9:30 a.m. to 5 p.m. Friday.

Building Permits

The cost of a building permit is determined by 23 construction factors listed on a building permit application (available at the Building Department, Kipling Building), and therefore varies widely from application to application. If construction is not started within 90 days from issuance of permit, a new permit must be purchased, unless otherwise specified. A building permit fee of approx. ½ of 1% of the contract figure is payable on approval of submitted drawings.

Car Rentals

Avis, Budget Rent-A-Car and Hertz all have offices at the Airport and on Royal Palm Way, either in or near the Atlantik Beach Hotel. Charges range from $43 for a small car to $70 for a large one, daily, plus $4 insurance and 5% surcharge.

Casinos and Night Clubs

A magnificent casino — one of the largest in the Western Hemisphere — is open for slot machines from 9 a.m., and from noon until the early hours of the morning for gambling. There is an excellent floor-show twice nightly.

The Monte Carlo Casino in the Lucayan Beach Hotel (both under reconstruction) is due to open by the end of 1983. There are also 12 night clubs on the island.

Chamber of Commerce

The Grand Bahama Chamber of Commerce has 90 members. It is affiliated with the Bahamas Chamber of Commerce in Nassau. The Chamber maintains an office at Pioneers Way and The Mall. Tel: 352-8329. P.O. Box F-808.

Churches

Twelve denominations have established churches in Freeport. Anglican-Episcopal: Christ the King; Baptist: First Baptist, Emmanuel Baptist, Zion Baptist and St. John's Native Baptist; Assembly of God: Calvary Temple; Freeport Hebrew Congregation; Catholic: Mary Star of the Sea; Lutheran: Our Saviour; Methodist: St. Paul's; Presbyterian: Lucaya Presbyterian Kirk; Seventh Day Adventist; Assemblies of Brethren in the Bahamas; Church of God: World Mission; Christian Science Society of Freeport. There is also a small Baha'i community in Freeport.

Cinemas

Freeport has one indoor twin theatre and a drive-in. The Columbus Twin Theatre, on the Mall, offers a variety of popular films. The Dolphin Drive-in Theatre, on Queen's Highway, shows two films nightly.

Climate

The northern Bahamas is generally cooler than the islands in the southeast since the latter extend into the tropics.

Grand Bahama has a slightly higher rainfall than New Providence (Nassau). The southeastern islands are the driest in the archipelago, although heavy rainfall is occasionally experienced due to their greater proneness to tropical disturbances.

Cost of Living

Food costs in Freeport are generally slightly higher than in Nassau. Individual items usually vary marginally higher in Freeport, and that variance is extended to the overall cost average.

Automobiles and clothing and other items are relatively the same in both cities.

Most homes and apartments are rented furnished. Furnishings include refrigerators and stoves, and washers and driers are usually included, either in the apartment or on the premises in the case of apartment buildings. Most apartment blocks have swimming pools. Duplex accommodations generally don't have pools.

Rents vary widely depending on the amenities offered. There are two different rental scales in Freeport: employees of Licensees can rent "bonded" (no duty paid) apartments at the lower end of the scale, but depending on location and amenities. Visitors must rent duty-paid apartments, which sometimes include maid service and linen, cutlery, etc., at the highest end of the scale. Efficiencies generally rent from $225 to $350 per month; one bedroom, $300 to $500; two bedroom, $500 to $750; three bedroom, $550 to $1,000 for bonded accommodation. A good three-bedroom house with garage and pool rents for $1,500 upwards.

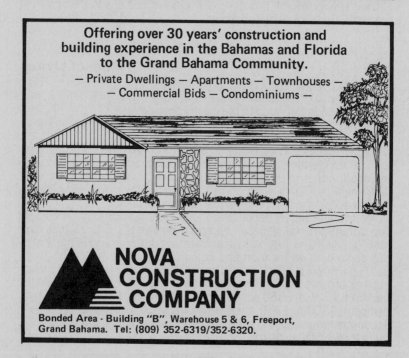
392

Cultural Activities

The Freeport Player's Guild present several plays throughout the year at the excellent 450-seat Regency Theatre, which has had a rehearsal room added. Recent plays (1982) included a new performance of "Separate Tables", also "Stagestruck", "Jesus Christ Superstar" and "Peter Pan". The Grand Bahama Players present occasional plays, usually by Bahamian authors.

The Freeport Friends of the Arts, a cultural group dedicated to bringing good music and dancing to Grand Bahama, presented in 1982 concerts by Russian pianist Boris Bloch and the Billy Taylor (Jazz) Trio, also repeat performances by the Alvin Ailey (Dance) Repertory Ensemble and the English Chamber Orchestra.

Customs

All persons entering Freeport/Lucaya, except licensees, must adhere to the Customs regulations set down in the Customs section of Bahamas Information, page 258. Licensees, however, have been granted certain exemptions from Customs duties upon import and export of goods until the year 2054 through the Hawksbill Creek Agreement.

The Agreement provides that supplies and manufacturing supplies may be imported or purchased without payment of duty.

Supplies are defined as: all materials, supplies, and things of every kind and description (and without limiting the generality of the foregoing words, all equipment, building materials and supplies, factory plant and apparatus, replacement parts, spare parts, machine and hand tools, contractor's plant, vehicles to be used for the business purposes of a licensee only, vessels, petroleum products, and nuclear fission products) **other than consumable stores.**

Manufacturing supplies are defined as: all materials, supplies and things, whether raw, partly processed or processed, or any combination thereof of every kind and description, **other than consumable stores,** that are imported for the purpose of any manufacturing, industrial or other business, undertaking, or enterprise within the Freeport area.

Consumable stores are defined as: Any article imported for personal use of any person or made available after its importation for personal use either by sale or gift. Also any article imported into the Freeport area and subsequently exported from the Port Area to any other part of the Commonwealth and any article assembled, processed or manufactured within the Freeport area, and subsequently exported from the Freeport area to any other part of the Bahamas, except pine lumber products or products consisting of or made out of the pine lumber or pine timber processed within the Freeport area.

The provisions of the Hawksbill Creek Agreement also permit a licensee to erect or purchase **one** private residence duty-free for the personal use and occupation of —

a. a licensee and his family or

b. a bona fide employee of a licensee and that employee's family. Contents of this residence that are duty-free include:
Cooking range or stove, dishwasher, refrigerator, vacuum cleaner, washing machine and dryer, non-portable TV sets, non-portable radios and record players, all permanent fixtures in the house, curtains, carpets, lamps and lamp shades, and pictures.

Conditions to Obtaining Customs Exemptions

The Hawksbill Creek Agreement places full responsibility upon each licensee to insure that duty-free materials are used only for the prescribed purposes within the Freeport area, since it is the use of any goods exclusively in a licensee's business that carries with it the freedom from customs duties conferred by the Agreement. Consequently, the licensee must either own the goods himself or he must be in such a close relationship to the true owner (e.g. as hirer or the fully responsible agent for an absent owner) as to be able to exercise full and effective control of the subsequent use of the goods.

The Agreement provides that there are only three points at which a licensee may claim duty-free privileges for his goods.
1. When the goods are imported into the Freeport area.
2. When the goods are taken out of a Customs-bonded warehouse in the Bahamas.
3. When the goods are purchased within the Bahamas, duty having already been paid and the licensee is claiming a refund of such duty.

When a licensee wishes to claim Customs duty exemption on any goods at these points, he must first enter the goods on a Conditionally Free Entry Form. By this form, the licensee makes a solemn declaration that the goods are intended to be used solely as supplies or manufacturing supplies within the Freeport area. It is a criminal offense to make a false declaration.

In addition to this declaration, the value of the imported goods and the rates of duty to which they would be liable must be declared. Where applicable, evidence of freight and insurance should be attached. Original invoices, copy bills of lading, packing lists should be submitted with the entry. To facilitate the calculation of varying rates of duty and to insure that importers may obtain any refund to which they are entitled, original invoices must in all cases show unit prices.

Licensee's Bond

Every licensee is required to enter a bond that legally binds him to pay double duty to the Government on any goods admitted duty-free which are subsequently used or applied to any purpose other than those permitted under the Hawksbill Creek Agreement.

The Customs authorities, if they see fit, may require a licensee to provide a satisfactory surety for his bond.

A licensee's bond is a continuing obligation, but he is released from it on any specific goods when he can produce satisfactory evidence that —
1. He has paid the proper duty on the goods.
2. The goods no longer exist.

3. The goods have been exported to foreign parts from the Bahamas either in their original state or in a different state resulting from manufacturing, processing or assembly in the Freeport area.
4. The goods have been transferred to the bond of another licensee.

Further information on Freeport Customs regulations can be found in **Guide to Customs Duties Exemptions and Procedures in Freeport, Grand Bahama Island, under the Hawksbill Creek Agreement,** published jointly by the Ministry of Finance and the Grand Bahama Port Authority.

There is a U.S. Customs & Immigration facility for pre-clearance at Freeport International Airport.

Dentists

Dr. Kenneth Alleyne, Antoni Clinic
Dr. Albert Antoni (Oral Surgeon), Antoni Clinic
Dr. Larry Bain, Antoni Clinic
Dr. Edward L. Colson, Antoni Clinic
Dr. Edward Johns (Orthodontist), Antoni Clinic
Dr. Michael G. Newton, Sun Alliance Building

Departure Tax

See Bahamas Information, page 265.

Doctors and Hospitals

Rand Memorial Hospital on East Atlantic Drive is government-owned and is a 50-bed community-type hospital. Departments: medical, surgical, obstetrics and gynaecology, pediatrics, accident and emergency, outpatients, clinical laboratories and radiography. Hospitalization charges are $10 per day in a ward, $14 in a semi-private ward, and double both prices for maternity cases, plus laboratory, pharmacy and other service fees.

The Antoni Clinic, East Sunrise Highway. Private outpatient clinic. Departments: medical, surgical, dental, general medicine and pediatric, obstetrics and gynaecology; general and plastic surgery, general dentistry and orthodontics, oral and maxillo-facial surgery. Facilities: pharmacy, pathological laboratory, X-ray department, minor and general surgery operating rooms. Staff: seven physicians — Dr. Robert Antoni, Dr. Amado Antoni, Dr. Albert Antoni, Dr. John Clement, Dr. David Jenkins, Dr. W. Pratt, Dr. Robert Bailey — which include a plastic surgeon, an oral surgeon, a specialist in obstetrics and gynaecology, and a (monthly) visiting ear, nose and throat specialist, Dr. W. Campbell. Also three full-time dentists, Dr. E. L. Colson, Dr. K. Alleyne, Dr. L. Bain, one orthodontist, four registered nurses, five practical nurses and nursing assistants; one registered

pharmacist; one X-ray technician, one laboratory technician, seven administrative and secretarial staff.

Lucayan Medical Centre, Adventurers Way. Departments: family medicine, internal medicine, obstetrics and anaesthetics. Facilities: X-ray, dispensary and laboratory. Staff: nine physicians – Dr. M. Bethel, Dr. P. Etuk, Dr. I. Horsfall, Dr. R. Philip, Dr. N. Sawyer, Dr. J. Evans, Dr. Jean Turnquest, Dr. R. McKeage and Dr. V. Burell, and a visiting orthopaedic specialist, Dr. Granville Bain, and a visiting ear, nose and throat specialist, Dr. W. Campbell. One nurse, one laboratory technician, six administrative staff.

Government Clinics at Hawksbill, Eight Mile Rock and West End are staffed with resident doctors and nurses who provide medical services at minimal fees.

Holistic Health-World Clinic — Dr. R. Roop, holistic physician.

Immunology Researching Centre (treatment of cancer) — Dr. Lawrence Burton, Ph.D., Dr. R. J. Clement, M.R.C.S., L.R.C.P., and Dr. Fred Weinberg, M.D.

Electricity

Electricity is generated by the Freeport Power Company, Ltd., at the Peel Street generating plant. Existing facilities consist of a 9,000-kilowatt diesel plant, two gas turbines totalling 40,000 kilowatts and a 75,000 kilowatt steam plant.

Total Net MwH Generated by Freeport Power Company

1977	262,656
1978	286,289
1979	338,500
1980	357,000
1981	258,000

Total Average Active Meters

1977	7206
1978	7263
1979	7563
1980	7969
1981	8184

Supply Voltages and Frequency

3 phase, 4 wire, 208/120 volts, 60 cycles
3 phase, 4 wire, 240/120 volts, 60 cycles
1 phase, 3 wire, 240/120 volts, 60 cycles ⎫ depending
1 phase, 3 wire, 208/120 volts, 60 cycles ⎬ upon location
3 phase, 4 wire, 480/277 volts, 60 cycles ⎭

Tariffs

The principal rates are:

(a)   Residential service

7¢ per kwh per month (this is the same for all kwh, the scale does not go down as your consumption increases)

(b)   Commercial Rate
First 5 kw of monthly maximum demand or less, $18.20
Next 25 and all additional kw of monthly maximum demand at $4.55 per kw

Energy charge —
First 2,000 kwh per month 6.25¢ per kwh
All additional kwh per month 5.75¢ per kwh

Fuel surcharge —
Based on monthly cost of fuel to Power Company.
The fuel surcharge for 1983 was averaging 6¢ at press time.

Employers Associations

There is a Grand Bahama Hotel Association and a Freeport Hotel Restaurant Employers' Association. Employers' interests are otherwise looked after by the Chamber of Commerce.

Engineers

Anthony B. Dean & Associates, Ltd. (consultant engineers)
Chee-A-Tow & Co. (G.B.), Ltd. — (land development and planning)
Island Electric Ltd.
L. & A. Industries (electrical and mechanical engineering)
Lucaya Engineering Services, Ltd. — (electric motor repairs, welding and metal work)
Lucayan Utilities, Ltd. — (sewage engineers)
Pan American Consulting International (chemical engineers)
Structural Engineering Consultants, Ltd.

Exchange Control

Regulations apply as in Nassau. See Bahamas Information, page 281.

Export Entry

An Export Entry is required for all goods exported by ship or air freight, and it is advisable to do the exporting through a freight service that will supply forms and deal with Customs. Ordinary parcels such as clothing and gifts sent through the Post Office at Explorer's Way do

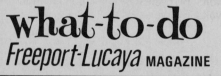

not require an Export Entry, but must have a post office-issued label affixed giving weight and value of contents.

Fishing
Gamefish found around Grand Bahama include sailfish, marlin, blue dolphin, kingfish, wahoo. Mrs. Lydia Blazer holds the record for kingfish (72 lbs) as well as for wahoo (84 lbs.), and the 1932 record (unconfirmed) for barracuda (103 lbs. 4 oz.) caught off West End by C.E. Benet still stands. There are marinas, boat dealers, repairers and charter agencies and fishing guides in Freeport, in Lucaya and at West End. If help is needed when boating in Bahamian waters, volunteers from the Bahamas Air Sea Rescue Association keep a 24-hour watch in collaboration with the U.S. Coast Guard. For Fishing Regulations, see Bahamas Information, page 284.

Freight Services
Freight can be shipped to and from Freeport/Lucaya by sea or air.
Scheduled airlines provide regular freight service, and a cargo airline, Skyfreight, offers service between Freeport and Miami. There is a minimum charge of $28 for 100 lbs. or less. From 100 lbs. to 1,000 lbs., the charge is 22¢ per pound, and over 1,100 lbs., 20¢ per pound. Nassau is served from either Freeport or Miami on a charter basis.
Two shipping lines provide freight service between Freeport and Florida. Universal-Alco and Tropical Shipping ply between Freeport, Ft. Lauderdale and West Palm Beach. There are two other shipping agents operating at Freeport. They are East End Shipping and United Shipping. Container service to England is available with delivery time approximately three weeks.
Cost of shipping depends on the commodity and weight.
Persons moving to the Bahamas are advised to contact a reputable international van line in their locality. They can offer complete door-to-door service from point-of-origin to island residence. There is paper work involved and Customs procedures that must be followed. Van lines and their agents in Freeport provide this service.
Original copies of all invoices and other documents must accompany goods or be sent on ahead. Clearance and delivery usually take about 24 hours.
Household and personal belongings coming to Freeport must undergo Customs inspection and take approx. a day-and-a-half to be cleared depending on the size of the shipment.
Freeport agents can ship door-to-door anywhere in the world.

Golf Courses
There are four 18-hole championship golf courses in Freeport/Lucaya.
These courses include the Lucayan Park Golf and Country Club, the Princess Golf Club, which has two courses on its property, the

400

Ruby and the Emerald, and the 18-hole layout at the Bahama Reef Yacht and Country Club.

The Fortune Hills Golf and Country Club presently operates a nine-hole layout.

Numerous local, inter-island and international tournaments are held at the various courses throughout the year.

Government Offices

Following is a list of Government Offices in Grand Bahama. (Unless otherwise noted, locations and postal addresses are in Freeport.)

Commissioner's Office
Sun Alliance & London Bldg.
P.O. Box 10765

Administrative Office
Sun Alliance & London Bldg.
P.O. Box F-1

Audit Office
Sun Alliance & London Bldg.
P.O. Box F-182

Treasury Dept.
Sun Alliance & London Bldg.
P.O. Box F-2485

Ministry of Works
Sun Alliance & London Bldg.
P.O. Box F-530

Customs Dept.
Administrative Office
The Harbour
P.O. Box F-2484

Dept. of Environmental
   Health Service
Hawksbill Clinic
P.O. Box F-680

Dept. of Statistics
Sun Alliance & London Bldg.
P.O. Box F-2561

Gaming Board
International Bldg.
P.O. Box F-2313

Immigration
Churchill Bldg.
Suite H East
P.O. Box F-62

Magistrates Court
Pioneers Way West
P.O. Box F-174

Ministry of Agriculture
   and Fisheries
West Mall
P.O. Box F-6

Ministry of Education
30 Kipling Bldg.
P.O. Box F-2595

Ministry of Health
Rand Memorial Hospital
P.O. Box F-71

Ministry of Labour
Sun Alliance & London Bldg.
P.O. Box F-589

Dept. of Social Services
International Bldg.
P.O. Box F-589

Ministry of Tourism
International Bazaar
P.O. Box F-251

Police Dept.
International Bldg.
P.O. Box F-82

Road Traffic Dept.
1A Kipling Bldg.
P.O. Box F-338

Bahamas Telecommunications Corp.
Pioneers Way West
P.O. Box F-2483

Ministry of Youth, Sports &
   Community Affairs
25B Kipling Bldg.
Box F-1

Gun Permits
Application in the first instance should be made to the Assistant Commissioner of the C.I.D. at Peel Street, Freeport. (See also Gun Permits, page 290.)

Harbour Control
Freeport Harbour Control went into operation in 1962, and gives clearance to all ships leaving and entering the harbour of Freeport. Permission must be obtained from Harbour Control for the movement from one berth to another while in the harbour. The office is in operation at all hours. Small fishing boats or small pleasure craft should telephone Freeport Harbour Control at 352-9651 before leaving the harbour, so that the whereabouts of these vessels can be ascertained in case they are overdue.

The VHF radio frequency of Harbour Control is initially Channel 16, after which further directions as to frequency will be given, from a choice of 14, 12, 68, 73, 74, 79, 20, 65, and 66. AM radio ship-to-ship frequencies are 2638, 2670 and 2182 kcs. The international emergency frequency, 2182 kcs., is controlled by Bahamas Telecommunications Corporation. For commercial traffic, AM frequency 2198 should be used.

Single band frequencies are 3300.0, 4139.5, 5057.0, 8100.0

Hawksbill Creek Agreement
The Hawksbill Creek Agreement, essentially a contract between the Bahamas Government and the licensed businesses of Freeport, was the foundation stone of Freeport. Signed in 1955, the agreement granted to the Grand Bahama Port Authority, under its founder, Wallace Groves, 50,000 acres of unused Crown Land to be developed as an international port. (Later, the Port Authority obtained additional land from the Crown and from private sources, making a total holding of about 149,000 acres — or 233 square miles.)

To encourage development of this land, the Government also granted certain concessions to the Port Authority and its licensees. Principal concessions are:
1. Freedom from taxation — There is a contractual guarantee that at least until 1990, there will be no personal income taxes, no corporate profit taxes, no capital gains taxes or levies on capital and no personal or real property or inventory taxes.
2. Freedom from Customs duties — At least until 2054 no excise or import duties will be levied on equipment or materials used by licensed businesses. Only goods for personal use or consumption are dutiable.

The Port area covers about one-third of the island, and should be checked with a map by drivers of bonded cars which cannot be driven outside the area without incurring penalties, e.g., Eight Mile Rock is outside the area.

Licensees are exempt from the Business Licence Tax which applies everywhere else in the Bahamas, provided that they run the type of business which can operate without a shop licence. A retail business like a pharmacy or news agency is **not** exempt.

History

Remains and artefacts have been found on the island which show that the Lucayan Indians lived here until the time of the Spanish conquerors. Grand Bahama was probably deserted for some time thereafter, then during the late 18th century a few settlements grew up as people drifted over from other islands. West End had spurts of activity (due to its proximity to the Florida coast) as a haven for gun-runners during the American Revolution and rum-runners during Prohibition.

It is only in the last quarter-century that the Island has been fully developed. With a population of about 4,000 in the 1950s, it has risen to over 33,000 in the 1980s, due entirely to the advent of American-born Wallace Groves and his Abaco Lumber Company. While cutting the island's crop of Caribbean pine, he devised a plan for making a huge free port and industrial centre in the midst of the scrub and swamp around Hawksbill Creek.

Groves started the Grand Bahama Port Authority with a grant of 50,000 acres of land (with an option of a further 50,000) from the Bahamian government. Houses, churches and schools were built, a magnificent deepwater harbour was dredged for oil tankers, an oil refinery was erected, an airport, hotels and casino were added.

By 1966, there were 214 miles of good roads and hundreds of buildings, and areas had been set apart for shops, light industries and heavy industries. The excellent hotels and beaches were soon to make it into a tourist haven.

Immigration

For information on Immigration, see page 296. For specific application to Freeport/Lucaya, contact the Immigration Department at its offices in the Churchill Building. Tel.: 352-9338, Box F-62. The procedure for applying for a work permit is exactly the same as in Nassau. Freeport applications are dealt with regularly when the Immigration Board meets in Freeport.

Import Information

Exchange Control approval is required from the Central Bank of the Bahamas for purchase of foreign currency for most current transactions, including payment for imports. However, approvals in Freeport for the purchase of foreign exchange for the purpose of paying for imports may be obtained directly at commercial banks upon the presentation of Form 1 together with supporting documents and invoices. Exchange Control forms are available from any bank. Approval

is given by the bank manager if appropriate, and there is no financial limit to his authority. There is no branch of the Central Bank of the Bahamas in Freeport.

Industry

Several large industries have been established in Freeport, attracted by tax advantages, a first class infrastructure and the availability of certain natural resources.

The first industry was established in 1958. This was a bunkering terminal which operated a successful service until it was absorbed in the late 1960s by BORCO, a huge oil refinery which was built by a consortium of New England Petroleum and Standard Oil of California. Charter Company now owns a 50 per cent interest in the refinery.

In 1979 International Development Corp., S.A., Luxembourg, acquired U.S. Steel's Bahama Cement Company. Terms of the transaction have not been disclosed, although it is known that U.S. Steel had invested over $75 million in the cement plant, which has a capacity of one million tons of cement a year. The main operation closed down in February 1982 due to the lack of building commitments. At press time it was producing sufficient cement to cope with the considerable amount of building in progress on Grand Bahama.

Another large industry is Syntex Corporation's chemical plant. It has also expanded its original facility for the production of compounds, some of which are used in the manufacture of birth control pills and Naproxen, an anti-arthritic drug.

In the pharmaceutical field are Cooper Laboratories (which manufacture drugs for Central and South America and Europe) and Franklin Chemicals, Ltd. The latter company, recently established in Freeport, is a division of Smith-Kline Corporation, and produces the compounds for Tagamet, the leading drug prescribed for treatment of ulcers. Tagamet is manufactured for export to Japan, Canada and other selected countries.

Todhunter-Mitchell Ltd., distillers and bottlers of wines and spirits, is another industry which has been in operation and expanding since the mid-1960s. It produces liquor for the Bahamas market as well as for export.

The Electric Auto Corporation is engaged in the assembly of electric automobiles, and Anglo-American Research Corporation in the research and development of these cars.

International Bazaar

One of Freeport's most popular attractions, the International Bazaar is a $3.5 million shopping complex featuring 80 businesses offering the merchandise and cuisine of three dozen countries.

Completed in 1967, the 10-acre Bazaar was designed by a motion picture special effects expert who took great pains with detail.

Visitors are greeted at the entrance of the Bazaar by a Torii gate, the Japanese symbol of welcome. The gate opens the way to Hong Kong Street where the shops are stocked with Oriental goods. Embroidery, jade and ivory carvings, brocades, beadwork, jewellery and expert tailoring are available. Two restaurants also offer the finest in Chinese food, with one featuring over 200 items on its menu.

Further along is the Japanese section where Ho-toi, the Japanese God of Fertility, stands guard at a restaurant featuring Kobe beef. Cameras, watches, radios, stereos and jewellery are available here.

Mexico, Spain, South America and the Caribbean are represented by a variety of stores selling superb Mexican, Guatemalan and Paraguayan clothing, Colombian emeralds for up to 30 per cent less than U.S. retail prices, leather goods, pottery and much more. Look for vivid Androsian (Bahamian) dresses, shirts and materials.

The Scandinavian section features glassware, figurines, china, jewellery and enamelware from Denmark, Norway and Sweden, also the best of English glass and china and unusual table-mats.

The Middle East is also represented with Jewish and Arabic gift items. Shops in the Indian section carry a wide range of beautiful silks and hand-carved brass plates and figurines. The African section has native wooden carvings, musical instruments and clothing from that part of the world.

The French area has colourful outdoor cafes where visitors may rest and enjoy a refreshing drink. French perfumes may be bought for up to 40 per cent less than U.S. retail prices.

There is an extensive Bahamian straw market selling hats, handbags, shopping bags, mats, wallets to hold letters and bills. The vendor will sew on a name or initials in raffia in less than five minutes.

A number of restaurants are also located in the Bazaar featuring food from Italy, Japan, France and China.

The Bazaar is open weekdays from 10 a.m. to 6 p.m., except Tuesdays and Thursdays, when it opens its doors at 9:30 a.m.

Judicial System

Freeport has one magistrate's court presided over by a stipendiary magistrate on weekdays. For summary criminal offences a case can be tried in this court, but indictable offences may be heard only as a preliminary hearing and then are referred to the Supreme Court in Nassau.

There is also an occasional court at Eight Mile Rock. Since hearing cases involves much expense in transferring police officers, witnesses and the accused from these two courts, it is anticipated that a larger court house will be built and that Circuit Judges will preside during the Law Terms.

Junkanoo

Junkanoo Parades are held in Grand Bahama on Boxing Day (December 26) and New Year's Day from 3 a.m. to 9 a.m. The Boxing Day Parade is held in West End, a settlement 25 miles west of Freeport.

The New Year's Day parade is staged at the Ranfurly Circle in downtown Freeport by the Grand Bahama Masquerade Committee, with groups competing for prizes up to $1,200.

Law Firms

	Freeport P.O. Box
* Bostwick & Bostwick	F-2912
* Callenders, Orr & Co.	F- 132
* Carson, Lawson, Klonaris, Sawyer & Knowles	F- 75
* Christie, Ingraham & Co.	F-2343
* Dupuch & Turnquest	F-2578
* Gomez, Dennis & Co.	F- 357
Gottlieb, Cay	F- 773
Hall, Carroll & Co.	F-2569
Henderson, J. Roy	F-2413
* McKinney, Bancroft & Hughes	F- 437
* Nottage, Miller, Johnson & Co.	F-2420
* Roberts, E. Dawson, Higgs & Co.	F- 427
* Seligman, Maynard & Co.	F-2445
Thompson, James Roosevelt	F-2912
J. Thompson & Co.	F-2698
* Wallace Whitfield, Cecil	F-2535
Wilchcombe, Stephen & Co.	F- 502

* Nassau office also.

Library

Located on the grounds of the Rand Memorial Hospital, the John Harvard Library is a lending library open to the public.

It was first organized in 1962, with headquarters in a downtown office building and is operated by an all-volunteer group.

Subscription fees are $15 per year. Each subscriber is entitled to check out four books for two weeks, but only one may be a current purchase. Library hours: Monday, Wednesday, Friday and Saturday, 10 a.m. to 5 p.m. (except holidays).

Licensing

All businesses operating in the Freeport area must be licensed by the Grand Bahama Port Authority, subject to the approval of the Bahamas Government. Licensees, whether individual, limited company or corporation, are eligible for all tax benefits granted through the Hawksbill Creek Agreement under Bahamian law. The Port Authority imposes an annual licence fee for operating in the Port area. This fee varies from company to company, and could be as little as $100 for

408

a small business or as much as $8,000 for a large one. An initial deposit is charged on application to cover paper work and is refundable if the licence is granted.

This fee is spent not only in maintaining the area around the licensee's business, but contributes towards the $2,000,000 per year spent by the Port Authority Group of Companies in landscaping, repairing the roads, picking up garbage, etc. Licence fees are paid for when issued and thereafter annually.

To apply for a licence:
1. A detailed description of the nature of business, including facilities, equipment and staff to be used, must be submitted to the Port Authority on a licence proposal form.
2. From information on the form, together with a detailed reference check, financial affidavit and business competence report, the project is analyzed by the Port Authority.
3. Upon approval by the licensing committee of the Port Authority and the Bahamas Government, a letter of intent is issued the licensee outlining the terms and conditions of the business and indicating the duration of the licence and the initial fee payable to the Port Authority.
4. Upon acceptance of these terms by the licensee, the formal licence agreement dictating the finalized terms and location of the business is drawn up. Any subsequent changes or additions require an amendment to the licence.

Marriage Licences

Marriage licences can be obtained on Grand Bahama from the Commissioner's Office, Sun Alliance & London Building, Freeport (tel: 352-6332), or the Commissioner's Office, Government Compound, Eight Mile Rock (tel: 348-2878). See also Bahamas Information, page 309.

Newspapers

One daily newspaper, **The Freeport News,** is published in Freeport. It is printed every afternoon, Monday-Saturday, except holidays, and sells for 25 cents. Also available are the two daily Nassau newspapers, **Tribune** and **Nassau Guardian.**

Some New York and Miami papers are available in Freeport the same day of publication and some a day later, at increased cost due to air freight charges. Magazines from abroad also cost considerably more than their marked price from the country of origin, for the same reason.

Passports

To obtain a passport, residents of Grand Bahama can obtain application forms from various couriers such as Fargo Mail, who will deliver the application to the Passport Office at the Ministry of External Affairs in Nassau, or to the consulate of the resident's own country. A visit to Nassau is not necessary.

Population

When the 1980 census was taken, the population of the entire island of Grand Bahama had risen to 33,102, from 25,859 in 1970. There are no figures available for Freeport alone, as the figures were provided by electoral constituencies.

Postal Information

The main Post Office on Grand Bahama is located on Explorers Way in Freeport, and provides the same service as the Post Office in Nassau. Airmail is delivered daily and surface mail weekly. Branch offices are located in West End, Eight Mile Rock, Smith's Point, High Rock, McClean's Town and Sweeting's Cay. Postal rates are the same as Nassau, i.e. airmail letters (½ oz.), Freeport/Europe 35¢, delivery three to ten days; Freeport/U.S. and Canada 31¢, delivery two to seven days; Freeport/Nassau airmail letters 10¢, postcards 8¢, delivery two to seven days. All other airmail postcards 25¢, air letters 25¢.

Property Transactions

The Government of the Bahamas charges a Stamp Duty (equivalent to a Transfer Tax) on all property conveyances, leases and agreements, and on mortgages.

The scale of Stamp Duty on conveyances is at present:

From	Up to and including	Stamp Tax (%)
$0	$6,000	¾ of 1%
$6,000.01	$20,000	1%
$20,000.01	$30,000	2%
$30,000.01	$50,000	3½%
$50,000.01	$100,000	4½%
Over $100,000		5%

The Stamp Duty is paid by the seller, unless otherwise agreed in writing. Where property is sold to non-Bahamians, the Stamp Duty is doubled, and the custom in Freeport is that in such instances each party pays one half, but again this should be agreed in writing.

On all mortgages, Stamp Duty is payable by the borrower at half scale. A separate scale is established for leases, agreements, wills and other recorded documents. The Bahamas Bar Association has established a scale of minimum fees for various services performed by an attorney, and for searching title and preparing or approving a conveyance, the usual minimum fee is 2% of the sale price. Each party retains, and pays, his own attorney.

Commissions charged by real estate agents vary according to the type of property and should be agreed in writing between the seller, who normally pays the commission, and his agent. In Freeport, much of the vacant land is owned by foreigners, and unlike Nassau, the majority of transactions still involve foreigners, either as buyers or sellers, or both, and this inevitably increases overheads.

When there is a glut of undeveloped land on the market, many sellers offer high incentive commissions for quick cash sales. As a guideline, the following commission scales apply: sale of undeveloped land, 10 to 15%; a house, 8%; a condominium or apartment building, 10%; commercial property, 10%.

Radio

ZNS-3, Radio Bahamas' Northern Service, is one of three stations operated by the Broadcasting Corporation of the Bahamas. Headquartered in Freeport, ZNS-3 is designed to cover Grand Bahama, Abaco and the Biminis, with local programming and advertising as well as national programming originating in the Nassau studios of the Corporation. See **Broadcasting,** Bahamas Information, page 242.

Schools

KINDERGARTEN/DAY CARE
Freeport Nursery School and Play Group - Calvary Academy — Kinglake Lane. Kindergarten, ages three to five. Three terms, September though June. Tuition: $245 per term. Nursery, $25 per week, or $245 per term, kindergarten to grade 2, $260 per term. Five qualified teachers, two nursery aides. Classes 9 a.m. to 2:30 p.m. Enrolment: 100. Day care: ages three months to five years, 8:00 a.m. to 5:30 p.m. (part-time care also). Operated by Calvary Temple. Headmistress, Mrs. L. Roberts, P.O. Box F-1880, Freeport, Grand Bahama. Tel. 352-5490.

PRIMARY SCHOOLS
Sunland Lutheran School — Gambier Drive. Under sponsorship of Our Saviour Lutheran Church. Nursery school through form 10. Coeducational. Three terms, but accounting is done in four parts (i.e. four bills are sent out). Term fees: nursery school, half-day, from 2½ years, $375; full-day, $415; kindergarten (full-day, 4 year-olds) $445; Form 1, $455; Forms 2-4, $475; Forms 5-7, $495; Forms 8 and 9, $525. There is a $50 yearly registration fee for all grades, of which $25 is refundable. Enrolment: 485; 35 teachers.

PRIMARY/JUNIOR HIGH SCHOOLS
Mary, Star of the Sea School — Sunrise Highway. Roman Catholic, Nursery through 8th grade. Co-educational. Three terms. Registration fee $30. Tuition: Nursery, half-day sessions $200; all day $265; Kindergarten and class 1, full day $275; grades 1-6 $275; grades 7-8 $295. Enrolment: 852; 2 Franciscan sisters, 39 lay teachers. Apply to Headmistress, Ms. Geneva Major, Mary, Star of the Sea School, P.O. Box F-2418, Freeport, Grand Bahama. Tel. 373-3456.

411

PRIMARY AND SECONDARY SCHOOLS

St. Paul's Methodist College — Clive Avenue. Administered by same Board of Trustees as Queen's College, Nassau. Co-educational. Ages 3 to 16. Three terms (Sept., Jan., April). Tuition: Infant Department, Grades Reception, $265; Kindergarten, 1 and 2, $275 per term; Junior Department, Grades 3 to 6, $295 per term; Junior High, Grades 7 to 9, $305 per term; Senior High, Grades 10 to 12, $325 per term. 10% discount for children other than oldest in school from one family. Registration fee: $15. Uniforms are same as Queen's College, Nassau. Students prepare for B.J.C., A.C.T., S.A.T. and London G.C.E. examinations. Enrolment: 800; 40 teachers. Apply to Principal, Mrs. S. Annette Poitier, St. Paul's Methodist College, P.O. Box F-897, Freeport, Grand Bahama. Tel. 352-6225.

SECONDARY SCHOOLS

Freeport High School — East Sunrise Highway. Administered by the Anglican Diocese of the Bahamas. Co-educational. Ages 11 to 19. Three terms. $320 (grades 7-12) per term. (Special course) College Board Exams, $420 per term; Commercial courses grades 11-12, $350 per term. $15 deduction per term for second child. Uniforms. All students pay $15 annual registration fee. Insurance $3 per year. Prepares candidates for G.C.E. Ordinary, Pitman examinations and American College Board exams. Enrolment: 400; 24 teachers. Apply to Principal, Mrs. Anita Osman, Freeport High School, P.O. Box F-667, Freeport, Grand Bahama. Tel. 373-3579.

Grand Bahama Catholic High School — Hawksbill. Roman Catholic. Four years, co-educational. Two semesters. Students may take American College Board, G.C.E., B.J.C. and City and Guilds examinations. Tuition: $992 yearly. Uniforms. Enrolment: 340. Teachers: 17 lay teachers. Apply to Principal, Mr. Joseph Darville, Grand Bahama Catholic High School, P.O. Box F-2635, Freeport, Grand Bahama. Tel. 352-2544.

Hawksbill High School — Hawksbill. Government-operated. Co-educational. Ages 11 to 18. Education to B.J.C., G.C.E. Ordinary and Advanced levels, plus technical and vocational courses, and R.S.A. Enrolment: 2,500. Three terms. Tuition free. Uniforms. 104 teachers. Apply to Principal, Hawksbill High School, P.O. Box F-1314, Freeport, Grand Bahama. Tel. 352-8513.

Service Clubs etc.

American Women's Club; Freeport/Grand Bahama Chamber of Commerce (P.O. Box F-808); Freeport Garden Club; Freeport Jaycees; Canadian Women's Club; Freeport Lions Club; Kiwanis Club of Freeport; Kiwanis Club of Lucaya; Pilot Club of Freeport; Rotary Club of Freeport; Rotary Club of Lucaya; Shriner's Club of the Bahamas; Freeport Toastmasters; Freeport Toastmistresses; an Association of Journalists and Professional Writers has been formed, also a Business and Professional Women's Association.

Y.M.C.A., open 9 a.m. to 9 p.m. Mon. through Fri., 10 a.m. to 12:30 p.m. Sat., offers a variety of activities for children and adults (P.O. Box F-253).

To contact any of the above clubs, write to the Chamber of Commerce; Ministry of Tourism, P.O. Box F-251, Freeport, Grand Bahama, or the Grand Bahama Island Promotion Board, P.O. Box F-650, Freeport, Grand Bahama.

Ship Services

At least eight cruise ships, including the *Dolphin, Amerikanis, Emerald Seas, Caribe* and *Sunward II,* make regular weekly visits throughout the year. Other cruise ships also call irregularly. There are fortnightly windjammer cruises on the *Fantome* and the *Yankee Trader* from Miami to Freeport.

Scandinavian World Cruises have introduced three new cruise ships: the **Scandinavia** leaves New York every five days on a two-and-a-half day cruise, bringing passengers and cars to Grand Bahama. It connects with the **Scandinavian Sun,** taking 434 passengers and 200 cars daily between Freeport and Miami. The **Scandinavian Sea** sails to Port Canaveral. All three ships are Bahamian-registered.

Supermarkets

There are two large supermarkets in the downtown area opening from 8:30 a.m. to 6 p.m. weekdays and 8 a.m. - 10 a.m. Sundays. A smaller one on Sunrise Highway with the same opening hours provides the essentials. Portion Control (Freeport) on Explorer's Way specializes in bulk sales and opens 8 a.m. to 9 p.m. Fridays and Saturdays, and 8 a.m. to 7 p.m. weekdays.

Surveyors

Claude Chee-a-Tow — Land Surveyor
John Cowdroy — Quantity Surveyor
John Doherty — Quantity Surveyor

Telephone

All long distance telephone service is provided over the facilities of the Bahamas Telecommunications Corporation (BATELCO). Toll telegram and telex billing is done by the Grand Bahama Telephone Company for all local Freeport/Lucaya customers.

There is Direct Distance Dialling to some countries. Consult the telephone directory.

Address all letters to Grand Bahama Telephone Co., Ltd., P.O. Box F-2478, Freeport, Grand Bahama.

Television

A CATV positive cable system relays seven television stations throughout Grand Bahama, and reception is good. Cable-TV is owned by Wometco Enterprises Inc. of Miami. Video machines are available for rent. See also page 346.

Tourism Information

Year	Air Arrivals	Sea Arrivals	Total
1979	433,920	74,250	508,170
1980	454,910	85,130	540,040
1981	557,605	67,884	625,489
1982	398,140	272,480	670,620

The tourist and promotion boards are situated above the Midnight Sun store in the International Bazaar. Their function is not only to give tourist information, but to keep a watching brief on standards in hotels and restaurants. They subsidize the Hotel Training Council, also.

Trade Unions

Bahamas Construction & Maintenance Workers' Union
Bahamas Hotel Catering & Allied Workers' Union
Bahamas Union of Teachers
Commonwealth Electrical Workers' Union
Commonwealth Transport Union
Commonwealth Union of Hotel Service & Allied Workers
Commonwealth Wholesale & Retail Workers' Union
Grand Bahama Commercial, Clerical & Allied Workers' Union
Grand Bahama Public Service Drivers' & Allied Workers' Union
Grand Bahama Telephone & Communications Workers' Union

Transportation

Taxi rates are set by the Government and are the same in Freeport as in Nassau; metered $1.20 for the first quarter mile and 20¢ for each additional quarter mile. For two passengers, the fare from the airport to Lucaya is $6.60; to Bahamas Princess $3.60, and to the downtown area, $3.60. From the Harbour area to Bahamas Princess the fare is $5.40; to Lucaya, $9.60, and to the airport, $6. The rates quoted are minimum fares for two passengers. Over two passengers, there is an additional charge of $1.50 per person.

Bicycles, scooters and automobiles are available for rent. Bicycles cost about $10 per day. Motor scooters rent for $22 from 9 a.m. to 5 p.m. or $14 from 9 a.m. to 1 p.m. Gas is supplied by the agency and there is no mileage charge. A valid driver's licence is required and both scooter drivers and passengers are required by law to wear helmets, which are supplied free of charge by the agency. A deposit of $20 is required.

Freeport/Lucaya has several car rental agencies and their prices are generally competitive. Cars rent from $43 per day, with unlimited mileage. Rates vary, depending on size of the car. Weekly rates are six times the daily rates.

Various types of boats are available for rent. Most beachfront hotels have two-passenger catamarans for rent on an hourly or daily basis. Runabouts are available from marinas on a limited basis and rent for about $35 half-day per person. Fishing boats and yachts are also available for charter.

Lucaya Beach Air Service, located at Freeport International Airport, operates an air charter service at a cost of $186 per hour (1-5 passengers) for flying around the island. For flying to another island, i.e. Treasure Cay, the price would be $265 each way, and $50 per hour of waiting. Helda Air Holdings operates charter flights anywhere and runs an air ambulance service.

See also **Air Service,** page 232.

Wages

Wages for housemaids (40-hour week) start at $70, with uniforms and meals left to the employer's discretion. Gardeners earn $19 upwards a day, working 9 a.m. to 4 p.m. Restaurant and hotel cooks (short-order, not chefs) earn about $140 upward per week.

A cocktail waitress at a large, oceanfront hotel makes about $82 weekly, basic pay, and a bartender about $145, excluding gratuities. Uniforms and meals are furnished by the employer.

A top secretary earns about $380 a week; an executive secretary about $365; a stenographer-secretary about $290; a junior secretary about $220.

Type of Job	Wage Average B$/Week
Stenographer-secretary	290
Hotel & Restaurant Manager	600
Head cook or Chef	220 upwards
Cook, except private service	140 upwards
Housemaids	70
Janitor	80
Farm helpers	80 upwards
Truck drivers	130-150
Fork lift operators	130
Labourers and handymen	80-100

Water Supply

The Grand Bahama Utility Company supplies water to Freeport and also provides a bulk supply for some nearby communities outside Freeport's borders. The company's developed well field capacity is 6,500,000 gals. per day. Average daily water consumption is about 5.2 million gals.

The residential water rate is now combined with the commercial rate at $2 per thousand gals. for the first 20,000 gals. per month, and $2.20 per thousand gals. for all additional usage.

(Continued from pg. 377)

were also at my table did not appear: they apparently had a continental breakfast in their cabin after playing the tables in the casino and then dancing in the discotheque until 4:30 a.m. They were later seen blindly groping for the "Bloody Marys" which were served on the Bahamas Deck between 8 a.m. and noon.

After breakfast, I had my hair shampooed and set at a cost of $12. I could also have had a massage, and a sauna and jacuzzi bath, but as the sun was shining brilliantly on a calm, deep-blue sea, I decided to take my book on deck.

The ship is extremely well provided with deck chairs, either around the swimming pool (which has an electric sliding roof for cool days) or in various spots which are sheltered from the wind and open to the sun.

The time passed all too quickly with another excellent lunch, dinner and floor-show, followed by a very interesting tour of the bridge after luncheon the next day. Perhaps one has been to the cinema too often and seen tough old mariners clad in oilskins and sou'wester struggling with a huge spoked wheel, but to my amazement here was a carpeted area like a very smart business executive's office, with picture windows and a dozen pots of poinsettias. The ship's wheel is about the size of that of a light aeroplane – you couldn't possibly have struggled with it – and the rest of the long stretch of electronic equipment resembled more closely the controls of a Jumbo-jet than anything I had envisioned on a ship.

What an absurd, childlike excitement, which everyone should experience just once, to sail up the busy Hudson River with its tooting tugs, its broad-beamed barges and its hovering helicopters, to see the sky-scrapers of Manhattan, golden in the evening sun, outlined against a clear blue sky. At least 1,000 cameras clicked simultaneously.

The cost of the cruise varies from $535, round trip, for an inside cabin, to $1,300 round trip for a deluxe suite ($750 one way), plus port charges of $26 (or $14). If you are not exactly "loaded", here are some tips: stay at the St. Regis or the Warwick hotels, which sometimes offer cheaper weekend rates. And if you must fly back rather than cruise, Pan American has a direct daily flight to Freeport, or you can take a slightly cheaper Arrow Airlines fare to Miami.

It was with real regret that I got off the ship a little while after we docked at 6 p.m. These lovely ships have proved to be of great benefit to the Bahamian tourist industry, for in the first year of operations they brought 243,206 passengers to Freeport.

Government

Cabinet Ministers & Portfolios

Pindling

Hanna

THE RT. HON. SIR LYNDEN O. PINDLING, K.C.M.G., P.C., M.P.,
Prime Minister, Churchill Bldg. Nassau

OFFICE OF THE PRIME MINISTER: Co-ordination of Ministers
THE CABINET OFFICE: Co-ordination of parliamentary business,
Ministry of Defence, national security, relations with the Hotel
Corporation of the Bahamas and Bahamas Information Services.
PRINTING DEPARTMENT: Printing and stationery, official gazette.
    (See also House of Assembly - Kemp's Bay, Andros)

THE HON. ARTHUR DION HANNA, M.P., Deputy Prime Minister and
Minister of Finance, Churchill Bldg., Nassau
OFFICE OF THE DEPUTY PRIME MINISTER: Leader of the House
DEPARTMENT OF PUBLIC PERSONNEL: Public personnel, office
accommodation, organization and methods, Whitley Council, pensions
and gratuities
TRAINING DIVISION: Public service training
MINISTRY OF FINANCE: Government finance, accounting and
borrowing. The Bahamas Development Bank, the Central Bank of the
Bahamas, banks, trusts, mutual funds and securities, companies, insur-
ance (excluding National Insurance), lotteries and gaming, relations
with the Gaming Board, racing, relations with the Racing Commission.
Rent control, weights and measures, consumer protection, monopolies,
hire purchase, price control, licensing of shops and businesses, including
the Port Area in Grand Bahama. Beers and spirits, treasure trove.
DEPARTMENT OF STATISTICS: Statistics, retail price index
CUSTOMS DEPARTMENT: Revenue
TREASURY DEPARTMENT: Budgetary control
    (See also House of Assembly — Ann's Town, New Providence)

Bethel

Christie

Maycock

THE HON. PHILIP M. BETHEL, M.P., Minister of Transport, General
Post Office, Nassau
MINISTRY OF TRANSPORT: Maritime affairs
PORT DEPARTMENT: Shipping and navigation, lighthouses, wrecks,
inter-island passenger, freight and mail services; ports and harbours,
abutments, boat registration
ROAD TRAFFIC DEPARTMENT: Road traffic, motor vehicles (cars
and carriages)
POST OFFICE DEPARTMENT: Postal services
METEOROLOGICAL DEPARTMENT: Meteorology (climatology,
aviation, marine and local weather reporting and forecasting)
CIVIL AVIATION DEPARTMENT: Aircraft registration, aircraft
air-worthiness, personnel licensing, aircraft accident investigation,
air navigation aids, airports, air-space, air traffic control. Air Transport
Licensing and relations with Nassau Flight Services Limited.
   (See also House of Assembly — Governor's Harbour, Eleuthera)

THE HON. PERRY G. CHRISTIE, M.P., Minister of Tourism,
Bay Street, Nassau
MINISTRY OF TOURISM: Promotion and development of tourism
DEPARTMENT OF TOURISM: Hotel encouragement, co-ordination
of applications for hotel and resort development
BAHAMAS NEWS BUREAU: Tourism publicity
   (See also House of Assembly - Centreville, New Providence)

THE HON. ALFRED T. MAYCOCK, M.P., Minister of Economic
Affairs, Rawson Square, Nassau
MINISTRY OF ECONOMIC AFFAIRS: Economic policy, project
review
REGISTRAR GENERAL'S DEPARTMENT: Registration of deeds,
business names, registration of commission merchants, copyrights,
patents, trademarks and registry of records
BAHAMAS AGRICULTURAL & INDUSTRIAL CORPORATION:
Promotion of agricultural and industrial development
   (See also House of Assembly - Fort Fincastle, New Providence)

Nottage

Roker

THE HON. KENDAL W. NOTTAGE, Minister of Youth, Sports and Community Affairs, Centreville House, Second Terrace, Collins Avenue, Nassau
BROADCASTING AND TELEVISION: Relations with the Broadcasting Corporation of the Bahamas
MINISTRY OF YOUTH, SPORTS & COMMUNITY AFFAIRS: Youth development, sports and recreation, parks, cultural affairs, junkanoo, women's affairs and community development.
   (See also House of Assembly — St. Agnes, New Providence)

THE HON. A. LOFTUS ROKER, M.P., Minister of Works & Utilities. John F. Kennedy Drive, Nassau
MINISTRY OF WORKS: Public works, building regulations, telegraphs, relations with the Bahamas Telecommunications Corporation; urban and island planning, department of physical planning
DEPARTMENT OF PUBLIC WORKS: Maintenance of public buildings, roads, bridges, beaches, parks and cemeteries, explosive and volatile substances, electricity, relations with Bahamas Electricity Corporation
DEPARTMENT OF WATER AND SEWERAGE: Water and Sewerage
   (See also House of Assembly - Nicoll's Town, Andros)

Maynard

THE HON. CLEMENT T. MAYNARD, M.P., Minister of Labour and Home Affairs, C.A. Bain Building, Oakes Field, Nassau
MINISTRY OF LABOUR AND HOME AFFAIRS: Labour employment and re-habilitation, prerogative of mercy, Justices of the Peace, nationality and citizenship, flags and coats of arms, cinemas and films
DEPARTMENT OF LABOUR: Trade unions, industrial relations, workmen's compensation, industrial inspection and safety, apprenticeship and training, employment agencies

420

POLICE DEPARTMENT: Internal security
PRISONS DEPARTMENT: Prisons, prisoners, probation, industrial schools
DEPARTMENT OF IMMIGRATION: Immigration and emigration
PARLIAMENTARY REGISTRATION DEPARTMENT: Parliamentary registration and elections.
(See also House of Assembly — Yellow Elder, New Providence)

Adderley

THE HON. PAUL L. ADDERLEY, M.P., Minister of Foreign Affairs and Attorney General, Post Office Building, Nassau
MINISTRY OF FOREIGN AFFAIRS: Foreign Affairs, Passports, visas, protocol matters, co-ordination of applications for technical assistance, political refugees, extradition, law of the sea, treaty succession
OFFICE OF THE ATTORNEY GENERAL: Legal affairs, legal education, law reform and revision
JUDICIAL DEPARTMENT: Law Courts, Coroners, enquiries, Notaries Public

Smith

THE HON. GEORGE A. SMITH, M.P., Minister of Agriculture, Fisheries and Local Government, East Bay Street, Nassau
DEPARTMENT OF AGRICULTURE: Regulation of the manufacture of food and beverages, quality control, testing and certification for food processing and preservation industries, wild animals and birds protection, plant protection, veterinary services, animal disease, public markets and slaughterhouses
DEPARTMENT OF FISHERIES: Fisheries, natural history specimens, Andros Reef and Blue Holes, relations with The Bahamas National Trust
DEPARTMENT OF LOCAL GOVERNMENT: Local government, local government administration, local government development and Family Islands Affairs

421

DEPARTMENT OF LANDS & SURVEYS: Lands and surveys, Crown Lands, commonage and forests, acquisition of lands and land surveys
DEPARTMENT OF CO-OPERATIVE DEVELOPMENT: Development of co-operatives
(See also House of Assembly — Rolleville, Exuma)

Ingraham

Rolle

Coakley

THE HON. HUBERT A. INGRAHAM, M.P., Minister of Housing and National Insurance, Citibank Bldg., Thompson Blvd., (Ministry of Housing, Social Services); Hawkins Hill (Housing Department); National Insurance Building, Farrington Road (National Insurance)
DEPARTMENT OF HOUSING: Housing, relations with the Housing Commission
GRANTS TOWN URBAN IMPROVEMENT PROGRAMME
DEPARTMENT OF SOCIAL SERVICES: Child protection, public assistance, indigent and aged persons, grants to institutions
NATIONAL INSURANCE: Benefits and assistance
(See also House of Assembly — Cooper's Town, Abaco)

THE HON. DARRELL E. ROLLE, M.P., Minister of Education, Shirley Street, Nassau
MINISTRY OF EDUCATION: Education and relations with the College of the Bahamas
DEPARTMENT OF EDUCATION: Scholarships, public libraries and museums, archives, public records and antiquities, arts and cultural development, relations with the National Trust on matters of historic interest. School Welfare Section; Industrial Training; Bahamas Hotel Training College
(See also House of Assembly — Mangrove Cay, Andros)

THE HON. LIVINGSTONE N. COAKLEY, M.P., Minister of Health, General Post Office, East Hill Street, Nassau
MINISTRY OF HEALTH: Responsible for all medical, nursing and health services
DEPARTMENT OF ENVIRONMENTAL HEALTH: Solid waste collection and disposal, Public Analyst, regulation of manufactures of drugs and pharmaceuticals, quarantine, dangerous drugs and poisons.
(See also House of Assembly - George Town, Exuma)

Senate

Government Members
(Progressive Liberal Party)

PRESIDENT
The Hon. Edwin L.
Coleby

VICE-PRESIDENT
The Hon. Bruce C.
Braynen

**GOVERNMENT
LEADER**
The Hon. Paul L.
Adderley, *Minister
of Foreign Affairs
and Attorney General*

The Hon.
Berlin Pratt

The Hon. Alfred
H. Stewart

The Hon. Clara
R. Hall-King

The Hon. Ishmael
Lightbourne

(cont'd overleaf)

423

The Hon. Ruby A.
Cooper-Darling

The Hon. Leroy
S. Hanna

The Hon. E. Andrew
Maynard

The Hon. Norris
R. Carroll

The Hon. Patricia
Coakley

OPPOSITION MEMBERS
(Free National Movement)

The Hon. J.
Henry Bostwick
Leader of the Opposition

The Hon. Merline
Hanna

The Hon. Warren
J. Levarity

The Hon. Charles
Virgill

424

House of Assembly

SPEAKER: The Hon. Sir Clifford Darling (see page 427).
DEPUTY SPEAKER: George W. Mackey (see page 429).
NOTE: There are 43 seats in the House of Assembly. Thirty-two are held by the Progressive Liberal Party (PLP), and 11 by the Free National Movement (FNM), the Official Opposition. Cabinet Ministers devote full time to Government. Occupations listed for House members who hold Cabinet posts are for background information only.

NEW PROVIDENCE

ANN'S TOWN
THE HON. ARTHUR DION HANNA, LL.B., M.P. (PLP). Deputy Prime Minister and Minister of Finance. Leader of the House. Barrister-at-law. Born Mar. 7, 1928, Acklins Island. Son of the late Joseph A. and Flora (nee Heastie) Hanna. Educated: Government High School, Nassau; Bristol University and Inner Temple. Married to the former Beryl Church of Bristol, England. Five children. Hobby: fishing. Residence: South Beach, Nassau. P.O. Box N-4877, Nassau.

BAIN'S TOWN
NORMAN RUPERT GAY, M.D., M.B.A., M.P. (PLP) Deputy Chairman, Tourism Advisory Board. Physician. Born Jan. 31, 1941, San Salvador. Son of James A. and Amy (nee Nairn) Gay. Educated: Canadian Union College, Alberta; Union College, Lincoln, Nebraska; Loma Linda University, California; Fellow Intl. Inst. of Holistic and Preventive Medicine. Member of the Natl. Honour Business Society of United States (Beta Gamma Sigma); Knight of the Round Table, Saarbrucken, W. Germany. Religion: Seventh Day Adventist. Hobbies: national sports and youth development work. Hon. Life Pres., Bahamas Volleyball Federation. President, Bahamas Bodybuilding, Weightlifting & Powerlifting Federation. Residence: West Bay Street, Nassau. P.O. Box N-3222, Nassau.

BAMBOO TOWN
CLAUDIUS LEANDER MINNIS, M.P. (PLP). Mechanical engineer. Born Jan. 20, 1931, Calabash Bay, Andros. Son of the late George Howard and Zelda (nee Edgecombe) Minnis. Founding member of the Amalgamated Building Construction and Allied Workers Union and of the Trade Union Congress. Educated: Calabash Bay Public School. Married to the former Mildred Ward of San Salvador. Ten children. Religion: Anglican. Hobbies: swimming, boating, travel. Residence: Carmichael Road, Nassau. P.O. Box N-4756, Nassau.

BLUE HILLS
ARTHUR A. FOULKES, M.P. (FNM). Journalist and public relations consultant. Born May 11, 1928, Mathew Town, Inagua. Son of the late Dr. William A. and Julie (nee Maisonneuve) Foulkes. Educated: Inagua Public School; Western Central School, Nassau. Ten children. Religion: Roman Catholic. Hobbies: reading politics, history and popular psychology. Residence: West Bay Street, Nassau. P.O. Box N-491, Nassau.

CARMICHAEL
FRANK HOWARD WATSON, M.P. (FNM). Managing Director/President, Bahama Divers (1976). Born March 24, 1940, Gordon's, Long Island. Son of William C. and Olga (nee Major) Watson. Educated: Government High School, Nassau; University of the West Indies. Married to the former June Wright of Aberdeen, Scotland. Two children. Religion: Anglican. Hobbies: tennis, fishing. Residence: Cunningham Acres, Nassau. P.O. Box SS-5004, Nassau.

CENTREVILLE
THE HON. PERRY GLADSTONE CHRISTIE. LL.B., M.P. (PLP). Minister of Tourism. Chariman, The Gaming Board. Barrister-at-Law. Born August 21, 1943, Nassau. Son of Gladstone and Naomi (nee Allen) Christie. Educated: Eastern Senior School, Nassau; University Tutorial College, London; Birmingham University and Inner Temple. Married to the former Bernadette Joan Hanna. One child. Residence: Cable Beach, Nassau. P.O. Box N-7940, Nassau.

DELAPORTE
THE HON. KENDAL GEORGE LAMON ISAACS, C.B.E., Q.C., M.A., LL.B., M.P. (FNM). Leader of the Opposition. Barrister-at-Law. Former Acting Chief Justice and Acting Judge. Served as Lieutenant Bahamas Battalion 1944-45. Born July 23, 1925. Son of Edward and Mary (nee Kemp) Isaacs. Educated: Government High School, Nassau. Degree of the Utter Bar, 1950, Middle Temple; B.A., LL.B., 1949, M.A., 1953, Queen's College, Cambridge. Married to the former Patricia Fountain of Nassau. Religion: Anglican. Hobbies: tennis, golf, music. Residence: West Bay Street, Nassau. P.O. Box N-1372, Nassau.

ENGLERSTON
THE HON. SIR CLIFFORD DARLING, Kt., J.P., M.P. (PLP) Speaker of the House of Assembly. Knighted 1977. Born Feb. 6, 1922, Acklins Island. Son of Charles and Aramelia (nee Johnson) Darling. Married to the former Ingrid Smith. Religion: Baptist. Hobby: water sports. Member: Masons, Elks and Acklins, Crooked Island and Long Cay Assn. Residence: South Beach Estates, Nassau. P.O. Box N-1050, Nassau.

FORT CHARLOTTE
VALENTINE SEBASTIAN GRIMES, M.P. (PLP). Chairman of the People's Penny Savings Bank. Attorney. Born June 19, 1948, Nassau. Son of the late George and Florence (nee Cartwright) Grimes. Educated: Quarry Mission School, St. John's College, Government High School, Nassau; University of the West Indies. Married to the former Thelma Barnett of Nassau. Three children. Religion: Anglican. Hobbies: sports, softball, tennis, swimming, basketball. Residence: Nassau East Boulevard, Nassau. P.O. Box N-9619, Nassau.

FORT FINCASTLE
THE HON. ALFRED T. MAYCOCK, M.P. (PLP). Minister of Economic Affairs. Chairman of Bahamasair Holdings and Bahamas Agricultural and Industrial Corporation. Born Dec. 22, 1933. Son of Alfred T. and Mary Eliza (nee Wallace) Maycock. Educated: Government High School, Nassau; Indiana Institute of Technology; University of Miami. Married to the former Aura Tynes of Nassau. Two children. Hobbies: sports, reading, music, civic work. Member: Bahamas Institute of Professional Engineers. Residence: Cable Beach, Nassau. P.O. Box SS-6322, Nassau.

FOX HILL
FRANK LEOPOLD EDGECOMBE, M.P. (PLP). Chairman, Road Traffic Authority. Attended the 25th Commonwealth Parliamentary Association meeting in Wellington, New Zealand, 1979. Born Mar. 3, 1928. Son of Courtney and Daisy (nee Cox) Edgecombe. Educated: Sandilands All-Age School and Bahamas Teachers College. Teacher for 26 years. Junior Cambridge Certificate, 1947; Teachers Certificate, 1954; London OL Certificate, 1965. Active in fraternal and church work. Married to the former Clementina Rahming. Eight children. Religion: Baptist. Hobbies: music, reading, sports, farming, carpentry. Residence: South Beach Road, Nassau. P.O. Box N-3008, Nassau.

427

GRANT'S TOWN

BRADLEY BERNARD ROBERTS, M.P. (PLP). Chairman, Bahamas Housing Commission. Businessman. Director, Sunshine Holdings Ltd., G.B. Oil Ltd., Bahamas Beverages Ltd.; Managing Director, Bethell-Robertson & Co., Ltd. Born Dec. 25, 1943, Nassau. Son of Rupert and Merle (nee Albury) Roberts. Educated: St. Augustine's College, Government High School Evening Institute, Nassau. Married to the former Hartlyn Mackey of Eleuthera. Four children. Religion: Roman Catholic. Hobbies: music, jogging. Member: Young Presidents Organization. Residence: Skyline Heights, Nassau. P.O. Box N-8208, Nassau.

HOLY CROSS

EDWARD CHARLES CARTER, M.P. (PLP). Chairman, Broadcasting Corporation of the Bahamas; Vice President, Restaurants (Bahamas) Ltd.; Chairman, Office Systems of the Bahamas, Ltd. Born April 13, 1943, Nassau. Son of Harcourt and Mary (nee Heastie) Carter. Educated: New York University; Ryerson Polytechnical, Toronto, and the University of Manchester, England. Married to the former Muriell Willhite of South Bend, Indiana. Two children. Religion: Anglican. Hobbies: tennis, reading. Residence: Highland Park, Nassau. P.O. Box SS-5753, Nassau.

MONTAGU

ORVILLE ALTON TURNQUEST, LL.B., M.P. (FNM). Barrister-at-Law. Born July 19, 1929, Nassau. Son of the late Robert and Gwendolyn (nee Wake) Turnquest. Educated: Government High School, Nassau. Articled law student to A.F. Adderley, and called to the Bahamas Bar. in June 1953. University of London; Lincoln's Inn; called to the English Bar in 1960. Married to the former Edith Thompson of Nassau. Three children. Religion: Anglican. Chancellor of the Anglican Diocese in Nassau and the Bahamas; on the Board of Governors of St. John's College & St. Anne's High School. Hobbies: tennis, swimming, music, reading. Residence: "Green Pines", Harrold Road, Nassau. P.O. Box N-682, Nassau.

PINEDALE

MILO BOUGHTON BUTLER, JR., M.P. (PLP). Businessman. Former Consul General in Miami. Born Nov. 30, 1936, Nassau. Son of the late Sir Milo B. Butler and Lady Butler (nee Caroline Loretta Watson). Educated: Eastern Senior School, Government High School, Nassau; Middle Temple. Married to the former Winifred Dorsett. Five children. Religion: Anglican. Hobbies: swimming, soccer, baseball, farming. Residence: Ernest Street, Nassau. P.O. Box N-9076, Nassau.

428

ST. AGNES
THE HON KENDAL WELLINGTON NOTTAGE, M.P. (PLP). Minister of Youth, Sports and Community Affairs. Lawyer. Born Mar. 24, 1940, Nassau. Son of the late Bernard and Olivia (nee Johnson) Nottage. Educated: Government High School, Nassau. Articled law student at P. L. Adderley Chambers, and called to the Bar in August, 1966. Married to the former Rubie Bethel of Nassau. Two children. Religion: Anglican. Hobbies: squash, reading. Residence: Prospect Ridge, Nassau. P.O. Box N-4691, Nassau.

ST. BARNABAS
SINCLAIR SILVIS OUTTEN, M.P. (PLP). Engineer, Marketing Director. Born Feb. 2, 1936, Turks Island. Son of Stina and Mable (nee Hamilton) Outten. Educated: Nassau Technical College; Chicago Technical College; University of Miami, M.B.A. 1981. Married to the former Avis Smith of Green Castle, Eleuthera. Four children by previous marriage. Founding member: Bahamas Association for Manpower Training and Development. Member: Masonic Lodge; Council Member, College of the Bahamas. Religion: Protestant. Hobbies: music, water sports. Residence: Sans Souci, Nassau. P.O. Box N-3562, Nassau.

ST. MICHAEL'S
GEORGE WILLIAM MACKEY, M.P. (PLP). Deputy Speaker of the House. Chairman, National Insurance Board. Businessman. President and managing director, P. & M., Ltd., and Bahamas Coin Amusement, Ltd. Born Jan. 19, 1938, Fox Hill. Son of Malachi and Olive (nee Mackey) Mackey. Educated: Government High School, Nassau. Married to the former Mary Elizabeth Thompson of Nassau. Two children. Religion: Anglican. Hobbies: sports, debating. President, Bahamas Baseball Association. Member: St. Anne's Vestry. Residence: St. Anne's Hill, Fox Hill. P.O. Box FH-14333, N.P.

SALEM
DAVID ALEXANDER KNOWLES, M.P. (PLP). Trade unionist. Born Jan. 4, 1940, Nassau. Educated: Eastern Senior School and Bosfield Johnson Private School. Attended Trade Union Educational Institute, University of the West Indies, and American Institute for Free Labour Development, Front Royal, Virginia. Married to the former Wilhelmina Bethel of Eleuthera. Two children. Residence: Sans Souci, Nassau. P.O. Box N-8680, Nassau.

SHIRLEA
PIERRE VALIANT LAUNCELOT DUPUCH, M.P. (FNM). Printing Executive. Shadow Minister of Health. Born April 23, 1938, Nassau. Son of Sir Etienne and Lady Dupuch (nee Marie Plouse). Educated: St. Augustine's College, Nassau; De La Salle, Canada; St. John's University, Minnesota; Carnegie Mellon University, Pennsylvania. Married to the former Susan Thompson of Kent, England. Four children. Religion: Roman Catholic. Hobbies: horses, fishing, boating. Residence: Camperdown Heights, New Providence. P.O. Box N-4555, Nassau.

SOUTH BEACH
EDWARD FRANCIS (BOBBY) GLINTON, M.P. (PLP). Trade Unionist. Born May 26, 1938, Nassau. Son of James and Miriam (nee Glinton) Glinton. Educated: Western Senior School, Nassau; Critchlow Labour College and Kuru-Kuru Co-operative College, Guyana. Married to the former Catherine Smith of Nassau. Seven children. Religion: Anglican. Hobby: softball, sports. Residence: Canterbury Park, Nassau. P.O. Box GT-2514, Nassau.

YAMACRAW
JANET GWENETT BOSTWICK, M.P. (FNM). Attorney. Born Oct. 30, 1939, Nassau. Daughter of Nick and Louise (nee Bethel) Musgrove. Educated: Government High School, Commercial Studies. Articled law student to Gerald Corbett, former Attorney General. Called to the Bahamas Bar in April 1971. Married to Senator J. Henry Bostwick (FNM). Four children. Religion: Anglican. Hobbies: fishing, reading, animal farming. Residence: Highbury Park, Nassau. P.O. Box N-1605, Nassau.

YELLOW ELDER
THE HON. CLEMENT TRAVELYAN MAYNARD, M.P. (PLP). Minister of Labour and Home Affairs. Born Sept. 11, 1928, Nassau. Son of Clement T. and Georgina (nee Symonette) Maynard. Educated: Eastern Secondary School, Nassau; Franklin School of Science and Arts, Philadelphia; School of Hygiene and Tropical Medicine, London University; Nova University. Founding member and first president, Bahamas Civil Service Union. Married to the former Zoe Ruth Cumberbatch of Trinidad. Five children. Religion: Anglican. Hobbies: boating, golf, reading, travelling. Residence: Five Acres, Adelaide Road, N.P. P.O. Box N-71, Nassau.

430

THE FAMILY ISLANDS

ABACO

THE HON. HUBERT A. INGRAHAM, M.P. (PLP).
Minister of Housing and National Insurance. Repre-
sentive for Cooper's Town. Attorney. Born Aug.
4, 1947. Son of Jerome and Isabella (nee Cornish)
Ingraham, Pine Ridge, Grand Bahama. Educated:
Cooper's Town Public School; Southern Senior School
and Government High School Evening Institute,
Nassau. Married to the former Delores Velmas Miller
of Miller's, Long Island. Two children. Religion: Anglican. Hobby: reading. Residence: Croton Avenue,
Nassau. P.O. Box N-7940, Nassau.

EDISON M. KEY, M.P. (PLP). Representative for
Marsh Harbour. Farmer. Born May 18, 1938, Nassau.
Son of Bunyan and Lillian (nee Bethel) Key. Educated: Abaco Government School, Abaco. Married
to the former Lorraine Roberts of Grand Rapids,
Michigan. Two children. Religion: Protestant. Hobbies: flying, skin diving, woodcraft. Residence: Pelican Shores. P.O. Box 439, Marsh Harbour, Abaco.

ANDROS

THE RT. HON. SIR LYNDEN OSCAR PINDLING,
K.C.M.G., P.C., LL.B., LL.D., D.H.L., M.P. (PLP).
Representative for Kemp's Bay. Prime Minister.
Barrister-at-Law. Born Mar. 22, 1930, Nassau. Son of
Arnold and Viola (nee Bain) Pindling. Educated:
Western Senior School, Government High School,
Nassau; University of London and Middle Temple.
Honorary degrees: LL.D., Howard University, Washing-
ton, D.C., D.H.L., University of Miami. Married to the
former Marguerite McKenzie of Andros. Four children.
Religion: Protestant. Hobbies: boating, jogging, div-
ing, swimming. Residence: Skyline Heights, Nassau.
P.O. Box N-1051, Nassau.

THE HON. DARRELL EARLIN ROLLE, LL.B., M.P.
(PLP). Minister of Education and Culture. Representa-
tive for Mangrove Cay. Barrister-at-Law. Born June 8,
1943, Lowe Sound, Andros. Son of the late Captain
Edgar L. and Prudence (nee Russell) Rolle. Educated:
Government High School, Nassau; Chiswick Polytech-
nic College of Arts, London; University of London;
University of Miami. Married to the former Beryl
Marie Smith of Green Castle, Eleuthera. Two children
(also one child by former marriage). Religion: Baptist.
Hobbies: tennis, fishing and reading. Member: Kiwanis
Club of Cable Beach. Residence: Cunningham Lake,
Nassau. P.O. Box N-8680, Nassau.

THE HON. ARCHIBALD LOFTUS ROKER, LL.B.., M.P. (PLP). Minister of Works and Utilities. Representative for Nicoll's Town. Chairman, Bahamas Water and Sewerage Corporation. Barrister-at-Law. Born Aug. 25, 1935, Acklins Island. Son of Elkin and Dolores Theodora (nee Hanna) Roker. Educated: Pompey Bay Public School, Acklins Island; University of London and Middle Temple. Married to the former Ruby Louise Livingston of Nassau. Religion: Anglican. Hobbies: fishing, water sports. Residence: Harrold Road, Nassau. P.O. Box N-4274, Nassau.

BIMINI/BERRY ISLANDS

GEORGE WARREN WEECH M.P. (PLP). Former Customs Officer. Born Mar. 25, 1939, Bimini. Son of the late Emmanuel and Olenia Weech. Educated: Primary School and privately at Bimini; La Salle University, Chicago. Married to the former Curlean Gwendoly Stuart of Bimini. Three children. Religion: Anglican. Hobbies: baseball, football, basketball, tennis. Residence: Alice Town, Bimini. P.O. Box 608, Bimini.

CAT ISLAND

ERVIN KNOWLES, M.P. (PLP). Building contractor and land developer. Born May 17, 1934, Nassau. Son of Daniel and the late Remelda (nee Major) Knowles. Educated: Eastern Junior and Senior Schools, St. John's College, Nassau. Married to the former Stella Symonette of Nassau. Six children. Religion: Anglican. Hobbies: athletics, fishing, tennis. Residence: Montagu Heights, Nassau. P.O. Box N-7772, Nassau.

CROOKED ISLAND AND ACKLINS

WILBERT ALEXANDER MOSS. M.P. (PLP). Businessman. Born Dec. 16, 1921, at McKi, Crooked Island. Son of the late Rev. James Robert and Marie (nee Winter) Moss. Educated: True Blue, Crooked Island Public School and Western Senior School Evening Institute. Married to the former Christina Ellen Pratt of Nassau. Four children. Religion: Pentecostal. Hobbies: swimming, reading, boating. Residence: Skyline Drive, Nassau. P.O. Box N-1512, Nassau.

432

ELEUTHERA

THE HON. PHILIP MICHAEL BETHEL, J.P., M.P. (PLP). Minister of Transport. Representative for Governor's Harbour. Born Dec. 16, 1940, Palmetto Point. Son of the late Herman and Alvord (nee Archer) Bethel. Received early education at Palmetto Point Public School. Married to the former Yvonne Carey of Tarpum Bay, Eleuthera. Six children and an adopted daughter. Religion: Baptist. Hobbies: softball, cycling, swimming, farming. Residence: Skyline Drive, Prospect Ridge, Nassau. P.O. Box N-3008, Nassau.

JAMES BERTRAM MOULTRIE, M.P. (PLP). Representative for Rock Sound. Parliamentary Secretary, Ministry of Foreign Affairs. Teacher and former Civil Servant. Born Dec. 27, 1944, Wemyss Bight. Son of Bertram and Mary (nee Dupuch) Moultrie. Educated: Wemyss Bight Public School; Bahamas Teachers' College; University of the West Indies; University of Miami. Former Deputy Permanent Secretary in three ministries. Married to the former Bernadette Williams. Three children. Religion: Anglican. Hobbies: basketball, soccer, reading, music. Residence: Danottage Estates, Nassau. P.O. Box N-3003, Nassau.

PETER J. BETHELL, M.P. (PLP). Representative for St. John's. Parliamentary Secretary to the Ministry of Agriculture, Fisheries and Local Government; Deputy Chairman, Bahamas Agricultural and Industrial Corporation. Born Nov. 16, 1950, Nassau. Son of Stanley and Emma (nee Albury) Bethell. Educated: Government High School, Nassau; University of Nebraska. Married to the former Paula L. Rogers of Dallas, Texas. One child. Religion: Anglican. Hobbies: baseball, cricket. Residence: Joan's Heights, South Beach, Nassau. P.O. Box N-3028, Nassau.

EXUMA

THE HON. LIVINGSTONE NATHANIEL COAKLEY, LL.D. M.P. (PLP). Minister of Health. Representative for George Town/Ragged Island. Accountant, educator. Born Apr. 3, 1925, at Simms, Long Island. Son of Amos and Aremina (nee McPhee) Coakley. Educated: Northeastern University, Boston, B.S., M.B.A., LL.D. Married to the former Marietta Armbrister of Nassau. Four children. Served as sergeant, Bahamas Bn., 1943-46. Religion: Anglican. Hobbies: tennis, soccer. Member: Kiwanis Club; Masonic Lodge; Fellow, Society of Commercial Teachers, London; Associate, National Society of Public Accountants, Washington, D.C. Residence: Imperial Park, Nassau. P.O. Box N-1446, Nassau.

433

THE HON. GEORGE ANDREW SMITH, M.P. (PLP).
Minister of Agriculture, Fisheries and Local Government. Representative for Rolleville. Businessman.
Born Dec. 14, 1940, George Town, Exuma. Son of
the late Richard F. and Mildred M. (nee Bullard)
Smith. Educated: St. Augustine's College, Nassau.
Married to the former Lourey C. Carroll of Deadman's Cay, Long Island. Two children. Religion:
Roman Catholic. Hobbies: swimming, yachting.
Member: Exuma Elevating Association, Prince Hall
Masonic Lodge. Address: P.O. Box N-1868, Nassau.

GRAND BAHAMA

MAURICE E. MOORE, M.P. (FNM). Representative
for High Rock. Businessman. Director, National Car
Rental. Born June 19, 1939, Grand Bahama. Son of
Elijah and Beatrice (nee Pinder) Moore of Grand Bahama. Educated: Grand Bahama Public School; St.
Augustine's College, Nassau; The R.C.A. Institute of
Technology, New York. Married to the former Sandra
Major of Nassau. Five children. Religion: Roman
Catholic. Hobbies: reading, fishing, travel. Residence:
Pinder's Point, Grand Bahama. P.O. Box F-843, Freeport, Grand Bahama.

CORNELIUS A. SMITH, M.P. (FNM). Representative
for Marco City. Business executive. Born April 7,
1937, North End, Long Island. Son of Sylvanus and
Susan Smith. Educated: Glinton Public School, Long
Island; Bahamas Teachers College, Nassau; University
of Miami, M.B.A. Married to the former Clara Knowles
of Tarpum Bay, Eleuthera. Three children. Religion:
Anglican. Hobby: fishing. Member: Jaycees, Kiwanis,
Freeport Chamber of Commerce, Bahamas Association
for Manpower Training and Development. Residence:
9, Sea-horse Lane, Freeport. P.O. Box F-3879, Freeport.

CECIL VINCENT WALLACE WHITFIELD, LL.B.,
M.P. (FNM). Representative for Pine Ridge. Barrister-at-Law. Born March 20, 1930, Nassau. Son of Kenneth Whitfield and Dorothy Rogers (nee Wallace).
Educated: University of Hull, Yorkshire, England;
Middle Temple, London. Divorced. Six children. Religion: Anglican. Hobbies: reading, gardening. Residence: Fox Hill, Nassau and East Sunrise Apts, Freeport.
P.O. Box N-753, Nassau.

MOSES ALONZO HALL, M.P. (FNM). Representative for West End. Barrister-at-Law. Born May 23, 1941, Eight Mile Rock, Grand Bahama. Son of Moses and Madelaine (nee Wildgoose) Hall. Educated: Bahamas, USA and England. Married to the former Anna Miller of Jamaica. Four children. Religion: Non-denominational. Hobbies: fishing, reading. Residence: Santa Maria Ave., Freeport, and West End, G.B. P.O. Box F-2569, Freeport.

INAGUA AND MAYAGUANA

VERNON JOSEPH SYMONETTE, M.P. (FNM). Accountant. Born Nov. 8, 1937, Mathew Town, Inagua. Son of W.A. Geoffrey and Ira G. (nee Glover) Symonette. Educated: Inagua Public School and Inagua Evening Institute. Married to the former Phyllis Estelle Hanna of Mathew Town, Inagua. Four children. Religion: Baptist. Hobbies: reading, fishing, shooting. Residence: Russell Street, Inagua.

LONG ISLAND

JAMES F. KNOWLES, M.P. (FNM). Representative for Clarence Town. Lawyer. Born Dec. 25, 1942, Fox Hill. Son of Alexander and Agnes (nee Pinder) Knowles. Educated: Sandilands All-Age School, Queen's College, Nassau. Married to the former Amarylis Rosien Treco. One child. Religion: Anglican. Hobbies: gardening, boating. Residence: Winton, New Providence. P.O. Box N-939, Nassau.

PHILIP PATRIC SMITH, M.P. (PLP). Representative for North Long Island, Rum Cay and San Salvador. Industrial Relations director and former trade unionist. Born Jul. 8, 1946 at George Town, Exuma. Son of the late Richard F. and Mildred M. (nee Bullard) Smith. Educated: St. Thomas More Grade School and St. Augustine's College, Nassau; Trade Union Institute of the University of the West Indies. Married to the former Hedda Cleare. Two children. Religion: Roman Catholic. Hobbies: cabinet making, music, reading. Residence: Village Court, Nassau. P.O. Box SS-5583, Nassau.

Parliamentary Secretaries

Ministry of Agriculture, Fisheries
      and Local Government . . . . . . .Mr. Peter Bethell, M.P.
Ministry of Foreign Affairs . . . . . . .Mr. James Moultrie, M.P.

Heads of Public Corporations

Bahamas Agricultural &
      Industrial Corp . . . . .Hon. Alfred T. Maycock, M.P.
Bahamas Development Bank . . . . . .Mrs. Ethlyn Isaacs
Bahamas Electricity Corp . . . . .Mr. Milo B. Butler, Jr., M.P.
Bahamas Telecommunications
      Corp . . . . .Mr. Sinclair Outten, M.P.
Bahamas Water & Sewerage
      Corp . . . . .Hon. A. Loftus Roker, M.P.
Broadcasting Corporation of
      The Bahamas . . . . .Mr. Charles Carter, M.P.
Gaming Board. . . . . .Hon. Perry G. Christie, M.P.
Housing Commission . . . . .Mr. Bradley Roberts, M.P.
Hotel Corporation of
      The Bahamas . . . . .Rt. Hon. Sir Lynden Pindling,
                             K.C.M.G., P.C., M.P.
Racing Commission . . . . .Mr. James Moultrie, M.P.

Permanent Secretaries

Secretary to the Cabinet . . . . .Mrs. Margaret McDonald, C.B.E.
Financial Secretary . . . . .Mrs. Ethlyn Isaacs
Labour and Home Affairs . . . . .Mrs. Jeanette Bethel
Youth, Sports and Community
      Affairs. . . . . .Mr. C.A.P. Smith
Health. . . . . .Mr. Harold Munnings
Works and Utilities . . . . .Mr. H.C. Walkine
Economic Affairs . . . . .Mr. Colin C. Deane
Legal Affairs. . . . . .Mr. Neville Smith
Education . . . . .Mr. Gurth Archer
Tourism. . . . . .Mr. Basil O'Brien
Director of Public Personnel . . . . . .Mrs. Lois Symonette
Transport. . . . . .Mrs. Vylma Thompson
Agriculture, Fisheries &
      Local Government. . . . . .Mr. Idris Reid (Acting)
Housing and National Insurance . . . .Mr. Kendric Williams (Acting)
Foreign Affairs . . . . .Mrs. Mary Sweetnam (Acting)

Public Service Officials

Agriculture and Fisheries Dept. . . . Sidney Russell, Director of Agriculture
Ronald Thompson, Director of Fisheries

Audit Dept. . . . . Richard Demeritte, Auditor General

Archives Dept. . . . . Mrs. D. Gail Saunders, Chief Archivist

Bahamas Development Bank . . . . Warren Rolle, Director

Bahamas Electricity Corp. . . . . .P.I. Bethel, General Manager

Bahamas Information Services . . . . Cyril Stevenson, M.V.O., Manager

Bahamas Telecommunications Corp. . . . . .R.I. Bartlett, General Manager

Bahamasair. . . . . .A. Curling, General Manager

Boys' Industrial School. . . . . . . Richard Dean, Superintendent

Broadcasting Corp. of The Bahamas . . . . Calsey Johnson, General Manager

Cabinet Office . . . . Mrs. Margaret McDonald, C.B.E., Secretary to the Cabinet

Central Bank of The Bahamas . . . William Allen, Governor

Civil Aviation Dept. . . . . .D.A.F. Ingraham, Director

College of The Bahamas . . . . . . Dr. Keva Bethel, Principal

Co-operatives Dept. . . . . Nathaniel Adderley, Director

Customs Dept. . . . . .J.E. Deleveaux, Comptroller

Ministry of Defence . . . . Commodore C. Belton, Commander

Ministry of Education . . . . Miss Marjorie Davis, Director

Governor General's Office. . . . . Mrs Juliette Barnwell, Secretary to the Governor General

Girls' Industrial School. . . . . . . Mrs. Enid Thompson, Superintendent

Ministry of Health . . . . Dr. Vernell Allen, Chief Medical Officer
Miss Hilda Bowen, M.B.E., Director of Nursing

Housing Dept. . . . . .I.D. Archer, Chief Housing Officer

Immigration Dept. . . . . Mrs. Barbara Pierre, M.B.E., Director

Judicial Dept.	Sir Denis Malone, Acting Chief Justice J. Henry, Justice B.O. Adams, Justice B.W. Prescod, Acting Justice J. Strachan, Acting Registrar of the Supreme Court
Labour Dept.	C.H. Turnquest, Director
Lands & Surveys Dept.	H.A. Hing Cheong, Director
Legal Dept.	Neville Smith, Director of Legal Affairs
Meteorological Dept.	N. Small, Director
Ministry of Finance	Mrs. Ethlyn Isaacs, Financial Secretary
Ministry of Tourism.	Baltron Bethel, Director General
Ministry of Works	Peter Gordon, Director
Parliamentary Registration Dept.	E. Davis, Parliamentary Registrar
Physical Planning Dept.	I. Davis, Director
Police Dept.	G.A. Bartlett, C.B.E., Q.P.M., C.P.M., Commissioner
Port Dept.	Leon Flowers, Port Controller
Post Office Dept.	John V. Saunders, Postmaster General
Prisons Dept.	Neville Taylor, M.B.E., Superintendent
Public Service Commission	Hanford W. Darville, C.B.E., Chairman
Registrar General's Dept.	Mrs. Sylvia Bonaby, Registrar General
Registrar of Insurance	Mrs. Octavia Johnson
Road Traffic Dept.	G.L. Pennerman, Controller
Social Services Dept.	Mrs. Lila Green, Director
Statistics Dept.	J.E. Tertullien, Director
Treasury Dept.	John Culmer, Treasurer
Water & Sewerage Corp.	E.G. Moss, General Manager

Consuls & Foreign Government Representatives

BRITISH HIGH COMMISSION
High Commissioner, His Excellency Mr. Peter William Heap
P.O. Box N-7516, Nassau. Tel. 5-7471/2/3/4
Deputy High Commissioner & Head of Chancery, Mr. Michael Holmes, M.B.E.
Naval Adviser - Caribbean: Commander Hugh L. Peers, R.N.

UNITED STATES EMBASSY
Ambassador, His Excellency Dr. Lev Eugene Dubriansky, P.O. Box N-8197, Nassau. Tel: 2-1181
Acting Deputy Chief of Mission: Mr. Charles L. Stephan
Political Economic Commercial Officer: Mr. Ishmael Lara
Naval Liaison Officer: Commander Helmuth Schlichting Jr.

EMBASSY OF THE REPUBLIC OF HAITI
Minister Counsellor, Mr. Max Charles, P.O. Box N-666, Nassau.
Tel: 2-2109

VICE CONSULATE OF BRAZIL
Vice Consul, Mr. Raul Correa de Smandeck, P.O. Box N-3431, Nassau.
Tel: 7-7945

HONORARY CONSULS, NASSAU
AUSTRIA — Mr. E. Michael Cadmus, P.O. Box N-8193, Tel: 5-5595/7
BARBADOS — Mr. Carlton I. Jones, P.O. Box N-4289, Tel: 5-5591/2
BELGIUM — Mr. Michael D. Ramsay, P.O. Box N-52, Tel: 2-2659
CANADA — Mr. Allan M. Duffield, P.O. Box SS-6371. Tel: 3-2123/4.
(Hon. Commercial Rep. — Phillip Cheetham, Tel: 5-5270)
COSTA RICA — Mr. Joaquin Bacardi, P.O. Box N-838, Tel: 7-4159
CYPRUS — Mr. Pericles A. Maillis, P.O. Box N-4014, Tel: 2-4292
DENMARK — Mr. Berlin W. Key, P.O. Box N-4005, Tel: 2-1340
DOMINICAN REPUBLIC — Mr. Shervin Thompson, P.O. Box N-4326,
Tel: 5-5521
FRANCE — Mr. Michael D. Ramsay, P.O. Box N-52, Tel: 2-2659
Honorary Consular Agent in Freeport — Mrs. Elizabeth Nash,
P.O. Box F-1023, Freeport, G.B.
GERMANY — Mr. Ernst Brokmeier, P.O. Box N-4360, Tel: 3-5227
GREECE — Mr. Anthony Klonaris, P.O. Box N-4360, Tel: 2-1381
GUYANA — Mr. Oscar Phillips, P.O. Box N-4613, Tel: 3-5491
ICELAND — Mr. Julian Maynard, P.O. Box N-7525, Tel: 2-8956
ISRAEL — Mr. Ralph Seligman, P.O. Box N-7525, Tel: 2-8956
ITALY — Mr. Everette Sands, P.O. Box N-51, Tel: 2-7586
JAPAN — Mr. Basil L. Sands, P.O. Box N-4665, Tel: 2-8560/1
MEXICO — Mr. Manuel Cutillas, P.O. Box N-838, Tel: 3-6211
MONACO — Mr. Eric Crowch, P.O. Box N-3618, Tel: 5-1166
NETHERLANDS — Mr. Oris S. Russell, C.M.G., O.B.E., P.O. Box
N-561, Tel: 3-1800
NORWAY — Mr. Berlin W. Key, P.O. Box N-4005, Tel: 2-1340
PERU — Mr. Francisco Caso Dagnino, P.O. Box N-10435, Tel: 2-2359
SPAIN — Mr. Orfilio E. Pelaez, P.O. Box N-4880, Tel: 2-4847
SWEDEN — Mr. Anders Wiberg, P.O. Box N-8333, Tel: 7-7944/7-7785
SWITZERLAND — Dr. J.J. Morger, P.O. Box N-4928, Tel: 2-8345/9

Representatives of The Bahamas Abroad

LONDON

His Excellency Mr. Richard Frederick Anthony Roberts. High Commissioner for the Bahamas in London. Born May 12, 1932, Nassau. Married former Melvern Hollis Bain of Miami and Nassau. Three children. Religion: Anglican.

Address: 39 Pall Mall, London, S.W.1, Tel: 01-930-6967/8.

Senior Official: Post of Deputy vacant at presstime.

WASHINGTON

His Excellency Mr. Reginald L. Wood, C.B.E. Ambassador for the Bahamas to the United States, Mexico, the Organization of American States and High Commissioner to Canada. Born November 14, 1924, Nassau. Married former Rita Edwards. Four children. Religion: Anglican.

Address: Suite 856, 600 New Hampshire Ave., N.W., Washington, D.C., 20037. Tel: (202) 338-3940.

Senior Official: Dr. Patricia Rodgers, Counsellor.

UNITED NATIONS

His Excellency Dr. Davidson L. Hepburn, Ambassador, Permanent Representative of the Bahamas to the United Nations. Born December 7, 1932, New Bight, Cat Island. Married former Ada M. Thompson, M.D. One child. Religion: Presbyterian.

Address: 767 Third Avenue, New York, N.Y. 10017. Tel: (212) 421-6925/6/9.

Senior Official: Dr. Peter Maynard, Counsellor.

NEW YORK

A Consulate is maintained in New York, at the same address as the U.N. Mission, under the direction of Mrs. A. Missouri Sherman-Peter, Consul. Tel: (212) 421-6420/1/2.

MIAMI

Mr. Carlton Wright, Consul for the Bahamas in Miami. Born April 28, 1947 in Nassau. Married former Audrey Dean. One child. Religion: Seventh Day Adventist.

Address: Suite 818, Ingraham Building, 25 S.E. Second Ave., Miami, Fla., 33131.

Senior Official: Miss Sheila Carey, Vice Consul.

Advertisers in this book

441

442

443

FREEPORT & GRAND BAHAMA

444

PHOTOGRAPHY CREDITS: Bahamas Ministry of Tourism; Bahamas National Trust; Captain Bill Crawford; Etienne Dupuch, Jr.; Graham Dupuch; Allanah Kay; William (Gus) Roberts; Roland Rose; Sally Smith; Stanley Toogood; Dave Woodward. Artwork by Ernie Alonzo, Vivien Archer and Deborah Johnson.

445

Index

G

H

I

T

Please rush me the
NEW
1985
Edition of
BAHAMAS
handbook

SOFTBACK EDITION	
	U.S.$
U.S.A.	.$18.15
CANADA	.$18.65
GT. BRITAIN.	.$23.20
(Price includes $13.95 book & airmail/handling)	
All others write to Publisher for mail rate.	

As soon as it is available

Name_____

(Please Print)

Street_____

City_____ State or _____
Province

Country_____

Payment must be enclosed Signed_____

Bahamas Handbook, P.O. Box N-7513, Nassau, Bahamas 1.

Please rush me the
NEW
1985
Edition of
BAHAMAS
handbook

SOFTBACK EDITION	
	U.S.$
U.S.A.	.$18.15
CANADA	.$18.65
GT. BRITAIN.	.$23.20
(Price includes $13.95 book & airmail/handling)	
All others write to Publisher for mail rate.	

As soon as it is available

Name_____

(Please Print)

Street_____

City_____ State or _____
Province

Country_____

Payment must be enclosed Signed_____

Bahamas Handbook, P.O. Box N-7513, Nassau, Bahamas 2.

Please rush me the
NEW
1985
Edition of
BAHAMAS
handbook

SOFTBACK EDITION	
	U.S.$
U.S.A.	.$18.15
CANADA	.$18.65
GT. BRITAIN.	.$23.20
(Price includes $13.95 book & airmail/handling)	
All others write to Publisher for mail rate.	

As soon as it is available

Name_____

(Please Print)

Street_____

City_____ State or _____
Province

Country_____

Payment must be enclosed Signed_____

Bahamas Handbook, P.O. Box N-7513, Nassau, Bahamas 3.